The Core-Periphery Divide in the European Union

Rudy Weissenbacher

The Core-Periphery Divide in the European Union

A Dependency Perspective

palgrave
macmillan

Rudy Weissenbacher
Institute for International Economics
and Development
Department of Economics
WU Vienna University of Economics
and Business
Vienna, Austria

ISBN 978-3-030-28210-3 ISBN 978-3-030-28211-0 (eBook)
https://doi.org/10.1007/978-3-030-28211-0

This Palgrave Macmillan imprint is published by the registered company Springer Nature Switzerland AG
The registered company address is: Gewerbestrasse 11, 6330 Cham, Switzerland

To Daphne and Primo

Preface

The idea to this book goes back to the time when the recent global economic crisis had hit Europe more than a decade ago. The crisis has not translated into a reformulation of the prevailing paradigm in economics. Rather, EU crisis management by austerity brought countries of the EU periphery to the brink of collapse. The term periphery experienced a revival but usually not in the context of an interdependence with a core. Such a holistic approach of core–periphery relationships to the analysis of global capitalism had been typical for the Latin American dependency school. Social scientists I categorize as 'European dependency school' (EDS) had applied aspects of the dependency paradigm to the European situation of core–periphery relations in the 1970s and 1980s. What I found surprising was the relevance of their analyses for the Europe of today, and the informed prospects formulated for the future of European integration. A call for a special issue of the *Journal of Contemporary European Studies* on core–periphery relations, an issue that would never materialize, was the first incentive to revisit the EDS in writing. The 20th Conference on Alternative Economic Policy in Europe (Euromemo Group) gave me the opportunity to draw on a few EDS authors for a paper presentation in Rome in 2014: *From Dependent Industrialization to Peripheral De-Industrialization in Europe: Considerations from Development Studies.* Joachim Becker and I presented a paper that attempted to bring together dependency school and regulation theory for the International Conference Research & Regulation in Paris in 2015: *Changing Development Models: Dependency School Meets Regulation*

Theory. Also in 2015, I gave a talk at a workshop of the Arbeitskreis kritische Europaforschung in Vienna: *Development Theory and Space—Questions of Core and Periphery in Europe* (Entwicklungstheorie und Raum—zu Fragen von Zentrum und Peripherie in Europa). Consequently, a first study appeared in German following discussions with Stefan Pimmer, who 'reloaded' dependency theories together with Lukas Schmidt in a special issue for the Austrian Journal of Development Studies (Journal für Entwicklungspolitik) in 2015: *Periphere Integration und Desintegration in Europa: Zur Aktualität der "Europäischen Dependenzschule"*. Subsequently, English versions were published in the *Journal of Contemporary European Studies* after all, as *Peripheral Integration and Disintegration in Europe: The 'European Dependency School' Revisited* in 2017 (online) and 2018 (print).

Besides these theoretical and methodical accounts, and contributions to the history of theory, the dependency paradigm influenced empirical studies in the course leading to this book. Based on a paper presented at the 18th Conference on Alternative Economic Policy in Europe (EuroMemo Group) in Poznań, Poland, in 2012, Joachim Becker and I contributed *Berlin Consensus and Disintegration: Monetary Regime and Uneven Development in the EU* to a book edited by Włodzimierz Dymarski, Marica Frangakis, and Jeremy Leaman (*The Deepening Crisis of the European Union: The Case for Radical Change*, 2014). A paper to the conference Beyond Financial Regulation: European Industrial Policies in the Wake of the Global Financial Crisis (Barcelona, Spain, 2013) led to a contribution together with Joachim Becker and Predrag Ćetković: *Financialization, Dependent Export Industrialization, and Deindustrialization in Eastern Europe*, in a book edited by Giovanni Cozzi, Susan Newman, Jan Toporowski (*Finance and Industrial Policy: Beyond Financial Regulation in Europe*, 2016).

Dependent Financialization and Uneven Development. Core and Periphery in the European Integration Process (Abhängige Finanzialisierung und ungleiche Entwicklung. Zentrum und Peripherie im europäischen Integrationsprozess) was published in the *Austrian Journal of Development Studies* (Journal für Entwicklungspolitik) 3 (2013) authored together with Joachim Becker and Johannes Jäger. Also with these two, I contributed *Uneven and Dependent Development in Europe: The Crisis and Its Implications* to a book edited by Johannes Jäger and Elisabeth Springler (*Asymmetric Crisis in Europe and Possible Futures: Critical Political Economy and Post-Keynesian Perspectives*, 2015).

Research groups of Giovanni Arrighi, an author I included in the EDS, inspired studies that were integrated in the book. An earlier version of these studies was published in the *Austrian Journal of Development Studies* (Journal für Entwicklungspolitik) 3/4, 2018: *A Ladder Without Upper Rungs: On the Limitations of Industrial Policies in TNC Capitalism: The Case of the European Union*. Preliminary studies on alternative regional policies were also published (in German language) in a special issue of the Journal *Kurswechsel* 2018, 2, which I edited together with Joachim Becker and Christina Plank: *Crisis as Normality: Capitalism, Regions, and Uneven Development* (Die Krise als Normalität: Kapitalismus, Regionen und ungleiche Entwicklung). Also in the Journal *Kurswechsel* a series of articles on the current situation of Italy was published, which would be a source for the case study of Italy in this book: *Berlusconismo with Good Manners: Remarks to the Government Reshuffle in Italy* (Berlusconismo mit guten Manieren. Anmerkungen zur Regierungsumbildung in Italien, *Kurswechsel* 2012, 2); *Not Another World, Just Another Europe: Lega North on the Right Path* (Keine andere Welt, nur ein anderes Europa. Die Lega Nord am rechten Weg, *Kurswechsel* 2015, 3); *'In a Few Months Nothing Will Ever Be the Same Again': The Yellow-Green Government and the Decline of Italy in European Capitalism* ("In wenigen Monaten wird nichts mehr wie früher sein": Die gelb-grüne Regierung und der Abstieg Italiens im europäischen Kapitalismus, *Kurswechsel* 2019, 1).

The dependency paradigm has never completely disappeared from the critical political economy in Vienna. I am grateful for these collaborations, discussions and joint authorships. I owe special thanks to Joachim Becker who accompanied the entire process of writing this book over the years, with discussions, reviews, and professional criticism. Moreover, discussions with Karin Fischer, Daniel Grabner, Stefan Pimmer, and Christian Reiner helped improving sections and arguments of this book.

The research leading to this book would never have been possible without the funding by the Austrian National Bank: I therefore gratefully acknowledge that research for this book was supported by funds from the Oesterreichische Nationalbank (Anniversary Fund, project numbers 15471 and 17058).

Last but not least, such research does not occur in a personal vacuum. I dedicate this book to Daphne and Primo who supported writing this book over many years, and accepted a family member that often was not able to find closing times or was diverted to an unfinished manuscript.

Vienna, Austria
August 2019

Rudy Weissenbacher

Acknowledgements

I gratefully acknowledge that research for this book was supported by funds from the Oesterreichische Nationalbank (Anniversary Fund, project numbers 15471 and 17058).

Contents

List of Figures

List of Tables

List of Boxes

CHAPTER 1

Introduction

> [D]espite the relevance of dependency theories to European problems, they have made little headway in our universities. There are other reasons, apart from our parochialism and [...] linguistic weaknesses [...]. First, an explicitly interdisciplinary school does not fit readily into the typical uni-disciplinary syllabi and research programmes. Perhaps more important, its style runs counter to prevailing academic fashions. An economist, in particular, who picks up a book by a dependency theorist is likely to notice the lack of algebra. [...] The fashionable models are mathematical, and to the greatest extent possible, quantifiable. This is understandable. It would be very convenient if only social problems could be reduced to algebraic functions: the solutions would then be straightforward. [...] Many of the propositions of dependency theory cannot easily be cast in mathematical terms, still less are they readily quantifiable. The theory is in large part about hierarchies, institutions and attitudes. (Seers 1981: 15)

Dudley Seers, the eminent representative of a group of researchers I subsume as 'European Dependency School' (EDS) in this book, emphasized the importance of core–periphery relations in Europe and for the Western European integration process in as early as the 1970s. Core–periphery relations in development studies reflect uneven socio-spatial

The original version of this chapter was revised: Reference and their citation have been updated in this chapter. The correction to this chapter is available at https://doi.org/10.1007/978-3-030-28211-0_10

R. Weissenbacher, *The Core-Periphery Divide in the European Union*, https://doi.org/10.1007/978-3-030-28211-0_1

developments. Behind the appearance of spatial hierarchy between regions and states in ‘late’ or ‘monopoly’ or ‘transnational’ capitalism, there lies a matrix of actors’ relations with unevenly distributed political, economic, and military power such as governments, classes, and transnational companies (TNC). These uneven power relations make core–periphery relations a complex issue. Core–periphery relations run through all countries and produce dependency relations within core and periphery countries alike.

This book inquires into core–periphery relations in the European Union from the perspective of the dependency paradigm. Uneven development, manifested in core–periphery relations in Europe and the integration model that would become the EU, has never disappeared. The way these core–periphery relations are being discussed, however, has changed distinctively. Crisis of Keynesian capitalism in the 1970s brought to the fore that despite the postwar boom with substantial economic growth structural uneven development had not been eliminated. EDS authors would talk of ‘growth without development’. EDS did show that structural problems of global uneven development were also visible on European soil but EDS did not prevail in establishing a lasting dependency paradigm of European research and alternative policy-making. Instead, the radical liberal paradigm of neoliberalism succeeded Keynesianism. The first enlargements of the Western European integration project happened during this paradigmatic change in the midst of the global crisis of the 1970s and 1980s. We will encounter the doubts in Southern European countries concerning the integration into the EC before they became member states (Greece in 1981, Portugal and Spain in 1986). These Southern enlargements were paralleled in their accession by austerity programs. However, the hope of leaving fascist dictatorship behind and joining a common prosperous and democratic future seems to have pushed hopes in integration high for many. When Central and Eastern European countries from the former Council of Mutual Economic Assistance (COMECON) entered the union, the integration model was in the tight grip of the neoliberal doctrine, which pictured a future of convergence if the forces of competition that now included territories (regions and states) could prevail. For the Southern periphery, a pseudo boom, made possible by low-interest capital import, appeared to make up for the austerity programs to meet the conditions of the currency union.

In the 1990s, the fact faded that behind the narrative of convergence there was still structural uneven development between core and periphery. With the defeat of the dependency paradigm, core–periphery relations were marginalized as analytical categories. Only recently, with the global economic crisis, that had started in the United States in 2007 and reached Europe in 2008, core–periphery relations have reentered discussions on uneven development in Europe, and the EU, respectively. However, the influence of core countries, governments, and companies have largely remained absent from discussions as if there was a periphery without a core.

This book focuses on core–periphery relations in Europe by readopting the notion of the dependency paradigm that relations between core and periphery form an analytical whole. It revisits the early analysis of core–periphery relations in the uneven development of Europe and the Western European integration project from the perspective of the dependency paradigm (history of theory). It will furthermore unfold, why such an approach is still important for an analysis of contemporary Europe, and will consequently estimate the current core–periphery relations in the EU empirically in order to offer a core–periphery typology. As a conclusion, it will consider the impasse of current European capitalism and perspectives of socio-ecological transformation.

Whether one uses the terms 'center' or 'core' depends pretty much on the linguistic frame of reference. Based on the literature in English that I mostly refer to, I will use the term 'core' in this book. Historically, Werner Sombart used distinctions between core and periphery in capitalism early in the twentieth century. He did not provide, however, a theoretical explanation of such relations. It was theory building from the periphery, namely Latin American structuralism (above all Raúl Prebisch and Celso Furtado), beginning in the 1940s, which started constructing such a theoretical framework. About the same time, however, in the 'global north', 'polarization theory' began deliberating on core–periphery relations: François Perroux in the 1940s, and Gunnar Myrdal and Albert Hirschman in the 1950s. In Latin America, the dependency paradigm gained momentum in the 1960s, when optimistic expectations on peripheral capitalism by Latin American structuralists (e.g. that import substitution would counter polarizing effects of international trade) were disappointed.

I am using the terms dependency *paradigm* or *school*, because some of the dependency authors explicitly denied the significance of working on a dependency *theory*. In the past, discussions of this heterogeneous group of authors used terms like school, conceptual framework, analysis, or perspective. Referring to Thomas Kuhn, Ronald Chilcote (1978: 56) suggested the use of dependency *model*, in the sense of the paradigm of a scientific community. The dependency paradigm has never become, however, a hegemonic 'normal science'. If a predominant paradigm generally shows persistent resistance against change, in social science, things are more complicated and resistance against a new paradigm is fiercer. As Paul Sweezy pointed out, a paradigm can break down not only due to internal factors but also if the society which is reflected in a paradigm changes. Other than with (natural) science, societal reality as a matter of social science is produced by interests of individuals, groups, classes, and nations. Thus revolutions in social sciences seem to correspond to changes in the social and political sphere (cf. Hurtienne 1984: 8f.).

Building on Latin American structuralist thinking, authors of the Latin American dependency school continued inquiries into the nature of core and periphery relations in the 1960s. They did so, however, without the structuralists' vision of a catching-up development. Industrial development and even convergence was and may be possible for peripheral countries but 'development' of societies in a broad sense was seen unlikely: the role models of modernization theories themselves, capitalist core countries, kept facing ongoing social conflicts and contradictions. *One* global capitalist system, they argued, was reproducing social and spatial relations of dependence with different socio-spatial consequences or situations.

TNC have become the most powerful global players, therefore I will use the term TNC capitalism. Companies have developed certain features of core and periphery in global commodity chains. This did not happen in a void. Such commodity chains run through core and (semi-)peripheral countries and regions, an argument elaborated by world-systems theorists (in this book above all Giovanni Arrighi) who followed dependency thinking. Core companies came into existence in symbiosis with core states, modeling a core–periphery scheme that made climbing the 'development' ladder from periphery to core difficult and unlikely. After World War II, a time when many peripheral countries gained formal independence, a new quality of core–periphery relations left a direct colonial rule behind. In Latin America, where most countries had reached independence during the nineteenth century already, dependency authors observed the ability of TNC to integrate and control economic sectors globally. We will see how they described the functional integration of peripheral countries into TNC capitalism with the penetrating and disintegrative effects that went along with this process of asymmetrical power. Osvaldo Sunkel called the ongoing symbiosis between TNC and core states neo-mercantilist.

As we will see, he suggested a socio-spatial concept of 'structural heterogeneity'. Uneven socio-spatial development thereby runs through both, core and peripheral states, which produces core and peripheral regions and privileges or marginalizes respective social classes. Johan Galtung called the core in the periphery a 'bridgehead in the Periphery nation' for the core in the core state. He observed a 'harmony of interest' between the core of a core state, and the core of a peripheral state. Vice versa he observed a 'disharmony of interest' between the periphery in core states and the periphery of peripheral states. Putting concisely the relations between space and class issues between core and periphery, Edward Soja used the terms vertical and horizontal class struggle.

The EDS worked on formulating an alternative paradigm as well. If it was disappointment with Latin American structuralist ideas and policies that opened the way to the more radical criticism of the Latin American dependency school, it was the crisis of Keynesian capitalism and disillusion with mainstream development models that stimulated criticism by the EDS. The crisis of global capitalism had reached the core countries in Europe, and similar to the dependency school in Latin America, the EDS challenged the prevailing paradigm from the left. From the end of the 1970s to the mid-1980s, these research networks inquired into uneven development in Europe. Similar to the dependency school in Latin America, they observed (and challenged) uneven patterns of integration into the capitalist system. I pool a very heterogeneous group of authors into a 'school'. Their common characteristics are that they apply—some more, some less explicitly—aspects and theoretical findings of the Latin American dependency paradigm to the situation in Europe. Scholars of the EDS were influenced by both, Latin American structuralists and dependency school, plus polarization theory (see Fig. 2.1). Their analysis of uneven development in Europe and the European integration process seems very topical in today's polarized EU. Moreover, the starting conditions of enlargement were considered an integration of unequal partners. The suggestions EDS scholars made for a more balanced mode of European integration were never taken up by policy-makers. Moreover, they themselves did not put much hope into a different mode of integration within the prevailing framework, because in a union of asymmetrical political and economic power, solidarity would end where competition begins. Consequently, drawing policy conclusions from the EDS for today does not offer reason to believe that the existing integration model EU can be reformed. The structural inequalities in Europe would require a complete remodeling. Moreover, there is also no reason to believe that a simple return to Keynesian economic policy can sustain remedy. The social and environmental problems the EDS scholars observed in the 1970s and 1980s—as observed by a variety of researchers at that time, e.g. in the first report for the Club of Rome (Meadows 1972) and the Cocoyoc Declaration of 1974, adopted by the United Nations Development Program jointly with the Environmental Program—were a result of post-war Keynesian type capitalism. The crisis that began 2007/8 was one of financialized capitalism (cf. Chapter 9). Since the 1970s, moreover, the capitalist mode of production evoked climate change with its ever more visible consequences (melting polar caps and glaciers, rising temperature, capricious weather conditions bringing droughts and floods).

For the peripheral European countries, dealing with the recent crisis, and the resulting increases in public debt, was much harder to digest than for the countries of the core. The financial/bank crisis turned into state crises in many countries of the periphery and then again into a currency crisis of the Euro zone. Even if Greece was an especially extreme case, it was no exception to the vulnerability of peripheral countries in an EU constructed by core countries. The neoliberal paradigm (see Chapter 9) succeeded also to the 1960s' modernization theory. The way to prevail was alleged as the saving national economy which in realty spelled austerity programs. A paradigmatic picture suggested Germany as role model personified as the saving Swabian housewife, and proposed mechanisms of private households for national accounts. In that way, everybody could become export champion with a positive trade balance. In reality, somebody has to import these exports, and somebody has to pay for them. In the case of the EU, the Southern periphery very much belonged to both of these somebodies until their debt situation slowed the process. German banks were among the important creditors that offered loans that again stimulated imports from German companies. In a broader picture, the Economic and Monetary Union (EMU) with a common currency first brought low interest rates to the Euro zone which poured 'cheap' money into the periphery: capital import and commodity import to the periphery.

The EU remains a union of nation states, even under the current structure of deeper integration that has given the EU parliament more rights. EU governments are still most powerful players in the EU legislative process. They form the Council of the European Union, the powerful chamber of the EU de facto bicameral legislative system.

Within the Council, the Federal Republic of Germany has a powerful stance in addition to its already substantial politico-economic power: It represents 16.10% of the EU28 population. The standard voting procedure in the Council requires a *qualified majority* for approval, which means 55% of governments or 16 governments, representing 65% of the EU population. A blocking minority consists of at least 4 Council members representing more than 35% of the EU population. Having said that, decision-making processes are often of informal nature, particularly within the informally organized Euro-zone group.

So far, only rarely governments have openly challenged the underlying neoliberal integration consensus. The government of pressured Greece may count as an example, with the well-known result of defeating the attempt of a left political alternative. The other example is the right-wing government of Italy elected in 2018. The government of Lega (formerly *Lega Nord per l'Indipendenza della Padania*) and Movimento Cinque Stelle defied the declining role of the Italian economy in European capitalism and therefore challenged the established neoliberal EU model. It had no intention of changing or socio-ecologically transforming the overall capitalist mode of production. As we will see in the course of this book, however, the neoliberalism following Friedrich Hayek is in no variance with authoritarian liberals, neo-nationalists, right-wing populists, and fascists.

Being the fourth largest economy of the EU28, Italy has more stamina to challenge EU regulations than Greece does. It belongs to the original rich club of six members of Western postwar integration, but it also brought the first larger peripheral area to the integration model: its Southern part *Mezzogiorno*. Spatial polarization between core and periphery does not stop at national borders but runs through countries, dividing core and peripheral countries into core and peripheral regions. While the postwar boom phase combined with a policy of state capitalism enabled Italy to enter the club of core countries, recent developments suggest a decline of Italy to the EU semiperiphery.

The case of an exit from the EU by the United Kingdom, originally expected on March 28, 2019 (Brexit), is not the result of the British government (of David Cameron) challenging the EU, because it did not have any intention to leave the EU when it decided to hold a referendum on British EU membership. Brexit seems to belong to the frequent popular opposition against the EU regime. However, the British situation, like the Italian, reflects a declining position in the European core-periphery system. While the decision by British voters would lead to a partial EU disintegration, other popular votes in the past had only postponing effects on integrative policies. As we will see in Chapter 5, European integration was historically an issue of European governments never put to popular vote. When there were popular votes in recent times, they were held in few member countries only. Adverse decisions, however, had only lasting effects when countries were able to negotiate special treatment for themselves. The popular votes against the introduction of an EU constitution in France and the Netherlands in 2005 opened the way to the Lisbon Treaty (a government treaty signed 2007, and put into force 2009). Much of the rejected constitution's content was integrated into existing integration provisions via amendments. Only in Ireland was the Lisbon Treaty put to popular vote (instead of the planned referendum on the constitution, which was never held, because French and Dutch voters had rejected the constitution). The referendum on the Lisbon Treaty in Ireland was granted a second round in 2009, after the treaty had been first rejected in 2008.

In other quarters, popular vote opened the way to special country treatment or even early disintegration: in 1973, the citizens of Norway decided against membership in the European Community (EC), which their government had negotiated earlier; the population of Greenland voted against membership in the Danish popular vote on EC membership, entered the EC with Denmark in 1973 but left the EC in 1985 (again by referendum decision); a Danish popular vote rejected the Maastricht treaty in 1992, opening the way for a special treatment (opt-out) in the second referendum in 1993. In 2000, again by popular vote, Denmark decided against membership in the European EMU.

With the exception of Greenland (that has—as part of the Danish state—a special relationship with the EU), Brexit would be the first incidence of a state leaving the Western integration process that had turned into the EU. In the UK and Italy, there seems considerable self-consciousness among decision-makers that these countries can challenge EU regulations and their economies can do well even if they resigned from EU membership. The story is different for peripheral countries, especially if they need to act alone.

The story told in this book is one of uneven and dependent development in Europe, especially the Western European integration model that turned into the EU. It is about the chances for the periphery that never were, because they never materialized in the integration context.

The view presented here is critical of the notion that the EU started as a 'good'—often alleged as solidary and peaceful—project aiming at socio-spatial equality that took a wrong turn toward neoliberalism. The thesis presented here indicates that this integration was neoliberal from the start, even if one might call it ordoliberal after a German subbranch of the ideological movement. Western European integration started as club of core countries plus Southern Italy. Liberal integration arrangements treated development of peripheral regions as a matter of market processes without conscious development policies. The reason why Southern Italy seemed to stand a chance of 'developing' was due to the fact that Italian state capitalism did ignore liberal policy demands by the commission, and consciously applied development policies. What made the lack of European development strategies bearable for postwar Italy, and brought partial and temporary success, was the combination of postwar boom and the strength of the nation states. This enabled Italy to ignore liberal visions by the commission in variance with Italian state capitalist development.

The original agreements of (Western) European integration were result of postwar power relations:

1. The end of realpolitik by the United States against the world war ally Soviet Union brought a beginning of the cold war after the death of US president Franklin Delano Roosevelt in 1945.
2. In order to strengthen its cold war ally, the United States granted or accepted a privileged position of Western Germany despite the fact that Nazi Germany had invaded and left destruction in most parts of Europe, employing industrial mass extermination.
3. Part of this privileged position was a benign treatment of elites from fascist Germany in Western Germany ('continuity') and sheltering Western Germany from demands of repayment of war destruction and forced wartime credits on part of the invaded countries.
4. In order to pacify the Western capitalist block against the Soviet Union, some kind of common structure deemed necessary.
5. Germany succeeded, however, in the negotiations on the common structure as far as economic policy is concerned. Accordingly, Western European integration would receive regulations inspired by economic liberalism suiting the strong economic position, Germany was soon able to recover with US support.

The structures aimed at freezing the capitalist mode of production, making it difficult for future governments of member states to leave that path.
6. France aimed at securing common political structures that were supposed to 'control' Western Germany institutionally.

In the founding years, peripheral Europe remained outside the political arrangements of Western European integration. The countries were first economically 'integrated' (via TNC) before they were able to participate in the integration model. When the political integration occurred, it was already after the postwar boom had ended, and in the era of the first global economic crises after World War II. The economic and geopolitical landscape first in the cold war and then within victorious capitalism did not seem to leave many other options. We will see that Dudley Seers (1979) called the integration of peripheral countries one of 'unequal partners' which was 'impossible: yet it simultaneously appears inevitable'. He, particularly among the EDS, dared prognoses on European integration without policies toward 'true integration'.

From the viewpoint of the periphery, and with a dependency perspective, respectively, questions regarding integration problems of the European Union today need to be posed differently. Socio-spatial polarization within the EU may not be caused by the inaptness of peripheral countries and regions to 'develop'. It may not be as much the periphery which causes problems for the EU. The structure and mode, the EU is organized as an integration model, seems to be the problem, and the reason behind continuing difficulty of peripheral countries and regions. This is not to say that peripheral countries outside the integration process could easily withdraw from polarizing developments of European and global capitalism—even if governments were elected that are able to challenge the EU consensus and the mode of production. Authors of the Latin American and EDS did emphasize exactly such dynamics. Within an integration project, borders that might offer some options to resist against penetration do not exist any longer. Even more so, a common currency union will lead to polarization if countervailing policies fail to appear. Such traditional economic means, in the sense that they would build on a flexibility of demand on global markets and downplay the role of the prevailing mode of production for global warming, would be the ability to devaluate the currency (which would counter productivity differentials and may reduce imports), conscious (balancing) industrial policies, or an adequate sort of remuneration of the periphery by the core. It is difficult to see, however, how a country with a small productive base can build up an industry capable of earning via exports in order to repay the accumulated debt. At one point, such a scenario might backfire to export-oriented core countries. For a while, exports may be shifted to other importers, especially outside the EU (as it happened in the case of Germany). Such a system, however, cannot be sustaining for the EU, even if austerity can squeeze debt from the periphery for a while.

Without 'real integration' policies, scholars from the European dependence school expected 'neocolonial scenarios', e.g. in Greece. They were not optimistic as far as the remedies were concerned they suggested for a more balanced integration. Similarly, they even perceived development policies like those Italy had applied for convergence of its Mezzogiorno as insufficient. The historical pattern of Southern Italian integration into the Italian state, and the world market, was seen beneficial for the Northern, in recent history more industrialized and 'developed', part of the country. For the Italian South, being part of the Italian state could be seen as similarly problematic as the membership in the EU for the EU periphery (cf. Chapter 3.6).

In the second chapter of this book, I am revisiting the main arguments by the Latin American dependency school. Who are important authors? How do they explain core–periphery relations? How does this affect peripheral societies? How do they explain global capitalism and the consequences of uneven socio-spatial development? Who are the actors of global capitalism? What is the role of the state? And: What are the options for a transformation?

Networks of authors I summarize as EDS feature in Chapter 3. Influenced by Latin American structuralism and dependency paradigm, and polarization theory, they apply aspects of the dependency paradigm on the European framework of core–periphery relations. I delineate research networks from the 1970s and 1980s and their concept of core and periphery states and regions. All of these networks had a critical attitude toward the old development paradigm. Some called it development 'from above' or 'to the outside'. A new paradigm was to include strategic elements of a 'selective spatial closure' and 'self-reliance'. For many, the European integration process played an important role in their estimates of current and future developments. They observed the integration critically and much of this analysis still seems relevant and topical today. What was formulated as an alternative to modernization theory and economic liberal theories (neoclassical, neoliberal, and Keynesian), however, was engulfed by the wave of neoliberalism and the globalization decade of the 1990s.

While Chapter 4 is dedicated to the critical analysis in these networks of the old development paradigm ('from above'), Chapter 5 focuses on a critical view on the history of European integration from a dependency perspective. Some myths of integration are critically questioned. In the framework of these core–periphery relations, the alleged German economic virtue is much related to the privileges originating with its Cold War position. Also in this chapter, alternatives are being presented that authors from the EDS suggested for a 'true integration'. Having said that, they themselves did not have much hope of such policies being implemented. Rather, they saw a 'neocolonial scenario' lurking around the corner. The principle alternative strategies by authors from the EDS (e.g. 'development from below', 'self-reliance') are being presented in Chapter 6, while Chapter 7 tells the story how the dependency paradigm 'was lost' in the globalization decade of the 1990s.

Chapter 8 inquires into the nature of core–periphery relations in the European Union today.

I will argue in this chapter that even if one considers industrial development as a proxy for development or leading to development in a broad sense, the prospects for 'progress' in contemporary capitalism are very limited. I will adapt the theory, method, and proxies for 'development' and 'industrial development' by Arrighi and Drangel (1986) and Arrighi et al. (2003) as I will present them in Chapter 3. I will adapt their approach for a core–periphery typology in the EU, and use it in order to estimate industrial convergence compared with convergence in 'development' (in EU language: convergence and cohesion). Furthermore, I will suggest additional proxies to estimate (spatial) politico-economic power in the hierarchy of core–periphery relations in TNC capitalism.

In the final Chapter 9, I will summarize the main arguments by the dependency paradigm relating to Europe and capitalism as a crisis-prone mode of production and organization of society, in the periphery as well as the core. After the first global crisis after World War II, 'development from above' as criticized by the EDS was not succeeded by any transformative movement that could have led to a post-capitalist formation of society. I will describe by the example of the most prominent and effective ideologue, Friedrich Hayek, the restoration of the development from above by a more radical liberal paradigm than Keynesianism, neoliberalism, the ideology of financialized capitalism. I will, furthermore, explain the change of forms of the capitalist mode of production using the model of transformation by Giovanni Arrighi, from what he calls 'signal crisis' to the 'terminal crisis'. Finally, I shall try to use elements of EDS suggestions to sketch an alternative political economy in the wake of recent developments.

References

Arrighi, Giovanni, and Jessica Drangel. 1986. The Stratification of the World-Economy: An Exploration of the Semiperipheral Zone. *Review* 10 (1): 9–74 (=Anniversary Issue: The Work of the Fernand Braudel Center).

Arrighi, Giovanni, Beverly Silver, and Benjamin Brewer. 2003. Industrial Convergence, Globalization, and the Persistence of the North-South Divide. *Studies in Comparative International Development* 38 (1): 3–31.

Chilcote, Ronald. 1978. A Question of Dependency. *Latin American Research Review* 13 (2): 55–68.

Cocoyoc Declaration, The. 1974. Adopted by the Participants in the United Nations Environmental Program (UNEP) and United Nations Conference on Trade and Development (UNCTAD) Symposium on 'Patterns of Resource Use, Environment and Development Strategies', October 8–12, Cocoyoc, Mexico.

Hurtienne, Thomas. 1984. Theoriegeschichtliche Grundlagen des sozialökonomischen Entwicklungsdenkens. Vol. 1. Rationalität und Sozialökonomische Entwicklung in der frühbürgerlichen Epoche. Saarbrücken et al. Breitenbach.

Meadows, Donella. 1972. *The Limits to Growth: A Report for the Club of Rome's Project on the Predicament of Mankind*. New York: Universe.

Seers, Dudley. 1979. The Periphery of Europe. In *Underdeveloped Europe: Studies in Core-Periphery Relations*, ed. Dudley Seers, Bernard Schaffer, and Marja-Liisa Kiljunen, 3–34. Sussex: Harvester Press (=Harvester Studies in Development 1).

Seers, Dudley. 1981. Introduction. In *Dependency Theory: A Critical Reassessment*, ed. Dudley Seers, 13–19. London.

CHAPTER 2

Studying Dependencies: A Conceptual Framework from the Periphery

2.1 Important Representatives of the Paradigm

'Yet, despite the relevance of dependency theories to European problems, they have made little headway in our universities', Dudley Seers (1981: 15) noted in the introduction to his 'critical reassessment' of 'development theory'. In German language, Dieter Senghaas (1972, 1974, 1979a; cf. Pimmer 2016) had very soon edited translations of selected 'dependency' authors. These new theoretical approaches seemed to have filled a theoretical void in development studies but did not affect mainstream economics: They 'formed the base for a new understanding of causes of underdevelopment and possible solutions to overcome it' (Thomas Hurtienne 1981: 106). It is import to see that there is no such thing as '*the*' dependency theory. The set of approaches has been called conceptual framework (Villamil 1979: 2), Gabriel Palma (1981) uses in his 'critical overview' the terms school, perspective, and analyses. Ronald Chilcote (1978: 56) suggests the use of 'dependency model', in the sense of a paradigm put forward by Thomas Kuhn: a 'scientific community's perspective of the world, its set of beliefs and commitments', guiding its 'selection of problems, evaluation of data, and advocacy of theory'. Since authors writing on dependency are very heterogeneous themselves, we might best talk of a set of theoretical approaches, not a strict testable scientific theory (Cardoso 1977a: 15f.). In order to give credit to the heterogeneity of approaches, I will preferably speak of dependency school. It is also the diversity of influences on this school

R. Weissenbacher, *The Core-Periphery Divide in the European Union*,
https://doi.org/10.1007/978-3-030-28211-0_2

of thought that contributes to its heterogeneity. Lall (1975: 800) talks of 'internal confusion due to the school's mixed parentage', namely the structuralist tradition of the Economic Commission for Latin America (ECLA, in Latin America: CEPAL, hence *cepalismo*), and a (also heterogeneous) Marxist tradition. To be sure, I am ignoring the discussion of who qualifies for a 'true' Marxist argumentation in dogmatic terms, a fierce but seemingly fruitless discussion in which Paul 'Baran [...] is usually cast as the wicked uncle who inspired the whole deviation' (Foster-Carter 1979: 216) that led to the Marxist inspired thread of the dependency paradigm. In the words of Palma (1981: 20), the intellectual traditions of the dependency paradigm consist of the 'Marxist debate concerning the development of capitalism in backward nations, and the post-1948 ECLA critique of the conventional theory of international trade and economic development'. '*Dependencia* economists thus range', as Lall (1975: 800) put it, 'from mildly socialistic nationalists like [Celso] Furtado or [Osvaldo] Sunkel, via writers of increasing radicalism like [Theotonio] Dos Santos and [Fernando Henrique] Cardoso, to explicit revolutionaries like [Andre Gunder] Frank'. Boianovsky (2015: 423) sees the dependency school as 'rebellious offspring of structuralism'. Cristóbal Kay (1989: 2) talks of a 'Latin American school of development', born in the late 1940s and consisting of two main strands: structuralism and dependency. The representatives of the latter strand are the heirs of the former (Kay 1989: 230, endnote 8):

> Structuralism developed as a critique of neoclassical analysis, while dependency analysis engaged in a critique of modernization theory. [...] The Marxist strand within dependency analysis is critical of orthodox Marxism as well as of structuralism. (Kay 1989: 2)

The structuralist or ECLA tradition, Palma (1981: 50ff.) calls 'dependency as a reformulation of the ECLA analysis of Latin American development'. It ties in with the analysis of development in Latin America by the United Nations Economic Commission of Latin America and the Caribbean (ECLA/CEPAL). Palma calls it 'first major Latin American contribution to the social sciences' (cf. also Kay 1989: 230, endnote 8). The driving force behind ECLA had been Raúl Prebisch, who was influenced by a variety of authors, among which were 'European structuralists' (e.g. Michal Kalecki, cf. Love 1996: 113) whose 'main impact [...] on Prebisch and the emerging school of Latin American structuralism [...] was a consequence of the Keynesian revolution [...]. Keynes's own influence was direct and "genetically" connected to Prebisch's work from the beginning', argues Love (1996: 112). However, due to an entirely different political-economic situation and political practice in the periphery than in the capitalist core countries, ECLA and Prebisch only very critically adapted Keynesian analysis to Latin America (CEPAL, n.y.). Moreover, Prebisch seems to have been influenced by Friedrich List (Seers 1983: 52) and pre-WWII European theorists using core–periphery concepts, such as the Romanian Mihail Manoilescu and the German Werner Sombart (Love 1996: 134f.). Celso Furtado, too, seems to have drawn on Sombart (Boianovsky 2015: 427).

We will encounter Sombart in Chapter 3.1 as possibly the first author using a core–periphery terminology, and one of the alleged influences on Prebisch. The controversial Sombart offered other concepts later to be found in either dependency or structuralist thinking. Sombart (1927: XIII) interpreted capitalism 'as [single] entity', arguing that 'therefore all [national] economic considerations, all country struggle are being eliminated'. What might have fallen on fertile ground in structural thinking of the twentieth century, however, was Sombart's assessment of the Mercantilist tradition (against Classical economic thinking). Sombart (1921: 920) counted Friedrich List toward the former. Love (1996: 111) argues that 'Sombart can [...] be associated with other corporatist and fascist writers' (such as Manoilescu) but that Sombart's position 'fits into this set [of peripheral fascist writers before 1945] only because of the exceptional position in which Germany found itself in the interwar period. It was potentially the leading European power but was a defeated, and for a time had been a partially occupied, country, stripped of its colonies'. 'Friedrich List [...] blew a first breach in the firm texture of liberal theory', Manoilescu (1937: 4f.) pointed out:

> For us Eastern Europeans, List is in this respect the intellectual pioneer of our defense in economic policy against Western Europe, and he is the trailblazer onwards to our own economic independence. Since then, the tradition has not discontinued. The preference for national interest over self-interest has received a new, fruitful, and central position in the economic policy of National Socialist Germany.

Sombart and Manoilescu had a 'bad odor in the triumphant liberal and neoclassical world of economics' (Love 1996: 110) after World War II. Sombart had been ambivalent before he started courting National Socialism (cf. Sombart 1934; Harris 1942). His admiration of the academic Karl Marx went along with nationalistic and chauvinist works (e.g. Sombart 1915). Moreover, Sombart's admiration of Karl Marx was dissimilar to many of the dependency authors who followed Marxian notions to overcome capitalism and its polarization. Sombart (1927: XVIII) celebrated Karl Marx purely academically but despised Marx' *Weltanschauung* and Marxism (ibid.: XXI).

ECLA, however, was opposed to both, notions of harmony of unregulated capitalism in liberal economic approaches but also to Marxist views that considered cumulating contradictions of capitalism as unmanageable. Prebisch shared with Manoilescu 'the separation of the critique of imperialism from that of capitalism' (Love 1996: 135). 'Exogenous' variables of conventional liberal economic thinking were introduced, such as income distribution, market imperfections, and the interests of individuals, groups, and nations. ECLA's analysis was a rejection of the international trade theory going back to Ricardo: International trade would not lead to a mutual benefit but was more advantageous to the core countries. The structure of production differed in the two poles core and periphery: the former was seen homogeneous and diversified, the latter heterogeneous and specialized. The periphery exported primary goods from low wage production and imported manufactured products from high wage production. In order to force an industrialization process in the periphery, state intervention, a 'healthy protectionism' (import substitution), exchange controls, and foreign capital (in order to close the capital gap in the balance of payment) were seen necessary. The expectations in ECLA policies, however, often did not materialize, or ECLA policies even aggravated the situation: import substitution industrialization (ISI) seemed to worsen the balance of payments, real wages were not rising quickly enough (to stimulate demand), and the income distribution was worsening in many countries. Unemployment was growing. Therefore, those members of the dependency school who reformulated the ECLA analysis of Latin American development did not share with ECLA the optimistic view of peripheral capitalist development. The new more pessimistic approach was seen as confirmation by the 'underdevelopment theorists' (that peripheral capitalist development was impossible) just at a time when cyclical changes of the global economy seemed to prove both wrong (and gave a boost to Latin American export of primary goods) in the Late 1960s (Palma 1981: 50ff.). Palma (1978: 898; 1981: 42) considers Celso Furtado and Osvaldo Sunkel among the representatives of this group of dependency thinkers. The difficulty of such characterizations seem obvious with Osvaldo Sunkel who quite as well might fit into the 'Cardoso and Faletto-group' ('a methodology for the analysis of concrete situations of dependency', see below). Similar to them, Osvaldo Sunkel (1977a: 11) demanded 'historical specificity' for the analysis:

> Even if not wholly satisfactory, the analytical frameworks of classical political economy and particularly of Marxism do at least go in the directions required to analyse development: globalism and wholism. But to be useful they require historical specificity, in terms of the analysis of the structural characteristics of particular societies at given times and places. Even if we assume that the basic laws of capitalist development are unchanged, the mode of operation of capitalist economies varies under different institutional arrangements and cultural traditions. Capitalist development is not, as macrodynamic growth models would have us believe, a cumulative process of mechanical dynamics where everything is determined by an unchanged set of initial conditions.

But also Celso Furtado seems to have contributed toward the 'methodology for the analysis of concrete situations of dependency'. Furtado drew on the French structuralist tradition. In the late 1940s, he was a student of the French polarization theorist François Perroux, 'a leading French structuralist economist who had taught Furtado during his doctorate at the Sorbonne' (Boianovsky 2015: 416). Furtado also 'referred to his interaction with [the French historian from the Annales-school Fernand] Braudel during the two decades he lived in Paris, and suggested that the notion of longue duree may be applied to the study of "external dependence" as the determining long-term feature of Brazilian economic history' (Boianovsky 2015: 428). 'In Furtado's [...] view, when concrete problems arise, the economist tends to abandon substance and retreat into "vague shadows"'. Such deficiency can be corrected only by the economist's 'carrying his knowledge of historical realities much further'. Therefore 'Furtado's suggested research program represented an attempt to combine elements from both structural and historical analyses' (Boianovsky 2015: 422).

The Marxist thread of capitalist development in the periphery, Palma (1981) described in detail. From the original writings of Marx and Engels, he proceeds to the Russian discussion of Lenin and others. With a gap of three decades to Marxist works on classical imperialism, theoretical work on imperialism was taken up after World War II: It was the work of the US-American Paul Baran that influenced the thread of the dependency school, Palma calls a 'theory of underdevelopment'. It carried the notion,

> almost as an axiomatic truth, of the argument that no Third World country can now expect to break out of a state of economic dependency and advance to an economic position beside the major capitalist powers. (Palma 1981: 22)

In this line of thought, the process of industrialization in the periphery (understood as progressive element of capitalism) was considered in contradiction to the needs of imperialism. Elites of advanced capitalist countries would form alliances with basically precapitalist domestic elites in Latin America which would prevent development in the periphery. This line of thought has provoked criticism in many a quarter (cf. Frank 1974). In political terms, Frank's intervention seems to have carried the notion that a popular front strategy (as put forward by Communist Parties in Latin America, except Cuba) was doomed to fail, because the 'Lumpenbourgeoisie' in Latin America was no reliable ally in order to fight the global imperialism. This excluded an 'auto-centered' capitalist industrialization process and aimed at an immediate transformation toward a socialist system. Palma (1981: 42ff.) distinguishes the 'CESO' school of the Centro de Estudios Sociales of the Universidad de Chile as representative of this line of thought, with its most famous member Andre Gunder Frank ('development of underdevelopment') but also Theotonio Dos Santos and Ruy Marini. Because he was most widely published in English language, Frank was (outside of Latin America) often perceived as the most important representative of overall Latin American dependency school (Seers 1981: 13). Frank (1974: 91) adheres, however, that

> though my work has been no more than part of a wider current many critics have singled me out for special and often exclusive treatment as supposedly representative of the remainder, sometimes going so far as to claim

> explicitly or implicitly that a (successful) critique of this one example will do and hold for all. Perhaps this (inverse) preference may be traced to the critics' supposition that Frank offers a more easily vulnerable or destructible target, or a more visible one, or an earlier encountered one, or a supposedly more extreme one, or some combination of these. One thing is sure, and it has been clarified by the author and universally appreciated by friend and foe alike: the work has been internationally and consciously political and substantially inspired by the Cuban Revolution. (cf. also Kay 1989: 156f.)

Cardoso (1977a: 14f.), too, emphasizes that the superficial and eclectic communication of what was seen as dependency theory had made it easily refutable, 'a straw man easy to destroy'. Working on such a radical theory was an effort that opens discussion on its weaknesses, something a 'method to analyse concrete situations' (Cardoso 1977a: 11) of dependency can better avoid. Relating to this approach, Palma (1981: 59ff.) calls the third thread, he distinguishes, 'a methodology for the analysis of concrete situations of dependency'. Main protagonists were Fernando Henrique Cardoso and Enzo Faletto. Here is not the place to go into detail of what some perceived as irony, namely the differences between Cardoso, the radical social scientist, and Cardoso, the Brazilian president (cf. Brown 1994). Cardoso and Faletto had recognized the first theory thread ('theory of underdevelopment') as too static, mechanical, and not in line with historical facts. Cardoso and Faletto (1976: 215ff., and 224ff.) even dissociate themselves from attempts to establish a theory of dependent capitalism because they deemed useless the search for laws of motion in dependent situations, i.e. characteristics of development that are being determined by global capitalism. Therefore, they prefer to talk of 'situations of dependency' and employ a historical-structural analysis with a nonmechanistic conception of history that includes social (class) struggles and sheds light on changing relations of classes and national states, in global and domestic terms. Such a concrete and dynamic approach allowed them to integrate processes of capital accumulation in their analysis that had begun in countries of Latin America, and therefore to show that industrial development was occurring (to a certain extent, under certain conditions) in countries of the periphery after all. They take issue with both, expectations of permanent stagnation in peripheral countries, and expectations that see solutions in capitalist development. Lastly, social problems in core capitalist countries remained unresolved as well (Fig. 2.1).

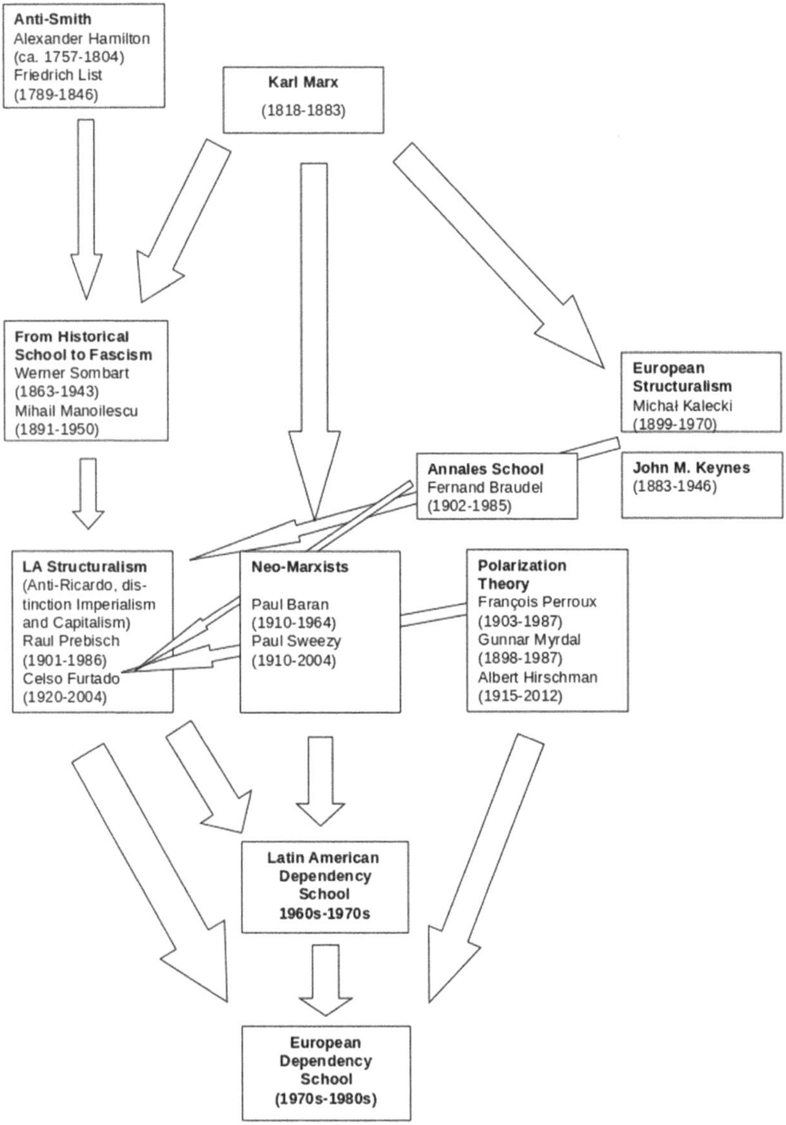

Fig. 2.1 Sketch of influences on dependency schools (*Source* Author)

2.2 No Primacy of the External Nor the Internal: Forms of Dependence in One Global Capitalist System

Internal and external factors had stimulated European developments toward industrial capitalism, a process that had lasted over centuries (cf. Weissenbacher 2007). Karl Marx put global expropriation alongside the internal English/European societal changes:

> The discovery of gold and silver in America, the extirpation, enslavement and entombment in mines of the aboriginal population, the beginning of the conquest and looting of the East Indies, the turning of Africa into a warren for the commercial hunting of black-skins, signalised the rosy dawn of the era of capitalist production. These idyllic proceedings are the chief momenta of primitive accumulation. On their heels treads the commercial war of the European nations, with the globe for a theatre. It begins with the revolt of the Netherlands from Spain, assumes giant dimensions in England's Anti-Jacobin War, and is still going on in the opium wars against China, &c. (Marx 1999: 533)

Some authors pointed out that European development 'started' from a peripheral position itself (e.g. Amin 1975: 46; Braudel 1992: 197), and Janet Abu-Lughod prefers to talk of 'restructuring' instead of 'rise' or 'fall' of systems: 'The old parts live on', writes Abu-Lughod (1989: 367),

> and become the materials out of which restructuring develops, just as the earlier system inherited not a tabula rasa but a set of partially organized subsystems. By definition, such restructuring is said to occur when players who were formerly peripheral begin to occupy more powerful positions in the system and when geographic zones formerly marginal to intense interactions become foci and even control centers of such interchanges.

What arguably has its roots in the twelfth and thirteenth centuries (Abu-Lughod 1989: 12; Braudel 1992: 197) gained new momentum with 'modern' restructuring beginning in the sixteenth century. The 'great divergence' (Pomeranz 2000) around 1800 seems to have been the visible 'take off' of English industrial capitalism spreading to what would become European global supremacy (cf. Weissenbacher 2007).

'Restructuring' in the (future) periphery meant for dependency theorists that European social structures (of feudalism and then capitalism) were being imprinted in the periphery of what was becoming one global capitalist system but did not overwrite completely existing structures. This must not be understood, as Cardoso (1977a: 13) pointed out, as

> a "mechanical" opposition between the internal and the external, in which the latter cancels out the existence of the former. The approach ought to be historical, and it therefore starts from the emergence of social formations. Underdevelopment then comes to be seen not merely as a process which is a concomitant of the expansion of mercantile capitalism and recurs under industrial capitalism, but as one which is actually generated by them.

'The distinction between "internal" and "external" factors', argues Osvaldo Sunkel (1973: 172, FN 3),

> should be taken essentially as a preliminary simplification. [T]he so-called "internal" structures are in turn the outcome of earlier historical processes of interaction between the external and the internal, and that "external" links have in fact very concrete and powerful internal manifestations.

He points out that 'underdevelopment' was not a transitional period but connected to the polarizing effects of the developments of one capitalist world system:

> [U]nderdevelopment is part and parcel of the historical process of global development of the international system, and therefore, [...] underdevelopment and development are simply the two faces of one single universal process. [...] Furthermore underdevelopment and development have been, historically, simultaneous processes which have been linked in a functional way, that is, which have interacted and conditioned themselves mutually. (Sunkel 1973: 135f.)

Cardoso and Faletto (1979: xvi) emphasize that they 'do not see dependency and imperialism as external and internal sides of a single coin', rather they

> conceive the relationship between external and internal forces as forming a complex whole whose structural links are not based on mere external forms of exploitation and coercion, but are rooted in coincidences of interests between local dominant classes and international ones, and, on the other side, are challenged by local dominant groups and classes.

They use the phrase 'internalization of external interests' (ibid.). The expansion of capitalism produces special situations of dependency. The interplay between internal and external forces again led to particular social formations with particular classes and forms of states. The social formation in the periphery must be seen as

> distinguishable from the classical pattern to the extent that "slaveholding colonialism," or some other form of colonial exploitation, is present as the basis of the articulation between dependent and dominant societies. (Cardoso 1977a: 13)

'[D]ependence should not and cannot', in Frank's (1972: 3) words,

> be considered a purely "external" relationship imposed on Latin Americans from abroad and against their wishes. Dependence is also, and in equal measure, an "internal," integral element of Latin American society. The dominant bourgeoisie in Latin America accepts the dependence consciously and willingly but is nevertheless molded by it.

Theotonio Dos Santos (1970: 232) distinguished three principle historical forms of dependency. Colonial dependence was characterized by trade export from the periphery, 'commercial and financial capital in alliance with the colonialist state dominated the economic relations of the Europeans and the colonies, by means of a trade monopoly complemented by a colonial monopoly of land, mines, and manpower (serf or slave) in the colonized countries'. The second form, financial-industrial dependence, 'consolidated itself at the end of the nineteenth century, [and was] characterized by the domination of big capital in the hegemonic centers, and its expansion abroad through investment in the production of raw materials and agricultural products for consumption in the hegemonic centers'. The post-World War II era saw the consolidation of a third (new) form of dependence, 'based on multinational corporations which began to invest in industries geared to the internal market of underdeveloped countries. This form of dependence is basically technological-industrial dependence'. Andre Gunder Frank (1972: 92ff.) labeled it 'neoimperialism and neodependence'.

Such different 'phases and forms of capitalist expansion (colonial-mercantile, mercantile-financial and industrial-financial capitalism, oligopolist forms of "multinationalized" capitalism, etc.)', emphasizes Cardoso (1977a: 13), must not be taken 'as an abstract and general conditioning factor' of dependency situations but 'reappear concretely in the analysis of their articulation in each local economy at different moments of time'. Cardoso (1977a: 13) exemplifies the interplay between the internal and external with the transition 'from the colonial situation to situations of dependency of national states' in Latin America in the nineteenth century. States were created 'in answer to the interests of local property-owning classes' but

> these, however, have their structural situation defined within the larger framework of the international capitalist system and are thus connected and subordinated to the conquering bourgeoisies of the western world and to those classes which succeed them; in this way alliances are established within the country, even though in contradictory form, to unify external interests with those of the local dominant groups; and [...] as a consequence, the local dominated classes suffer a kind of double exploitation. The "movement" that had to be understood, then, was that deriving from the contradictions between the external and the internal, viewed in this complex fashion and summed up in the expression "structural dependency". If imperialism was embodied in the penetration of foreign capital (invasions by Americans in the Caribbean, by the English in South America, etc.)', it also implied a structural pattern of relations that "internalized" the external and created a state which was formally sovereign and ready to be an answer to the interests of the "nation," but which was simultaneously and contradictorily the instrument of international economic domination. (Cardoso 1977a: 13)

Such a process of 'internalization of external interest' draws the actors, i.e. social classes, into the focus of attention.

2.3 The 'Ideology of National Bourgeois Development'

International crises that affected core countries, offer room to maneuver to reduce dependence relations for peripheral countries. World economic crisis and World War II, for example, opened up the way for ISI in some Latin American countries from the 1930s on (Frank 1972: 75f.). The inability of the national bourgeoisies in Latin America (and Africa and Asia, for that matter, ibid.: 91) to initiate, however, some sort of independent national development inspired Frank to label these classes 'with perhaps a touch of poetic license' (ibid.: 8) 'lumpenbourgeosie' and the policies they implemented 'lumpendevelopment'. Using 'lumpen' has drawn criticism. 'The local bourgeoisie become lumpen', writes Cardoso (1977b: 58),

> incapable of rational accumulation, dilapidated in their consumerism, blind to their "real interest." Here, the error has to do with the distinction between a real process and an ideological process. What ceased to have any function was the "ideology of national-bourgeois development," not the local bourgeoisies. I, myself, have done what I could, in works written since 1962, to demonstrate that the thesis, which saw a drive towards economic and social progress in the politics of the national bourgeoisie, lacks foundation. [...] [T]he facts [have not] suggested that there has been support for policy strengthening at local decision-making centers and transform the State into an instrument of opposition to foreign penetration.

If one takes Frank's (1972: 9) clarification and answer to critics, however, the positions of Cardoso and Frank do not seem to differ in this respect.

> I have been told that I ought never to use the word "bourgeoisie" because it denotes a social process which has never existed and will never exist in colonial and neocolonial Latin America. But I have been unable to replace it with another term. I find "dominant class" unsatisfactory: "oligarchy" has even more ambigous implications in connection with the Latin American reality; and I cannot even consider "aristocracy" or "middle class," which are terms used by the ideologists of imperialism and their Latin American counterparts. Thus, I have chosen to retain "bourgeoisie" and to add "lumpen" to it.

The lumpenbourgeoisie is an 'active' tool of foreign industry and commerce, but both share an interest in the status quo of keeping the dependence (ibid.: 5). Obviously, dependency theorists rejected modernization theoretical visions of capitalist development in the periphery following role models of core countries. They did

> generalize the criticisms of the theory that the national bourgeoisies could repeat the function they served in the center as the leaders of the capitalist process in underdeveloped countries. It also displayed the insufficiencies of the theory of modernization and the expectation that there would be stages of development identical to and in the same sequence as those in Europe. (Cardoso 1977a: 19)

'The penetration of [TNC] in Latin American industry had started after the Great Depression', argued Celso Furtado (1968, quoted in Sunkel 1973: 168):

> After the Second World War, this penetration becomes intensive [...]. In this way, [...] the process of formation of a national class of industrial entrepreneurs was interrupted. [...] The elimination of the national entrepreneurial class necessarily excludes (therefore) the possibility of self-sustained national development, in the line of classical capitalist development.

The dependent relations between core and periphery cannot be seen as purely 'external' argues Frank, because otherwise,

> it could be argued that objective conditions exist which would permit the "national" bourgeoisie to propose a "national" or "autonomous" solution to the problem of underdevelopment. But in our view, such a solution does not exist – precisely because dependence is indivisible and makes the bourgeoisie itself dependent. (Frank 1972: 3f.)

The functional link between core and periphery brought polarization in all parts of the (one) global economy:

> The evolution of this global system of underdevelopment-development has, over a period of time, given rise to two great polarizations which have found their main expression in geographical terms. First, a polarization of the world between countries: with the developed, industrialized, advanced, "central northern" ones on one side, and the underdeveloped, poor, dependent, and "peripheral southern" ones on the other. Second, a polarization within countries, between advanced and modern groups, regions and activities and backward, primitive, marginal and dependent groups, regions and activities. (Sunkel 1973: 136)

'[I]t is not possible', adds Cardoso (1977b: 58),

> to explain the dynamics of capital accumulation in the periphery without the changes occurred in the central economies. All of this accentuates the contradictory (but I insist, dynamic) character of associated development.

Frank (1967, quoted in Frank 1972: 3) argues that 'the impregnation of the satellite's domestic economy with the same capitalist structure and its fundamental contradictions' was more important for the 'generation of structural underdevelopment' than 'the drain of economic surplus from the satellite after the incorporation as such into the world capitalist system'. Cardoso (1977a: 19f.) distinguishes two ways, dependency authors understood the 'process of capitalist development' in the periphery:

> 1. There are those who believe that "dependent capitalism" is based on the hyper-exploitation of labor, that it is incapable of broadening the internal market, that it generates constant unemployment and marginality, and that it presents a tendency to stagnation and a kind of constant reproduction of underdevelopment (thus Gunder Frank, Marini, and to a certain extent, Dos Santos). 2. There are those who think that, at least in some countries of the periphery, the penetration of industrial-financial capital accelerates the production of relative surplus-value; intensifies the productive forces; and, if it generates unemployment in the phases of economic contraction, absorbs labor-power in the expansive cycles, producing, in this aspect, an effect similar to capitalism in the advanced countries, where unemployment and absorption, wealth and misery coexist. Personally I believe the second is more consistent, although the "dependent-associated development" model is not generalizeable [sic] to all the periphery.

These deliberations suggest a variety of integration scenarios into the (one) global capitalist system but closing the gap in international (political, military, and economic) power relations and development in a broad societal sense are unlikely to be reached in the framework of transnational capitalism. Role models in terms of modernization theory (which consider 'underdevelopment' as transitional period) were rejected by all dependency authors. They observed polarizing effects of capitalism in the global north and south. Furthermore, the developmental head start of core 'role models' changed the international framework long-lasting by establishing power hierarchies between core and peripheral countries which were difficult or even impossible to overcome. But it is important to see that the terminology of 'development' is insufficient or ambiguous. Dependency theorists did not expect capitalism to 'develop' in order to reach an overall societal progress, 'a good life for all', not within core capitalist countries and least of all globally. Such a development needed a socialist mode of production. What was deemed possible for some countries was capitalist *industrial* development, with positive social welfare effects for some fractions of society but also with polarization: 'If the capitalist pattern of development in industrialized dependent countries pushes toward internal fragmentation and inequalities, argues Cardoso (1972: 95),

> values related to national integrity and social participation might be transformed into instruments of political struggle. To permit the State and bourgeois groups to command the banner of nationalism – conceived not only in terms of sovereignty but also of internal cohesion and progressive social integration – would be a mistake with deep consequences.

Therefore 'denunciation of marginalization as a consequence of capitalist growth, and the organization of unstructured masses, are indispensable tasks of analysis and practical politics'. He does not deem it 'very realistic to expect the national bourgeoisie to lead resistance against external penetration' (ibid.). As a (political) consequence,

> **denunciation of the dependency perspective** cannot rest on values associated with **bourgeois nationalism**. National integrity [...] means primarily popular integration in the nation and the need to struggle against the particular form of development promoted by the large corporations. In the same way that trade unionism may become a danger for workers in advanced capitalist societies, development is a real ideological pole of attraction for middle class and workers' sectors in Latin American countries. The answer to that attractive effect cannot be a purely ideological denial of economic progress, when it occurs. A reply must be based on values and political objectives that enlarge the awareness of the masses with respect to social inequalities and national dependency. (Cardoso 1972: 95, bold by RW)

2.4 Classes and States in Transnational Capitalism and New Dependency

Since their analysis rejected the idea of a national 'bourgeois class' playing a role as actor in a modernization theory kind of developmental progress, dependency authors also found the idea of stages in capitalist development implausible. Such ideas of stages (and corresponding actors) seem to have been popular among Communist parties in Latin America: A national bourgeoisie was to promote industrial development that would also lead to overall societal development (such as perceived in the cases of European role models). Consequently, the bourgeoisie was seen as an ally against transnational companies (TNC) which again were considered as having no interest in industrial development (cf. Cardoso 1977a: 18). Dependency authors on the other hand separated visions of overall societal development from industrial development, and challenged the view that imperialism and capitalist industrialization in the periphery were mutually exclusive.

> The dependentistas showed that a kind of industrialization was occurring under the control of the multinationals, and they drew certain conclusions from it. There was even an attempt to propose a more general model of the process, to characterize a 'transnational capitalism' and to estimate its effects, not only on the periphery, but also on the very center of the capitalist economies. (Cardoso 1977a: 18)

Again, it is important to define what is meant by 'development'. Cardoso and Faletto (1976: 225f.) make sure that when they talk about dependent development they mean development of productive forces, a capitalist development with similar contradictory and polarizing consequences as can be found in core countries:

> So, we do not mean by the notion of 'development' the achievement of a more egalitarian or more just society. These are not the consequences expected from capitalist development, especially in peripheral economies.

What Cardoso and Faletto (1976: 226) put down as their aim, seems to somewhat bridge over differences in content to the 'theory of underdevelopment' group in Palma's categorization, and maybe unites most dependency authors except those very strongly committed to the 'structuralist' or 'developmentalist' ECLA tradition:

> It is not realistic to imagine that capitalist development will solve basic problems for the majority of the population. In the end, what has to be discussed as an alternative is not the consolidation of the state and the fulfillment of 'autonomous capitalism,' but how to supersede them. The important question, then, is how to construct paths toward socialism. (ibid.)

Theotonio Dos Santos (1970: 232), whom Palma counts to thread one ('theory of underdevelopment'), had coined the concept of 'new dependence'. After colonialism and financial-industrial dependence (consolidated by the end of the nineteenth century), a third form of dependence was being established after World War II, based on multinational corporations. Osvaldo Sunkel (1973: 291f., 305f., and 309f.) calls transnational capitalism neo-mercantilist because TNC belong to core countries and—even if they are not congruent to core states in their policy agenda—are seen as main actors of asymmetrical power between core and periphery, influencing peripheral countries' politics and economics, and penetrating industries due their financial power. TNC are able to integrate and control economic sectors globally. In peripheral countries, those sectors are being privileged that are linked to the core of international capitalism, the other parts of the economy and society are separated and marginalized, major parts of the population are segregated. Particularly in those countries that have experienced the first phase of industrial development, argues Celso Furtado (1967: 333f.), the penetration of US TNC had reached high intensity after World War II. Often countries faced an interrupted process of formation of national industrial bourgeoisies. The financial power of TNC took over the most dynamic sectors of manufacturing industries and the national bourgeoisie capable of running and supporting national industries were absorbed into the new managerial class ('nueva clase gerencial'). The effect was that national entrepreneurship was subordinated to the needs of TNC: 'The elimination or annulment of the autonomous national entrepreneurs excludes necessarily the possibility of a self-generated development along the lines of classical capitalism' (Furtado 1967: 335). Extending Furtado's argument of absorption of the industrial bourgeoisie, Sunkel (1973: 311) uses the integration/non-integration of different classes (entrepreneurs, middle class, workers, absolutely not integrated) to illustrate the segregation of classes and groups and the national disintegration by integration into TNC capitalism. Furtado (1967: 335) points out that

> [t]he only domestic companies that can reach strategic positions are those directly supported by the state. These two decision systems, the TNC superstructure and the national states were to define the future of economic development in Latin America.

Cardoso and Faletto (1979: 210) use these strategic systems to extend their class analysis. In those Latin American countries, where industrial development in the framework of this 'new dependency' occurred (e.g. Argentina, Brazil, Mexiko),

> the state embodies an alliance between the interests of the internationalized sector of the bourgeoisie and those of public and entrepreneurial bureaucracies. The local bourgeoisie links itself to these sectors.

The states connected to foreign enterprises via 'public enterprises created by the state, which come to function as *corporations*' and 'married foreign interests with the local bourgeoisie' (Cardoso and Faletto 1979: 203). It is the states 'productive function [...] to assure capital accumulation, and since in performing this function, it creates a sector of public entrepreneurs' (Cardoso and Faletto 1979: 210) and its social base. This 'state bourgeoisie' does not simply consist of bureaucrats:

> They function, sociologically, as the "officeholders of capital." For they support the accumulation of capital in the state enterprises. Both the accumulation of capital by public enterprises and the placing of national wealth (mineral ore, impounded taxes, lands, roadways, etc.) at the disposal of private capital are fundamental requirements for the advancement of associated-dependent capitalism. (Cardoso and Faletto 1979: 210)

The class alliance that dominates such states consists of 'the local entrepreneurial sector, associated with the multinational foreign enterprises, and the state productive sector'. It

> may organize itself institutionally within the context of authoritarianism, restricted democracy, or totalitarianism. There is little credibility in its structural compatibility with substantive forms of mass-democracy, populism, or even traditional caudillo (bossist) authoritarianism, since in these regimes the requisite policies leading to the expansion of industrial dependent capitalism become difficult to implement, because of the masses' interests in economic redistribution and political participation. (Cardoso and Faletto 1979: 210f.)

The integration of peripheral economies into global TNC capitalism bore the chance to develop the productive forces and bring wealth to sections of societies but for the price of polarization and disintegration: Sunkel (1973: 291f., and 309f.) talks of a process of national disintegration by integration into transnational capitalism. The national sectors of production (integrated into the international system) exert influences on technological, cultural, and ideological levels. 'STRICTU SENSU', argue Cardoso and Faletto (1979: 201),

> the capacity for action of various Latin American states has increased. In this sense, one might consider that they are "less dependent". Our concern is not, however, to measure degrees of dependency in these terms, - which fail to ask, "less for whom? for which classes and groups?" Which classes have become more sovereign? Which alliances and class interests within each country and at the international level lead the historical process of economic development?

Consequently, Cardoso and Faletto (1976: 217ff.) were rather sober as far as expectations into transnational capitalism were concerned. If there was a progressive element, it was the development of productive forces. What was now labeled 'new' dependency in neo-imperialism and transnational capitalism brought 'more dynamic forms of dependence' replaced 'quasi-colonial situations' and allowed 'greater degrees of maneuver to the national states and to the bourgeoisies locally associated to the state and to the multinationals' (Cardoso 1977a: 20). But still, multinational companies based in core countries had a monopoly on technological progress. The international division of labor continued, it was based on 'unequal forms of appropriation of the international surplus, and on the monopolization of the dynamic capitalist sectors by the central countries' (Cardoso 1977a: 20).

> In fact, dependency, monopoly capitalism and development are not contradictory terms: there occurs a kind of dependent capitalist development in the sectors of the Third World integrated into the new forms of monopolistic expansion. [...] Today for G.M. or Volkswagen, or General Electric, or Sears Roebuck, the Latin American market, if not the particular market in each country where those corporations are producing in Latin America, is the immediate goal in terms of profit. So, at least to some extent, a certain type of foreign investment needs some kind of internal prosperity. There are and there will be some parts of dependent societies, tied to the corporate system, internally and abroad, through shared interests. (Cardoso 1972: 89f.)

There were efforts to radically break with types of 'development that is tied to international capitalist-oligopolistic expansion', as Cardoso and Faletto (1979: 200) put it, which 'were not limited to the politics of the guerrilla' but included the 'Chilean popular unity of the Allende period' where

> the state was viewed not as a "bourgeois institution" to be destroyed, but as the lever for a possible total transformation of society, on condition that its control remain in the hands of popular forces. Both the battle between classes and the basic dependency relationship find in the state a natural crossroads. The contradiction of a state that constitutes a nation without being sovereign is the nucleus of the subject matter of dependency. (Cardoso and Faletto 1979: 200)

Divorcing the state from the nation seems to have been essential for the new—and more strained—class relations. Despite economic growth, increasing wealth, and urbanization, 'the existential, social, and economic problems of a majority of the population' (Cardoso and Faletto 1979: 201) were not eliminated, but sometimes even aggravated:

> Under these conditions, the state and the nation have become separated: all that is authentically popular, even if lacking the character of specific class demands, has come under suspicion, is considered subversive, and encounters a repressive response. (ibid.: 202)

Problems that were being confronted and absorbed in capitalist core countries like income distribution, minority movements, feminist or youth demands

> appear threatening to the existing order. From the perspective of dominant classes, the nation has become increasingly confused with the state, and the latter in turn has identified its interest with theirs, resulting in the confusion of the public interest with the defense of the business enterprise system. (ibid.: 202)

Consequently, the character of the state changed drastically in transnational capitalism. 'If the state has expanded and fortified itself', emphasize Cardoso and Faletto (1979: 201),

> it has done so as the expression of a class situation which has incorporated both threats of rupture with the predominant pattern of capitalist development [...], and policies of the dominant classes favorable of the rapid growth of the corporate system, to alliances between the state and business enterprises, and to the establishment of interconnections, at the level of the state productive system, between "public" and multinational enterprises. To accomplish this, the state has assumed an increasingly repressive

> character, and dominant classes in a majority of countries have proposed policies increasingly removed from popular interest. They have rendered viable a "peripheral" capitalist development, adopting a growth model based on replication - almost in caricature of the consumption styles and industrialization patterns of the central capitalist countries.

2.5 Development and Socialism: Waiting for the 12th of Never?

Dependency theorists envisaged overcoming dependence and transcending capitalism into a socialist model of society. What this socialism would look like, was not much elaborated. Frank, in retrospect, assessed the dependency schools efforts critically:

> The question we did not adequately address was how to eliminate dependence. True there were different schools that offered in part similar and in important respects different anti-dependence theory, policy and praxis. They reigned from the most social democratic reformist "dependent development" of Fernando Henrique Cardoso to the most "revolutionary socialist" "Underdevelopment or Revolution" of Frank, Rui Mauro Marini, and Theotonio Dos Santos and others in between. Samir Amin and I saw delinking or deconnexion from the world capitalist economy externally and socialism internally as the only paths to salvation. In retrospect our positions were not nearly as different as we claimed at the time, and on the question of what to do to eliminate dependence we were all wrong [all of us and altogether]. (Frank, n.y.)

Already at that time, there were not many policy options. A bourgeois revolution against transnational capitalism was seen unrealistic, dependency theorists offered substantial critique of modernization theory, pointed out the interrelation between the internal and the external, and advanced a more sophisticated approach toward class relations. As a consequence, alliances with the national bourgeoisie were not deemed constructive or feasible. Dos Santos called the national bourgeoisie 'dominated dominators' (cf. Bienefeld and Godfrey 1982: 5). Industrial development was possible in the periphery but without overall (societal) development. With the 'new dependence' the use of immediate force as means of expropriation retreated to the background:

> At an advanced stage of peripheral development the reproduction of the system can be guaranteed without directly controlled investment or direct political intervention merely through technological domination based on an increasing technological gap and combined with the existence of local social classes and strata, integrated through their consumption patterns (therefore their real interests) and through the ideology which usually accompanies it (renunciation of patriotic nationalism, the reduction of all ideology to consumerism, etc.). This is precisely the major significance of neo-colonialism and neo-imperialism. (Amin 1974: 22)

And a socialist utopia? Stalin used the concept of 'socialism in one country'. There was a remarkable industrialization process after revolutionary Russia had remained victorious against internal and external counterrevolutionary armies on its soil and showed resilience against international isolation. However, the quick process of 'socialist primitive accumulation' was—as the original capitalist version—based on immense atrocities. As a matter of fact, world-systems theorists discussed whether state socialist countries should be explained as catching-up process within the capitalist world system (Chase-Dunn 1982). Dieter Senghaas (1979b: 412, endnote 50) seems to have followed a similar notion. He argued that socialism in the periphery had the function to homogenize structural heterogeneous societies which would become partners of capitalist metropolis again after consolidation (but without peripherization).

Already in the international arena of the cold war, political alternatives were difficult to establish, especially outside the Soviet sphere of interest. Arrangements with the Soviet Union were necessary and could fail for ideological or geopolitical reasons (or both). While the Soviet Union protected Cuba, it did little to support the democratically elected government of Salvador Allende in Chile. Furthermore, the ability of the Soviet Union to intervene in the periphery was being impaired by growing dependency on food imports in the 1970s, furthermore it became unable to fully meet the oil supply of its allies (Seers 1983: 85). Yugoslavia was a communist experiment that emancipated from Soviet influence but needed benevolent support from the capitalist core—which was possible due to its geopolitical position (cf. Weissenbacher 2005). But without strong Soviet support the contradictions for the peripheral Marxist experiment in Yugoslavia were more accentuated. On the one hand, the Yugoslav state was to form the productive forces which should enable and build the base for a socialist society, on the other hand the state was to whither away in preparation for a communist society. The consequence was a 'self-dissolving of the development state' (Weissenbacher 2009). Ultimately, also the group of non-allied countries (Yugoslavia was a founding member) could only unsuccessfully challenge core capitalist countries with a common strategy in order to reduce dependencies ('collective self-reliance'). These countries of the periphery pushed for a new international economic order (NIEO). But a key difficulty for common policies was that such a heterogeneous group of countries then also included those with authoritarian rulers (Villamil 1979: 8).

One could argue a lack of world revolutionary perspective in dependency thinking (cf. Brenner 1977). The expropriation of the periphery by the core is a constituent element of global capitalism as perceived by dependency authors. Instead of an overall movement of workers in core and periphery against the global bourgeoisie, the dependency school would imply a complicity of core countries' workers with core capitalists against the periphery. And indeed, one could derive such thinking from a thread of the dependency school: The complicity of workers in core countries in the expropriation of workers in the periphery prominently reentered the discussion via the controversial work of Arghiri Emmanuel on unequal exchange (1972; cf. Fischer and Weissenbacher 2016) who seems to have run into difficulties and contradictions by trying to press his observations into empirical laws. Marxist critique also pointed at the difference between exploitation of workers and appropriation of surplus value:

> It is, to say the least, curious that Emmanuel should [...] draw the explosive conclusion that the labourers of the underdeveloped countries are more exploited than those of the developed countries, in the sense that the latter benefit from imperialist exploitation. The ultimate consequence is the absence of international solidarity between workers, the class struggle being henceforth between rich countries and poor countries. But, looking closely at the schemes of inequality of exchanges one simply notices that the transfer of surplus value takes place from the hands of the capitalists in [the peripheral country] to the hands of the capitalists in [the core country]; the appropriation of surplus-value – not to be confused with exploitation – is made by one capitalist class at the expense of another, and not by one working class from another. Without any transfer of surplus-value from [the peripheral to the core country] nothing would be changed in the rate of exploitation of the workers of [the peripheral country], except that then the capitalists of the dominated nation would keep for themselves the surplus-value that they have extracted from their own workers. (Palloix 1972 [1970]: 85)

Similarly the Belgian Marxist Ernest Mandel emphasized that—other than Emmanuel's assumption of an average international rate of profit—national rates of profits continue to coexist with uneven rhythm of capital accumulation adding to uneven development. Wages—value and price of labor—were not the root of unequal exchange, as argued by Emmanuel, but the consequence of uneven global capitalism (Fischer and Weissenbacher 2016: 147ff.).

Johan Galtung (1971: 83f., and 112; 1972: 36ff.) also uses the 'general idea' of a labor aristocracy which he draws from Lenin. But Galtung incorporates this idea into the relations of his imperialism theory, where the periphery of the core nation has a certain shared interest with the core of a core nation. He defines imperialism as 'relation between a Center and a Periphery nation' (Galtung 1971: 83):

> The basic idea is [...] that the center in the Center nation has a bridgehead in the Periphery nation, and a well-chosen one: the center in the Periphery nation.

Galtung (1971: 83) delineates international relations in his 'structural theory of imperialism' as follows:

> (1) there is *harmony of interest* between *the center in the Center* nation and the *center in the Periphery* nation,
> (2) there is more *disharmony of interest* within the Periphery nations than within the Center nations,
> (3) there is *disharmony of interest* between the *periphery in the Center* nation and the *periphery in the Periphery* nation.

Osvaldo Sunkel (1972: 278ff., and 309ff.) offers an analysis of regions, sectors, and classes in the global capitalist economy that seems much more elaborated. The structural heterogeneity is not only a matter of peripheral countries but also core countries. Since integration into the global TNC sector determines structural heterogeneity, and this overall integrated sector is dominated by TNC from core countries, not-integrated, marginalized sectors are bigger in peripheral and small in core countries. Classes are not separated into integrated versus marginalized sector, they are being more structured by the penetration of TNC capitalism than just along the lines of workers-capitalists, similar to the production of a spatial 'structural heterogeneity'. Integrated and marginalized sector, both consist of entrepreneurs, middle class, and workers. To put it another way, international TNC capitalism divides all classes into integrated and non-integrated/marginalized sectors, except that the not-integrated sector also has a big subsector consisting of 'absolutely marginalized groups'. Class relations are therefore much more differentiated.

Certainly the restructuring process of the 1970s, which outsourced production into peripheral low wage and low production standards economies, increased the ability of core capital to increase pressure on workers in core countries as well (and still preserve the social peace, cf. Weissenbacher 2008: 103ff.; Fischer and Weissenbacher 2016): imports of low wage products allowed maintaining levels of consumption despite downward wage pressure, and both added to stabilizing the inflation rate. This might have bought off revolts. Outsourcing and pressure on workers in core countries were the strategic answer to the twin crisis (decreasing profitability and overproduction) by the economic and political elite in core countries, argues Smith (2012). This seems to suggest an ability to divide and fraction workers on a global level to a much larger extent than it was suggested by Johan Galtung. Edward Soja would later talk of vertical and horizontal class struggles (see below). As with the European Dependency School later on, socialism in the periphery seemed for Latin American dependistas—with no global radical change in sight—an immediate defensive action against penetrative global capitalism.

2.6 Self-Reliance: Concept and Development Theory in Progress

Among the vast literature treating self-reliance, the peace researcher Johan Galtung has written very extensively and prominently on the concept of 'self-reliance' (SR). He drew on multiple origins of the concept, e.g. Chinese, Korean, Tanzanian, and Indian (Galtung 1976a). The European dependency school would again draw on SR (and on Galtung) in the concepts of 'collective' or 'selective' self-reliance. Galtung proposed the politics of SR as

> an important part of the contemporary history – an effort to undo five centuries of dependency on the West [...]. [...] If self-reliance is the antithesis of dependence [...], then there is something to gain in

> understanding using the English language as a guide. For "dependence" has two negations in English, both of them implicit in the idea of self-reliance: independence and interdependence. The meaning of independence is autonomy, that invaluate combination of self-confidence, a high level of self-sufficiency and fearlessness out of which invulnerability is forged. The meaning of interdependence is equity, which means a style of cooperation that does not engender new patterns of dependence. Very often this can best be done by cooperating with one's geographical neighbor – but there may be social neighbors further out in space. (Galtung 1976b: 1f.)

SR was seen as an 'open-ended' concept that had a certain 'nucleus of content' (Galtung 1976a: 1). The

> basic rule of self-reliance is this: produce what you need using your own resources, internalising the challenges this involves, growing with the challenges, neither giving the most challenging tasks (positive externality) to somebody else on which you become dependent or export negative externalities to somebody else to whom you do damage (who may also become dependent on you). Self-reliance cuts both ways: it preserves the positive externalities by trading much less upwards, protects others against the negative externalities by trading much less downwards. It is a measure of economic defence as well as a pact of economic non-aggressiveness. (Galtung 1985: 6)

Internalizing externalities is, for Galtung (1976a: 12), one of the most important factors in favor of SR:

> [B]y relying on one's own forces, a genuine development of oneself, individually and collectively takes place. Much less is lost by reinventing something invented elsewhere already than by casting oneself in the role of the learner and imitator. In conventional terms: the research and development facilities may be clumsy – whatever that means – but they are one's own, as are the mistakes, and it is from own mistakes, not from those made by others, there is more to learn.

'The whole theory of self-reliance is a total rejection' (Galtung 1985: 6) of the capitalist division of labor but SR is not against trade (when production is short of consumption). Trade should be arranged, however, best between equal partners (periphery–periphery is preferable to core–periphery) with equal structures, intra-sectoral and not inter-sectoral (like primary products against industrial goods or services) in order to keep 'the exchange [...] as equal as possible' (Galtung 1985: 7).

> One field of production should be carried out in such a way that the country is at least potentially self-sufficient, not only self-reliant: production for basic needs, particularly food, clothing and shelter, energy, arms or whatever is needed for home defence. (Galtung 1985: 7f.)

Galtung's concept of SR builds on solidarity and participation, mobilizing of own resources, development of own capabilities, adoption of new methods and technology in the own environment. '[S]elf-reliance is profoundly anti-capitalist' (Galtung 1976a: 6), 'is psycho-politics as much as economics, or both' (Galtung 1985: 8). It includes material and nonmaterial production and values, and strongly safeguards the natural environment and its resources. The economic principle of SR prioritizes use to exchange values (Galtung 1976a: 6). All in all, there is a clear tendency to overcome contradictions seen inherent to the capitalist mode of production. SR can be applied to the regional, the national, and the local level,

> through increased cooperation and innovative behavior of a type that respects local conditions a horizontal infra-structure will emerge as a basis for true autonomy. Through mutual aid the Periphery of today will be weaned off its dependency on the Center of today – through partial withdrawal from the Center and increased reliance on itself – in which case the terms "Center" and "Periphery" as applied to the global system will no longer be valid. (Galtung 1976a: 13)

SR must not be confused with autarky or self-sufficiency. While

> SR policy calls for a certain amount of decoupling from the Center, for some time, [...] it also calls for recoupling on more equal terms, e.g. for intra-sector exchanges. The time for recoupling is not necessarily when the former Center is willing to import manufactured goods on equal (tariff and nontariff) terms – that is a very limited perspective on the matter. Equally important is probably the level of general population autonomy, of sufficient self-confidence no longer to be afraid of meeting challenges from other self-reliant units. (Galtung 1976a: 18)

In the preface to the collection 'self-reliance' (Galtung 1983: 16), it becomes clear, however, why the alternative development concept of self-reliance was difficult to realize. Concept, principles, and praxis of self-reliance require without doubt joint action of a strong elite and of conscious people, but above all of an elite that is ready or forced to forfeit a rash of typical classical group privileges. Our approach is therefore neither colored capitalist 'blue' nor socialist 'red' – it is green, with an emphasis on the local level and on participation.

What if the bourgeois classes did not intend or cannot be persuaded to transfer power in favor of a new mode of production with an anti-capitalist structure and motivation? As the editor of the self-reliance collection (Ferdowsi 1983: 10) put it:

> A [...] problem of the self-relience concept that needs to be resolved relates to the question as to who is able to put such a strategy into practice. Because it is not enough to know why a target is being striven for but also: how can it be reached and by whom. If these questions are not being settled, this strategy will indeed influence our thinking but will not contribute to bring concrete changes to the contemporary reality. Because many elites in the Third World that might serve as carrier of such a strategy did not – with a few exceptions – fullfill such hope.

Galtung's idea to keep SR an open concept (a work in progress that started from a 'nucleus of content') seems to have led to a use of aspects of self-reliance in a way that carried the danger to contradict the original intention. In his introduction to Galtung's collection, Mir Ferdowsi (1983) pointed at the examples of the basic needs strategy and the political project of a 'collective self-reliance'. The basic needs strategy was taken up by the World Bank but harbored the suspicion that the basic needs strategy aimed at pacifying the poor by reforms and by some (financial) support. Capitalism was stabilized with a policy for the periphery instead of changing capitalism with a policy by the periphery that enabled people in the periphery to reconstruct their own economies (Ferdowsi 1983: 8).

In September 1970, the third conference of non-allied countries proposed collective self-reliance and the spirit of self-reliance in order to organize the countries' socioeconomic progress. In 1976, they agreed that only collective self-reliance was an instrument to reach economic independence (Ferdowsi 1983: 11). Furthermore, the obvious structural imbalances between core and periphery in the global economy had led to attempts to implement a *New International Economic Order*

(NIEO), e.g. the Sixth Special Session of the UN Assembly approved a *Declaration and Action Program* on the establishment of an NIEO in 1974 (Villamil 1979: 7f.; Galtung 1983 [1978]: 23f.). Galtung (1983 [1978]: 25ff.) was optimistic regarding implementation of an NIEO in the 1970s, although he saw aspects of the NIEO skeptically. The old economic order would change into the NIEO, and then to self-reliance. The latter process would not happen without violence.

> The reaction of the core will consist of supporting the New Economic World Order. It hoped it could thereby stop drastically and still in time a movement that would destroy the entire classical core-periphery system. Another option would be a military solution, particularly staging a military coup d'etat at a local level, or an economic manipulation before single countries were able to establish a system of self-reliance. But there are many other methods to preserve Western predominance, and the elites of these countries are very well aware of this fact – they have been able to gain much hands-on experience recently. (Galtung 1983 [1978]: 31)

Indeed, initiatives to change the international mode of production, which was considered unjust and wasteful by many, faced open and covered resistance. The directors of the UN Ecological (UNEP) and Development (UNCTAD) Programs received a 'three feet long telegram' (Galtung w/o year) by US foreign minister Henry Kissinger disapproving the Cocoyoc Declaration (1974). The Trilateral Commission, a private organization founded in 1973, brought together leading figures from transnational capitalism and politicians from the USA, Europe, and Japan. It meant to coordinate governments from core countries in order to shape a corporate-friendly globalization process and counter the influence of periphery governments in the global decision-making process (Villamil 1979: 8ff.).

The group of non-allied countries was very heterogeneous, the common interest was overcoming dependence on the core. As the Tanzanian president Nyere (quoted in Hein 1980: 68) put it at the conference of the Group of 77 in Arusha in 1977:

> The Group of 77 does not share an ideology. Some of us are avowedly "Scientific" Socialists, some just plain socialists, some capitalist, some theocratic, and some fascist! ... What we have in common is that we are all, in relation to the developed world, dependent – not interdependent – nations.

Clearly a 'collective' strategy meant something else for such a heterogenous group than in the SR concept of Johan Galtung. Alternative development could mean certain success in capitalist industrial development for some and possibly climbing the ladder in the international hierarchy. The accumulation crisis in the core had strengthened capitalist subcenters in the periphery, and south-south economic relations also increased. But the effect was a more differentiated polarization and uneven development in the global south. This has to be seen in the framework of the development process of global capitalism (Hein 1980: 96f., and 108ff.). Mir Ferdowsi (1983: 11) drew sober conclusions:

> The development of a privileged group of developing countries did not only impede the development of other, poorer countries. It also contributed to a situation in which countries in Africa, Asia, and Latin America rose to regional predominance which produced new power relations and dependencies in the Third World. Only before this background one can explain the attractiveness of collective self-reliance – without individual and national self-reliance – for the elites of the Third World. Because collective self-reliance is by all means suitable to contribute to the power of the elites without influencing internal structures, respectively power relations within the countries being influenced or even contributing to a transformation of societies' relations.

In such a framework alternative development could easily be reduced to industrial development. Those scenarios that envisaged TNC as the (only) carrier and diffuser of capital and technology (also necessary in collective self-reliance considerations), TNC needed to be ('collectively') controlled (cf. Wohlmuth 1980). But, again, this would at best lead to industrial development but neither to core type capitalism nor to a change in the mode of production envisaged by a broader sense of alternative development (Amin 1981: 534ff.). There was indeed hope that industrial development could be brought to the periphery. The Lima Declaration of the UN organization for industrial development (UNIDO) in 1975 encouraged industries of the industrialized countries to redeploy production to the periphery. This process of reorganization, however, tended to give multinational companies the opportunity to regain profitability through outsourcing (Fiejka 1981).

Given these divergent approaches, and particularly if changing the mode of production is seen important for an alternative development, one can follow Hein's (1980: 69) definition:

> [T]he term "Collective Self-Reliance" (CSR) [is being] reserved for the cooperation between such countries that also pursue an individual strategy of "Self-Reliance", i.e. having separated themselves – among other things by state control of external economic relations – from an integration into the capitalist world market predominantly connected by market relations, i.e. having "dissociated" them. All other measurements are for the time being simply called "cooperation among developing countries". Thereby one not only avoids a mystification connected with a not justified use of the term "Self-Reliance" but also resolves the common ambivalence in using the term "CSR" in works that confront the "New Economic World Order" critically.

What remained of NIEO was in fact a 'New International Division of Labor', as described by Fröbel et al. (1977). More recently it has been interpreted at the crossroads between Fordism and the age of financialization as 'strategic response to the twin crises of declining profitability and overproduction that resurfaced in the 1970s in the form of stagflation and synchronized global recession' (Smith 2012: 40). The Volcker Shock 1979 helped restoring US hegemony and sparked the credit (debt) crisis in the periphery (and Comecon countries). Conditions for new credits and debt restructuring subordinated countries in the periphery under policies later called 'Washington Consensus'.

References

Abu-Lughod, Janet L. 1989. *Before European Hegemony: The World System A.D. 1250–1350*. New York and Oxford: Oxford University Press.

Amin, Samir. 1974. *Accumulation on a World Scale: Acritique of the Development of Underdevelopment*, vol. 1. New York and London: Monthly Review Press.

Amin, Samir. 1975 [1973]. *Die ungleiche Entwicklung. Essay über die Gesellschaftsformationen des peripheren Kapitalismus*. Aus dem Französischen von Hildegard und Hartmut Elsenhans. Hamburg.

Amin, Samir. 1981. Some Thoughts of Self-Reliant Development, Collective Self-Reliance and the New International Economic Order. In *The World Economic Order: Past and Prospects*, ed. Sven Grassman and Erik Lundberg, 534–552. London and Basingstoke: Macmillan.

Bienefeld, Manfred, and Martin Godfrey. 1982. Introduction. In *The Struggle for Development: National Strategies in an International Context*, ed. Manfred Bienefeld and Martin Godfrey, 1–24. Chichester et al.: Wiley.

Boianovsky, Mauro. 2015. Between Lévi-Strauss and Braudel: Furtado and the Historical-Structural Method in Latin American Political Economy. *Journal of Economic Methodology* 22 (4): 413–438.

Braudel, Fernand. 1992 [1985]. Chinesen, Araber … hatte nur Europa eine Chance? In *1492: die Welt zur Zeit des Kolumbus. Ein Lesebuch*, ed. Rainer Beck, 187–197. München (=Beck'sche Reihe 460).

Brenner, Robert. 1977. The Origins of Capitalist Development: A Critique of Neo-Smithian Marxism. *New Left Review* I/104 (July–August): 25–92.

Brown, Ken. 1994. Word for Word/Fernando Henrique Cardoso; Having Left Campus for the Arena, Winner in Brazil Shifts to Right. *New York Times*, November 20. http://www.nytimes.com/1994/11/20/weekinreview/word-for-word-fernando-henrique-cardoso-having-left-campus-for-arena-winner.html, http://www.nytimes.com/1994/11/20/weekinreview/word-for-word-fernando-henrique-cardoso-having-left-campus-for-arena-winner.html (November 26, 2014).

Cardoso, Fernando Henrique. 1972. Dependency and Development in Latin America. *New Left Review* 74: 83–95.

Cardoso, Fernando Henrique. 1977a. The Consumption of Dependency Theory in the United States. *Latin American Research Review* 12 (3): 7–24.

Cardoso, Fernando Henrique. 1977b. Current Theses on Latin American Development and Dependency: A Critique. *Boletín de Estudios Latinoamericanos y del Caribe* 13 (22): 53–64.

Cardoso, Fernando Henrique, and Enzo Faletto. 1976. *Abhängigkeit und Entwicklung in Lateinamerika*. Frankfurt/Main: Suhrkamp.

Cardoso, Fernando Henrique, and Enzo Faletto. 1979. *Dependency and Development in Latin America*. Berkeley, Los Angeles, and London: University of California Press.

CEPAL (ed.). n.y. *Raúl Prebisch and the Challenges of Development of the XXI Century. Textos Esenciales: Introduction to Keynes*. http://prebisch.cepal.org/en/works/introduction-keynes (August 11, 2015).

Chase-Dunn, Christopher (ed.). 1982. *Socialist States in the World System*. Beverly Hills: Sage.

Chilcote, Ronald. 1978. A Question of Dependency. *Latin American Research Review* 13 (2): 55–68.

Cocoyoc Declaration, The. 1974. Adopted by the Participants in the United Nations Environmental Program (UNEP) and United Nations Conference on Trade and Development (UNCTAD) Symposium on 'Patterns of Resource Use, Environment and Development Strategies', October 8–12, Cocoyoc, Mexico.

Dos Santos, Theotonio. 1970. The Structure of Dependence. *American Economic Review* 60 (2): 231–236.

Emmanuel, Arghiri. 1972. *Unequal Exchange: A Study of the Imperialism of Trade*. New York: Monthly Review Press.

Ferdowsi, Mir. 1983. Editorisches Vorwort. In Galtung, Johan, *Self-Reliance. Beiträge zu einer alternativen Entwicklungsstrategie*, ed. Mir Ferdowsi, 5–11. München: Minerva.

Fiejka, Zdisław. 1981. Implementing the New International Economic Order (NIEO): Attempts at Regulating the Structure of World Industry. In *Dependency Theory: A Critical Reassessment*, ed. Dudley Seers, 150–159. London: F. Pinter.

Fischer, Karin, and Rudy Weissenbacher. 2016. Ungleicher Tausch – Grundannahmen, Widersprüche und aktuelle Bedeutung eines umstrittenen Theorems. *Z. Zeitschrift Marxistische Erneuerung* 27 (105): 140–157.

Foster-Carter, Aidan. 1979. Marxism Versus Dependency Theory? A Polemic. In *Millennium: Journal of International Studies* 8 (3): 214–234.

Frank, André Gunder. 1972. *Lumpenbourgeoisie: Lumpendevelopment. Dependence, Class, and Politics in Latin America*. New York and London: Monthly Review Press.

Frank, André Gunder. 1974. Dependence Is Dead, Long Live Dependence and the Class Struggle: An Answer to Critics. *Latin American Perspectives* 1 (1): 87–106.

Frank, Andre Gunder. n.y. Personal Research Interests for Public Policy Practice. In *Andre Gunder Frank Official Website*, ed. Róbinson Rojas. http://rrojas-databank.info/agfrank/research.html#DEPENDENCE (April 26, 2016).

Fröbel, Folker, Jürgen Heinrichs, and Otto Kreye. 1977. *Die neue internationale Arbeitsteilung: strukturelle Arbeitslosigkeit in den Industrieländern und die Industrialisierung der Entwicklungsländer*. Reinbek bei Hamburg: Rowohlt.

Furtado, Celso. 1967. La concentración del poder económico en los Estados Unidos y sus proyecciones en América Latina. *Estudios Internacionales* 1 (3–4): 323–336.

Galtung, Johan. 1971. A Structural Theory of Imperialism. *Journal of Peace Research* 8 (2): 81–117.

Galtung, Johan. 1972. Eine strukturelle Theorie des Imperialismus. In *Imperialismus und strukturelle Gewalt. Analysen über abhängige Reproduktion*, ed. Dieter Senghaas, 29–104. Frankfurt/Main: Suhrkamp.

Galtung, Johan. 1976a. Self-Reliance: Concept, Practice and Rationale. In *Transcend International*. https://www.transcend.org/galtung/papers/Self-Reliance%20-%20Concept,%20Practice%20and%20Rationale.pdf (May 23, 2017).

Galtung, Johan. 1976b. The Politics of Self-Reliance. In *Transcend International*. https://www.transcend.org/galtung/papers/The%20Politics%20of%20Self-Reliance.pdf (May 23, 2017).

Galtung, Johan. 1983 [1978]. *Self-Reliance. Beiträge zu einer alternativen Entwicklungsstrategie*, ed. Mir Ferdowsi. München: Minerva.

Galtung, Johan. 1985. Towards a New Economics: On the Theory and Practice of Self-Reliance. In *Transcend International*. https://www.transcend.org/galtung/papers/Towards%20a%20New%20Economics-On%20the%20Theory%20and%20Practice%20of%20Self-Reliance.pdf (May 23, 2017).

Harris, Abram. 1942. Sombart and German (National) Socialism. *Journal of Political Economy* 50 (6): 805–835.

Hein, Wolfgang. 1980. Zusammenarbeit zwischen Entwicklungsländern – Ansatz für "Kollektive Self-Reliance" oder Voraussetzung für die weitere Entfaltung abhängiger Akkumulation? In *Self-Reliance als nationale und kollektive Entwicklungsstrategie*, ed. Khushi Khan, 67–127. München und London: Weltforum (=Weltwirtschaft und internationale Beziehungen 20).

Hurtienne, Thomas. 1981. Peripherer Kapitalismus und autozentrierte Entwicklung – Zur Kritik des Erklärungsansatzes von Dieter Senghaas. *Prokla* 11 (3): 105–136.

Kay, Cristóbal. 1989. *Latin American Theories of Development and Underdevelopment*. London and New York: Routledge.

Lall, Sanjaya. 1975. Is 'Dependence' a Useful Concept in Analysing Underdevelopment? *World Development* 3 (11 and 12): 799–810.

Love, Joseph. 1996. *Crafting the Third World: Theorizing Underdevelopment in Rumania and Brazil*. Stanford: Stanford University Press.

Manoilescu, Mihail. 1937. *Die nationalen Produktivkräfte und der Außenhandel*. Berlin: Junker und Dünnhaupt.

Marx, Karl. 1999 [1887]. *Capital: A Critique of Political Economy*, vol. I. Marx/Engels Internet Archive. https://www.marxists.org/archive/marx/works/download/pdf/Capital-Volume-I.pdf.

Palloix, Christian. 1972 [1970]. The Question of Unequal Exchange: A Critique of Political Economy. *Bulletin of the Conference of Socialist Economists* 2 (1): 67–94.

Palma, Gabriel. 1978. Dependency: A Formal Theory of Underdevelopment or a Methodology for the Analysis of Concrete Situations of Underdevelopment. *World Development* 6 (7–8): 881–924.

Palma, Gabriel. 1981. Dependency and Development: A Critical Overview. In *Dependency Theory: A Critical Reassessment*, ed. Dudley Seers, 20–78. London: F. Pinter.

Pimmer, Stefan. 2016. Ich war damals einfach interessiert an diesen neuen Paradigmen. In *Dieter Senghaas über die deutschsprachige Rezeption der Dependenztheorien*, ed. Mattersburger Kreis für Entwicklungspolitik. http://www.mattersburgerkreis.at/site/de/aktuelles/interviews/article/269.html (March 31, 2017).

Pomeranz, Kenneth. 2000. *The Great Divergence: China, Europe, and the Making of the Modern World Economy*. Princeton and Oxford: Princeton University Press.

Seers, Dudley (ed.). 1981. *Dependency Theory: A Critical Reassessment*. London: F. Pinter.

Seers, Dudley. 1983. *The Political Economy of Nationalism*. London et al.: Oxford University Press.

Senghaas, Dieter (ed.). 1972. *Imperialismus und strukturelle Gewalt. Analysen über abhängige Reproduktion*. Frankfurt/Main: Suhrkamp.

Senghaas, Dieter (ed.). 1974. *Peripherer Kapitalismus: Analysen über Abhängigkeit und Unterentwicklung*. Frankfurt/Main: Suhrkamp.

Senghaas, Dieter (ed.). 1979a. *Kapitalistische Weltökonomie. Kontroversen über ihren Ursprung und ihre Entwicklungsdynamik*. Frankfurt/Main: Suhrkamp.

Senghaas, Dieter. 1979b. Dissoziation und autozentrierte Entwicklung. Eine entwicklungspolitische Alternative für die Dritte Welt. In *Kapitalistische Weltökonomie. Kontroversen über ihren Ursprung und ihre Entwicklungsdynamik*, ed. Dieter Senghaas, 376–412. Frankfurt/Main: Suhrkamp.

Smith, John. 2012. Outsourcing, Financialisation and the Crisis. *International Journal of Management Concepts and Philosophy* 6 (1–2): 19–44.

Sombart, Werner. 1915. *Händler und Helden. Patriotische Besinnungen*. München und Leipzig: Duncker & Humblot.

Sombart, Werner. 1921. *Der moderne Kapitalismus. Historisch-systematische Darstellung des gesamteuropäischen Wirtschaftslebens von seinen Anfängen bis zur Gegenwart. Zweiter Band. Zweiter Halbband. Das europäische Wirtschaftsleben im Zeitalter des Frühkapitalismus, vornehmlich im 16., 17., und 18. Jahrhundert. Vierte, unveränderte Auflage*. München und Leipzig: Duncker & Humblot.

Sombart, Werner. 1927. *Das Wirtschaftsleben im Zeitalter des Hochkapitalismus. Erster Halbband. Die Grundlagen – der Aufbau*. München und Leipzig: Duncker & Humblot (=Der moderne Kapitalismus. Dritter Band, erster Halbband).

Sombart, Werner. 1934. *Deutscher Sozialismus*. Berlin: Buchholz & Weisswange.

Sunkel, Osvaldo. 1972. Transnationale kapitalistische Integration und Nationale Desintegration: Der Fall Lateinamerika. In *Imperialismus und strukturelle Gewalt. Analysen über abhängige Reproduktion*, ed. Dieter Senghaas, 258–315. Frankfurt/Main: Suhrkamp.

Sunkel, Osvaldo. 1973. Transnational Capitalism and National Disintegration in Latin America. In *Social and Economic Studies* 22 (1): 132–176 (Based on earlier works in 1968, see FN 2).

Sunkel, Osvaldo. 1977. The Development of Development Thinking. *The IDS Bulletin* 8 (3): 6–12.

Villamil, José. 1979. Introduction. In *Transnational Capitalism and National Development*, ed. José Villamil, 1–15. Sussex: Harvester Press (=Harvester Studies in Development 2).

Weissenbacher, Rudy. 2005. *Jugoslawien. Politische Ökonomie einer Desintegration*. Wien: Promedia.

Weissenbacher, Rudy. 2007. Historical Considerations of Uneven Development in East Central Europe. In *Dollarization, Euroization and Financial Instability: Central and Eastern European Countries Between Stagnation and Financial Crisis?* ed. Joachim Becker and Rudy Weissenbacher, 35–83. Marburg: Metropolis.

Weissenbacher, Rudy. 2008. Keeping Up Appearances: Uneven Global Development in a System of Structural Imbalances. *Journal für Entwicklungspolitik* XXIV (4): 78–121.

Weissenbacher, Rudy. 2009. Sozialismus in Jugoslawien. Die Selbstauflösung des Entwicklungsstaats. In *Sozialismen. Entwicklungsmodelle von Lenin bis Nyerere*, ed. Joachim Becker and Rudy Weissenbacher, 74–97. Wien: Promedia and Südwind (=Historische Sozialkunde/Internationale Entwicklung 28).

Wohlmuth, Karl. 1980. Collective Self-Reliance und die Kontrolle Transnationaler Konzerne. In *Self-Reliance als nationale und kollektive Entwicklungsstrategie*, ed. Khushi Khan, 323–365. München and London: Weltforum (=Weltwirtschaft und internationale Beziehungen 20).

CHAPTER 3

Development Studies and the Dependency Approach in European Research Networks of the 1970s and 1980s

The dynamic of theoretical and political developments in Latin America had an appeal well beyond the region. Not only had the works of the Latin American dependency school been translated. Some of the researchers of the research networks presented in this book looked back at personal experiences in Santiago de Chile, which had been an important center of the Latin American dependency school before the coup d'état against the government of Salvador Allende in 1973. The Viennese regional development scientist Walter Stöhr and the US-American regional planner John Friedmann had been advisors to the newly founded Chilean planning bureau in the 1960s (Soms García 2010: 45). This advice seems to have been financed by the US-American Ford Foundation, for which Stöhr had been 'senior regional planning adviser [...] in Santiago' (Stöhr et al. 2001: 269), and which published Friedmann's 'Generalized Theory of Polarized Development' in 1967. Already a year earlier, Friedmann and Stöhr had presented a paper in Vienna, with the title 'The Uses of Regional Science: Policy Planning in Chile' (Friedmann 1967: 56). The political scientist Dieter Nohlen (n.y.), again, was representative of the German Christian-Democrat *Konrad Adenauer Stiftung* in Chile from 1969 to 1972. The British development economist, development advisor, and later researcher in development studies, Dudley Seers (1983a: xi), had worked for the United Nations Economic Commission of Latin America and the Caribbean (ECLA/CEPAL) 'in 1957–1961 under Raul Prebisch [...], and alongside Osvaldo Sunkel, as well as many other Latin American

R. Weissenbacher, *The Core-Periphery Divide in the European Union*,
https://doi.org/10.1007/978-3-030-28211-0_3

economists, who were evolving the "structuralist" and "dependency" approaches'. Seers had been advisor in 35 smaller countries:

> If I had undertaken research mainly in, say China, India, the United States and the Soviet Union, my approach would, without doubt be very different. I would, for example, be less aware of the special problems of small countries (especially vis-a-vis the great powers) and more conscious of the importance of regional differences within countries - and of the economic, political and social costs of central bureaucracies. (Seers 1983a: x)

In the 1970s, social scientists from the Institute of Development Studies (IDS) at the University of Sussex started dealing with questions of the European periphery by using methods from development studies on the European situation (Seers 1977), e.g. Manfred Bienefeld and Dudley Seers visited Portugal on behalf of the IDS in order to advise the Portuguese government in development planning in 1976 and 1978, respectively (Seers 1978: i). Members of the European Association of Development Institutes (EADI) joined in and formed a 'European Periphery Group' (Seers 1983b: ixff.). EADI identified parallels between countries and regions of the European periphery with those of the global periphery:

> The Association's main focus is the field of development studies, which used to mean studies of the problems of the 'less-developed' or 'underdeveloped' or (still more euphemistically) 'developing' countries of Africa, Asia and Latin America. This, however, was not merely patronising but also scientifically indefensible, since it implied that these countries were facing fundamental problems which had been solved in Europe – a position much harder to defend now than a decade ago. (Seers 1983a: ix)

EADI had been founded in Linz in 1975, and was originally also based in Austria. Dudley Seers from IDS was elected first EADI president (Van Bilsen 1976: 9f.) and also convenor of the 'European periphery group'. EADI should look at problems familiar from non-European regions within the European context: 'Development studies deal with relationships between a dominant "core" of countries and a dependent "periphery". In Europe we can see a core of rich countries and a periphery' (Seers 1983b: 518). 'Periphery' was soon dropped from the name because core countries also had peripheral regions, which were to be analyzed as well (Seers 1983c: 519f.). Many publications on core–periphery relations originated with this group, among which were *Underdeveloped Europe: Studies in Core-Periphery Relations* (Seers et al. 1979), *Integration and Unequal Development: The Experience of the EEC* (Seers and Vaitsos 1980), *European Studies in Development: New Trends in European Development Studies* (De Bandt et al. 1980), *The Second Enlargement of the EEC: The Integration of Unequal Partners* (Seers and Vaitsos 1982), *The Enlargement of the European Community: Case-Studies of Greece, Portugal, and Spain* (Payno and Sampedro 1983), and *The Crisis of the European Regions* (Seers and Öström 1983). This network was very heterogeneous. Moreover, this book discusses a group of researchers from the German Development Institute (GDI), above all Stefan Musto (1977, 1982, 1985a, 1985b), as a sideline of EADI. Musto (1985c), head of the Department of Political Sociology at GDI, drew heavily on Seers and dedicated a book to the late Seers (Musto and Pinkele 1985). GDI researchers did a number of important studies on the peripheral enlargement of the (back then) European Community (e.g. Claus et al. 1977; Hummen 1977; Eßer et al. 1978, 1980; Eußner 1983).

The collection *Underdeveloped Europe: Studies in Core-Periphery Relations* (Seers et al. 1979) marked 'a new departure by inquiring whether one can apply in Europe some of the theoretical insights obtained from work in the field conventionally called "development studies"' (Seers 1979a: xiii). Using Latin American theories of dependency on Europe was seen fruitful because

> the economics taught in Western Europe [...], even in its periphery, ignores hierarchical relationships between countries, or within them. Further, the experience of the 'Third World' could well be relevant in some respects to some problems of the European periphery – for example in dealing with the governments and corporations of the core – if we are prepared to study them. (Seers 1979a: xix)

The discussion about the enlargement of what was still the Western European integration project of a European Economic Union in the 1970s brought core–periphery relations even more to the fore. Governments from three Southern European peripheral countries had applied for membership (Greece, Portugal, and Spain), with possibly more to be considered (Turkey and Cyprus):

> The incorporation of these countries into a predominantly core organisation raises structural issues that are familiar in the development field: If unemployment in them were not so great and so chronic, if they had no severly depressed regions, if wages were as high in the candidates as in the core of Europe, if their economies were diversified and political systems stable, enlargement would not raise the profound difficulties it does for the existing members of the EEC. (Seers 1979a: xix)

Another network was strongly influenced by the dependency paradigm: The school of world-systems analysis of the Fernand Braudel Center in Binghamton organized discussions on European core–periphery relations in the early 1980s (Arrighi 1985a). Giovanni Arrighi coordinated a large and important research program investigating Calabria and three of its sub-regions (for researchers and publications see: Arrighi and Piselli 1987) and published a concept for a core–semiperiphery–periphery systematic (Arrighi and Drangel 1986). A third group met for a symposium on 'Regional policies and political decentralization in Southern Europe' in Heidelberg in 1984. Its geographical focus was on Italy, Portugal, and Spain, its research questions dealt with uneven development, political decentralization, and regional policies. The network used theoretical approaches from development studies, especially the 'dependency paradigm', for the analysis of European regions (Nohlen and Schultze 1985a: 7).

I distinguish between these networks in their temporary organizational form, and not in a strict sense. Walter Stöhr (1983a, 1985) participated in the EADI—and Heidelberg networks, but in his work he also referred to Immanuel Wallerstein from the Binghamton network (Stöhr 1983b: 117). John Friedmann (1983) took part in the EADI network but was also a reference for a number of other authors (e.g. Nohlen 1985: 12). He was editor and author of a collection on *Self-Reliant Development in Europe* (Bassand et al. 1986), based on a conference of the Swiss research program on regional problems, held in cooperation with the Swiss National Commission for UNESCO: '[T]he strategy of self-reliance was accepted *from the outset* as a legitimate theoretical and political alternative to the long dominant export-oriented nature of regional studies and regional policies' (Brugger and Stuckey 1986: 2). Having its concepts applied to capitalist core countries, the dependency paradigm had become close to the threshold of being accepted in the mainstream of social science. In this book, I cannot offer a comprehensive overview of all networks and authors that used aspects of the dependency paradigm on Europe, not even in English or German. I will focus on networks and authors closer to international or regional development studies.

There were a couple of other important contributions influenced by the Latin American Dependency School. Dieter Senghaas very early did translation work of the Latin American dependency school into German (cf. Pimmer 2016). He and his doctoral student Ulrich Menzel spurred a dynamic in development research by using findings from the theory of peripheral capitalism on core countries themselves. Not only were modernization theory's conclusions inadequate to be transferred from core to periphery but the 'metropolitan' experience was much more differentiated itself (e.g. Senghaas and Menzel 1979). The renowned Hungarian economic historians Iván Berend and György Ránki (e.g. 1982) 'started out as dependency theorists critical of nationalist interpretations of Hungarian economic history' (Reill 2011: 5), 'having borrowed the terms [core and periphery] from [Immanuel] Wallerstein' (Love 2011: 33). Here, however, György Ránki (1985) is included in the 'European Dependency school', because he participated in the Binghamton network. Last but not least, I will refer to the state and class theorist Nicos Poulantzas who did not participate in the networks but was an important reference for authors (within and outside the networks) concerned with dependencies in Europe. He engaged with Latin American scholars of dependency (Fernando Cardoso and others at a seminar in Mexico in 1971, cf. Benítez 1998: 353–398) and seems to have been influenced by the Latin American dependency school (Poulantzas 1974: 90). Otto Holman (2002: 409) called the works of Alan Lipietz (cf. 1987: 13), an early author of the (French) Regulation Theory, who also followed Latin American dependency authors, and of Poulantzas versions 'of dependency theory for Southern Europe'. Poulantzas appears as a prominent single author in this book because he goes beyond mere structural analysis and seems to transfer class and state analysis from the Latin American dependency paradigm to the European context.

Furthermore, there were other research networks engaging with questions of uneven development and the European periphery at that time. A conference at the University of Durham in 1982 ('National and Regional Development in the Mediterranean Basin') led to a collection selecting 13 contributions (Hudson and Lewis 1985a). In context of the 'Durham-network', Southern Europe included six countries

(France, Greece, Italy, Portugal, Spain, and Turkey) 'that are most closely associated with Northern Europe' (Hudson and Lewis 1985b: 2). Empirical case studies should close a research gap in order to refine the theoretical framework for systematic comparative analysis. It was hoped

> that we will be able to build up comparative studies during the 1980s which will give generalizations about Southern European 'Models of Development' a closer relationship to contemporary reality than they now enjoy. (Hudson and Lewis 1985b: 1)

Hudson and Lewis (1984), again, were among the twelve contributors of a volume that was the outcome of a colloquium at the University of Exeter (Williams 1984a), where considerations from the dependency school and world-systems analysis were included (Williams 1984b).

3.1 States, Regions, and Struggles Between Classes and Spaces in Transnational Capitalism

After World War II, the observation that social inequality in capitalism is being manifested also in spatial terms was labeled as backward areas and then developing countries. This carried the perception of modernization theory that catching-up to powerful and successful states would be possible for all (if the 'right' policies were being applied). The Latin American dependency school used the concept of 'periphery' and argued a dependence on the political economy of the capitalist core. The European Dependency School used the dependency framework for the European situation. Selwyn (1979: 35), for example, argued that any system of 'spatial inequality' has to be seen in the context of 'systems of social inequality which may be defined in terms of class, occupation or ethnic group'. Among the European dependency scholars there had been advocates of regional or national alternatives to counter spatial inequalities. Friedmann (1983: 149ff.) pointed at the conflicting interests behind the conceptual categories of 'core' and 'periphery'. Different natures of conflict had been suggested, region vs. region, capital vs. region, or capital vs. capital 'though fought out on the terrain of regions, with multinationals pitted against national and regional fractions of the bourgeoisie'. Friedmann distinguishes between 'two geographies' that together constitute a 'unity of opposites', namely 'life space' and 'economic space'.

The imperative of the economic space (and its actors firms and corporations) dominate life spaces. Economic space is seen as abstract, open, and unlimited but also superposing over concrete and territorial life spaces such as nations, regions, and communities. Modern societies need both spaces for sustenance but they are also in conflict with each other. The nature of the economic space is destructive,

> its continuous expansion is vital to the reproduction of capitalist relations as a whole. Expansion occurs ruthlessly, through the destruction of inefficient producers and their replacement by firms that are more viable. (Friedmann 1983: 151)

In the dominant economic space, with an ideology of capital, values had been confused. Life is subordinated and reduced to (earning a) livelihood, becoming equal to consumption, 'reducing life to a function of economic calculation' (ibid.). The dialectic, Friedmann (1983: 157f., FN2) uses, resembles the conflict between 'life' and 'economic' space. It is not one in the Hegelian tradition but

> a traditional Eastern concept in which two opposing forces meet and clash without ever resolving the contradictions between them. In such a Taoist dialectic, the victory of one force over the other would imply the destruction of the particular system of order they comprise, a system which sustains itself only through conflict [...].

The consequence of such reasoning appears to be the end of the capitalist mode of production, either by ending forces of (capitalist) expansion, or by capitalist expansion destroying the life spaces necessary for its reproduction. Class and spatial dynamics are interwoven in Friedmann's analysis. Capitalist actors of the economic space are seen in firms and companies but Friedmann's antagonisms do not exclude regional capitalists siding with workers against TNC. Traditional Marxists often eyed such dependency arguments critically (Szentes 1983: 108; cf. Chapter 6.2). Dudley Seers (1980: 9f.) found that 'Marxist economics [...] in its official textbook versions [...] shows little interest in geographical differences, which would only blur the picture of class conflicts'. The political geographer with dependency leaning, Edward Soja (1985: 176), criticized what he labeled 'new territorialism' (regionalists from the 'European dependency school': Friedmann and Weaver (1979) and Stöhr and Taylor (1981), 'for its overly romantic and utopian presentation of regionalism, regional planning, and the territoriality of social life; and for its obfuscating interpretation of the history of capitalist development, the role of the state, and the nature of territorial politics'. But Soja (1980: 209 and 222, cf. also Hadjimichalis (Soja and Hadjimichalis 1979), who contributed to the EADI network) also offered a contribution to reconcile the opposing poles in the discussion, namely 'spatial determinism' and 'socially constructed space', respectively. He suggests the concept of 'socio-spatial dialectic'. Space was socially produced and organized. Two axes of conflict arise from the capitalist mode of production, a vertical (class conflicts) and a horizontal (core–periphery) one. Both are seen as inseparable, both can be explained in their interrelation only. He defines two forms of class struggle: 'Thus the transformation of capitalism can occur only through the combination and articulation of a horizontal (periphery vs. center) and vertical (working class vs. bourgeoisie) class struggle, by transformation on both the social and spatial planes' (Soja 1980: 224). In the process, spatial resistance must not be monopolized by anti-egalitarian policies:

> The two forms of class struggle can be made to appear in conflict, especially with the manipulation of territorial identities under bourgeois nationalism, regionalism, and localism. But when territorial consciousness is based on the exploitative nature of capitalist relations of production and reproduction, and not on parochialism and emotional attachment to place, it is class consciousness. The production of space has indeed been socially obfuscated and mystified in the development of capitalism, and this has allowed it to be used against class struggle. (ibid.: 224)

What was not elaborated, however, was the characteristics of classes and how power was organized on a state level. But what are the classes in this 'horizontal class struggle' between core and periphery? If one abandons the simplistic logic of modernization theory—as scholars of dependency do—then classes in countries and regions where capitalist industrialization was introduced later, the influence from the outside helped shaping structures and agents of development that could lead to different development paths, with progressive and regressive elements. Leon Trotsky called such processes 'uneven and combined development' (cf. Weissenbacher 2008). The class and state theorist Nicos Poulantzas was familiar with Latin American dependency analysis, which he incorporated into his variant of neo-Marxist writing. There are direct references to the Latin American dependency school (Poulantzas 1974: 112 and 2001: 28), but one can find also particular language of dependency theorists. Furthermore, Poulantzas had attended an international seminar (on social classes) in Mexico in 1971, where Fernando Cardoso was his commentator (cf. Benítez 1998). It is hardly a surprise that many of the following accounts by Poulantzas seem to resemble writings of the dependency authors presented in Chapter 2. As with the Latin American dependency theorists and the authors of the European dependency networks, Poulantzas analyzed transnational capitalism (he used the term 'mondialization'—globalization) in the era of imperialism and monopoly capital: Transnational companies (TNC) form joint ventures and the (new) international division of labor runs across borderlines (Poulantzas 1974, 2001). They control an 'institutional space' that runs across regions and nations, as Constantine Vaitsos (1980: 24) wrote in the EADI network:

> For a significant part of production activities and exchange relations, the underlying economic and behavioural forces can no longer be adequately understood or interpreted on an inter-national or an inter-areas basis. Instead, the appropriate framework of analysis appears to be one of corporate internalization. In such a context, decisions and information management, production and exchange activities, as well as the accumulation of resources and capabilities are integrated within the consolidated boundaries of a single enterprise control system, with affiliated or related firms operating in a number of national jurisdictions.

This corporate internalization alters the economic space of regions and nations which thus do not necessarily coincide with political boundaries. Corporations are not limited to their economic space of origin, they can shift between economic spaces (regions, nations) in order to determine where profits are realized, where they are declared, and where processes of accumulation and growth take place (Vaitsos 1980: 26). The internationalization of production and capital accumulation, argues Poulantzas (2001: 25ff.), affects the 'imperialist chain' of countries as well as every single country's society. Uneven development had always been integral for capitalism but now domination of countries (as power relation between countries) is being replaced: Core countries (metropoles) establish, in the imperialist stage, their immediate rule and their mode of production within the dominated and dependent social formations themselves. This reproduction of power relations chains the periphery to the core (metropoles), each country in its own form. Each dependent social formation therefore organizes its class and state structures according to the structure of these power relations and internalizes them. Poulantzas stresses that precapitalist, pre-imperialist (competitive capitalism), and imperialist characteristics coexist. He describes social formations as the geographical 'place of the reproduction process and therefore intersections of uneven development in the conditions of modes and forms of productions within the class struggle' (Poulantzas 2001: 30). He expected that the internationalization of modes of productions and a 'socialization' of labor (due to its high level of organization in very big companies) would 'objectively increase the international solidarity of workers' (Poulantzas 2001: 59). 'At the same time', and this is important for our discussion of the 'vertical and horizontal class struggle', 'the national form prevails in their struggle that is essentially an international struggle' (ibid.).

Similar to Latin American dependency thinking, for Poulantzas the state in the era of monopoly capitalism differs from the one in the liberal era of competitive capitalism. What he labeled 'authoritarian statism' gives the executive (government) more power in this era. Authoritarian statism, however, seems to be the form for core countries, while in peripheral countries, 'for example in Latin America, we are witnessing the emergence of *a new form of dependent State* which [...] involves significant points of dissimilarity with the new form of State in the dominant countries' (Poulantzas 2014: 204). 'Authoritarian statism', argues Poulantzas (2014: 204), 'is thus dependent upon those structural modifications in the relations of production and the processes and social division of labour which characterize the present phase at both the world and the national levels'. In the era of transnational capitalism, the (authoritarian) state needs to intervene into the economy to an extent that actually also produces crisis although it is meant to counter structural problems. It seems unclear from this discussion whether for Poulantzas the Southern European periphery is in a similar position as Latin American states. In any respect, '[i]n certain European countries (France, Italy, Spain, Greece, Portugal) contradictions condense into veritable political crises finding expression in a crisis of the State itself' (Poulantzas 2014: 214). Drawing on Poulantzas, Hadjimichalis

(1983: 136) argues that 'deep historical roots of authoritarian rule in southern Europe – due to the mode of articulation of these countries with the international division of labour and their internal class structure – permitted the development of authoritarian statism, parallel with the development of formal democratic liberties. The outcome is a direct political crisis and a crisis of the State itself'. Among the consequences are the strengthening *and* weakening of the state, and also a regional crisis that leads to 'new forms of struggle in Spain, Italy and Greece which combine class consciousness with regional and community identity'. Regional social movements 'arise from both objective conditions of uneven regional development and subjective conditions of rising regional consciousness', 'a certain type of [...] social practices' that has a 'territorial and a multi-class base' (petty bourgeoisie, peasantry, working class) (ibid.: 137f.).

Poulantzas' analysis sounds like what we have seen from the Latin American dependency school in Chapter 2. Frank and Dos Santos had been—too strictly if we look at the discussion in Chapter 2—criticized for emphasizing external against internal factors of dependence. Especially with Cardoso and Faletto, and their analysis of one global capitalism with yet special situations of dependence, the similarity between Poulantzas and the Latin Americans seems striking. They talk of a complex whole of external forces and 'internalization of external interests' and the interplay between internal and external forces had led to particular social formations with particular classes and forms of states. Poulantzas as well perceived internal and external elements of the state which he saw coined by class relations. The state 'must be considered [...], as a material condensation (apparatus) of a relation of force between classes and fractions of classes as they are expressed in a specific manner (the relative separation of the state and the economy giving way to the very institutions of the capitalist state) at the very heart of the state' (Poulantzas 2008a: 307f.). '[T]he state', argues Poulantzas (2008a: 309),

> establishes the general and long-term interests of the power bloc (the unstable equilibrium of compromises) under the hegemony of a given fraction of monopoly capitalism. The concrete functioning of its autonomy, which is limited in the face of monopoly capitalism, seems to be a process whereby these intrastate contradictions interact, a process that, at least for the short term, seems prodigiously incoherent and chaotic.

But this establishment of the long-term interest of the power bloc is result of struggles between dominating and dominated classes that are (also) taking place at the state level (and in its institutions) (Poulantzas 2014: 40ff.). Poulantzas calls this indirect class rule via the state and its institutions 'relative autonomy of the state' vis-à-vis the dominant classes (Poulantzas 2008b: 280). This relative autonomy seems to allow the modern capitalist state to represent

> itself as embodying the general interest of society as a whole, as the substantiation of the 'will' of the 'political body' that is the 'nation'. Here the concept of hegemony (hegemony-as-political-practice) refers to the moment when the political structuration of the dominant classes - ideological function, organizational function, leadership, and so on - assumes decisive importance in class relations. (Poulantzas 2008c: 89)

It is important for Poulantzas to stress that the state is not a 'monolithic bloc' (Poulantzas 2008a: 308). Rather, 'the dominant classes or fractions in the capitalist formation emerge as structured into a particular ensemble, via *state mediation*, by "the hegemony of one social group over a series of subordinate groups"' (Poulantzas 2008c: 103). But there are 'class contradictions found, particularly, those between fractions of the power bloc that constitute the state':

> They manifest themselves in the form of internal contradictions between the diverse branches and apparatuses of the state, while having a privileged representative of a particular interest of the power bloc: executive and parliament, army, justice, regional-municipal and central apparatuses, various ideological apparatuses, and so forth. (Poulantzas 2008a: 309)

Poulantzas (2008d: 179) refers to Marx, Engels and Lenin in arguing that 'members of the state apparatus, which it is convenient to call the "bureaucracy" in the general sense, constitute a specific social category - not a class' (Poulantzas 2008e: 41f.). '[T]he term social category', Poulantzas (2008f: 201) argues,

> designates an ensemble of agents whose principal role is its functioning in the state apparatuses and in ideology. This is the case, for example, with the administrative bureaucracy which is composed in part of groups of state functionaries (civil servants). [...] [T]he senior personnel, the top of the administrative bureaucracy, generally belong to the bourgeoisie, while

> the intermediate and lower echelons may belong either to the bourgeoisie or to the petty bourgeoisie. These social categories belong to classes and do not in themselves constitute classes: they have no specific role of their own in production.

In a dependent state, Poulantzas (1976: 12) argues, the 'state petty bourgeoisie' has substantial weight 'due to the parasitic growth of the state bureaucracy characteristic of this dependent situation'. He calls a 'caste' the 'administrative bureaucracy' of capitalist societies which 'cannot actually function as a factor totalizing private interests and the general interest' nor 'as a 'neutral' mediator between social classes, as the neo-capitalist doctrines of the welfare state would have it' (Poulantzas 2008e: 41f.):

> This means that, although the members of the state apparatus belong, by their class origin, to different classes, they function according to a specific internal unity. Their class origin - class situation - recedes into the background in relation to that which unifies them - their class position: that is to say, the fact that they belong precisely to the state apparatus and that they have as their objective function the actualization of the role of the state. This in its turn means that the bureaucracy, as a specific and relatively 'unified' social category, is the 'servant' of the ruling class, not by reason of its class origins, which are divergent, or by reason of its personal relations with the ruling class, but by reason of the fact that its internal unity derives from its actualization of the objective role of the state. The totality of this role itself coincides with the interests of the ruling class. (Poulantzas 2008d: 179)

This presentation of a flexible model of a capitalist the state whose apparatus consists of a state bureaucracy that mediates between fractions of capitalist classes but also represents the interests of a dominant bloc in power reminds of the analysis by Cardoso and Faletto presented in Chapter 2. For them as well, the state was not only at the crossroads of dependency relationships but also of class struggles in order to win state power and institutions first, and then change society as a whole (see Chapter 2). In Poulantzas' (2008e: 43) words,

> it is not a question, here and now, of seizing power by direct armed struggle - from the very beginning - but of conquering power. On the other hand, still more than in the case of any seizure of power, this conquest can

> and must be carried out by a hegemonic organization of the working class, by an organization which, from its subaltern position, raises itself up to the level of a class that already envisages the concrete exercise of power, while struggling to conquer it. The ultimate goal of this power in the hands of the proletariat is to impart to the 'democratic' values of liberty and equality, negated by the contemporary state and its division from civil society - the base – a concrete, material content and meaning that are 'human' and 'true', extending to all levels.

While this sounds like a gradual takeover of power, Poulantzas (1976: 82) seems to suggest, however, otherwise:

> There is certainly always a unity of state power related to the state's representation of the interests of the hegemonic class or fraction, and this is the reason why the popular classes can never occupy the state apparatus bit by bit, but have to smash it in the transition to socialism; but this should not give rise to the idea of the state as a bloc devoid of fissures.

As we have seen in Chapter 2, the Latin American dependency writers estimated lowly the role of a national bourgeoisie in Latin America to be a promotor of development or put up resistance against transnational capital. Poulantzas differentiates capital fractions (sections and size) but also offers two principal types of capital groups, the national bourgeoisie and the comprador bourgeoisie:

> Reference to political and ideological criteria is also important in defining fractions of the bourgeoisie. Some of its fractions are to be located already at the economic level of the constitution and reproduction of capital: industrial, commercial and financial capital, big and medium capital at the stage of monopoly capitalism (imperialism). But precisely at the imperialist stage, a distinction arises which is not to be located at the economic level alone - the distinction between the 'comprador' bourgeoisie and the national bourgeoisie. The comprador bourgeoisie is that fraction of the class whose interests are constitutively linked to foreign imperialist capital (capital belonging to the principal foreign imperialist power) and which is thus completely bound politically and ideologically to foreign capital. The national bourgeoisie is that fraction of the bourgeoisie whose interests are linked to the nation's economic development and which comes into relative contradiction with the interests of big foreign capital. (Poulantzas 2008f: 200)

While the comprador bourgeoisie lacks an own independent base of capital accumulation and is an intermediary of the interests of foreign (US) capital, the national bourgeoisie can, under certain conditions of struggles for national liberation, position itself as ally of popular struggles (Poulantzas 1974: 110ff.). It seems as if the very weakness of the national bourgeoisie (including the prospect that there was no fraction of bourgeoisie that would have some amount of independence or could stand up against penetrating US capital) led Poulantzas to introduce a further analytical category: interior or domestic bourgeoisie. Above all, the domestic bourgeoisie is a category based in (European) imperialist countries competing with the United States. It has its own economic and accumulation base and is a result of the internationalization of production and its internalization (Poulantzas 2001: 52f.). However, 'the new forms of dependence characterizing the relationships that certain dependent countries have with the imperialist centres', argues Poulantzas (1976: 41), 'permits the emergence or development of a new fraction of the bourgeoisie in these countries [Greece, Portugal, Spain]: a fraction which I have referred to elsewhere as the domestic bourgeoisie'. We remember that Dos Santos (1970), Cardoso (1977), and Cardoso and Faletto (1979) called 'new dependency' the core–periphery relations of TNC capitalism that also had significance in terms of class relations of dependent states within the international division of labor. For Poulantzas (1976: 41), this means

> on the one hand, the rapid destruction of pre-capitalist modes and forms of production, on account of the forms assumed by the present imports of foreign capital in these countries; on the other hand, the process of dependent industrialization, due to the tendency of foreign capital to invest in the directly productive sectors of industrial capital, in the current context of internationalization of production and capital. [...] As this industrialization gets under way, there develop nuclei of an autochtonic bourgeoisie with a chiefly industrial character (directly productive capital) [...].

I can only briefly point at what seem to be contradictions in Poulantzas' class analysis. An important element of his strategic efforts appears to have been his criticism of those communists (as in France) who argued for an alliance with fractions of the national bourgeoisie as part of an anti-monopolist strategy. He considers these efforts futile which is reminiscent of the arguments of Latin American dependency writers against strategies building on a popular front including Latin American bourgeoisies. Having said that, Poulantzas analytical escape seems to be the introduction of a domestic bourgeoisie, and he, indeed, argues that this domestic bourgeoisie cannot 'necessarily' be reduced 'to what Gunder Frank called Lumpenbourgeoisies' (Poulantzas 2001: 53) but has a certain leeway to act autonomously from US capital. The domestic bourgeoisie does not seem to function like a 'real' national bourgeoisie from modernization theory. There are

> characteristics that prevent this domestic bourgeoisie from becoming an effective national bourgeoisie, in particular its heterogeneity, its division due to the contradictions that run through it, and its political and ideological weakness and ambiguity. Events in Greece and Portugal, therefore [...] are far from proving the possibilities often ascribed to them of a strategic alliance between the popular masses and fractions of the bourgeoisie on the basis of a process of national liberation and transition to socialism - as if these were genuine national bourgeoisies. (Poulantzas 1976: 58)

Despite this disappointment over the alleged role of a national bourgeoisie, an alliance of socialist parties with the domestic bourgeoisie was possible in order to overthrow dictatorships: 'Under the hegemony of the domestic bourgeoisie' in Greece, Portugal, and Spain, an 'overthrow of the dictatorships is possible even without the process of democratization being telescoped together with a process of transition to socialism and national liberation':

> This fact was far from evident to all who were involved in the resistance; we most often considered that this bourgeoisie was unable to have such a place, to play this role in a genuine break with the regime and the replacement of one form of state (dictatorship) by another (bourgeois 'democracy') – a decisive difference, even within the bourgeois state. This indicates that the domestic bourgeoisie has often been doubly underestimated: not just as a possible ally, but also, and this matters far more here, as an adversary, for even if experience shows that it can be an ally in certain particular conjunctures, it does not cease to be at the same time an adversary. (Poulantzas 1976: 66f.)

But the domestic bourgeoisie in Greece, Portugal, and Spain was weak and 'unable, for the most part, to wield long-term political hegemony over the other fractions of the bourgeoisie and the dominant classes, i.e. over the power bloc' (ibid.: 44). It was itself fragmented and only 'certain important sectors of the domestic bourgeoisie [...] have turned towards a policy of integration into the Common Market' (ibid.: 52) and against dictatorships, namely 'its monopoly sectors [...] modestly known as the "enlightened" or "neo-capitalist" bourgeoisie' (ibid.: 57). This was a 'genuine tactical alliance between broad sectors of the domestic bourgeoisie and the popular forces on a precise and limited objective, i.e. the overthrow of the military dictatorships and their replacement by "democratic" regimes' (ibid.: 59). And there it stopped:

> And if it could already be predicted in advance that no fractions of the bourgeoisie would be found ready to support a process of transition to socialism, there has not even been any sign up to now of any fractions ready to support even limited anti-monopoly objectives such as are contained in the 'Common Programme' of the French Communist and Socialist Parties. (ibid.: 58f.)

Maybe the domestic bourgeoisie could be a useful category for a bourgeoisie in countries of late industrialization. Poulantzas' intention, however, was not a concept for late industrializers. It seems to have been at least equally important for him to explain inner-imperialist struggles: European bourgeoisies of the EC as against the United States (cf. Poulantzas 2008g: 244ff.). Since the domestic bourgeoisie is in itself fragmented, it remains unclear why it poses an essential category and could not be replaced by capital fractions (of the entire bourgeoisie) after all (for a state analysis that operates with capital fractions, cf. Agnoli 1995 [1978]). A fraction of the comprador bourgeoisie, for example, could quite as well be defined as 'more modern', not entirely dependent on US capital, and able to reach temporary hegemony over the power bloc. The situation in Europe seems to have been changing, a pax Germanica started to replace pax Americana in Europe (cf. Chapter 5). European monopoly capitalists or fractions of them might have started an interest in replacing fascist dictatorships in Europe and support a 'Europeanized' comprador bourgeoisie. In such a case, neither a domestic nor a national bourgeoisie was necessary for such political changes. As Pollis (1983: 210) put it:

> Nationalistic right wing regimes that engage in protectionist policies threaten the economic interests of European industrialists whose access to markets is restricted, as is their ability to make investment decisions free of controls. Left-wing revolutionary regimes, on the other hand, would threaten the entire foundation of bourgeois states and the EC itself.

Lastly, Poulantzas did not empirically establish the difference between the domestic and comprador bourgeoisies. For Lipietz (1987: 115), it was 'unclear how it [the domestic bourgeoisie, RW] differs from the national bourgeoisie'. Bob Jessop (1985: 280) quotes various critical studies that 'have denied that a domestic bourgeoisie exists in Spain, Greece, or Portugal'. And Poulantzas (1976: 45) himself concedes that

> [t]he distinction between comprador and domestic bourgeoisie, while being based on the new structure of dependence, is not a statistical and empirical distinction, fixed rigidly once and for all. It is rather a tendential differentiation, the concrete configuration it takes depending to a certain extent on the conjuncture.

3.2 Core and Periphery: Characteristics and Definitions

The crisis that reached Europe in 2008 has led to a wide use of the terms peripheral and periphery, again, in order to group countries within the European Union (EU) and the Economic and Monetary Union (EMU). Often the use of such concepts seems purely figurative. The term 'core' is ostentatiously absent for the most part. It does not make sense, however, to talk about periphery without also dealing with the core, and the relationship between periphery and core, respectively. Periphery is—especially if one pays attention to socioeconomic processes and certainly in the terms of the 'dependency school'—part of a dialectic totality with a conceptual duality of core and periphery (plus in some cases an intermediate form of a semiperiphery). Such a relational concept very much depends on the focus of analysis. This becomes clear in the different approaches of the EADI network and the 'Binghamton-network'. The former observes core–semiperiphery–periphery relations within Europe (Seers 1979b) while the latter tries to grasp whether Southern Europe should be treated as part of a global semiperiphery (Arrighi 1985b). The core–periphery metaphor is geographic only in the sense of geography as social science which is concerned with political economy. 'Regional theory', argues Friedmann (1983: 148),

> relies to a large extent on the core-periphery model and its related concepts of dependency, unequal development, and geographical transfer of value. Despite its simplifications, it is, in many respects, a convenient model: used with circumspection, it can lead to significant results, both for analysis and practice.

Latin American structuralism and the dependency school had decisively shaped the core–periphery model, and the 'European Dependency School' used it in the European circumstances of uneven (spatial) development. Bevor that, Karl Marx and Marxist writers had early emphasized uneven spatial development (Weissenbacher 2008: 97ff.; Love 2011:15f.) but it was 'Werner Sombart, the maverick of the last generation of the German Historical School of economic development', whose '*Der moderne Kapitalismus* was probably the first work to distinguish between center and periphery in the world economic system' (Love 2011: 26). Sombart, however, 'did not provide any theory of relations between Center and Periphery' (Love 1996: 134). Although the Argentinian structuralist Raúl Prebisch did not seem to recall how he came to use the terms 'center' and 'periphery' (Love 2011: 39, Fn41), Sombart might have had an impact on Prebisch via the Romanian structuralist (and Fascist) Mihail Manoilescu (who did not use the terms literally). 'Sombart specifically referred to Center and Periphery in the same sense as Prebisch did', argues Love (1996: 134). 'The process of reconfiguration [of capitalism] has taken place', writes Sombart (1927: XIV),

> by developing intensively to its highest form at a tiny little spot on the surface of the earth. From here it has utilized the rest of the world. In order to negotiate one's way through the imbroglio of occurrences, we need to distinguish between a capitalist center, capitalist central countries, and a – seen from this center – mass of peripheral countries. Those are the leading, active nations, these are the serving, passive countries.

Prebisch started to refer to 'center' and 'periphery' in a series of lectures in 1944, and in print in 1946 (Love 1996: 126ff.; 2011: 19 and 21ff.). But also theorists of the European and US-American core have formulated core–periphery models: François Perroux developed his theoretical framework parallel to Prebisch (Love 1996: 112), Gunnar Myrdal and Albert Hirschman in 1957 (cf. Hirschman 1975: 143), and in 1958 (Friedmann 1983: 148). As regards the 'European Dependency School', John Friedmann, claims to have coined the term 'core region' in English language in order to replace the 'growth poles' in Perroux's language, and later 'core and periphery' to replace Hirschman's 'underdeveloped' south and 'developed' north (Friedmann and Weaver 1979: 116, cf. Friedmann 1967: 22 and 1966: Chapter 2). He argues to have

> developed this model of core-periphery relations still further, with a view to undergirding the practice of regional planning with appropriate theory. In a work published in 1972, I brought together economic, geographic, and political variables into a set of interconnected hypotheses. 'A general theory of polarized development' proved too unwieldy, however, to gain much popularity. In any event, it was soon overtaken by Marxist approaches to regional analysis which, though they made extensive use of the core-periphery imagery, did so essentially to illuminate the mechanisms of uneven development on a world scale [...]. (Friedmann 1983: 148f.)

But about the same time, Johan Galtung (1971, 1972) had published his 'structural theory of imperialism' (cf. Chapter 2.5), building on core–periphery relations (Galtung used the term 'center'). Prebisch, Friedmann, and other non-Marxists started to use the 'core-periphery imagery' to analyze uneven development on a world scale (or European scale, for that matter). It became an important tool in development studies. Dudley Seers departed from the observation that using hierarchies among countries was very common. Most often the top countries were called 'rich', 'developed', 'imperialist', or 'industrialized'. It had been a 'convenient metaphor' to describe these countries as 'core' and the remainder as 'periphery':

> Between the two groups of countries are big differences in level of income, structures of employment, rates of fertility and social conditions. In the hands of some, especially dependency theorists, this is not just a metaphor; it is shorthand for a set of structural relationships, in which the core countries are dominant. (Seers 1979a: xiii)

Visible signs of the structural imbalances between core and periphery in Europe are tourism flows to the periphery and flows of migrant workers to the core (France from Portugal, Spain, and Algeria; Western Germany from the Balkans and Turkey; both from Italy; Seers 1979b: 9ff.). Casparis (1985: 111, 127ff.), writing in the Binghamton network on the example of Switzerland, suggests an immediate relationship between the establishment of core countries and their drawing of labor from peripheral areas abroad, including Southern Europe. Such dependent migration flows, however, only emerged

> after big differences in income levels have appeared, and to explain these we have to examine commercial, financial, technological, military and cultural asymmetries, such as can be found influencing countries further out from a core. (Seers 1979a: xiv)

Demetrios Papademetriou (1983: 243f.) placed migration in the context of the 'European framework of uneven development' with a 'reserve labor army' that was 'raised, paid for, and maintained by the periphery and placed at the disposal of international capital at a critical juncture in the development of the center' (Papademetriou 1978 quoted in Papademetriou 1983: 243). He analyzed the negative consequences of labor migration for the sending but also receiving societies. Geographic neighborhood is not seen as a precondition for core–periphery relations. However, vicinity (as with the European case) can accelerate and intensify changes via economic, political, and cultural channels. Transport costs are lower (for tourists and migrants), exports can easier compete in neighboring markets which bears a potential danger for industrialization processes in peripheral countries (Seers 1979a: xv–xviii; 1979b: 22ff.).

Clearly processes that determine core–peripheral relations reach across national borders, eventually creating core regions in the periphery and peripheral regions in overall core countries. Characteristics for peripheral regions (within states) were being described by Walter Stöhr (1983a: 8f.; 1983b: 121) and Nohlen and Schultze (1985b: 46, for Andalusia, the *Mezzogiorno*, and Southern Portugal):

- disproportionate importance of the agricultural sector and tourism,
- industries oriented on raw material and primary production,
- predominance of traditional and labor-intensive technology, dominance of small companies,
- few modern capital-intensive heavy industries located in the growth poles of the region,

- low per capita income,
- high unemployment and underemployment,
- high migration and brain drain,
- signs of structural heterogeneity and marginality, poor social infrastructure
- dependence on financial transfers from and (industrial) investment decisions (capital and technology transfer) outside the region.

3.3 Semiperiphery and Division of Labor

For the 'Binghamton-network', the theoretical analysis of Immanuel Wallerstein (1985) is central. His concept follows ideas from the Latin American dependency school and suggested a zero-sum game for the relations between core and periphery:

> The more one zone became 'core-like,' the more another became 'peripheral.' (Wallerstein 1985: 33)

Core and periphery are connected economically by commodity chains that reach across national borders. Until the 1960s production and distribution within such commodity chains could be 'fairly well' categorized as primary products in the periphery versus industrial goods as core products. Changes in production ever since have shown that such a dualism does not work as universal criterion. Wallerstein suggests assessing concrete pairs of core–periphery relations along an axial division of labor in commodity chains (production processes and locations, investment patterns, pricing policies). That would show which part of the pair was more core-like or peripheral. Such a conception was working well for the world economy as a whole '[b]ut when we seek to understand state policies in relation to the ongoing process of the world accumulation of capital, a simple binary tension doesn't seem to work as well' (Wallerstein 1985: 33f.). He goes further beyond the core–periphery dichotomy in order to understand state policies in relation to global accumulation of capital. Commodity chains are seen as going across national borders, each state hosts core and peripheral processes, for those states that have an even mix of both types of activities, he suggests the name semiperiphery. State policies can influence capital accumulation in different ways.

> They include, among others, the control of flows across frontiers, the control of the internal work force, taxation, redistributive expenditures, and expenditures on social overhead. This is in addition to any involvement of the state as customer or producer. There are also the expenditures on the military, which is a key weapon that creates the space for the state to make these other decisions. (Wallerstein 1985: 34)

Semiperipheral states can change their status to a core state and also the structure of global commodity chains. Wallerstein (1979a: 21f.) considered the existence of a semiperiphery as 'needed to make a capitalist world-economy run smoothly', it had an important political role in stabilizing the capitalist world-system:

> This semiperiphery is then assigned as it were a specific economic role, but the reason is less economic than political. That is to say, one might make a good case that the world-economy as an economy would function every bit as well without a semiperiphery. But it would be far less *politically* stable, for it would mean a polarized world-system. The existence of a third category means precisely that the upper stratum is not faced with the *unified* opposition of all others because the *middle* stratum is both exploited and exploiter. It follows that the specific economic role is not all that important, and has thus changed through the various historical changes of the modern world-system. (Wallerstein 1979a: 21f.)

Within the Binghamton network, there had been a controversial debate on the concept of semiperiphery. Giovanni Arrighi (1985c: 243) attributes the controversy within the group, whether Southern European states have been semiperipheral, to 'a lack of operational criteria for identifying semiperipheral states':

> Wallerstein's criteria as set out in his contribution to this volume are rather vague and formal. They are vague mainly because we are not told what weight to assign to the mix of economic activities that fall within a state's boundary, on the one hand, and to its position in the interstate system, on the other. They are formal mainly because we are not told, substantively, which activities in the various commodity chains are core-like and which are periphery-like, how the two types of activity have changed over time, above all, how peripherality, semiperipherality, and coreness can be operationally measured.

Using 'an ill-defined combination of criteria' (Arrighi 1985c: 244) has led to the classification of 'a wide range of countries in terms of economic strength and political background' (Wallerstein 1979c: 100) as semiperipheral, from Brazil to Cuba, Algeria to Saudi Arabia, Israel, Nigeria and (back then) Zaire in Africa, and finally Asian countries: Turkey, China, Korea, and Vietnam. Overall, the countries of Wallerstein's semiperiphery made up about the size of 2/3 of world population, as Arrighi (1985c: 244ff.) commented tersely. We will return to Arrighi's model further down below.

Wallerstein explains 'unequal relation' between core and periphery by referring to Arghiri Emmanuel (1972, who popularized the notion of 'unequal exchange'), but Wallerstein avoids the controversy around the theorem (cf. Fischer and Weissenbacher 2016). Wallerstein observes the ability of core capitalists to appropriate parts of the surplus value realized in the periphery:

> Surplus-value, once created, gets distributed among a large number of people beyond the person who first obtains that segment of created value. In the whole circuit of capital that value may get distributed to a multiplicity of people. And the core-periphery relationship indicates the degree to which surplus-value is unevenly distributed in the direction of the core. What we are talking about now is a process. The degree to which the economic relationship is core-peripheralized is the degree to which there is an increasingly unequal distribution of the surplus product between two different bourgeoisies. (Wallerstein 1978: 221)

Furthermore, Wallerstein (1979b: 71) argues an unequal exchange based on the exchange of high against low-wage production,

> in which a peripheral worker needs to work many hours, at a given level of productivity, to obtain a product produced by a worker in a core country in one hour. And vice versa. Such a system is necessary for the expansion of a world market if the primary consideration is profit. Without *unequal* exchange, it would not be profitable to expand the size of the division of labor.

Lastly Wallerstein (2004: 28) stresses the importance of monopoly production within the axial division of labor between core and periphery:

> Since profitability is directly related to the degree of monopolization, what we essentially mean by core-like production processes is those that are controlled by quasi-monopolies. Peripheral processes are then those that are truly competitive. When exchange occurs, competitive products are in a weak position and quasi monopolized products are in a strong position. As a result, there is a constant flow of surplus-value from the producers of peripheral products to the producers of core-like products. This has been called unequal exchange.

It seems to me that the way Giovanni Arrighi and Jessica Drangel (1986) clarify, adapt, and qualify the world-systems analysis as introduced by Wallerstein and others adds very much to the understanding and concretion of the core–semiperiphery–periphery model. In order to avoid ambiguities, they use the term semiperiphery 'exclusively to refer to a position in relation to the world division of labor and never to refer to a position in the interstate system' (ibid.: 15). Although both spheres are important and interrelated it is 'the separation of the two types of command [that] is a peculiarity of the capitalist world-economy (as opposed to world-empires)' (ibid.: 16). The economic activities of this world economy are being pursued in (overall) commodity chains (Box 3.1), therefore it is not a sectoral distribution that decides upon the allocation of states as belonging to core, semiperiphery, or periphery. It is 'the unequal distribution of rewards among the various activities that constitute the single overarching division of labor defining and bounding the world-economy' (ibid.: 16). These economic activities are called 'nodes of the commodity chain' (ibid.: 16).

Box 3.1: 'Chain research': the terminology

The terminology has changed alongside the turns in content in 'chain' research from commodity chains toward global commodity chains and global value chains. 'By the early 2000s', writes Bair (2014: 2), 'the commodity chain terminology was frequently being used interchangeably with other constructs, such as global production networks (GPNs). In recent years, one such alternative nomenclature – global value chains (GVCs) – has become hegemonic, especially within more applied or policy-oriented studies of global industries. Global value chain analysis has even been taken up enthusiastically by international financial institutions [...]'.

Global commodity chains and global value chains 'are analytically oriented toward the micro (individual firm) or meso (sector) level as opposed to the macro and holistic perspective characteristic of the world-system conceptualization of commodity chains' (Bair 2005: 164). I will stick, therefore, to the original world-systems terminology throughout this book: 'World-systems theorists understand commodity chains as consisting not only of the steps involved in the transformation of raw materials into final goods, but also as webs connecting that set of productive activities with the social reproduction of human labor power as a critical input into this process. Additionally, world-systems theorists are most fundamentally interested in how commodity chains structure and reproduce a stratified and hierarchical world-system' (Bair 2005: 155f.; see Bair 2005 and 2009 for a literature overview of the different strands of 'chain' literature).

Arrighi and Drangel reject or amend a variety of assumptions important for authors in a similar paradigmatic context (dependency and world-systems). They decline the perception that a single type of sectoral reward (profit, wage, rent) could explain a differentiation into core, semiperiphery, or periphery. This is by no means trivial, because Arghiri Emmanuel, for example, who is Wallerstein's reference for unequal exchange, assumes that institutionally determined wage inequality between core and periphery determines the respective characteristics. Furthermore, Emmanuel based his model of a homogenous world market on full competition in which profits of single capitals converge to an average international rate of profit. International monopolies were only capable of disturbing the convergence of national but not international rates of profits (cf. Fischer and Weissenbacher 2016: 145ff.).

Consequently, Arrighi and Drangel reject the idea of pure competition (and therefore also assumptions of classical political economists and Marx, ibid.: 16f.). They acknowledge 'the level of wages (or of profit) as a [single] criterion for distinguishing core and peripheral activities' only 'under a most restrictive set of assumptions' (ibid.: 18). They regard them as not useful 'in capturing the variety of situations (in terms of factoral distribution of rewards) in and through which core–peripheral relations have historically been reproduced'. Instead they 'take only the level of aggregate rewards as indicative of the core and peripheral status of an activity' (ibid.: 18). What is the nature of these activities? Are there core and peripheral activities? These questions seem to have utmost importance for development studies (a) in the light of historical experience of core–periphery categorization, and (b) for possible future development scenarios. Other than modernization theoretical accounts that more or less regard progress a movement from agricultural production to industrial production (as alleged in the British experience), Arrighi and Drangel reject the idea of invariant characteristics:

> We further assume that no particular activity (whether defined in terms of its output or of the technique used) is inherently core-like or periphery-like. Any activity can become at a particular point in time core-like or periphery-like, but each has that characteristic for a limited period. Nonetheless, there are always some products and techniques that are core-like and others that are periphery-like at any given time. (Arrighi and Drangel 1986: 18)

We will return to this question shortly. Since Arrighi and Drangel's model is a three-tier system, we first need to explain the logic behind it (the relations between enterprises and the states), and the identification of the three tiers. For that reason, the authors outline their interpretation of the capitalist enterprise that they perceive as engaging in a mix of activities and creating competitive pressure by introducing profit-oriented innovations. The success of an enterprise lies in the ability to upgrade its mix of activities at the expense of other enterprises:

> [A]s the capitalist enterprise is a locus of "accumulation" (of assets, expertise, specialized knowledge, and organization), the present capability of an enterprise to upgrade its mix of activities will to some extend depend upon its past success in doing so. (ibid.: 21)

The core enterprises that successfully upgrade their activities are, Arrighi and Drangel (1986: 21) claim, quoting Schumpeter, 'aggressor by nature and wield the really effective weapon of competition'. Arrighi and Drangel (1986: 19ff.) draw on Schumpeter's conception of 'creative destruction' but they interpret it spatially instead of chronologically. With Schumpeter, profit-oriented innovations create windfall profits for a few and losses for the majority of enterprises. In the phase of economic prosperity, a productive revolution occurs which then leads in a depression phase to the elimination of old and outdated elements of the industrial structure. The competition is being dampened in the prosperity phase but in the depression phase the majority of enterprises overrates their chances to be equally successful and engages in a cut-throat competition. While this was a 'cluster in time', Arrighi and Drangel (1986: 20) use this concept for a 'cluster in space': zones of predominating prosperity and zones of predominating depression (cf. also Arrighi et al. 2003: 17). Core enterprises compete by outsourcing the consequences of competition to peripheral enterprises (or peripheral capital). A relatively small group of core enterprises cluster in a 'core zone' and produce a spatial polarization. Such an arrangement would be volatile (if core and periphery arrangements changed easily), but core enterprises and core states have developed together which produced a rather stable form of spatial polarization. Arrighi and Drangel (1986: 22) observe that the

> competitive struggle among capitalist enterprises has not taken place in a political void, but has been closely interrelated with the formation of states – that is, of formally sovereign territorial jurisdictions.

States have been integral to the formation of the world economy, and commodity chains have operated across state boundaries. However, states differ in their ability to influence the commodity chains, 'the modalities by which the social division of labor operates' (ibid.: 22). The position of states in their relation to enterprises (or commodity chains) contains weaknesses. States are seen as having a priority of securing their monopoly of power on their territories, and not the creation of wealth. They compete against other states attempting to upgrade their position in the division of labor.

> The main difficulty is that economic command is largely dependent upon an innovative participation in the world division of labor [...], and that capitalist enterprises have progressively become specialized agencies of such participation [...]. The problem of upgrading a state's mix of core-peripheral activities is thus largely a problem of being able to attract and develop organic links with "core capital" [...]. This capacity is only in part reflection of state's political power [...] it depends equally if not more on the extent to which a state has already developed organic links with core capital and, therefore, already encloses within its jurisdiction a predominantly core mix of activities. (ibid.: 24)

However, core states have, and peripheral states lack, the capability

> (1) to control access to the most remunerative outlets of all major commodity chains, (2) to provide the infrastructure and services required by core-like activities, and (3) to create a political climate favorable to capitalist entrepreneurship. This means that core states control advantages of core locations and can use that control to develop a symbiotic relation with the core capital that is already located within their jurisdiction, and to attract more core capital from peripheral locations. (ibid.: 25)

This symbiotic relationship between core states and core capital enhances, for both, the ability 'to consolidate and reproduce their association with predominantly core-like activities' (ibid.: 26), while the opposite is true for peripheral states which face an 'endemic inability [...] to escape their association with predominantly peripheral activities' (ibid.: 26). Semiperipheral states are those which have an about even mix of core-like and peripheral activities. They may try and strengthen linkages between the two types of activities within their boundaries and by doing so escape of some world market pressure. Also they can compete with core activities outside their territory but also with peripheral activities. Action of semiperipheral state makes a difference, they are not passive recipients of mixes of core–peripheral activities (upgrading or prevent from downgrading, ibid.: 27f.). Actual upgrading from semiperiphery to core status, however, seems possible in exceptional cases only:

> [T]he inability of the bulk of semiperipheral states to move into the core (and of peripheral states to move into the core) is the obverse of the success of some states to upgrade their mix of core-peripheral activities and move to a higher position. (ibid.: 28)

Candidates for upgrades to core or semiperiphery are being found at the borders between the three tiers. Arrighi and Drangel (1986: 29) adapt the concept 'perimeter' (introduced by Peter Lange 1985, cf. Chapter 3.6), they call these upper areas perimeter of the core and perimeter of the periphery. Arrighi (1985c: 247) 'redefines' these perimeters as

> no man's land that separates the unambiguously semiperipheral from the unambiguously core states, the perimeter of the core is not a line demarcating two zones but is itself a zone – a relatively empty but quite wide zone. Indeed, the two perimeter zones may even be subject to a progressive widening consequent upon core-periphery polarization.

In their empirical analysis, Arrighi and Drangel (1986: 30) emphasize 'that there is no operational way of empirically distinguishing between peripheral and core-like activities and therefore of classifying states according to the mix of core–peripheral activities that falls under their jurisdiction'. There is no complete map of commodity chains and consequently no assessment of the competitive pressure at their nodes. Furthermore, the relationships of competition and cooperation are constantly changing. Arrighi and Drangel (1986: 31) point out, however, that such problems were not unique to their concept:

> Mixes of core-peripheral activities play in world-systems theory a role analogous to that played by "marginal utility" in neo-classical price theory or "labor embodies" in Ricardian and Marxian theories of value. All such "quantities" play a key role in their respective conceptualizations but cannot be subjected to direct measurement. What matters is to be able to derive from the conceptualization a set of empirically verifiable hypotheses that can provide us with indirect measurements of key variables.

Rather conventionally, Arrighi and Drangel (1986: 31ff.) use GNP per capita in a common currency (US dollar) as proxy for the aggregate rewards to test their hypothesis of a three-tier system. I emphasize a few of their findings: The state composition of the three-tier system has not changed substantially from 1938 to 1983: 'In sum, 95% of the states for which we could find data (and 94% of total population) were in 1975/83 still on or within the boundaries of the zone in which they were in 1938/50' (ibid.: 44). There were (temporary) downward movements, however, from 1938/1950 to 1960/1970 (Germany and UK from core to perimeter of the core, and France and Belgium from perimeter of the core to the semiperiphery). 74 out of 93 states remained in one of the three zones (10 in the core zone, 20 in the semiperiphery, and 44 in the periphery) and are being qualified as 'organic members' (ibid.: 49). The organic members are then used to approximate the 'economic activities' prevailing in different zones.

We have already seen that Arrighi and Drangel reject the idea of invariant characteristics for core-like or peripheral activities. Especially as far as industrialization and industrial production is concerned, this aspect seems important for development studies. The findings of Arrighi and Drangel (1986: 53ff.) suggest that modernization theoretical views of progress (from agricultural to industrial production) are of limited explanatory value. Furthermore, they question that the capability to industrialize qualifies as means or sign of an overall development or dependency characteristic. Using data of the average labor force employed in 'industry' and of the share of 'manufacturing' in GDP for the countries in the three tiers they found that 'the gap between the degree of industrialization' of the core vis-à-vis the semiperiphery and the periphery was narrowing significantly after 1960. In the late 1970s, 'the semiperiphery not only caught up with but overtook the core in terms of industrialization' (ibid.: 55). These findings seem to fit well the analysis on dependent industrialization in Chapter 4.4.

Arrighi and Drangel (1986: 55f.) argue that semiperipheral countries lost economic command in terms of industrialization in the period of 1938–1948,

> so there are good reasons for supposing that in this period core-like activities were largely industrial activities. Interestingly enough, it was at the end of this period that Prebisch and his associates first introduced the concept of core-periphery relations and formulated it in terms of a primary activities-industrial activities dichotomy. (ibid.: 55)

From the 1950s to 1960s, 'a positive correlation between industrial activities and core-like activities is still in evidence' (ibid.) but gaps in industrialization and GDP between core and semiperiphery and periphery are narrowing. 1960–1965, the authors call transitional years: The gaps in industrialization are decreasing 'but there is no corresponding relative decline in core states' economic command'. The authors interpret this by 'the fact that the positive correlation between industrial and core-like activities was losing strength'. In the following two decades 'a weakened positive correlation turned into an increasingly strong *negative* correlation'. In the period from 1965 to 1980, 'the periphery and the semiperiphery continued to industrialize' and 'the core began to de-industrialize'. While the industrialization gap narrowed (core–periphery) or almost disappeared (core–semiperiphery), the economic command of the semiperiphery (compared to the core) remained constant, and of the periphery (compared to the core) worsened (ibid.: 55f.).

> The implication is that industrial activities were being peripheralized – they were, that is, losing their previous core status. Interestingly enough, it was toward the end of this period that Wallerstein suggested that the core-periphery dichotomy should be disentangled from the primary activities-industrial activities dichotomy [...]. [...] In sum, the industrialization of the semiperiphery and periphery has ultimately been a channel, not of subversion, but of reproduction of the hierarchy of the world-economy. (ibid.: 56)

But what replaces industrial production as core activity? Arrighi and Drangel (1986) draw on Arrighi (1985c: 275) who argues that

> the growing importance of vertically integrated TNC's in all branches of economic activity (from agriculture and mining to manufacturing, distribution, and banking) dissolves and blurs any previously existing correlation between the core-periphery dichotomy [...] and distinctions based on the kind of commodity produced (e.g., industry versus agriculture) or even on the techniques of production used (e.g., high productivity versus low productivity).

Such integrated and joint processes take place in different states. The distinguishing mark between core, semiperiphery, and periphery seems to have become the control over the commodity chain:

> The relevant distinction is between activities that involve strategic decision making, control and administration, R&D, and other "brain" activities, on the one hand, and activities of pure execution, on the other. [...] [C]ore states are those where TNC's concentrate their brain activities, and peripheral states are those where they concentrate their muscle-and-nerve activities. Under these circumstances, semiperipheral states would be of two types: states that have attained the core position of the previous stage of development of the world economy but that have not yet moved on to the core position of the new stage; and countries where TNC's locate a fairly balanced mix of brain and muscle/nerve activities. (Arrighi 1985c: 275)

These inquires suggest that there is a persistent path dependence in the spatial division of labor that makes an upgrading of a state's position difficult. Core states and core enterprises grow and develop together in a symbiotic relationship but the nature of the commodity chains is changing. The control over the commodity chain gained importance in relation to the industrial production and its geographical distribution. Semiperipheral or peripheral countries could close the gap to core countries as far industrialization is concerned without closing the gap in terms of distribution of GNP per capita. Based on this research, Arrighi (1990) talked of a 'developmentalist illusion', arguing against the assumption 'that "industrialization" is the equivalent of "development" and that "core" is the same as "industrial" [...] cuts across the great divide between the dependency and the modernization schools' (Arrighi 1990: 11). Possibly the identification of core countries as 'industrial' countries was prevailing among dependency authors, Arrighi and Drangel themselves considered the first half of the 1960s as transitional years, when industrial activities were still core activities in terms of economic command. But the discussion in Chapter 2 suggests that there was an understanding among dependency authors that industrial development was no synonym for development. In 1996, Arrighi et al. saw, however, the predictive capacity of the dependency perspective and the world-systems analysis alike as more accurate than modernization theory:

> [W]hichever way we look at the patterns latent in the data, we find evidence that invalidates the catching-up hypothesis shared by all variants of modernization theory. Interestingly, the hypothesis has become even less plausible from the mid 1980s onwards, that is, precisely when the rise of highly dynamic capitalist economies in East Asia and the demise of Soviet communism have led many to declare the dependency and world-systems perspectives obsolete and to advocate a revival of the modernization perspective. In fact, the evidence presented here shows that, not just the world-systems perspective, but also the dependency perspective has predicted the basic trends of the world economy in the 1980s and 1990s far more accurately than the modernization perspective. [...] For all that has changed over the last 10–15 years, the hierarchy of wealth of the global economy has remained pretty much the same, as truly predicted, and not just "retrodicted", by world-systems theorists. (Arrighi et al. 1996: 14)

Following Arrighi and Drangel (1986), Arrighi et al. (2003, cf. also Chapter 8)

> demonstrate [that] industrial convergence has not been accompanied by a convergence in the levels of income and wealth enjoyed on average by the residents of the former First and Third Worlds. In other words, the divide between the rich nations of the former First World and poor nations of the former Third World – the North-South divide – remains a fundamental dimension of contemporary global dynamics. (ibid.: 4)

They base their empirical analysis on studies that found evidence of a core or OECD 'convergence club' at the upper end of the world income distribution (ibid.: 6 and 8). The convergence among these countries was not accompanied by an overall (global) convergence of income. In order to show the convergence of industrial production against the non-convergence of income they relate a country's income (measured by the Gross National Product per capita—GNPPC—in relation to the weighted average of core countries' income of a given year) to its industrial development (measured by the share of GDP in manufacturing of a country in relation to the share of GDP for core countries in any given year). Measured by 'the proportions of GDP in manufacturing' in core and periphery and semiperiphery, 'industrial convergence in this period was due exclusively to First World de-industrialization', argue Arrighi et al. (2003: 15), while the unevenness in economic performance between peripheral and semiperipheral countries increased significantly.

3.4 The Core of Western Europe: An Incomplete Egg

From a world perspective, Europe started as periphery but also uneven development in Europe has been observed for precapitalist times. The particular way the feudal mode of production and feudal societies had formed—as a synthesis of the vanishing Roman Empire and the intruding Germanic communal clan system—did shape European uneven development (up to today, as some authors argue, cf. Weissenbacher 2007). Core–periphery relations in Europe are, therefore, not seen as something entirely new. The European center of political and economic gravity shifted to the Atlantic (from the Northern Italian city-states) during the sixteenth century, Portugal and Spain were later replaced by the Netherlands, France, and then England. The center of gravity

> returned to the European heartland in the last two decades with the growing industrial leadership of Germany, the collapse of the colonial empires and the contraction of European influence overseas. The economic (though not of course the political) precursor of the present system was Continental Europe in 1939–1945. Germany was able to control effectively all of Southern Europe (except Portugal). The German government and its corporations harnessed the occupied and allied countries to the German war economy. Labour was imported from the periphery on a large scale: German armed forces also lived in it rather like tourists,

> making use of hotels. But the military importance of proximity, especially common land frontiers, was shown by the lack of success of the attempt to incorporate North Africa as well. This system collapsed with the defeat of Germany, but something formally similar reappeared in the 1960s, with the revival of industrial output and a new phase of technological advance. (Seers 1979b: 22)

Under pax Americana, US allies in the cold war regained strength, profiting from US reconstruction aid. High economic growth rates and low growth of working age population soon allowed Western European countries to absorb migrant workers (and refuges from Eastern Europe). In principle, Seers' (1979b: 8f.) delineations contain therefore two core regions for Europe, the United States and Western Central Europe. Papadantonakis (1985: 86) from the Binghamton network talks of a 'consolidation of North European capitalism under U.S. hegemony', that is reflected in the 'overbearing influence exerted upon [Southern Europe] by the North European core' in the three decades before. Seers (1979b: 8f.) concentrates, however, on the European core countries among which he counts Western Germany, France, the Netherlands, Belgium, Switzerland, Austria, Denmark, Norway, and Sweden. These countries were the origin of most of the tourists and offered almost all jobs for migrant workers. He perceived them culturally 'fairly' homogenous, with social and economic indicators that suggested a similar situation to the United States. They had comparatively moderate inflation rates and a currency policy of appreciation toward all non-state socialist countries (except Japan) after the Smithonian Agreement of 1971 (when US president Nixon suspended the Bretton Woods System).

Arrighi and Drangel (1986: 66) from the Binghamton network (cf. the discussion in Chapter 3.3) defined 'organic' members of the core zone, namely countries that were considered members of the core the first and last period of their analysis, from 1938–1950 to 1975–1983. The European 'organic' core members were Denmark, Germany, the Netherlands, Norway, Sweden, Switzerland, and the United Kingdom. There were, furthermore, four members that managed to climb from perimeter of the core (cf. Chapter 3.2) in 1938–1950 to core status in 1975–1983: Austria, Belgium, Finland, and France. Finally there was the case of Italy that upgraded from semiperiphery to core in the respective period (cf. also Chapters 3.6 and 8).

Core–periphery relations, however, do not adhere to national borders, therefore they can be analyzed in national *or* spatial terms (Seers 1979b: 16ff.). Core regions in Europe extend into states that are being described as semiperipheral or even peripheral. An early attempt to estimate core–periphery relations for Europe was offered by Werner Sombart (1927: XIVf.):

> During the first half of the 19th century, the capitalist center was England, then, during the longest period of high capitalism, it was "Western Europe", which means except England an area confined by a line that runs from Southern Sweden over Antwerp, Amiens, Mühlhausen, Milano, Vorarlberg, Lower Austria, Moravia, Lodz, Berlin and back to Sweden; finally the East of the United States of America has joined as a part of such a center during the recent generation, whereby world economic relations have become more entangled.

In the second half of the twentieth century, still in Cold War times and almost an anticipation of a future dividing line of Yugoslavia, Seers (1979b: 18 and 21) starts his account of regions, that he includes as edge to the core, with Slovenia. These regions form an incomplete egg (we will complete the picture later), with 2700 km in the longest axis and a breadth of 1500 km:

> If we go round the rim of the core clockwise, starting with Yugoslavia, the most dynamic area is the North-West, Slovenia; in Italy, the North; in Spain, the Basque provinces and Catalonia, which lie to the North and North-East; in Britain, the South-East; in Finland, the South-West. (Seers 1979b: 18)

These boundaries must not be taken as exact ones:

> Broadly speaking, those living inside the egg are less likely to be working in agriculture or tourism, to be unemployed, to see their families broken by migration, or to receive a very low income, than those outside. Nearly all the big European transnational companies (including banks) have their headquarters inside, as well as most of the television studios, newspaper offices, book publishers, etc. (Seers 1979b: 19)

Finally, there are regional disparities within the countries of the core as well, such as between Brittany or Corsica, and Alsace-Lorraine or the Paris region, respectively, but 'the contrasts are mild in comparison with those in the periphery' (Seers 1979b: 9). 'And generally, the closer to the center of the egg', so Seers (1979b: 19) (Fig. 3.1),

Fig. 3.1 The regional core of Europe in the 1970s (*Source* This 'incomplete egg' was redrawn from Dudley Seers [1979b: 19] by the author. The map used is from the US Central Intelligence Agency [1972])

> the greater the concentration of power. One could imagine a 'yolk', which would include Denmark, West Germany, the Benelux countries, Paris, the Lyon area, Switzerland and Lombardy.

3.5 The Periphery and the Semiperiphery of Western Europe

The EADI group included the 'North-Western periphery' (Finland, Ireland, Scotland) in its analysis (Bryden 1979; Crotty 1979; Kiljunen 1979; Schaffer 1979; Seers 1979b) and Seers (1979b) made projections for the regions of European Comecon and Yugoslavia. The 'Binghamton'-research network concentrated on the 'political economy of Southern Europe' and included Greece, Italy, Portugal, Spain, and Turkey. The Heidelberg group focused on Italy, Portugal, and Spain. On the country level, Seers (1979b: 17) considers—starting southeast—Turkey, Cyprus, Greece, Yugoslavia, Spain, Portugal, and Ireland as peripheral. Vicinity to the center of the egg is also seen important for the development patterns outside the egg. As a general rule, the farther away from the center, the poorer a region tends to be. This might suggest a circle shape rather than an egg, reasons Seers, but this would produce anomalies:

> Ireland, the Highlands and the islands of Scotland and central Wales hardly seem to be core areas; nor do Sardinia or Southern Italy (or parts of Albania). I am unable to rationalize the egg shape. (Seers 1979b: 31, Endnote 10)

As for the European periphery, Seers (1979a: xiii) observes similarities with countries from the global periphery which they seem to have similarities with (i.e. Mexico). To establish a classification, he searches for characteristics to qualify an 'underdeveloped Europe':

> There are two obvious candidates in Southern Europe: Portugal and Greece. They are both countries which are short of technological capacity and capital goods industries, and much of local manufacturing is foreign-owned. Militarily they are weak, and their governments have to cope with considerable political pressures from outside. (Seers 1979b: 3)

Spain and Yugoslavia were seen similarly except for the industrial structures that were larger, better integrated, and more nationally owned. But also Spain's exports, for example, were predominantly going to the main (European) core country Western Germany, and consisted of food and raw material mainly, whereas the reciprocal imports were manufactures and semi manufactures (Seers 1979b: 3; Kiljunen 1979: 319f.). Semiperipheral countries in Seers' (1979b: 7) analysis are dependent on the core but have features that suggest a differentiation from the periphery. In the case of Finland, the main industries were nationally owned and had a significant technological capacity. The currency was more independent from a core currency (i.e. Ireland was following the British Pound), tourism was not a significant industry, exports were more diversified in terms of structure and destination, and the per capita income was relatively high. On the other hand, there were Britain and Italy that did not appear to fit a clear core classification. Italy had a distinctive North–South divide that influenced its average characteristics. Furthermore, it was dependent on tourism and had sent net labor migrants to Europe's core. These features were, however, in the Italian case less important for the balance of payments than in the other South-European countries. A much smaller portion of the industrial structure was foreign controlled and Italy was seen as a substantial producer of equipment, steel and chemicals. Moreover, Italian unions had managed to reduce the wage differentials between North and South and to put pressure on public corporations to locate new factories in the South. Institutions had been founded to develop regions with disadvantages (i.e. Cassa per il Mezzogiorno). The social situation in Southern Italy seemed much better than in comparative regions of the periphery (such as the South of Portugal) and the dependence in economic, political, and cultural terms less distinctive.

Britain had a double character as exporter and importer of capital and labor. It was being more and more penetrated by foreign capital, which gained a big share of North Sea oil concessions, and on the other hand successfully conquered the domestic market for consumer goods, especially electronic equipment. For a long time Britain had been importer of labor (Caribbean, South Asia, and the Irish Republic, to a lesser extent from Southern Europe) but also labor exporter to the United States and the old Commonwealth. At that time, labor import had slowly dried up and Britain had become a small-scale exporter of labor. Furthermore, it was a net importer of tourists. Social conditions in Scotland, Wales, and

Table 3.1 EU15 Core–semiperiphery–periphery in the 1960s

	GNI per capita (EU15)	*Arrighi/Drangel (EU 14 in the world scheme)*
Core	Denmark, Germany, Luxembourg, Netherlands, Sweden, UK	Sweden
Perimeter of the core	XXX	Denmark, Germany, UK
Semiperiphery (SP)	Austria, Belgium, Finland, France Italy	Austria, Belgium, Finland, France, Greece, Ireland, Italy, Netherlands, Spain
Perimeter of the Periphery	XXX	Portugal
Periphery	Greece, Ireland, Portugal, Spain	XXX

For calculation of GNI per capita see Chapter 8

the southwest of England were perceived worse than in most countries of the core but the fiscal policy of the state was seen to have prevented (even more than in the case of Italy) that social disparities between regions grew too high. In both, Britain and Italy, state financed R&D was weak and both countries displayed characteristics of 'underdevelopment': chronic inflation and reoccurring currency problems. Very generally, Seers classifies those countries as semiperipheral where more than half of the population lives in core regions (Seers 1979b: 9–16).

As far as the Binghamton network is concerned (cf. the discussion in Chapter 3.3), Arrighi and Drangel's (1986: 66) 'organic' members of the semiperiphery (countries that were considered semiperipheral in the first and last period of their analysis, from 1938–1950 to 1975–1983) in Europe (where data was available) consisted of Greece, Hungary, Romania, Turkey, USSR, and Yugoslavia. The European semiperiphery consists, argues Wallerstein (1979c: 100) of 'the whole outer rim', namely

> the southern tier of Portugal, Spain, Italy and Greece; most of eastern Europe; parts of the northern tier such as Norway and Finland.

There is an apparent similarity between Arrighi and Drangel's and Wallerstein's European candidates for membership in the global semiperiphery and Dudley Seers‘ European peripheral countries. For Seers,

Finland and Britain count toward the European semiperiphery. The Binghamton network does not operate with a strictly European core–periphery relationship but operates on a global scale (world-systems analysis). Seers, again, has no elaborated theoretical concept of the core–semiperiphery–periphery model and how upgrades and downgrades might function. Wallerstein and Arrighi and Drangel on the other hand attempt to grasp such changes. Authors from the 'Binghamton'-group cautiously assessed this concept of a global semiperiphery in the European context (Tables 3.1, 3.2, and 3.3).

Table 3.2 EU15 Core–semiperiphery–periphery in the 1970s

	GNI per capita (EU15)	*Arrighi/Drangel 1975–83 (EU 14 in the world scheme)*	*Seers' (1979b: 17) European scheme (EU 15)*
Core	Austria, Belgium, Denmark, France Germany, Luxembourg, Netherlands, Sweden	Austria, Belgium, Denmark, Finland, France, Germany, Italy, Netherlands, Sweden, UK	Austria, Belgium, Denmark, France Germany, Luxembourg, Netherlands, Sweden
Perimeter of the core	XXX	Ireland, Spain	XXX
Semiperiphery (SP)	Finland, Greece, Italy, UK	Greece, Portugal	Finland, Italy, UK
Perimeter of the Periphery	XXX	XXX	XXX
Periphery	Ireland, Portugal, Spain	XXX	Greece, Ireland, Portugal, Spain

For calculation of GNI per capita see Chapter 8

Table 3.3 EU15 Core–semiperiphery–periphery in the 1980s

	GNI per capita
Core	Austria, Belgium, Denmark, France, Germany, Italy, Luxembourg, Netherlands, Sweden
Semiperiphery	Finland, Greece, UK
Periphery	Ireland, Portugal, Spain

For calculation of GNI per capita see Chapter 8

3.6 Italy: A Perimeter of the Core?

Particularly the space between core and periphery left room for analytical clarification. The Italian case was subject of such deliberations and drew attention of authors in all the networks of the European dependency school, e.g. Robert Wade (1979, 1980) writing in the EADI network, Peter Lange (1980, 1985, also: Lange and Tarrow 1980), John Logan (1985), and Sidney Tarrow (1985, 1990) writing in the Binghamton network, and Mario Caciagli (1985) and Raimondo Catanzaro (1985) in the Heidelberg network.

Italy was particularly interesting because it had a pronounced internal core–periphery structure between North and South resembling domestically what development studies observed internationally. At the same time, as a state, Italy was integrated in the international core–periphery system, with the North and South of Italy having particular functional specialization. Peter Lange (1985: 180ff.) introduced an extension of the concept of the semiperiphery ('perimeter of the core'), discussing Italy as newly arrived in the core status (from semiperiphery) in the boom years of the early 1960s. By using such periodization, he contradicts Immanuel Wallerstein's thesis who had stressed that above all a phase of economic downturn offered the opportunity for a government's policy to trigger such a transformation. Sidney Tarrow (1985) also saw Italy as having arrived in mature capitalism. John Logan (1985: 173ff.), however, pleaded to treat Spain similar to Italy, emphasizing a common European heritage and similar developments in the 1970s. He shows reservations against Wallerstein's concept of semiperiphery, especially if used to distinguish Southern Europe. György Ránki (1985: 82), again, stressed that 'to put Italy entirely into the same category as the other Southern nations would certainly make the whole model in some way too general, too vague'. And Kostis Papadantonakis (1985: 89) had to exclude significant regions, but if one exempted 'Turkey's more backward hinterland and the Italian and Spanish regions that have historically been more closely integrated with the European core leaves the five Mediterranean countries in a fairly uniform economic situation'.

Peter Lange's (1985: 186ff.) 'perimeter of the core' stands for a country's newly arrival in the core status during the boom phase of the 1960s. He uses wage levels as 'most easily distinguishable (and last to arrive) characteristics' (ibid.: 189) for the core industrial productive structure. This turned out to be a constraint for international trade (high wage economy) when the global economy entered a phase of economic downturn: Workers in the Northern Italian export industries had eked out higher wages. Italy was neither able to react to the crisis like a low-wage semiperipheral country anymore but its institutional set-up (and the behavior of main actors from capital, labor, and the state) prohibited a response that other core countries used. Lange (1985: 192ff.) distinguishes two main forms of core governments' response to the crisis of the 1970s. In what he describes as predominantly Anglo-American approach, capital strove to reduce the economic role of the state (regulations, tax reduction) and to challenge labor power (which was fragmented) and wage levels. In Italy, however, labor strength had only recently risen and was an essential part of becoming (high-wage) core. Therefore an 'Anglo-American solution' appears to have been too costly, politically and economically, in a democratic setting. In the second variant—that was archetypically found in neo-corporatist countries like Austria, Norway, and Sweden—the state played an important role by creating 'a climate for compromise over the terms of transition and restructuring between capital and labor' (ibid.: 193).

The Italian state, however, was unable and unwilling to play such a 'rational' role in Italy, argues Lange, due to the semiperipheral framework of its creation after World War II—a clientelistic, quasi one-party political system of the Christian Democratic Party (Democrazia Cristiana-DC). 'Equipped with a comfortable electoral majority', as Mario Caciagli (1985: 76f.) put it in the Heidelberg network, 'the Christian Democrats began to understand the structures of a centralist and quasi-authoritarian state as guarantor of their own political hegemony'. With the help of the United States, DC had established a wide range of power (from which it managed to keep away the Italian Communist Party – PCI): But '[t]he DC allowed other parties a share of patronage – if not power [...]' (Tarrow 1990: 319), even the Socialist Party (PSI). 'The Italian state is not simply the instrument of capitalist class interests, unable to intervene powerfully against those interests', Robert Wade (1980: 166) pointed out in his Poulantzas-type analysis, 'but nor is it so autonomous from that dominant class that it can sustain intervention to secure political support regardless of the effects on capital accumulation'. The Italian Christian Democratic Party (DC) was able to manage also the Italian state's policy toward the Italian periphery, the Mezzogiorno. Not all capital fractions agreed with the industrialization policy in Southern Italy, but DC was able to broker between fractions (and secure political hegemony). In 1980, 'the political representation of organised business is still primarily provided by the Christian Democrats' (Martinelli 1980: 85). However, with the crisis of the 1970s, which was also a crisis of the Keynesian economic model, the institutional set-up of postwar Italy seems to have begun eroding. Above all, what we have discussed in previous chapters, reactions to the crisis in international capital accumulation in the 1970s a) led to a new international division of labor and outsourcing of production, b) increased the pressure on workers in core countries, and c) sounded the bell for the age of financialization and neoliberal capitalism. Robert Wade (1980: 167) summarized aptly the different forces tearing on the fabric of the Italian society:

> [T]he "needs of capital" set limits on the extent to which the state can operate against national capital accumulation in pursuit of clientelistic political support in the South. In a competitive world economy, the crisis in national capital accumulation, to which inefficient "modern" heavy industry in the South is a substantial contributor, is expressed in the country's chronic balance of payments deficit; which in turn prompts other adjustments, such as deflationary measures wanted by the country's creditors. These in turn prompt reactions from those who feel deprived or threatened, one of which may be a switch in political support, producing a change in the basis of legitimacy, and perhaps a change in the balance of class forces.

The Italian unions were also in an uneasy position which impaired their role as trustworthy actors for compromises. Their influence among workers was limited due to the self-consciousness, workers acquired when they successfully (often decentrally and/or wildcat organized) challenged Italy's (semiperipheral) low-wage regime in the 1960s. Consequently, Lange (1985: 194ff.) introduces a third mode of core crisis reaction, 'modern dualism':

> The political conditions for this type of response appear that capital is unable to dominate [as in the Anglo-American solution] and, at the same time, both the historical and contemporary conditions for a stable class compromise [as in the neo-corporatist models] do not exist. [...] [C]apital (and to some extent workers as well) undertakes internal exit from the sphere of the state and establishes a second, "hidden," zone of the economy, which falls outside of the effective jurisdiction of government and the unions. (ibid.: 195)

The result was a decentralization of Italian politics that caught substantial international attention (e.g. Putnam et al. 1993, Chapter 2). Arnaldo Bagnasco (1977) had popularized the notion of three Italian regions for the Italian political economy: The 'third Italy' of North-Eastern Italy (Bagnasco 1977 described as 'peripheral') may have seen a greater resilience against crisis due to an economy of small and medium size companies (as compared to what he called the 'marginalized' South or the 'Fordist' North-West) but it was still rooted in an overall (national) Keynesian development regime of the Italian state. 'Third Italy‘ inspired, however, international economic research on an alternative (idealized) capitalism in clusters and networks (cf. Chapter 7). Political decentralization, however, seems to have been a matter of power considerations. Caciagli's (1985: 76ff.) analysis on the political decentralization supports Lange's account: The Christian Democratic Party (DC) had originally supported the idea of decentralization to be included in the Italian constitution but then changed positions and impeded its political implementation. DC perceived left administrations governing in regions as potential challenge of its claim to power and therefore denunciated regionalization as danger for democracy. It was only in the crisis of the 1970s when some regionalization policies were implemented. Radical workers and students demanded participation and reforms that the central state was seen unable to pursue, but also capitalists from modern industrial sectors stipulated new forms of conflict regulations. Unable to cope with the conflict situation along the established lines, DC had begun perceiving the regional level as puffer for conflict to the central state level. Johannes Agnoli (1977: 215f.) talked of reversion of polarity toward regional elections as reaction to distortions of capital accumulation and state efficiency (due to wildcat workers resistance that had spread to urban quarters). But also Communists seem to have hoped to be able to use the regional government (in some they had strongholds) to advance reforms of state and society. Much of the regionalization process remained, however, programmatic wishful thinking. In terms of regional planning, autonomous regional industrial policies failed, economic policies were still oriented on concerns of the national government, which was also able to keep control on the distribution of financial means (Caciagli 1985: 78f.).

In Southern Italy, however, unemployment remained high and wages low despite massive labor migration from Southern Italy to Northern Italy and Central Europe. Writing in the EADI network, Robert Wade (1979: 203) called extreme irony the situation of capital-intensive investments in Southern Italy. A staunch (sevenfold) increase in industrial investment led to an increase of 45% in industrial employment only. While the Souths share of national industrial investment rose, its share in national industrial employment shrank. Still, these investments accounted for most of the industrial employment created. But neither on the input side nor on the output side were these investments much linked to local producers but rather to the North (cf. also Catanzaro 1985: 92f.). Managers from the North controlled transregional companies or commodity chains headquartered in the North. These investments in the South were described as 'cathedrals in the desert'. One account of these industrial 'growth poles' (in Gela) was titled 'industrialization without development' (Hytten and Marchioni 1970). Wade (1979: 200ff.; 1980: 161ff.) argues against the development orthodoxy that conceived Northern and Southern Italy as separate economies and largely ignored that progress in Northern Italy and 'underdevelopment' in Southern Italy were connected. The type of integration—with improved infrastructure—opened the Southern economy. Southern Italy industrialized without tariff barriers, the traditional small manufacturing sector—that used to produce for local markets—was no match for the competition from the North and therefore declined. Net imports from the North increased. Capital inflow by social transfer payments (production subsidies, pensions, family allowance) provided for the payments of imports. These transfer payments supported growth in the Northern industry and secured electoral majorities: The new class of bureaucrats that administered Italian public expenditure in the South was an important factor in the Christian Democratic Party's hegemonic system, the Northern ruling class dependent upon for safeguarding electoral stability. 'The alliance of the new southern bureaucratic elite with the northern industrialists through the state', writes Wade (1980: 167) on the Italian situation, 'is thus the partial equivalent at country level of [Osvaldo] Sunkel's transnationalization thesis [cf. above]: elites of peripheral states integrate their interests with those of the owners and managers of transnational capital, using the state apparatus to redistribute part of the surplus to themselves'. Moreover, the Italian industrialization strategy was one of 'development from above' as criticized by authors from the European dependency school: economic growth during overall boom phases and arranged via 'growth poles' (unbalanced growth) would only lead to economic growth without societal development.

If one looks at the Italian system of capital accumulation as a whole, as pointed out by Wade (1979: 210ff.; 1980: 159ff.), the North–South divide shows an interesting parallel to the functional division of labor in the North–South relations of Yugoslavia (with a different politico-economic system, cf. Weissenbacher 2005). Three linkages seem worth noting: (1) The national (federal in the case of Yugoslavia) transfer system subsidized prices in the heavy industry of the South. The resulting primary or intermediate goods were recycled as low-price input into the export industry of the North; (2) national/federal development programs did not create enough employment in the South to endanger Northern industry's demand for migrant labor; (3) the limited increase in wealth ('development') led to demand for Northern industry's consumer goods in the South. Recently, the economist Gianfranco Viesti (2009: 31 and 70ff.; Caporale 2015, cf. also Mania 2015: 2) has brought forward similar arguments. Investments in the South stimulate production in the North. Viesti challenges what he considers a myth, namely that Northern regions money is sunk in the Italian South. This strikingly resembles the Yugoslav discussion in the 1980s of who profited more of the common economy, the industrialized North or the peripheral South (cf. Weissenbacher 2005). Viesti presents per capita data of territorial expenses in favor of Northern regions. Generally, Italy might be more a problem for the Mezzogiorno than the Mezzogiorno is for Italy: Due to dependent integration into the Italian nation state and national economy, the Italian South has restricted development perspectives.

3.7 Eastern Europe: Completing the Egg?

Dudley Seers had categorized, as we have seen, the Yugoslavia of workers' self-management with the typology of Capitalist Europe. The state socialist countries of European Comecon receive extra treatment. Seers observed some similar dynamics. He deemed the most powerful economy the German Democratic Republic (GDR), 'which lies in fact very close to the Western European core' (Seers 1979b: 20). It was geographically located in the center of the egg and showed core characteristics: It exported equipment and technology, employed migrant labor, and net exported tourists. Average social conditions were seen not much below of the Federal Republic of Germany (FRG), about the level of Austria. As in the Western European system, the social situation of a country was observed the worse the farther away it was from Germany. The indicators show 'strikingly' that—similar to Britain, Finland, and

Italy—Czechoslovakia, Hungary, and Poland can be considered intermediate countries between core and periphery, even if social conditions and income display more similarities to the Western European periphery. Bulgaria and Romania are considered clearly more peripheral in their economic structure, income level, and social conditions. They are also more dependent on technology imports (especially from the GDR). Seers (1979b: 20) completes the egg of the European core (cf. the map, cf. Fig. 3.1) with Bohemia, Silesia, former Eastern Prussia, and the Baltic countries. Similar to the United States for Western Europe, Eastern Europe had a second core, namely the Soviet Union that was strong in economic relations to the Comecon (export of energy, arms, and technology but import of industrial products) and an overwhelming military power (Warsaw Pact, military interventions in the semiperiphery of Eastern Europe). It sent, however, relatively few tourists and employed little migrant labor. Also, the cultural influence of the USSR on the East European system was weak, where there was US influence. The USSR's income level and its level of consumer technology were below US standards:

> So it is not fully able to act as a major core, though its population size alone, together with its resource base, and the fear in Eastern Europe of German expansion, enable it still to exert a dominant influence. (Seers 1979b: 20)

Clearly, anew research agenda dealing with Seers' classification would seem a fruitful endeavor. What made Eastern Germany core and Czechoslovakia semiperiphery in the indicators used by Seers? Was it more peripheral Slovakia that influenced average accounts? Both, GDR and ČSSR had been considered most developed industrial countries of Comecon. As far as GDP per capita was concerned, GDR had overtaken the ČSSR in 1967, and both were well above the USSR, the third country above Comecon average. The situation seems to have been similar as far as industrial per capita production was concerned. GDR overtook the ČSSR from 1955 to 1963, both countries being above the USSR numbers (Kosta 1974: 132 and 222f.). Can the situation of the USSR in Fordist times be compared with the United States in the age of financialization, insofar as industrial production (alone) is not necessarily a feature of a core country? Seers implicitly considers similar mechanisms of core–periphery development for Capitalist and State Socialist systems which is reminiscent of the world-systems analysis. Last but not least. Seers' model had been perceptive as far as the Western European situation is concerned, and as regards the Yugoslav dividing line (with Slovenia being at the rim of the core), anticipating the fault line.

With the end of the system confrontation, however, Eastern Europe forfeited its core and integrated into the Western capitalist system as periphery. Especially striking is the degrading of the Eastern core country Eastern Germany to a periphery of Western Germany, as subordinated workbench of Western Germany's industries (Heimpold 2010: 727ff., 737). Consequently, Seers' egg remained incomplete.

References

Agnoli, Johannes. 1977. Wahlkampf und Sozialer Konflikt. In *Auf dem Weg zum Einparteienstaat*, ed. Wolf-Dieter Narr, 213–241. Opladen: Westdeutscher.

Agnoli, Johannes. 1995 [1978]. Der Staat des Kapitals. „Zivilgesellschaft" oder bürgerliche Gesellschaft? In *Der Staat des Kapitals und weitere Schriften zur Kritik der Politik*, ed. Johannes Agnoli. Freiburg i.Br.: Ça ira, 21–89 (=Gesammelte Schriften 2).

Arrighi, Giovanni (ed.). 1985a. *Semiperipheral Development: The Politics of Southern Europe in the Twentieth Century: Beverly Hills, London, and New Delhi* (Explorations in the World-Economy 5).

Arrighi, Giovanni. 1985b. Introduction. In *Semiperipheral Development: The Politics of Southern Europe in the Twentieth Century*, ed. Giovanni Arrighi, 11–27. Beverly Hills, London, and New Delhi (=Explorations in the World-Economy 5).

Arrighi, Giovanni. 1985c. Fascism to Democratic Socialism: Logic and Limits of a Transition. In *Semiperipheral Development: The Politics of Southern Europe in the Twentieth Century*, ed. Giovanni Arrighi, 243–279. Beverly Hills, London, and New Delhi: Sage (=Explorations in the World-Economy 5).

Arrighi, Giovanni. 1990. The Developmentalist Illusion: A Reconceptualization of the Semiperiphery. In *Semiperipheral States in the World-Economy*, ed. William Martin, 11–42. Westport, CT: Greenwood Press.

Arrighi, Giovanni, and Fortunata Piselli. 1987. Capitalist Development in Hostile Environments: Feuds, Class Struggles, and Migrations in a Peripheral Region of Southern Italy. *Review* 10 (4): 649–751 (Fernand Braudel Center).

Arrighi, Giovanni, and Jessica Drangel. 1986. The Stratification of the World-Economy: An Exploration of the Semiperipheral Zone. *Review* 10 (1): 9–74 (=Anniversary Issue: The Work of the Fernand Braudel Center).

Arrighi, Giovanni, Beverly Silver, and Benjamin Brewer. 2003. Industrial Convergence, Globalization, and the Persistence of the North-South Divide. *Studies in Comparative International Development* 38 (1): 3–31.

Arrighi Giovanni, Roberto Korzeniewicz, David Consiglio, and Timothy Moran. 1996. Modeling Zones of the World Economy: A Polynomial Regression Analysis (1964–1994). Paper Presented at the 1996 Annual Meeting of the American Sociological Association. New York, NY.

Bagnasco, Arnaldo. 1977. *Tre Italie. La Problematica territoriale dello svilluppo italiano.* Bologna: Il Mulino.

Bair, Jennifer. 2005. Global Capitalism and Commodity Chains: Looking Back. *Going Forward. in: Competition & Change* 9 (2): 153–180.

Bair, Jennifer. 2009. Global Commodity Chains: Genealogy and Review. In *Frontiers of Commodity Chain Research*, ed. Jennifer Bair, 1–34. Stanford: Stanford University Press.

Bair, Jennifer. 2014. Editor's Introduction: Commodity Chains in and of the World System. *Journal of World-Systems Research* 20 (1): 1–10.

Bassand, Michel, Ernst Brugger, John Bryden, John Friedmann, and Barbara Stuckey (eds.). 1986. *Self-Reliant Development in Europe.* Theory, Problems, Actions: Aldershot and Vermont.

Benítez Zenteno, Raúl (ed.). 1998 [1973]. *Las clases sociales en américa latina. Congress at the Universidad Nacional Autónoma in Mérida, Yucatán.* Mexico: Siglo XXI.

Berend, Iván, and György Ránki. 1982. *The European Periphery and Industrialization 1780–1914.* Cambridge: Cambridge University Press.

Brugger, Ernst, and Barbara Stuckey. 1986. Introduction: Self-Reliant Development in Europe. In *Self-Reliant Development in Europe: Theory, Problems, Actions*, ed. Michel Bassand, Ernst Brugger, John Bryden, John Friedmann, and Barbara Stuckey, 1–5. Aldershot and Vermont: Gower.

Bryden, John. 1979. Core-Periphery Problems: The Scottish Case. In *Underdeveloped Europe: Studies in Core-Periphery Relations*, ed. Dudley Seers, Bernard Schaffer, and Marja-Liisa Kiljunen, 257–277. Sussex: Harvester Press (=Harvester Studies in Development 1).

Caciagli, Mario. 1985. Dezentralisierung und Regionalpolitik in Italien. In *Ungleiche Entwicklung und Regionalpolitik in Südeuropa: Italien, Spanien, Portugal*, ed. Dieter Nohlen und Rainer-Olaf Schultze unter Mitwirkung von Wolfgang Merkel, 75–81. Bochum: Brockmeyer (=Politikwissenschaftliche Paperbacks 6).

Caporale, Antonello. 2015. Sfatiamo I falsi miti: si spende als Sud per arricchire il Nord. Interview with Gianfranco Viesti. In Il fatto quotidiano, August 1, 19.

Cardoso, Fernando Henrique. 1977. The Consumption of Dependency Theory in the United States. *Latin American Research Review* 12 (3): 7–24.

Cardoso, Fernando Henrique, and Enzo Faletto. 1979. *Dependency and Development in Latin America.* Berkeley, Los Angeles, and London: University of California Press.

Casparis, John. 1985. Core Demand for Labor from Southern Europe: The Case of Switzerland. In *Semiperipheral Development: The Politics of Southern Europe in the Twentieth Century*, ed. Giovanni Arrighi, 107–131. Beverly Hills, London, and New Delhi: Sage (Explorations in the World-Economy 5).

Catanzaro, Raimondo. 1985. Unequal Development in Southern Italy: Features, Causes, and some Suggestions for Research: A Preliminary Report. In *Ungleiche Entwicklung und Regionalpolitik in Südeuropa: Italien, Spanien, Portugal*, ed. Dieter Nohlen und Rainer-Olaf Schultze unter Mitwirkung von Wolfgang Merkel, 83–94. Bochum: Brockmeyer (=Politikwissenschaftliche Paperbacks 6).

Claus, Burghard, et al. 1977. Zur Erweiterung der Europäischen Gemeinschaft in Südeuropa. Berlin (=Schriften des Deutschen Instituts für Entwicklungspolitik (DIE) 52).

Crotty, Raymond. 1979. Capitalist Colonialism and Peripheralisation. In *Underdeveloped Europe: Studies in Core-Periphery Relations*, ed. Dudley Seers, Bernard Schaffer, and Marja-Liisa Kiljunen, 225–235. Sussex: Harvester Press (=Harvester Studies in Development 1).

De Bandt, Jacques, Péter Mándi, and Dudley Seers (eds.). 1980. European Studies in Development: New Trends in European Development Studies. London and Basingstoke: Palgrave Macmillan.

Dos Santos, Theotonio. 1970. The Structure of Dependence. *American Economic Review* 60 (2): 231–236.

Eßer, Klaus, et al. (eds.). 1978. *Europäische Gemeinschaft und südeuropäische Beitrittsländer.* Berlin (=Schriften des Deutschen Instituts für Entwicklungspolitik (DIE) 54).

Eßer, Klaus, et al. 1980. *Überlegungen zur portugiesischen Industriepolitik angesichts des Beitritts zur EG.* Berlin (=Schriften des Deutschen Instituts für Entwicklungspolitik (DIE) 60).

Emmanuel, Arghiri. 1972. *Unequal Exchange: A Study of the Imperialism of Trade.* New York: Monthly Review Press.

Eußner, Ansgar. 1983. *Industriepolitik und Süderweiterung der EG am Beispiel der Werftindustrie.* Berlin (=Schriften des Deutschen Instituts für Entwicklungspolitik (DIE) 72).

Fischer, Karin, and Rudy Weissenbacher. 2016. Ungleicher Tausch – Grundannahmen, Widersprüche und aktuelle Bedeutung eines umstrittenen Theorems. *Z. Zeitschrift Marxistische Erneuerung* 27 (105): 140–157.

Friedmann, John. 1966. *Regional Development Policy: A Case Study of Venezuela.* Cambridge, MA: MIT Press.

Friedmann, John. 1967. *A General Theory of Polarized Development.* Santiago: The Ford Foundation: Urban and Regional Advisory Program in Chile.

Friedmann, John. 1983. Life Space and Economic Space: Contradictions in Regional Development. *Seers/Öström* 1983: 148–162.

Friedmann, John, and Clyde Weaver. 1979. *Territory and Function: The Evolution of Regional Planning*. London: Edward Arnold.

Galtung, Johan. 1971. A Structural Theory of Imperialism. *Journal of Peace Research* 8 (2): 81–117.

Galtung, Johan. 1972. Eine strukturelle Theorie des Imperialismus. In *Imperialismus und strukturelle Gewalt. Analysen über abhängige Reproduktion*, ed. Dieter Senghaas, 29–104. Frankfurt/Main: Suhrkamp.

Hadjimichalis, Costis. 1983. Regional Crisis: The State and Regional Social Movements in Southern Europe. In *The Crisis of the European Regions*, ed. Dudley Seers and Kjell Öström, 127–147. London and Basingstoke: Palgrave Macmillan.

Heimpold, Gerhard. 2010. Zwischen Deindustrialisierung und Reindustrialisierung. *Informationen zur Raumentwicklung* 37 (10/11): 727–743.

Hirschman, Albert. 1975. Interregional and International Transmission of Economic Growth. In *Regional Policy: Readings in Theory and Applications*, ed. John Friedman and William Alonso, 139–157. Cambridge, MA; and London: MIT Press.

Holman, Otto. 2002. Die Neue Europäische Peripherie. Ost- und Süderweiterung der Europäischen Union im Vergleich. *Prokla* 32 (2): 399–420.

Hudson, Ray, and Jim Lewis. 1984. Capital Accumulation: The Industrialisation of Southern Europe? In *Southern Europe Transformed: Political and Economic Change in Greece, Italy, Portugal and Spain*, ed. Allan Williams, 179–207. London: Harper & Row.

Hudson, Ray, and Jim Lewis (eds.). 1985a. *Uneven Development in Southern Europe: Studies of Accumulation, Class, Migration and the State*. London and New York: Methuen.

Hudson, Ray, and Jim Lewis. 1985b. Introduction: Recent Economic, Social and Political Changes in Southern Europe. In *Uneven Development in Southern Europe: Studies of Accumulation, Class, Migration and the State*, ed. Ray Hudson and Jim Lewis, 1–53. London and New York: Methuen.

Hummen, Wilhelm. 1977. *Greek Industry in the European Community—Prospects and Problems*. Berlin (=Schriften des Deutschen Instituts für Entwicklungspolitik (DIE) 45).

Hytten, Eyvind, e Marco Marchioni. 1970. *Industrializzazione senza sviluppo.* Gela: una storia meridionale. Milano: Franco Angeli.

Jessop, Bob. 1985. *Nicos Poulantzas: Marxist Theory and Political Strategy.* Basingstoke: Macmillan.

Kiljunen, Kimmo. 1979. Finland in the International Division of Labour. In *Underdeveloped Europe: Studies in Core-Periphery Relations*, ed. Dudley Seers,

Bernard Schaffer, and Marja-Liisa Kiljunen, 279–302. Sussex: Harvester Press (=Harvester Studies in Development 1).

Kosta, Jiří. 1974. *Sozialistische Planwirtschaft. Theorie und Praxis.* Opladen: Westdeutscher Verlag.

Lange, Peter. 1980. Crisis and Consent, Change and Compromise: Dilemmas of Italian Communism in the 1970s. In *Italy in Transition. Conflict and Consensus*, ed. Peter Lange, and Sidney Tarrow, 110–132. London: Frank Cass.

Lange, Peter. 1985. Semiperiphery and Core in the European Context: Reflections on the Postwar Italian Experience. In *Semiperipheral Development: The Politics of Southern Europe in the Twentieth Century*, ed. Giovanni Arrighi, 179–214. Beverly Hills, London, and New Delhi: Sage (=Explorations in the World-Economy 5).

Lange, Peter, and Sidney Tarrow (eds.). 1980. *Italy in Transition: Conflict and Consensus.* London: Frank Cass.

Lipietz, Alain. 1987. *Mirages and Miracles. The Crisis of Global Fordism.* London: Verso.

Logan, John. 1985. Democracy from Above: Limits to Change in Southern Europe. In *Semiperipheral Development: The Politics of Southern Europe in the Twentieth Century*, ed. Giovanni Arrighi, 149–177. Beverly Hills, London, and New Delhi: Sage (=Explorations in the World-Economy 5).

Love, Joseph. 1996. *Crafting the Third World: Theorizing Underdevelopment in Rumania and Brazil.* Stanford: Stanford University Press.

Love, Joseph. 2011. The Latin American Contribution to Center-Periphery Perspectives: History and Prospect. In *Cores, Peripheries, and Globalization: Essays in Honor of Ivan Berend*, ed. Peter Hanns Reill and Balázs Szelényi, 15–42. Budapest and New York: Central European University Press.

Mania, Roberto. 2015. Mezzogiorno, la Grecia d'Italia. *La Repubblica, Affari & Finanza* 30 (27): 1–2 (July 20).

Martinelli, Alberto. 1980. Organised Business and Italian Politics: Confindustria and the Christian Democrats in the Postwar Period. In *Italy in Transition: Conflict and Consensus*, ed. Peter Lange and Sidney Tarrow, 67–87. London: Frank Cass.

Musto, Stefan. 1977. Spanien und die Europäische Gemeinschaft. Der schwierige Weg zur Mitgliedschaft. Bonn (=Europäische Schriften des Instituts für Europäische Politik 48).

Musto, Stefan. 1982. Structural Implications. In *The Second Enlargement of the EEC: The Integration of Unequal Partners*, ed. Dudley Seers and Constantine Vaitsos (with the assistance of Marja-Liisa Kiljunen), 67–91. London and Basingstoke: Macmillan (=Studies in the Integration of Western Europe 2).

Musto, Stefan. 1985a. The Loss of Hegemony: Sensitive Industries and Industrial Policies in the European Community. In *Europe at the Crossroads: Agendas of the Crisis*, ed. Stefan Musto and Carl Pinkele, 85–102. New York et al.: Praeger.

Musto, Stefan (ed.). 1985b. *Endogenous Development: A Myth or a Path? Problems of Economic Self-Reliance in the European Periphery.* Tilburg (=European Association of Development Research and Training Institutes: EADI Book Series 5).

Musto, Stefan. 1985c. In Search of a New Paradigm. In *Endogenous Development: A Myth or a Path? Problems of Economic Self-Reliance in the European Periphery*, ed. Stefan Musto, 1–13. Tilburg: EADI (=European Association of Development Research and Training Institutes: EADI Book Series 5).

Musto, Stefan, and Carl Pinkele (eds.). 1985. *Europe at the Crossroads.* Agendas of the Crisis. New York et al.: Praeger.

Nohlen, Dieter. n.y. Dieter Nohlen—Curriculum Vitae. http://www.nohlen.uni-hd.de/de/cv.html (December 2, 2014).

Nohlen, Dieter. 1985. Ungleiche Entwicklung und Regionalpolitik in Südeuropa (Italien, Spanien, Portugal). Eine Einführung. In *Ungleiche Entwicklung und Regionalpolitik in Südeuropa: Italien, Spanien, Portugal*, ed. Dieter Nohlen und Rainer-Olaf Schultze unter Mitwirkung von Wolfgang Merkel, 9–15. Bochum (=Politikwissenschaftliche Paperbacks 6).

Nohlen, Dieter, and Rainer-Olaf Schultze. 1985a. Vorwort. In *Ungleiche Entwicklung und Regionalpolitik in Südeuropa: Italien, Spanien, Portugal*, ed. Dieter Nohlen and Rainer-Olaf Schultze unter Mitwirkung von Wolfgang Merkel. Bochum, 7–8 (=Politikwissenschaftliche Paperbacks 6).

Nohlen, Dieter, und Rainer-Olaf Schultze. 1985b. Ungleiche Entwicklung und Regionalpolitik in Südeuropa. Externe Verursachungsdfaktoren und endogene Entwicklungschancen. In *Ungleiche Entwicklung und Regionalpolitik in Südeuropa: Italien, Spanien, Portugal*, Hg. Dieter Nohlen und Rainer-Olaf Schultze unter Mitwirkung von Wolfgang Merkel, 17–73. Bochum (=Politikwissenschaftliche Paperbacks 6).

Papadantonakis, Kostis. 1985. Incorporation Is Peripheralization: Contradiction of Southern Europe's Economic Development. In *Semiperipheral Development: The Politics of Southern Europe in the Twentieth Century*, ed. Giovanni Arrighi, 86–106. Beverly Hills, London, and New Delhi: Sage (=Explorations in the World-Economy 5).

Papademetriou, Demetrios. 1983. A Retrospective Look at Mediterranean Labor Migrations to Europe. In *The Contemporary Mediterranean World*, ed. Carl Pinkele and Adamantia Pollis, 237–256. New York: Praeger.

Payno, Juan Antonio, and José Luis Sampedro (eds.). 1983. *The Enlargement of the European Community: Case-Studies of Greece, Portugal, and Spain.*

London and Basingstoke: Macmillan (=Studies in the Integration of Western Europe 3).

Pimmer, Stefan. 2016. „Ich war damals einfach interessiert an diesen neuen Paradigmen." Dieter Senghaas über die deutschsprachige Rezeption der Dependenztheorien. In ed. Mattersburger Kreis für Entwicklungspolitik. http://www.mattersburgerkreis.at/site/de/aktuelles/interviews/article/269.html (March 31, 2017).

Pollis, Adamantia. 1983. The Southern European Semiperiphery and the European Community. In *The Contemporary Mediterranean World*, ed. Carl Pinkele and Adamantia Pollis, 202–220. New York: Praeger.

Poulantzas, Nicos. 1974 [1973]. Die Internationalisierung der kapitalistischen Produktionsverhältnisse und der Nationalstaat. In Multinationale Konzerne. Entwicklungstendenzen im kapitalistischen System, ed. Otto Kreye, 81–129. München: Hanser.

Poulantzas, Nicos. 1976 [1975]. *The Crisis of the Dictatorships. Portugal, Greece, Spain*. London: NLB.

Poulantzas, Nicos. 2001 [1974]. Die Internationalisierung der kapitalistischen Verhältnisse und der Nationalstaat. In *Die Zukunft des Staates*, ed. Joachim Hirsch, Bob Jessop, and Nicos Poulantzas, 19–69. Hamburg: VSA.

Poulantzas, Nicos. 2008a [1976]. The Political Crisis and the Crisis of the State. In *The Poulantzas Reader: Marxism, Law and the State*, ed. James Martin, 294–322. London and New York: Verso.

Poulantzas, Nicos. 2008b [1976]. The Capitalist State: A Reply to Miliband and Laclau. In *The Poulantzas Reader: Marxism, Law and the State*, ed. James Martin, 270–293. London and New York: Verso.

Poulantzas, Nicos. 2008c [1965]. Preliminaries to the Study of Hegemony in the State. In *The Poulantzas Reader: Marxism, Law and the State*, ed. James Martin, 74–119. London and New York: Verso.

Poulantzas, Nicos. 2008d [1969]. The Problem of the Capitalist State. In The Poulantzas Reader: Marxism, Law and the State, ed. James Martin, 172–185. London and New York: Verso.

Poulantzas, Nicos. 2008e [1964]. Marxist Examination of the Contemporary State and Law and the Question of the 'Alternative'. In *The Poulantzas Reader: Marxism, Law and the State*, ed. James Martin, 25–46. London and New York: Verso.

Poulantzas, Nicos. 2008f [1972]. On Social Classes. In *The Poulantzas Reader: Marxism, Law and the State*, ed. James Martin, 186–219. London and New York: Verso.

Poulantzas, Nicos. 2008g [1979]. Interview with Nicos Poulantzas. In *The Poulantzas Reader: Marxism, Law and the State*, ed. James Martin, 387–402. London and New York: Verso.

Poulantzas, Nicos. 2014 [1978]. *State, Power, Socialism*. London and New York: Verso.

Putnam, Robert, Robert Leonardi, and Raffaella Nonetti. 1993. *Making Democracy Work: Civic Traditions in Modern Italy*. Princeton: Princeton University Press.

Ránki, György. 1985. Problems of Southern European Economic Development (1918–38). In *Semiperipheral Development: The Politics of Southern Europe in the Twentieth Century*, ed. Giovanni Arrighi, 55–85. Beverly Hills, London, and New Delhi: Sage (Explorations in the World-Economy 5).

Reill, Peter Hanns. 2011. Introduction. In *Cores, Peripheries, and Globalization: Essays in Honor of Ivan Berend*, ed. Peter Hanns Reill and Balázs Szelényi, 1–11. Budapest and New York: Central European University Press.

Schaffer, Bernard. 1979. Regional Development and Institutions of Favor. In *Underdeveloped Europe: Studies in Core-Periphery Relations*, ed. Dudley Seers, Bernard Schaffer, and Marja-Liisa Kiljunen, 237–256. Sussex: Harvester Press (=Harvester Studies in Development 1).

Seers, Dudley. 1977. Back to the Ivory Tower? The Professionalisation of Development Studies and Their Extension to Europe. *IDS Bulletin* 9 (2): 6–11.

Seers, Dudley. 1978. *Development Planning in Portugal: Report of a Mission Under the OECD Technical Co-operation Service*. Brighton: Institute of Development Studies (IDS), University of Sussex.

Seers, Dudley. 1979a. Introduction. In *Underdeveloped Europe: Studies in Core-Periphery Relations*, ed. Dudley Seers, Bernard Schaffer, and Marja-Liisa Kiljunen, xiii–xxi. Sussex: Harvester Press (=Harvester Studies in Development 1).

Seers, Dudley. 1979b. The Periphery of Europe. In *Underdeveloped Europe: Studies in Core-Periphery Relations*, ed. Dudley Seers, Bernard Schaffer, and Marja-Liisa Kiljunen, 3–34. Sussex: Harvester Press (=Harvester Studies in Development 1).

Seers, Dudley. 1980. Theoretical Aspects of Unequal Development at Different Spatial Levels. In *Integration and the Unequal Development: The Experience of the EEC*, ed. Dudley Seers and Constantine Vaitsos (with the assistance of Marja-Liisa Kiljunen), 9–23. London and Basingstoke: Macmillan (=Studies in the Integration of Western Europe 1).

Seers, Dudley. 1983a. Preface: Regional Problems and Development Theory. In *The Crisis of the European Regions*, ed. Dudley Seers and Kjell Öström, ix–xiii. London and Basingstoke: Macmillan.

Seers, Dudley. 1983b. The Applications of Development Theories within Europe. In *Emerging Development Patterns: European Contributions*, ed. István Dobozi and Péter Mándi, 517–521. Selected Papers of the 3rd General Conference of EADI, November 11–14, 1981, Budapest, Hungary.

Budapest, European Association of Development Research and Training Institutes (EADI) and Institute for World Economy of the Hungarian Academy of Sciences.

Seers, Dudley. 1983c. *The Political Economy of Nationalism*. London et al.: Oxford University Press.

Seers, Dudley, Bernard Schaffer, and Marja-Liisa Kiljunen (eds.). 1979. *Underdeveloped Europe: Studies in Core-Periphery Relations*. Sussex: Harvester Press (=Harvester Studies in Development 1).

Seers, Dudley, and Constantine Vaitsos (with the assistance of Marja-Liisa Kiljunen) (eds.). 1980. *Integration and Unequal Development: The Experience of the EEC*. Macmillan: London and Basingstoke (=Studies in the Integration of Western Europe 1).

Seers, Dudley, and Constantine Vaitsos (with the assistance of Marja-Liisa Kiljunen) (eds.). 1982. *The Second Enlargement of the EEC: The Integration of Unequal Partners*. Macmillan: London and Basingstoke (=Studies in the Integration of Western Europe 2).

Seers, Dudley, and Kjell Öström (eds.). 1983. *The Crisis of the European Regions*. London and Basingstoke: Routledge.

Selwyn, Percy. 1979. Some Thoughts on Cores and Peripheries. In *Underdeveloped Europe: Studies in Core-periphery Relations*, ed. Dudley Seers, Bernard Schaffer, and Marja-Liisa Kiljunen, 35–43. Sussex: Harvester Press (=Harvester Studies in Development 1).

Senghaas, Dieter, and Ulrich Menzel. 1979. Autozentrierte Entwicklung trotz internationalem Kompetenzgefälle. Warum wurden die heutigen Metropolen Metropolen und nicht Peripherien? In *Kapitalistische Weltökonomie. Kontroversen über ihre Entwicklungsdynamik*, ed. Dieter Senghaas, 280–313. Frankfurt/Main: Suhrkamp.

Soja, Edward. 1980. The Socio-Spatial Dialectic. *Annals of the Association of American Geographers* 70 (2): 207–225.

Soja, Edward. 1985. Regions in Context: Spatiality, Periodicity, and the Historical Geography of the Regional Question. *Environment and Planning D: Society and Space* 3 (2): 175–190.

Soja, Edward, and Costis Hadjimichalis. 1979. Between Geographical Materialism and Spatial Fetishism: Some Observations on the Development of Marxist Spatial Analysis. *Antipode* 11 (3): 3–11.

Sombart, Werner. 1927. Das Wirtschaftsleben im Zeitalter des Hochkapitalismus. Erster Halbband. Die Grundlagen – der Aufbau. München und Leipzig: Duncker & Humblot (=Der moderne Kapitalismus. Dritter Band, erster Halbband.).

Soms García, Esteban. 2010. ODEPLAN/MIDEPLAN: Una escuela para el cambio social. Ministerio de Planificación, Gobierno de Chile, Santiago.

Stöhr, Walter. 1983a. Alternative Strategies for Integrated Regional Development. In *The Crisis of the European Regions*, ed. Dudley Seers and Kjell Öström, 6–14. London and Basingstoke: Macmillan.

Stöhr, Walter. 1983b. Alternative räumliche Entwicklungsstrategien endogener 'selektiver Eigenständigkeit'. *Österreichische Zeitschrift für Soziologie* 8 (3): 117–134.

Stöhr, Walter. 1985. Selective Self-reliance and Endogenous Regional Development—Pre-conditions and Constraints. In *Ungleiche Entwicklung und Regionalpolitik in Südeuropa: Italien, Spanien, Portugal*, ed. Dieter Nohlen und Rainer-Olaf Schultze unter Mitwirkung von Wolfgang Merkel, 229–249. Bochum (=Politikwissenschaftliche Paperbacks 6).

Stöhr, Walter, and Fraser Taylor (eds.). 1981. *Development from Above or Below? The Dialectics of Regional Planning in Developing Countries*. Chichester et al.: Wiley.

Stöhr, Walter, Josefa Edralin, and Devyani Mani (eds.). 2001. *New Regional Development Paradigms. Vol. 3. Decentralization, Governance, and the New Planning for Local-level Development*. Westport: Greenwood Press in cooperation with the United Nations Centre for Regional Development (=Contributions in Economics and Economic History 225).

Szentes, Tamás. 1983. The TNC Issue: Naive Illusions or Exorcism and Lip-Service. In *Emerging Development Patterns: European Contributions*, ed. István Dobozi and Péter Mándi, 97–118. Selected Papers of the 3rd General Conference of EADI. Budapest (=EADI Book Series 1).

Tarrow, Sidney. 1985. The Crisis of the Late 1960's in Italy and France: The Transition to Mature Capitalism. In *Semiperipheral Development. The Politics of Southern Europe in the Twentieth Century*, ed. Giovanni Arrighi, 215–241. Beverly Hills, London, and New Delhi (=Explorations in the World-Economy 5).

Tarrow, Sidney. 1990. Maintaining Hegemony in Italy: "The Softer They Rise, the Slower They Fall!" In *Uncommon Democracies: The One-Party Dominant Regimes*, ed. Thomas Jefferson Pempel, 306–332. Ithaca and London: Cornell University Press.

US Central Intelligence Agency. 1972. Europe 9–72. In Library of Congress, Washington, DC. https://urldefense.proofpoint.com/v2/url?u=https-3A__www.loc.gov_item_75693732_&d=DwIFAw&c=vh6FgFnduejNhPPD0fl_yRaSfZy8CWbWnIf4XJhSqx8&r=PQelu8ZjKbjEbRfu6o6YYu5Z6-FCD-MUN5ZxrvBFQbwSpLC9r6iMWlQG1R8s1JamK&m=C3u-s8CQ_iV-Qx-AEPP-jCYX52s_TZqLSUa1qrPQxRZY&s=nJu_jZWEGVsw5YDn8Qb-V1GHAOrF4fhIGQVkhNwKV8qQ&e= (August 30, 2019).

Vaitsos, Constantine. 1980. Corporate Integration in World Production and Trade. In *Integration and Unequal Development: The Experience of the EEC*, ed. Dudley Seers and Constantine Vaitsos (with the assistance of Marja-Liisa

Kiljunen), 24–45. London and Basingstoke: Macmillan (=Studies in the Integration of Western Europe 1).

Van Bilsen, Anton. 1976. Report by the Chairman of the Provisional Committee. In *The New International Economic Order—Economic, Social and Political Imolications*, ed. European Association of Development Research and Training Institutes (EADI), 8–10. Report on the 1975 General Conference of EADI Linz/Austria, September 11–13, 1975. Vienna, EADI.

Viesti, Gianfranco. 2009. Mezzogiorno a tradimento. Il Nord, il Sud e la politica che non c'è. Roma and Bari: Laterza.

Wade, Robert. 1979. Fast Growth and Slow Development in South Italy. In: Dudley Seers, Bernard Schaffer, Bernard, and Marja-Liisa Kiljunen, (eds.) (1979): Underdeveloped Europe: Studies in Core-periphery Relations. Sussex: Harvester, 197–221 (=Harvester Studies in Development 1).

Wade, Robert. 1980. The Italian State and the Underdevelopment of South Italy. In *"Nation" and "State" in Europe*, ed. Ralph Grillo, 151–171. London et al.: Academic Press.

Wallerstein, Immanuel. 1978. World-System Analysis: Theoretical and Interpretative Issues. In *Social Change in the Capitalist World Economy*, ed. Barbara Hockey Kaplan, 219–235. Beverly Hills and London: Sage (=Political Economy of the World-System Annuals, 1).

Wallerstein, Immanuel. 1979a [1974]. The Rise and Future Demise of the World Capitalist System: Concepts for Comparative Analysis. In *The Capitalist World-Economy*, ed. Immanuel Wallerstein. Cambridge et al.: University Press and Editions de la Maison des Sciences de l'Homme, 1–36 (=Studies in modern capitalism).

Wallerstein, Immanuel. 1979b [1974]. Dependence in an Interdependent World: The Limited Possibilities of Transformation Within the Capitalist World Economy. In *The Capitalist World-Economy*, ed. Immanuel Wallerstein, 66–94. Cambridge et al.: University Press and Editions de la Maison des Sciences de l'Homme (=Studies in modern capitalism).

Wallerstein, Immanuel. 1979c [1976]. Semiperipheral Countries and the Contemporary World Crisis. In *The Capitalist World-Economy*, ed. Immanuel Wallerstein, 95–118. Cambridge et al.: University Press and Editions de la Maison des Sciences de l'Homme (=Studies in modern capitalism).

Wallerstein, Immanuel. 1985. The Relevance of the Concept of Semiperiphery to Southern Europe. In *Semiperipheral Development: The Politics of Southern Europe in the Twentieth Century*, ed. Giovanni Arrighi, 31–39. Beverly Hills, London, and New Delhi: Sage (=Explorations in the World-Economy 5).

Wallerstein, Immanuel. 2004. *World-Systems Analysis: An Introduction*. Durham: Duke University Press.

Weissenbacher, Rudy. 2005. *Jugoslawien. Politische Ökonomie einer Desintegration*. Wien: Promedia.

Weissenbacher, Rudy. 2007. Historical Considerations of Uneven Development in East Central Europe. In *Dollarization, Euroization and Financial Instability: Central and Eastern European Countries Between Stagnation and Financial Crisis?*, ed. Joachim Becker and Rudy Weissenbacher, 35–83. Marburg: Metropolis.

Weissenbacher, Rudy. 2008. Keeping Up Appearances: Uneven Global Development in a System of Structural Imbalances. *Journal Für Entwicklungspolitik XXIV* 4: 78–121.

Williams, Allan (ed.). 1984a. *Southern Europe Transformed: Political and Economic Change in Greece, Italy, Portugal and Spain*. London: Harper & Row.

Williams, Allan (ed.). 1984b. Introduction. In *Southern Europe Transformed: Political and Economic Change in Greece, Italy, Portugal and Spain*. London: Harper & Row, 1–29.

CHAPTER 4

Old Paradigms and New Crises

EDS writers observed the global economic crises of the 1970s and 1980s, some of them had been development practitioners/advisers during the postwar boom decades. Consequently, EDS writers had a very sober view concerning development perspectives within the capitalist system and criticized respective explanatory theories and models. Existing paradigms of economic and regional development deemed odd and unsuitable or were even thought to have collapsed (Öström 1983: 2). If the concept of a 'Fordist' postwar model was of limited explanatory strength (cf. Becker and Weissenbacher, forthcoming), Fordism was at best 'incomplete' in the global and European South. Giunta and Martinelli (1995: 196) would call the 'Fordist' model for the South of Italy 'limited and biased'. With the crisis of the 1970s, however, it became apparent that core countries were passing through a period of structural change as well. This very broadly dashed remaining hopes on 'trickle-down' and 'spill-over' effects.

The original version of this chapter was revised: Reference and their citation have been updated in this chapter. The correction to this chapter is available at https://doi.org/10.1007/978-3-030-28211-0_10

R. Weissenbacher, *The Core-Periphery Divide in the European Union*,
https://doi.org/10.1007/978-3-030-28211-0_4

4.1 The Old Development Paradigm 'From Above'

In both, core and periphery, theory and practice had been dominated by modernization theory and liberal economic theory in its neo-classical and Keynesian variant (Nohlen and Schultze 1985: 26). These conventional theories were unapt to overcome dependencies because they were, as Seers (1979: 25) put it, 'developed in the interest of dominant countries and for dominant countries, taking for granted their structural characteristics and interest in free trade'. Furthermore, they had shaped also social scientists in the global periphery. 'In a sense', argued Seers (1980: 6),

> their theoretical equipment was twice removed from reality – it reflected the doctrines developed for *other* countries in response to *earlier* events.

Seers held the nineteenth-century European tradition of political economy responsible for the shortcomings of economic development doctrines in the twentieth century. They were being Eurocentric and full of belief in 'the civilizing role of modernization' and (technological) progress (Box 4.1). Ironically 'colonial powers felt little need for planning their own future, but became increasingly concerned about the economic plight of their territories' (Seers 1983: 98). 'Developments plans' were first mostly lists of public infrastructure programs (roads, ports, schools, etc.), in the neo-colonial era, economic growth projections became the nature of 'development':

> The underlying model is crude, often a simplistic version of Keynesianism, with no place for the major strategic issues, especially greater self-reliance. [...] In the last quarter century, plans have mostly been derived from the Harrod-Domar model [...], which treats investments as the determinant of economic growth. Estimates of investment needs have relied heavily on incremental capital output ratios (ICORS): [...] these show great variation, especially over periods as short as five years. In fact, they can have little meaning if they cover groups of industries with very different technologies, less if they refer to the whole economy. Output is anyway also affected by many factors besides capital – e.g., apart from education, improvements in the health of the workforce. [...] In brief, the plans have not been about development, which surely implies social and political progress as well as economic [...]. (Seers 1983: 98 and 100)

Box 4.1: Development of productive forces: the fetish of TNC capitalism?

Dudley Seers (1983: 38) argued that 'after the mainstream of classical thought split in two', the Chicago school and the traditional Marxist school, which Seers both labeled neo-classical schools, 'both continued to develop in the same buoyant atmosphere of the nineteenth century, a time when the possibilities opened up by industrialization still seemed limitless'. But then, after the second world war,

> the economism of the main neo-classical schools has implied treating development as a largely, even purely economic phenomenon. They [...] take some definition of national income based on neo-classical conventions as measure. [...] The important test of even a capitalist country's progress is, in Marxist terms, the growth of its 'productive forces': by one route or another, economic growth will – in their view – ultimately force a change in social relationships, to the benefit of the people as a whole. It is, of course, this emphasis on economic growth which largely explains the touching neo-classical faith that there has been development in the last few decades, despite increasing inequalities and political repression [...]. Since these appear implicit in some high-growth patterns, one could make out a case for arguing that growth is negatively correlated with development. (Seers 1983: 40f.)

Indeed, contrary to Karl Marx's nineteenth-century expectations, the development of productive forces (labour/workers in combination with the means of production) has not lead to such conflicts with the relations of production (the economic material base with class relations between owners and not-owners of the means of production) that would change the social formation and the mode of production. Moreover, twentieth-century philosophers who followed Marx' work pointed out that the very force that Marx saw as instrumental to overcome capitalism turned into a force helping to justify or even to maintain it. The same Marx, as Ernst Bloch (2000: 241) put it,

> who drove the fetish character out of production, who believed he had analyzed, exorcised every irrationality from history as merely unexamined, uncomprehended and therefore operatively fateful obscurities of the class situation, who had banished every dream, every operative utopia, every telos circulating in religion from

> history, plays with his "forces of production," with the calculus of the "process of production" the same all too constitutive game, the same pantheism, mythicism, upholds for it the same ultimately utilizing, guiding power which Hegel upheld for the "Idea [...]".

The expectations of Marx had been overly optimistic, Theodor Adorno (1972: 363) argued similarly, that the productive forces would burst the relations of production. Marx, the sworn enemy of German idealism, had kept its key historical narrative: Emphasizing the role of productive forces for social change resembled Hegel's 'Weltgeist' and turned into justifications for later versions of the social order that Marx intended to change.

Twentieth-century TNC capitalism fragments global workers to a higher degree (with highly polarised incomes), employs ever less wage labor due to high productivity (but accepts extreme labor-intensive conditions in the periphery), wastes resources (with the consequences for mankind), and establishes uneven consumption patterns. The relations of production are treated as 'given' in mainstream thinking, technological innovations are being sought for in order to cure social and environmental problems related to the global mode of production. The 'development of the productive forces' experiences a 'strange non-death' (to borrow a phrase from Colin Crouch 2011). Theodor Adorno (1972) had elaborated as early as 1968, shortly after the period Arrighi and Drangel consider transitional years (when industrial production ceased to be a core activity), the underlying issues of contemporary capitalism: 'Late capitalism or industrial society?' It was 'the current form of socially necessary appearance', he argued (Adorno 1972: 368f.), '[t]hat productive forces and relations of productions are seen as one today and therefore one could readily design society from the productive forces'. It was a necessary appearance for society because it integrated formerly distinctive elements of the 'social process', including people. Material production, distribution, consumption are administered in common, the boundaries of which become blurred: 'All is one. The totality of mediation processes ["Vermittlungsprozesse"], truly of the exchange principle, produces another deceptive immediacy. It allows for the possible forgetting of differences and antagonisms, contrary to one's own perception, or to repress them from consciousness' (Adorno 1972:

369). The ideology of core countries in late capitalism blocks the view at different development experiences (and narratives that might diverge from bottom-up capitalism as free market success story). Relations of production go beyond ownership of the means of production and include elements of the state and its administration. Adorno (1972: 363) calls this the 'role of the state as institutional capitalist ["Gesamtkapitalist"]' which seems compatible with the symbiotic relationship between states and companies which Arrighi and Drangel talked about (above). The productive forces seem to resemble general technical rationality, and a situation is created that appears as if 'the universal interest is that in the status quo, and full employment is the ideal and not the liberation from dependent labor. This situation, however, which is with regard of foreign affairs extremely unstable, anyway, constitutes a mere temporal balance, the resultant of forces which threaten to tear it apart. Within the dominant relations of production, mankind is virtually its own reserve labor force which must be supported' (ibid.).

The relations of production have survived, argues Adorno (ibid.), and have 'continued to subjugate the productive forces. The signature of this age is the predominance of the relations of production over the productive forces, which have mocked the conditions for some time' (ibid.). 'It is exactly this fetishism of the productive forces', the French sociologist Pierre Bourdieu (2005: 176) tied in with Ernst Bloch, 'that is echoed by the prophets of neoliberalism and the archpriests of monetary stability and D-mark'.

Stöhr (1983b: 120) described as development paradigm 'from above', 'center-down', and 'from outside' a dependency on global demand and on effects of global innovation centers that are being diffused to the periphery in hierarchical processes by means of private capital transfer and public funds (Stöhr 1983c: 284ff.; Stöhr 1981: 61). Development 'from above' for countries and regions aimed at reaching a high degree of

> industrialization and urbanization resembling the structures of the most developed countries today, by a unilineal process of increasing the use of capital, technology, and energy, and by utilizing ever-increasing agglomeration and scale economies in order to participate with increasing specialization in the world market according to their comparative advantages in

> factor endowment, which in fact rarely occurs precisely in this fashion [...]. (Stöhr 1981: 61)

Different approaches were seen as belonging to the 'center-down' paradigm:

> The center-down paradigm has its roots in the balanced versus unbalanced growth controversy of the 1950s. It was argued that the poverty of the developing countries and of less-developed subnational areas is a result of the low productivity of labour, which is in part a function of an inadequate supply of physical capital. But the shortage of capital is attributable in large measure to the persistently low levels of saving – caused in turn by low income, thus completing the vicious circle of poverty. Because low incomes and a consequent lack of effective demand generally spell failure for any heavily concentrated investment in a single consumer-goods industry, the balanced growth advocates proposed that investment should be diversified over a broad range of such industries. Each industry, it was argued, would then generate, through its factor payments, a demand for the goods of the other industries sufficient to keep all of them viable. Investment projects that might be individually unprofitable would, taken together, be profitable [...]. (Hansen 1981: 15)

The theory of ***balanced growth*** (important proponents were Ragnar Nurkse and Paul Rosenstein-Rodan) was soon questioned regarding the costs and state planning abilities of such a 'big push' of industrialization. Furthermore an open economy would have to deal with the import pressure on infant industries. Famous theorists of ***unbalanced growth*** are often referred to as polarization theorists. They formulated concepts of positive and negative effects from core on peripheral regions: Albert Hirschman (leading sectors, 'trickle down'-effects, polarization), John Friedmann (core–periphery model of regional development), Gunnar Myrdal ('spread effects' and 'backwash effects'), and François Perroux (growth poles of industrial sectors, originally in purely economic terms), whereupon the latter two were distinctively more pessimistic regarding the development of peripheral regions (Hansen 1981: 16ff.; Friedmann 1983: 148f.). The 'polarization school' was by no means a homogeneous group either. They seemed indeed mostly theorists and development planners from the core, drawing from 'development experience' in the core but also from work experience in the periphery. But Hirschman, for example, believed into market forces in order to counter inequalities and disparities, while Myrdal urged for government intervention, and Friedmann was markedly critical of the prevailing 'polarized' development doctrine (Friedmann and Weaver 1979: 115f.). 'Basically this model assumed', as Stöhr (1983b: 120) points out:

> that development has to emanate largely from world-wide effective innovation centers and world-wide demand, and to spread 'downwards' towards less developed nations and regions. This was supposed to have been enabled by a hierarchic diffusion of demand multipliers (for instance via the export base model), by a hierarchic process of diffusion of innovation, and by a transfer of private capital and public funds, respectively, from the highly developed to the low developed regions. Hereby this model assumed – even if often tacitly – that the development of weaker developed countries and regions had to be based on impulses 'from above' and 'from outside'.

Crucially, development theories 'from above' followed similar assumptions as the prevailing liberal economic perceptions of regional policy that assumed, economic backwardness and development disparities had endogenous causes leading to 'modernization deficits'. The remedy was seen to come from outside impulses. The proposed solutions were following objectives of a national or global economic policy and should be market-based. Economic imbalances were meant to be overcome by functional and spatial integration, structural differentiation and specialization through division of labor (Nohlen and Schultze 1985: 27). Such a liberal market-based paradigm of regional policy was following a special modeling logic:

1. The logic of modeling treated regions as functional regions without history and geography. There is no regional unity that is historically grown. The region is functionally determined by the framework of overall national economic development;
2. Functional integration and specialization by division of labor is necessary to reach equilibrium (facilitated through 'trickle-down' effects). Market equilibrium was to be reached in the long-term. Development disparities are being accepted in the short run (or even stimulated) because the economy overall must first grow before wealth reached by economic growth can be distributed regionally (convergence theory);

3. Regional policy was subordinated to the national economy, whereby infrastructure investments furthered functional integration (functional barriers to growth, allocation and integration are being removed) (Nohlen and Schultze 1985: 27c.).

Nohlen and Schultze (1985: 30c.) emphasize that Keynesian and neoclassical concepts of regional development do not differ in their strategies but in the instruments they apply. When neoclassical economic convergence between rich and poor regions had not appeared, argue (Stöhr and Tödtling 1979: 138), regional policies were introduced—'as crutches to try to make the neo-classical model work'—such as manipulation of factor prices (capital and employment incentives) and distribution of external resources (public infrastructure investments)' (Stöhr and Tödtling 1979: 138). Both concepts, so Nohlen and Schultze (1985: 30c.), assumed endogenous causes and exogenous impulses to overcome market imbalances. Functional integration and specialization were deemed necessary to reach equilibrium, which was made possible by trickle-down effects from growth poles of modern industries. Both concepts focus on growth of the overall economy and link regional policy to the needs of the entire state. They follow the logic of capital utilization that depends on constant growth and concentration, the negative impact of which they wanted to counter in the first place. Therefore the framework of the original processes is not being overcome. As far as the instruments are concerned, the neoclassical visions trusted that imbalances could be overcome by self-healing effects of market mechanisms. Labor migration into core regions would also increase the peripheral regions income. Keynesian remedies went beyond such a 'passive rehabilitation'. Funding for infrastructure development was accompanied by direct and indirect investment incentives (subsidies, tax incentives) in order to stimulate growth and employment. Often such stimulation efforts for modern and capital intensive sectors could not recruit employment regionally and therefore had effects outside the region. 'The current doctrine', as Friedmann and Weaver (1979: 172) pointed out,

> which is based on the theory of polarized development, is fully consistent with the transnational ideology of development; it is a willing instrument in the hands of managers of unequal development.

Two basic strategies for regional development came from neoclassical economic theory. The export base model developed in the 1950s relied on an expansion of (international) demand outside the region, in order to stimulate growth within the region and reduce imbalances. The main focus was the comparative advantage in strategic raw material production plus attached industrial production. It was assumed that the setup and stimulation of an export production will increase overall demand because income for the region would also raise demand for goods and services from the region itself. This was supposed to have an expansive multiplier effect. Diversifying export production and increasing real income would create endogenous growth, short-time imbalances, and long-term equilibrium of development disparities via market mechanisms (Nohlen and Schultze 1985: 27c.). Also from the 1950s on, the growth poles concept assumed a pilot effect of modern industries being outsourced into peripheral regions. It was based on the perception that expectations of specialization and division of labor from sectoral process optimization would also work in a regional context and hence stimulate growth. Industries with above average expectation of growth in gross production, employment, and value-added were to be established. Such modern key industries in peripheral regions would have a high elasticity of demand and should be competitive in an interregional context. These growth poles would send manifold development impulses to the region by producing input and output linkages between up- and downstream companies. By doing so, growth poles also produce sectoral and regional polarization. Similar to the export base model the phase of polarization was considered temporal. Political measures and market forces would spike trickle-down effects that lead to equilibrium (Nohlen and Schultze 1985: 29).

In the late twentieth European framework 'development from above' policies had decreasing explanatory value because the economies were ever more differentiating, as Musto (1985: 2f.) put it: (a) 'Europe's industrial metropoles are experiencing a partial de-industrialization, a new type of underdevelopment', and (b) the newly industrialized countries that had managed to stimulate capitalist industrialization tended 'to impede the industrialisation process in the remaining part of the developing world'. In some countries, these policies included decentralization and increasing regional autonomy (i.e. Spain, Italy) but the result was perceived as 'blatant and meanwhile from all side stated failure' (Nohlen 1985: 10).

Moreover, industrialization and class relations in the European South markedly differed from alleged role models in modernization theory (cf. Hadjimichalis 1983; Giner 1985; Woodward 1985). Based on their study on Calabria, Arrighi and Piselli (1987) suggested that development paths could lead into different directions (core or periphery), even if points of departures were similar. Macro-processes of integration into the world market or into a nation-state could alter experiences decisively. 'Qualitative processes' could lead to peripheralization—as in the case of three subregions of Calabria—although 'the same kind of relations of production may be associated [...] in another place [Prussia, Switzerland, the US, RW] with ascent to core position' (Arrighi and Piselli 1987: 694). They (Arrighi and Piselli 1987: 687) understand by 'peripheralization'

> a process whereby some actors or locals, that participate directly or indirectly in the world division of labor, are progressively deprived of the benefits of such participation, to the advantage of other actors or locales. The redistribution of benefits can take different forms, and each of our three roads to wage labor – as they unfolded in Calabria – illustrates a specific form of peripheralization: transfer of surplus, unequal exchange, and direct surplus appropriation.

Arrighi and Piselli (1987: 694) argue that the same microstructural relations and developments can lead to different paths of development because ascending to the core and peripheralization

> are macroprocesses of the world-economy, which have only indirect and partly indeterminate connections with the microstructures of production and reproduction. As a macroprocess, peripheralization is determined primarily by the relations in time and space among microstructures and only secondarily by the nature of the microstructures themselves.

Lastly, 'primitive accumulation' and free movement of labor was not a sufficient characteristic for future development toward a core region. 'The Calabrian case provides compelling evidence', concludes Piselli (2011: 37f.),

> in support of the need to critically rethink the assumptions about 'primitive accumulation' by means of which the dispossession of the peasantry is seen as a natural condition of successful capitalist development. In short: In the first place, systems of production that are often construed as successive stages in the development of capitalism (subsistence-production, small-scale commodity production, and large-scale commodity production) developed in Calabria next to each other and at about the same time. In the second place, if none of the three roads to wage labour can be construed as representing successive stages of capitalist development, neither can any of them be construed as a feature of core positions or of peripheral positions.

Geopolitical position, the state level, and the substate level (such as Calabria) influence the development path of microstructures. In the case of the three Calabrian subregions, historical developments at the level of the state, the geopolitical order, and integration into the world market and its developments converged their own development paths toward one peripheral region of Calabria:

'Actors, activities, and locals are shaped by history and geography, ecology and sociology, in complex ways', argue Arrighi and Piselli (1987: 696) against economism in development (economic growth or development of productive forces). But 'once a locale has entered a given path of development', they add laconically,

> the direction of change, if not its speed, is pretty much set for long periods of time. [...] [E]conomic activities become embedded in social relations that form a cultural totality can only change as a totality. This is of course also true of economic activities in in core locales. However, it is plausible to assume that the greater command over world-economic resources of the actors endows them with better possibilities to do two things: one, to establish new activities in addition to, or substitution for, existing activities; and two to overcome social constraints and resistance to innovation.

The alleged modernization path was once more altered when transnational companies (TNC) began integrating Southern European countries into their realm in the 1960s, well before the Southern enlargement of the EC brought political integration (Vaitsos 1982: 143; Hadjimichalis and Varou-Hadjimichalis 1980; cf. Chapter 5.5). (A similar process of TNC activity was observed when Eastern Europe 'integrated' into the Western integration model from the 1970s onwards, Hager 1985: 67;

cf. Komlosy 2006: 85–91.) The expectation that development processes would be triggered by market mechanisms did not materialize. Instead, the institutional, cultural, legal and often military penetration of peripheral regions eroded the development potentials and increased dependencies (Stöhr 1985a: 229f.). With fading faith in trickle-down and spill-over effects, peripheral regions 'increasingly needed to consider making regional development more endogenous' (Stöhr 1983a: 7; cf. also Stöhr 1983c: 284f.; 1985a: 230). As a solution to the crisis, however, more spatial specialization prevailed, establishing a new international division of labor and further spatial hierarchization (Stöhr 1983b: 121; 1985b: 7 and 12). Regional policies of nation-states led to deeper integration into the world market, and motivating export orientation further increased the functional disintegration of regions: 'The increased opening up of regional structures to external influence, particularly in peripheral areas, led to an increased exposure to external shocks and a reduced resilience' (Stöhr 1983a: 11).

4.2 Transnational Companies: 'New' Actors Disguised by an Old Paradigm

TNC have been the dominant actors in transnational capitalism in Europe long before political integration (cf. Chapter 5.5). TNC capitalism appears to contradict drawing board assumptions by economic scientists that aim at constructing invariant empirical laws. But also some dependency thinkers had been criticized for not acknowledging the deep structural penetration of transnational capitalism which was perceived as dividing line among dependency theorists. As a Marxist economist, EADI member, and dependency school critic Tamás Szentes (1983: 109) put it:

> Contrary to those variants of the [dependency theory] which attribute primary importance to the type of dependence (and of exploitation) manifested in the exchange relations or in the transferred technology and consumption patterns [Immanuel Wallerstein, Arghiri Emmanuel, Oscar Braun, Celso Furtado], it can be proved both logically and historically that the most deeply-rooted, far-reaching and intensive type of economic dependence and of the asymmetrical relations in the international economy is the foreign control by ownership (not necessarily majority ownership) over the key sectors of economy, over the 'commanding heights'.

> This restricts the national sovereignty over the economy far more than any other type, and besides reproducing itself as a result of the local accumulation process of foreign capital, it also provides, by its structural effects, the basis for the rise or perpetuance of the other types of dependence. In so far as the investment decisions in the key sectors are made or strongly influenced by foreign capital, particularly by the giant TNCs, the production structure of the country is shaped according to foreign interests. What follows is that the biased production structure will largely determine a biased trade structure, and will also affect the technological and training conditions, the financial bottlenecks and the consumption pattern, too. Though there is, of course, an interaction, as long as ownership control exists (in its internationally asymmetrical pattern), and exerts its structural effects, the other forms of dependence appear rather as derivatives.

Following our discussion in Chapter 2, it seems as if neither Furtado nor Wallerstein would count towards authors underestimating TNC power. Also among the European Dependency School, there was awareness of the role of TNC. Eminently dealing with issues of TNC in the European Dependency School was Constantine Vaitsos (1980: 24):

> For a significant part of production activities and exchange relations, the underlying economic and behavioural forces can no longer be adequately understood or interpreted on an inter-national or an inter-areas basis. Instead, the appropriate framework of analysis appears to be one of corporate internalization. In such a context, decisions and information management, production and exchange activities, as well as the accumulation of resources and capabilities are integrated within the consolidated boundaries of a single enterprise control system, with affiliated or related firm operating in a number of national jurisdictions.

Central planning has long entered the capitalist mode of production but the appearance of market capitalism prevailed. TNC constitute meta-market institutions that operate on a dual structure, argued (Vaitsos 1980: 42): market mechanisms to the outside (if on oligopolist markets) and central planning, control, and discretionary decision-making to the inside. TNC 'have developed', as Vaitsos (1980: 34) put it almost four decades ago,

> into the most centrally planned, monitored, controlled and managed economic entities in the world economy. The Soviet or Chinese economies

> fall short of them in the extent of non-participation by constituent parts in central planning and overall decision-making. They also fall short in the locational concentration of certain strategic assets, such as technology and top managerial capabilities. Through the internalisation of decision-making on a worldwide scale, the apex of the capitalist system, namely the transnational enterprise, has evolved in an institution which, in its sizeable international operations, negates the foundations of pluralism upon which the market system was founded. In this case, serious conflicts exist between efficiency (in managing global operations) and distributional implications. One area where this administrative and non-participatory structure of decision-making is visible is the setting of transfer prices on goods and services exchanged among affiliates.

Also the 'regionalists' of the European dependency school were aware of the role TNC played in the capitalist mode of production. When dependency analyses were written in the 1970s, a power struggle in the international economy was prevailing. Friedmann and Weaver (1979: 163ff.) gave an account on the power struggle between states/governments and transnational companies which was, on an international level, carried out by and in organizations like the international labor organization (ILO) or the Club of Rome.

> Every national economy is, to a degree, both functional and territorial, but the actions to which these principles of social cohesion give rise often result in bitter struggle. In any event, the complexity of the response space does not allow of ideologically 'pure' answers. Territory and function are both needed for development. The real question is which principle is to be master: shall function prevail over territory, or territory over function. At the moment the transnationals appear to be gaining in this contest for dominion, but the arguments favouring the territorial principle are very strong, and territorial systems are, in any case, essential to the survival of corporate (functional) power. Without territory, corporate power could not shift the burdens of production on society. (Friedmann and Weaver 1979: 171)

Spatial development planning based on the theory of polarized development and with the 'growth centre doctrine as its principle tool' had become 'the handmaiden of transnational capital' and 'a willing instrument in the hands of the managers of unequal development' (Friedmann and Weaver 1979: 171). TNC had a strong influence on regional development, leading to monopolistic structures without modernization in industry (cf. Chapter 4.2). John Logan (1985: 150ff.) argued that integration into transnational capitalism had aggravated contradictions between traditional and 'modern' capitalist elites, which had finally led to the end of dictatorships in Southern Europe. He pointed out 'that "modern" elites [...] are intimately interlocked with international capital. Their future is not a development pattern leading to a more independent national economy, but indeed in some ways to a more dependent role in the world-system' (Logan 1985: 150). Çağlar Keyder (1985: 147) emphasized 'the conflict between pro-European and pro-American fractions during the late 1960s and the early 1970s'. Following Poulantzas, Costis Hadjimichalis (1983: 136) refers to authoritarian statism, which 'corresponds to the current phase of advanced monopoly capitalism, in the way that the liberal state referred to the competitive stage of capitalism'. Most Western European countries had seen 'intensified State control over every sphere of socio-economic life, combined with extensive spatial policies' since the 1960s. In Southern Europe (Greece, Italy, Portugal, and Spain) this new form of state acquired distinctive features since 1975. They seemed 'to be more "open" and "democratic" compared to the recent experience of fascism and military dictatorship' (ibid.). New democratic liberties developed but integration into (new) international division of transnational capitalism brought a new authoritarian statism as well (cf. Chapter 3.1).

4.3 Spatial Specialization, External Dependency, and Disintegration of Peripheral Regions

Spatial specialization was seen to have increased markedly after 1945 (Stöhr 1983a: 7f.; 1985b: 2ff.): Single regions produced less products for growing markets. Specialization applied not only for products but also for factors of production and their functional relations. It supported the social and political differentiation among regions in terms of political power, social innovation, but also the degree of dependencies. To the consequences of such economic, political, and social interrelations belonged a narrow concentration of economic activities on few resources (raw materials, tourism) because there was demand in the 'large-scale interaction system'. Other resources remained little or not utilized. Century-old mechanisms that had regulated the relations among people, or between people and nature were often

> put out of action and are substituted by behavioural patterns and institutions from the outside, which cannot be adapted to regional requirements. Decision-making structures of trans-regional enterprises and national or international institutions are catalysts for this process. (Stöhr 1983a: 8)

With the global crisis of the 1970s, the dilemma of regional policy, which aimed at reducing the divergence of regional living and working conditions, became also manifest in industrialized countries (Tödtling 1983: 36). The studies by Stöhr and Tödtling (1977, 1978) suggested that 'spread-effects' were smaller than 'backwash effects', and that there was little sign of regional convergence (Stöhr and Tödtling 1979: 148ff.; Stöhr 1975). Where regional convergence was visible, it seemed to be accompanied by disparities at other levels (intra-regional or intra-personal). Regional policies had been based on the mentioned external conditions and following assumptions that ran out of validity in the early 1970s (Stöhr 1983c: 284). Regional disparities had not been eliminated during the upswinging conjuncture, and built henceforth the base for a new 'spatial division of labor' as it was called by Doreen Massey (1979) in her contribution to the conference 'The Death of Regional Policy': She considered it unclear if the level of convergence was owed to regional policies or rather to the behavior of industry during the conjectural upswing, and the consequences of interregional and international division of labor. Stöhr (1983b: 120f.) emphasized the role of economic growth in the temporary quantitative success of regional transformation that covered the (negative) qualitative and structural changes of transformation in peripheral regions, such as a decline in sectoral and functional diversification of peripheral economic spaces, a growing structural dependency from external key functions and decision-making, global economic and structural fluctuations, and external factors like capital and technology. The structural transformation would go along with the new spatial division of labor, which was introduced by multi-regional and multinational companies. They took advantage of existing disparities and were, as Herzog and Tödtling (1983: 111) showed in their critical study on funding institutions of Austrian regional policies, able to use incentives most successfully (access to public funding, inner division of labor in order to use regional division of labor).

Key functions of this new spatial division of labor (R&D, planning, decision-making) were concentrated in core regions, while executing parts of the production, with low rates of innovation and small sectoral differentiation, and routine functions were outsourced into peripheral regions:

> This can also be seen as process of *successive hierarchical outsourcing of production processes* into peripheral regions [...]. This process of outsourcing often happens in many steps, as routine production from low developed regions in industrial countries relocates to developing countries that display a still lower wage level and an again lower organizational level of their labor force [...]. (Stöhr 1983b: 121; cf. also Stöhr 1985b: 7 and 12)

A specialization pursued in accordance to the needs of core regions had—despite temporal growth successes also in some quarters of the periphery—undermined 'the substance of weakly developed regions and therefore [...] reduces their medium term and long term development potentials', which led to a functional disintegration of peripheral regions (Stöhr 1983b: 122).

> This is manifested in the discontinuities of local and regional economic circuits as well as of social and political interaction patterns (caused, for example, by out-migration or long-range commuting), in the idleness of regional resources, and in the decline of facilities catering to the daily needs of the population [...] - access to employment, consumer goods, services, etc. (Stöhr 1983a: 9)

Regional policies in most countries tended to accelerate functional disintegration. 'Development' was promoted by world market integration ('integration into large-scale interaction systems'): development of transport infrastructure between core and periphery, new factories to transfer production from the core, investment incentives, and public transfers, 'export-base activities', facilitating tourism industry (Stöhr 1983a: 10). Regional economic cycles were being interrupted but satellite industries led to instable employment situations. Decision-making processes were being transferred to core regions (for example central government planning institutions). Setbacks in demand caused by the crisis of the 1970s confronted peripheral regions with 'negative export-base multipliers' (closing of factories, cut in public funds). It became obvious that qualitative economic, social, and institutional aspects of development had been neglected: production displayed a low level of diversification, employment was instable and export-dependent, local supply had become less accessible and of lower in quality: 'The increased opening up of regional structures to external influence, particularly in peripheral areas, led to an increased exposure to external shocks and a reduced resilience' (Stöhr 1983a: 11).

4.4 Dependent Industrialization and Peripheral Deindustrialization

Early departures to industrial development in Southern European countries had been frustrated, and 'the belated rise of industrial capitalism [...] before and during the First World War was only the most visible trace of a deeper current, with a much longer past', argues Salvador Giner (1985: 316) from the 'Durham-network':

> What happened was not so much that these countries were 'late joiners' to the capitalist industrial transformation, but rather that their bourgeoisies had failed in their efforts to be among the 'first comers'.

Attempts of 'capitalist modernization' and 'catching-up' industrialization came in many countries of the European periphery in the form of Fascist regimes (as pointed out by the Binghamton network working on European dependency). Loukas Tsoukalis (1981: 96ff.), an author who wrote in Seers' EADI-network, seems to use a language that distorts the view on the nature of this 'modernization' when he talks of an 'economic miracle' and of 'rapid industrialisation' for the cases of Greece, Portugal, and Spain. He concedes, however, that it had been the opening of the three economies to the world market during the boom years of the 1960s and early 1970s that stimulated such tendencies. Acknowledging the critical view of dependency authors (Muñoz et al. 1979) he adds:

> If we approach the problem from a more critical angle, we can talk of an industrialization process which has led to an increasing dependence on foreign trade and technology. This has in turn created a dualistic economy, serious regional and structural disequilibria and a highly unequal distribution of income. It has also brought about the adoption of foreign consumption habits which do not correspond to the standard of living already achieved in those countries. Last but not least the rapid process of industrialization did not solve the problem of unemployment and this forced hundreds of thousands of workers to leave their country [...]. (Tsoukalis 1981: 96)

Dudley Seers' (1978) report on the Portuguese situation unmistakably shows the legacy post-Fascist governments inherited from the period of Fascist modernization: growth without development.

> So, although economic growth was moderately fast (about 6–7% a year in real terms), social problems remained severe and some of them grew worse, aggravating the regional imbalance. Wages were held to levels which were becoming very low by comparison with those in France and West Germany, but nevertheless, the economy was incapable of absorbing the growth in the labour force. Two quasi-solutions emerged in response to the widening gap between wage levels in Portugal and elsewhere in Europe: labour emigrated in increasing numbers and a growing flow of foreign tourists commenced. By 1974, the economy was relying on emigrants' remittances and tourist earnings to cover a large part of import needs, including food. Thus, the country had become heavily dependent on events in North Western Europe as well as Africa. (Seers 1978: 2)

With the global economic crisis, the vulnerability of the three peripheral Mediterranean countries became obvious. They had few options compared to the core countries, 'while profoundly affected by the economic crisis and by the policies adopted by the core', they 'are severely constrained in their ability to respond or react in an autonomous fashion' (Pollis 1983: 212). If transnational capitalism could foster industrial development, it apparently also led to regional deindustrialization. Different authors have observed processes of deindustrialization in European regions of the periphery, such as for Eastern and Southeastern European countries during transformation processes (Becker et al. 2016) or the Greek, Portuguese, and Spanish EC/EU integration processes (Etxezarreta et al. 2014: 65; López and Rodríguez 2010: 8; Stathakis 2010: 110; Santos and Jacinto 2006).

Deindustrialization often appears to be used intuitively, this is why Francesco Lissoni (1996: 1) tried 'to put some order in the debate', and suggested two main views, a macroeconomic and a geographic one. The former equals a process of tertiarization, the latter describes changes in local areas, 'once specialized in a few traditional manufacturing activities, and nowadays threatened by plant closures and layoffs [...]'. More recently, UNIDO (2013: xv) defined deindustrialization as '[l]ong-term decline in manufacturing relative to other sectors. Typically measured in terms of share of manufacturing employment in total employment'. Changes in the share of the manufacturing sector in GDP or employment seem to be the typical measurement of changes in industrial development (Tregenna 2011: 5).

A reduction of employment, however, could also be caused by a higher productivity which could lead to constant or growing output—if not a sign of deindustrialization on the output side than still on the employment side. Furthermore a shrinking share of manufacturing in relation to the service sector (tertiarization) does not necessarily mean shrinking output or employment if both sectors grow overall. Last but not least, a definition of 'long-term' seems necessary in order to distinguish deindustrialization from short term effects. Of course, as Louri and Pepelasis Minoglou (2001: 398) put it nicely, '[f]or an economy to reach de-industrialization, it is thought that it has first to be industrialised'. Therefore the focus of the attention had been the advanced capitalist countries, with a peak in manufacturing output and employment between the 1950s and 1970s, and a steady decline afterwards (ibid.). Nicholas Kaldor is recognized as first having coined the term deindustrialization in the 1960s (Lissoni 1996: 2; Louri and Pepelasis Minoglou 2001: 398), relating relative decline of manufacturing (employment and output shares) to GDP growth. Later the role of manufacturing was extended to contributing to exports and structural effects (technical progress and productivity growth) (Louri and Pepelasis Minoglou 2001: 398f.). All in all the literature Louri and Pepelasis Minoglou (2001: 398ff.) review, suggest external dependence (demand for tradable products) and domestic failure to adapt to pressures by international demand (transition to high wage and high productivity production) as reasons for deindustrialization. A classification of 'three alternative hypotheses for explaining de-industrialization' is being offered, referring to a study by Rowthorn and Wells (1987):

> (a) the *maturity hypothesis*, according to which once a certain per capita GDP is reached, the share of manufacturing industry will inevitably start falling in favour of services (provided that the share of agriculture is already small), (b) the *specialization hypothesis*, according to which the trading patterns of an economy shape the structure of its product and employment and (c) the *failure hypothesis*, according to which it is the failure of manufacturing, possibly due to its structural weaknesses, to compete internationally, that makes its reduction inevitable. (ibid.: 399; cf. also Tregenna 2011: 6f.)

For overall processes of industrialized countries, a *maturity hypothesis* can then be interpreted in the framework of the phasing-out or 'maturing' postwar accumulation model in industrial societies that set in at the end of the 1960s, with shrinking profitability in the manufacturing sector. It heralded the age of 'postfordism' and 'financialisation'. A *specialization hypothesis* would then belong to the structural consequences of this transformation: tertiarization in the industrial countries and outsourcing of low-technology production to the periphery. (Fröbel et al. 1977; Smith 2012) Furthermore

> the 1980s switch in 'policy regime' in OECD countries (broadly speaking, from post-war Keynesianism to demand constraining monetarism) did also contribute to the huge 1980s drop in manufacturing employment[…] and [t]he technological revolution that took off in the 1980s also played a major role […]. (Palma 2008: 4)

For peripheral countries in Europe as latecomers in industrial development, the maturity hypothesis can be pretty much neglected. These countries ran through a process of dependent industrialization (and integration into the world market). From the 1950s to the 1970s, they were 'still showing signs of industrial dynamism' but

> in the 1980s and 1990s, many intermediate countries entered the stage of de-industrialisation without having reached either the high levels of industrial activity or the high per capita incomes of the advanced capitalist economies. Thus, their relative place in the global economy in terms of growth potential and living standards deteriorated, diminishing prospects of convergence. (Louri and Pepelasis Minoglou 2001: 398)

From the perspective of development studies, a 'failure hypothesis' (failure to reach full-fledged industrialization) is a relative of modernization theory, Palma (2008) uses a concept of 'pre-mature de-industrialization'. Modernization theory assumes that there are role models whose ideal path (or stages) latecomers in development can or should follow in order to reach a similar status. Modernization as a role model, however, is more an exception than the rule. If failure to reach full-fledged modern industrialization is the norm, then the few leading nations plus a couple of runners-up from the semiperiphery might be exceptions due to special circumstances. Moreover, if we take the analysis of Arrighi and Drangel (1986; cf. Chapter 3.2 above) than industrialization was just a temporal 'core-like' economic activity that was historically 'necessary' to attain or keep a core status. According to this analysis it is the control of commodity chains ('brain activities') in TNC capitalism that determines core status. Furthermore, it must be repeated that a symbiotic relationship between core enterprise and core state create a kind of 'path dependence' that is difficult to overcome in an attempt to upgrade, e.g. from semiperiphery to core status (cf. Chapter 3.2). Therefore it appears doubtful that a peripheral country can just ignore economic activities that have been considered core-like historically (industrialization) and just turn toward economic activities that are considered core-like today ('brain activities' and control).

However, historical tendencies toward policies of 'self-reliance' faced harsh adverse winds on part of the 'developed' countries, above all the United States, which included coups d'etat.

> The simple fact was however that it seemed increasingly clear that no amount of repression [...] could contain the emerging social and political pressures as long as the manufactured export alternative did not become a more realistic option, at least in 'key' countries with particular geo-political significance. (Bienefeld 1982: 48)

Such considerations had the already discussed beneficial effect that they could also take pressure from the contradictory scheme within the developed block of OECD countries (outsourcing production and offering privileged market access):

> As competitive pressures between OECD producers intensified, the temptation for the lagging economies to improve their position (and hence sustain their profits and contain inflation) by taking advantage of cheap labour in the developing world became more and more irresistible. What the UK and the US had begun on a minute scale in Hong Kong and Puerto Rico, was now expanded dramatically to South Korea, Brazil, Taiwan, Singapore, Mexico and the European periphery. In addition a growing number of Export Processing Zones established as pure enclaves in a variety of countries [...]. (Bienefeld 1982: 48f.)

The notion among the dependency school, namely that capitalist industrial development was possible in the periphery, had a double ironic twist: first, economic progress in industrial production happened under authoritarian rule, second, the obvious contradictions of capitalist development were covered by new success stories:

> [A] relatively heterogeneous set of economies, all (except Mexico and Yugoslavia) under extremely authoritarian right-wing regimes, emerged more or less simultaneously as the NICS [newly-industrialized countries], to be eventually acclaimed as models which vindicated the market as an adequate, and indeed, the optimal engine of rapid development [...]. Their experience has become the basis for the militant application of equilibrium economics to development, as implicit in the use of cost-benefit techniques based on the practically unqualified use of international prices as relevant opportunity costs [...], and effectively ignoring the many earlier counsels that this frame of analysis was inappropriate to the development context [...]. It is somewhat ironic that this should have happened just when the inadequacies of that frame of analysis have become most evident in the developed countries. (Bienefeld 1982: 49)

The special cases of the cold war frontier 'tiger states' belonged to the set of arguments for a generalized capitalist development path and success. As Manfred Bienefeld (1982: 49) described this in the early 1980s:

> The new faith was immensely strengthened during the 1970s when a few of the smaller NICs - South Korea, Taiwan, Singapore, Hong Kong - attained effective full employment, and as a consequence saw real wages rise significantly in spite of continued political, and trade union, repression. This crucial evidence strengthened the argument that market-based policies which accepted initial inequalities could be economically and socially desirable in developing economies. The experience demonstrated once again that if the process of capitalist accumulation can be sufficiently concentrated in a particular economic space for an adequate period it has the capacity to generate full employment, and consequently to diffuse material benefits within this economic space. In this sense the notion of trickle down lives, as it has lived in Japan, and in the other industrialized countries before that. It still remains, however, to determine what conditions, both national and international, might allow such a concentration of accumulation to be sustained over time. In this respect the end of full employment in the industrial countries represents a strong warning against simplistic generalizations or undue optimism.

References

Adorno, Theodor. 1972 [1968]. Spätkapitalismus oder Industriegesellschaft. In *Gesammelte Schriften. Band 8. Soziologische Schriften I*, ed. Theodor Adorno, 354–370. Frankfurt/Main: Suhrkamp.

Arrighi, Giovanni, and Jessica Drangel. 1986. The Stratification of the World-Economy: An Exploration of the Semiperipheral Zone. *Review* 10 (1): 9–74 (=Anniversary Issue: The Work of the Fernand Braudel Center).

Arrighi, Giovanni, and Fortunata Piselli. 1987. Capitalist Development in Hostile Environments: Feuds, Class Struggles, and Migrations in a Peripheral Region of Southern Italy. *Review* 10 (4): 649–751 (Fernand Braudel Center).

Becker, Joachim, Predrag Ćetković, and Rudy Weissenbacher. 2016. Financialisation, Dependent Export Industrialization, and Deindustrialisation in Eastern Europe. In *Finance and Industrial Policy: Beyond Financial Regulation in Europe*, ed. Giovanni Cozzi, Susan Newman, and Jan Toporowski, 41–64. Oxford: Oxford University Press.

Becker, Joachim, and Rudy Weissenbacher. Forthcoming. Fordism in the Americas. In *Rethinking the Americas Vol. III: Key Topics in Political Economy and Governance*, ed. Anne Tittor, Bernhard Leubolt, and Daniel Hawkins.

Bienefeld, Manfred. 1982. The International Context of National Development Strategies: Constraints and Opportunities in a Changing World. In *The Struggle for Development: National Strategies in an International Context*, ed. Manfred Bienefeld and Martin Godfrey, 25–64. Chichester and New York: Wiley.

Bloch, Ernst. 2000 [1964, 1923]. *The Spirit of Utopia*. Stanford: University Press.

Bourdieu, Pierre. 2005 [1997]. Neo-Liberalismus als konservative Restauration. In *Das PRAXIS-Konzept im Zentrum gesellschaftskritischer Wissenschaft*, ed. Horst Müller, 175–180. Norderstedt: Books on Demand.

Etxezarreta, Miren, et al. 2014. Boom and (Deep) Crisis in the Spanish Economy: The Role of the EU in Its Evolution. In *The Deepening Crisis of the European Union: The Case for Radical Change*, ed. Wlodzimierz Dymarski, Marica Frangakis, and Jeremy Leaman, 58–89. Poznan: Poznan University of Economics Press.

Friedmann, John. 1983. Life Space and Economic Space: Contradictions in Regional Development. In *The Crises of the European Regions*, ed. Dudley Seers and Kjell Öström. London: Palgrave Macmillan.

Friedmann, John, and Clyde Weaver. 1979. *Territory and Function: The Evolution of Regional Planning*. London: Edward Arnold.

Fröbel, Folker, Jürgen Heinrichs, and Otto Kreye. 1977. *Die neue internationale Arbeitsteilung: strukturelle Arbeitslosigkeit in den Industrieländern und die Industrialisierung der Entwicklungsländer*. Reinbek bei Hamburg: Rowohlt.

Giner, Salvador. 1985. Political Economy, Legitimation and the State in Southern Europe. In *Uneven Development in Southern Europe: Studies of Accumulation, Class, Migration and the State*, ed. Ray Hudson and Jim Lewis, 309–350. London and New York: Methuen.

Giunta, Anna, and Flavia Martinelli. 1995. The Impact of Post-Fordist Corporate Restructuring in a Peripheral Region. In *Behind the Myth of*

European Union: Prospects for Cohesion, ed. Ash Amin and John Tomaney, 190–225. London and New York: Routledge.

Hadjimichalis, Costis. 1983. Regional Crisis: The State and Regional Social Movements in Southern Europe. In *The Crisis of the European Regions*, ed. Dudley Seers and Kjell Öström, 127–147. London and Basingstoke: Palgrave Macmillan.

Hadjimichalis, Costis, and Dina Varou-Hadjimichalis. 1980. Penetration of Multinational Capital into Backward Regions: A Policy Analysis in Greece. *Antipode* 12 (2): 17–24.

Hager, Wolfgang. 1985. Fortress Europe: A Model? In *Europe at the Crossroads: Agendas of the Crisis*, ed. Stefan Musto and Carl Pinkele, 65–84. New York et al.: Praeger.

Hansen, Niles. 1981. Development from Above: The Centre-Down Development Paradigm. In *Development from Above or Below? The Dialectics of Regional Planning in Developing Countries*, ed. Walter Stöhr and Fraser Taylor, 15–38. Chichester et al.: Wiley.

Herzog, Hubert, and Franz Tödtling. 1983. Versuch einer Einschätzung der österreichischen Regionalpolitik für periphere entwicklungsschwache Regionen. *Österreichische Zeitschrift Für Soziologie* 8 (3): 100–113.

Keyder, Çağlar. 1985. The American Recovery of Southern Europe. Aid and Hegemony. In *Semiperipheral Development: The Politics of Southern Europe in the Twentieth Century*, ed. Giovanni Arrighi, 135–148. Beverly Hills: Sage (=Explorations in the World-Economy 5).

Komlosy, Andrea. 2006. Österreichs Brückenfunktion und die Durchlässigkeit des „Eisernen Vorhangs". In *„Zarte Bande": Österreich und die europäischen planwirtschaftlichen Länder*, ed. Gertrude Enderle-Burcel, Dieter Stiefel, und Alice Teichova, 73–105. Wien: Studienverlag (=Mitteilungen des Österreichischen Staatsarchivs/Sonderband 9).

Lissoni, Francesco. 1996. *Deindustrialization in Lombardy: An Empirical Assessment*. European Regional Science Association. 36th European Congress, August 26–30. ETH Zurich: Switzerland.

Logan, John. 1985. Democracy from Above: Limits to Change in Southern Europe. In *Semiperipheral Development: The Politics of Southern Europe in the Twentieth Century*, ed. Giovanni Arrighi, 149–177. Beverly Hills, London, and New Delhi: Sage (=Explorations in the World-Economy 5).

López, Isidro, and Emmanuel Rodríguez. 2010. *Fin de ciclo. Financiarización, territorio y sociedad de propietarios en la onda larga del capitalismo hispano (1959–2010)*. Madrid: Traficantes de Sueños.

Louri, Helen, and Ionna Pepelasis Minoglou. 2001. On the Determinants of (De-)Industrialization: A Quantitative Exploration. *International Review of Applied Economics*, 15 (4): 397–410.

Massey, Doreen. 1979. In What Sense a Regional Problem? *Regional Studies* 13 (2): 233–243.

Muñoz, Juan, Santiago Roldán, and Angel Serrano. 1979. The Growing Dependence of Spanish Industrialization on Foreign Investment. In *Underdeveloped Europe: Studies in Core-periphery Relations*, ed. Dudley Seers, Bernard Schaffer, and Marja-Liisa Kiljunen, 161–175. Hassocks: Harvester (=Harvester Studies in Development 1).

Musto, Stefan. 1985. In Search of a New Paradigm. In *Endogenous Development: A Myth or a Path? Problems of Economic Self-Reliance in the European Periphery*, ed. Stefan Musto, 1–13. Tilburg: EADI (=European Association of Development Research and Training Institutes: EADI Book Series 5).

Nohlen, Dieter. 1985. Ungleiche Entwicklung und Regionalpolitik in Südeuropa (Italien, Spanien, Portugal). Eine Einführung. In *Ungleiche Entwicklung und Regionalpolitik in Südeuropa: Italien, Spanien, Portugal*, ed. Dieter Nohlen and Rainer-Olaf Schultze unter Mitwirkung von Wolfgang Merkel, 9–15. Bochum (=Politikwissenschaftliche Paperbacks 6).

Nohlen, Dieter, and Rainer-Olaf Schultze. 1985. Ungleiche Entwicklung und Regionalpolitik in Südeuropa. Externe Verursachungsdfaktoren und endogene Entwicklungschancen. In *Ungleiche Entwicklung und Regionalpolitik in Südeuropa: Italien, Spanien, Portugal*, ed. Ungleiche Entwicklung und Regionalpolitik in Südeuropa: Italien, Spanien, Portugal, 17–73. Bochum (=Politikwissenschaftliche Paperbacks 6).

Öström, Kjell. 1983. Introduction. In *The Crisis of the European Regions*, ed. Dudley Seers and Kjell Öström, 1–5. London and Basingstoke: Palgrave Macmillan.

Palma, Gabriel. 2008. De-industrialization, 'Premature' De-industrialization and the Dutch Disease. In *The New Palgrave Dictionary of Economics*, 2nd ed., ed. Steven Durlauf and Lawrence Blume. Basingstoke. http://www.dictionaryofeconomics.com/dictionary.

Piselli, Fortunata. 2011. Reflections on Calabria: A Critique of the Concept of 'Primitive Accumulation'. *Austrian Journal of Development Policy* XXVII (1): 25–43.

Pollis, Adamantia. 1983. The Southern European Semiperiphery and the European Community. In *The Contemporary Mediterranean World*, ed. Carl Pinkele and Adamantia Pollis, 202–220. New York: Praeger.

Rowthorn, Robert, and John Wells. 1987. *De-Industrialisation and Foreign Trade*. Cambridge: Cambridge University Press.

Santos, Vitor, and Ana Jacinto. 2006. A industria portuguesa: Desindustrialização – progresso ou declinio? In *A economia portuguesa 20 anos após a adesão*, ed. António Romão, 184–213. Coimbra.

Seers, Dudley. 1978. *Development Planning in Portugal: Report of a Mission Under the OECD Technical Co-operation Service*. Brighton: Institute of Development Studies (IDS), University of Sussex.

Seers, Dudley. 1979. The Periphery of Europe. In *Underdeveloped Europe: Studies in Core-Periphery Relations*, ed. Dudley Seers, Bernard Schaffer, and Marja-Liisa Kiljunen, 3–34. Sussex: Harvester Press (=Harvester Studies in Development 1).

Seers, Dudley. 1980. The Cultural Lag in Economics. In *The Relevance of Economic Theories*, ed. Josef Pajestka and Charles Feinstein, 3–16. London and Basingstoke: Macmillan.

Seers, Dudley. 1983. *The Political Economy of Nationalism*. London et al.: Oxford University Press.

Smith, John. 2012. Outsourcing, Financialisation and the Crisis. *International Journal of Management Concepts and Philosophy* 6 (1–2): 19–44.

Stathakis, George. 2010. The Fiscal Crisis of the Greek Economy. In Kurswechsel, No. 3, 109–114. http://www.iippe.org/wiki/images/d/db/CONF_GREEKCRISIS_Stathakis.pdf.

Stöhr, Walter. 1975. *Regional Development: Experiences and Prospects in Latin America*. The Hague: Mouton.

Stöhr, Walter. 1981. Development from Below: The Bottom-Up and Periphery-Inward Development Paradigm. In *Development from Above or Below? The Dialectics of Regional Planning in Developing Countries*, ed. Walter Stöhr and Fraser Taylor, 39–72. Chichester et al.: Wiley.

Stöhr, Walter. 1983a. Alternative Strategies for Integrated Regional Development. In *The Crisis of the European Regions*, ed. Dudley Seers and Kjell Öström, 6–14. London and Basingstoke: Palgrave Macmillan.

Stöhr, Walter. 1983b. Alternative räumliche Entwicklungsstrategien endogener 'selektiver Eigenständigkeit'. *Österreichische Zeitschrift Für Soziologie* 8 (3): 117–134.

Stöhr, Walter. 1983c. Changing External Conditions and a Paradigm Shift in Regional Development Strategies. In *Europe at the Crossroads: Agendas of the Crisis*, ed. Carl Pinkele and Stefan Musto, 283–307. New York: Praeger.

Stöhr, Walter. 1985a. Selective Self-Reliance and Endogenous Regional Development—Pre-conditions and Constraints. In *Ungleiche Entwicklung und Regionalpolitik in Südeuropa: Italien, Spanien, Portugal*, ed. Dieter Nohlen and Rainer-Olaf Schultze unter Mitwirkung von Wolfgang Merkel, 229–249. Bochum (=Politikwissenschaftliche Paperbacks 6).

Stöhr, Walter. 1985b. Industrial Structural Change and Regional Development Strategies: Towards a Conceptual Framework. Paper presented at the joint UNIDO/IGU Symposium on Regional Development Processes/Policies and the Changing International Division of Labour, Vienna, August 20–24, 1984. Wien (=IIR Discussion 21).

Stöhr, Walter, and Franz Tödtling. 1977. Evaluation of Regional Policies: Experiences: Experiences in Market and Mixed Economies. Wien (=IIR-Discussion 1).

Stöhr, Walter, and Franz Tödtling. 1978. Evaluation of Regional Policies: Experiences in Market and Mixed Economies. In *Human Settlement System:*

International Perspectives on Structure, Change and Policy, ed. Niles Hansen, 85–119. Cambridge, MA: Ballinger Publishing.

Stöhr, Walter, and Franz Tödtling. 1979. Spatial Equity: Some Anti-thesis to Current Regional Development Doctrine. In *Spatial Inequalities and Regional Development*, ed. Hendrik Folmer and Jan Oosterhaven, 133–160. Boston, The Hague, and London: Nijhoff.

Szentes, Tamás. 1983. The TNC Issue: Naive Illusions or Exorcism and Lip-Service. In *Emerging Development Patterns: European Contributions*, ed. István Dobozi and Péter Mándi, 97–118. Selected Papers of the 3rd General Conference of EADI. Budapest (=EADI Book Series 1).

Tödtling, Franz. 1983. Regionale Unterschiede der nichtlandwirtschaftlichen Betriebs- und Arbeitsplatzstruktur in Österreich. *Österreichische Zeitschrift für Soziologie* 8 (3): 36–44.

Tregenna, Fiona. 2011. *Manufacturing Productivity, Deindustrialization, and Reindustrialization.* Helsinki (=UNU-WIDER Working Paper 2011/57).

Tsoukalis, Loukas. 1981. *The European Community and Its Mediterranean Enlargement.* London, Boston, and Sydney: Allen and Unwin.

UNIDO (ed.). 2013. *Industrial Development Report 2013. Sustaining Employment Growth: The Role of Manufacturing and Structural Change.* Vienna.

Vaitsos, Constantine. 1980. Corporate Integration in World Production and Trade. In *Integration and Unequal Development: The Experience of the EEC*, ed. Dudley Seers and Constantine Vaitsos with the assistance of Kiljunen, Marja-Liisa, 24–45. London and Basingstoke: Macmillan (=Studies in the Integration of Western Europe 1).

Vaitsos, Constantine. 1982. Transnational Corporate Behaviour and the Enlargement. In *The Second Enlargement of the EEC: The Integration of Unequal Partners*, ed. Dudley Seers and Constantine Vaitsos with the assistance of Marja-Liisa Kiljunen, 137–162. London and Basingstoke: Houndmills (=Studies in the Integration of Western Europe 2).

Woodward, Susan. 1985. The Economic Crisis in Southern Europe: Origins and Political Responses. In *Europe at the Crossroads: Agendas of the Crisis*, ed. Carl Pinkele and Stefan Musto, 103–132. New York: Praeger.

CHAPTER 5

Core and Periphery from Cold War to Monetary Integration

5.1 Reconstruction of the European Core

Before we turn to the way the European dependency school judged the European integration process, we should revisit the turmoil immediately after World War II, where the origins of the European Union lie. It is easy to see why today's EU mythology stresses the aspect of a peace union. However, peace seems to have been a pacification of the capitalist sphere of interest in Europe which bore the imprint of continuity and block confrontation. The US realpolitik of a war alliance with the Soviet Union had ended with the death of Franklin Delano Roosevelt 1945. His successor Harry Truman returned to the US prewar foreign policy, which had been hostile against the Soviet Union from the very beginning. But other than after World War I, the United States took decisive stance in shaping the international postwar order, arriving in their role as hegemonic power of the capitalist core. Truman's more confrontational stance with the Soviet Union was made possible by the US monopoly of the atomic bomb—which lasted until 1949—and the demonstration (against Japan) that the United States was willing to use it. Reshaping the Western European core, above all Germany against the Soviet Union, the United States allowed significant fractions of the German Fascist elite to regain positions in the Federal Republic of Germany (cf. Weissenbacher 2007: 30ff.). The European Recovery Program (ERP, 'Marshall Plan') belongs to the policy of stabilizing and integrating the Western European Capitalist bloc

R. Weissenbacher, *The Core-Periphery Divide in the European Union*,
https://doi.org/10.1007/978-3-030-28211-0_5

(Haller 2009: 92; Marsh 2011: 13) as does being soft on German War criminals (Schwartz 1990: 406). The ERP had an importance besides the geopolitical function: the stabilization of Western Europe served the investment strategies and the very economic stability of the US economy that had been in full war production as the factory of the Allied armies (Harvey 2004: 188; Panitch and Gindin 2012: 99ff.).

For the European countries that were invaded and exploited by Fascist Germany, there is a bitter irony in the German ERP success story. The economic historian Alice Teichova (1988: 174–178, 188–193) called the economic relations Germany had established in Eastern and Southeastern Europe already before 1938—the year Germany annexed Austria and parts of Czechoslovakia—'informal empire'. World War II would accentuate exploitation. 'Germany's deficits during World War II were mostly robbery at gunpoint', as Albrecht Ritschl (2012), economic historian and advisor to the German ministry of economics, put it. After the war, the United States immediately helped the economy of the defeated enemy Germany to its feet again—at the expense of the victorious but exploited and damaged European countries. All countries that received funds from US ERP had to accept that their claims (reparations, debt) were blocked until Germany had fully repaid ERP funds. Furthermore,

> German pre-1933 debt was to be repaid at much reduced interest rates, while settlement of post-1933 debts was postponed to a reparations conference to be held after a future German unification. No such conference has been held after the reunification of 1990. The German position is that these debts have ceased to exist. (Ritschl 2012)

The United States privileged its former enemy Germany after the war, against the allies and the countries that had suffered immense casualties, destruction, and plundering by German invasion during World War II. Such a war is the most extreme version of core–periphery relations. In pure economic terms it means that modernization of German capital stock and industries during the war was based on robbed resources and slave labor. It belongs to the privileges that it was clear for all allies that the German society would never pay back what German war and occupation caused in European societies. Despite destruction on German soil, Germany was still considered the economic engine of Europe. A European recovery without rebuilding the German economy was deemed not very likely. What was there concerning allied agreement on partial reparations faded with the cold war (cf. Roth and Rübner 2017). With the vanishing interest in German reparations, also research on the topic suffered. Roth and Rübner (2017: 195) estimate the German total debt relating to World War II at 5.9 (European) billion Euro of 2015, 79% of which (equal to 152.5% of German GDP in 2015) they consider as not compensated. Small countries like Greece appear as extreme cases. The authors argue that Greece remained virtually not compensated, they estimate outstanding accounts at 185 thousand million Euro (2015, ibid.). A limited final compensation (either the amount Germany used as transfer payments to integrate Eastern Germany—1.2 (European) billion Euro—or at least the provisions Germany paid to the functional elite of the Nazi dictatorship—306 thousand million Euro) should be paid to those societies that had remained largely uncompensated although they suffered most by German occupation, and were not able to participate in the core prosperity of postwar reconstruction boom, respectively (ibid.: 198).

The London conference, which dealt with German foreign debt, began in 1951. It can be seen as an example of yet another challenge for countries that had been invaded by Germany. In the negotiations with the new German government, representatives of the invaded and exploited countries met staff from old (Fascist) Germany. The leader of the German delegation in London was Hermann Josef Abs, a member of many supervisory boards of German banks and industrial companies (for example IG Farben, Deutsche Bank), first in Fascist Germany and then in the Federal Republic of Germany (Hilberg 1990: 1259ff.; Czichon 1995: 169ff., 221, 242ff., 370ff., 386; James 2001: 214f.; 2004: 214ff., 224ff.). With the agreement on German foreign debt, signed on February 27, 1953, the German government was able to postpone the reparation issue. When state socialist Eastern Germany was integrated into the Federal Republic, the related international treaty (2 + 2 treaty) alarmed the German government. Such a treaty had the potential to reopen the reparation issue. An internal brief for chancellor Helmut Kohl (dated March 15, 1990, reprinted in Roth and Rübner 2017: 504f.) summarized the German legal opinion on the reparation issue. It states that 'currently none of our former wartime enemies is entitled to reparations'. [...] [W]e have only agreed to a provision whereupon '"an assessment of claims resulting from World War II ... is postponed up to the final regulation of the reparation question". When the "final regulation of the reparation question" shall occur, has not been regulated in the London debt agreement'. And also the transition agreement with the three Western allies, the paper continues, only stipulated that reparations should be regulated by a peace treaty of Germany with its opponents or by reparation settlements. Therefore, the document makes clear that 'the federal government and also the government of a future united Germany has an overriding interest to defy any claim on the conclusion of a peace treaty'. Germany's legal opinion argued that (a) there never was a legal agreement to reopen the reparation issue, (b) there was a 'lack of specific, contractually agreed commitments' by Germany, (c) the former enemies had relinquished their claims, and (d) Germany had provided benefits already. Therefore, 'the complex of reparation problems [...] is, 45 years after the end of the war, de facto settled' (ibid.). The Greek government, however, kept die reparation claims open and has re-issued them in 2019 following the findings of a Greek parliamentary commission from 2016 that estimated outstanding reparations of Germany for Greece with 288 thousand million Euro (GFP 2019).

With the German currency reform of 1948, the US Army had introduced the Deutsche Mark and also 'wiped out domestic public debt, the largest part of the 300% of 1938 GDP' (Ritschl 2012). Quite Ironic in the light of today's discussion, the privileged treatment allowed Germany to establish the mythology of being the embodiment of economic virtue:

> The Marshall Plan had an outer shell, the European Recovery Programme, and an inner core, the economic reconstruction of Europe on the basis of debt forgiveness to and trade integration with Germany. The effects of its implementation were huge. While Western Europe in the 1950s struggled with debt/GDP ratios close to 200%, the new West German state enjoyed debt/GDP ratios of less than 20%. This and its forced re-entry into Europe's markets was Germany's true benefit from the Marshall Plan, not just the 2-4% pump priming effect of Marshall Aid. As a long term effect, Germany effortlessly embarked on a policy of macroeconomic orthodoxy that it has seen no reason to deviate from ever since. (Ritschl 2012)

Clearly, European integration was motivated by geopolitical requirements of reconstructing capitalist Europe. Jean Monnet, one of the political operators of European integration, 'owed much to American encouragement', his 'decisive advantage [...] was the closeness of his association with the US political elite' (Anderson 2011: 14):

> Monnet's strength as an architect of integration did not lie in any particular leverage with European cabinets – even if he eventually came to enjoy the confidence of Adenauer – but in his direct line to Washington. American pressure [...] was crucial in putting real – not merely ideal – force behind the conception of 'ever greater union' that came to be enshrined in the Treaty of Rome. (Anderson 2011: 17)

To be sure, Monnet himself seems to have been 'remarkably free from the Cold War fixations of the period, looking forward to a united Europe that would balance between America and Russia' (Anderson 2012: 55). The Western European integration process, however, had an economic, political, and military agenda from the very beginning, and received important dynamics from outside in the atmosphere of Cold War and decolonization (Korean War, Suez-Crisis, and Hungarian Uprising). When the United States demanded from France a coherent policy toward Germany, it appears to have been Monnet who came up with the idea of a supranational pooling of coal and steel resources. It was this European Coal and Steel Community (ECSC) that in 1952 formed the nucleus of European integration, which should enable France to politically control what was about to become German economic superiority again (Anderson 2011: 14f. and 21; 2012: 54f.; Moravcsik 1998: 90; Hobsbawm 1996: 241; Leonard 1992: 4ff.; Luif 1988: 3; Scherb 1988: 51ff.).

An important fraction of the German 'economic miracle'-elite seems to have eyed the integration process critically. Similar to Friedrich Hayek, who envisaged institutional arrangements beyond reach of the susceptible influence of national electorates, ordoliberals, the 'German variant of neoliberalism' (Oberndorfer 2012b: 421), despised propositions for European integration they deemed statist or dirigiste (Anderson 2011: 64f.). The first wave of ordoliberals (e.g. Eucken) and neoliberals like Hayek shared an admiration of the German state theorist Carl Schmitt, and the authoritarian liberalism by the government of Heinrich Brüning (with the emergency law of the Weimar constitution) which laid the ground for the succeeding Fascist government of Adolf Hitler. There is a tradition of questioning parliamentary democracy and repudiating the welfare state and economic democracy that runs from the Weimar Republic to postwar Europe, culminating in a renaissance of Hayek in the 1970s (cf. Chapter 9.3), the authoritarian competition state, and authoritarian constitutionalism (Scheuerman 1997; Oberndorfer 2012a, b).

As Ralf Ptak (2004: 62ff.) pointed out, postwar construction of ordoliberal economists as opponents of National Socialism are apologetic. German neoliberal/ordoliberal economists were able to publish freely in NS times and belonged to advisors of the NS state in questions of economics, market and spatial research, and war economics, e.g. Ludwig Erhard, Alfred Müller-Armack, Walter Eucken.

Ludwig Erhard, Secretary of Economics in the Konrad Adenauer administration and later German chancellor, was one important and decisive figures in continuity and tradition. Erhard 'was a pragmatic in the service of different principals' (Roth 1998: 99) who hired particularly many Nazi-cadres with expertise in economic administration and enemy territory occupation for leading posts in his Ministry of Economic Affairs (Roth 2001: 36; for Erhard's role in Nazi Germany, where he did groundwork for the German social market economy ['soziale Marktwirtschaft'], see Plehwe 1998; Roth 1998, 1999a, b; Wünsche 1999). From 1950, Erhard belonged to the larger ordoliberal current of the neoliberal Mont Pèlerin-Society (MPS). He subsidized MPS and tried to counter macroeconomic regulation models that he perceived dominating in other ministries (Roth 2001: 13f. and 26ff.). Walter Eucken participated in the founding meeting of MPS in 1947, among the ordoliberal 'German School of Social Market Economy' were Müller-Armack and many others (Ptak 2004: 261).

Erhard and the ordoliberal German group took an important role in shaping the European integration process. A decade after WWII, Germany was freed from many of its responsibilities accumulated through German fascism. Western European integration process would allow the Western part of Germany to regain even more room to maneuver in postwar Europe. Stuart Holland, contributor to the EADI network—who was drawing on the Latin American Dependency School (Holland 1980: 114)—and British labor politician, described the German approach to European integration with these words:

> For Konrad Adenauer, as for Walter Hallstein – not only first president of the Commission, but also former West German Foreign Minister – it was important for the Federal Republic to regain a place in the sun of international affairs, but not at the cost of denuding herself of commitment to the dominance of a market economy and the competitive process. (ibid.: 13)

As the study by Thomas Rhenisch (1999: 91ff., 154ff.), shows, however, parts of German industry would have preferred a more functionalist integrative (free trade) solution in the context of the European Economic Co-operation (OEEC) to an institutional integration of EEC6. OEEC was the predecessor of OECD, the important institution of Western European integration and cold war that also administered the European Recovery Program (ERP, 'Marshall Plan'). As far as the Western German government's position is concerned, there was going on—behind the scenes—a stiff quarrel between the foreign secretary, backed by chancellor Konrad Adenauer, and secretary of economics Ludwig Erhard, who also favored a free trade arrangement in a wider context of OEEC including Britain. Erhard considered the OEEC the ideal example of an open liberal integration, while he saw in institutions like the EEC6 integration model, as Rhenisch (1999: 91) put it, 'instruments from the dirigiste torture chamber'. He preferred an economic functional integration instead. Erhard was backed by important fractions of German industries. Representing an uncompromising economic liberal position—against the pragmatic stance of Adenauer and the foreign secretary—Erhard tried to topple or at least postpone the integration concept of the EEC6 before the treaty of Rome. He tried in vain to be authorized with the government's integration negotiations. Only after the treaty of Rome was signed, Erhard's economic ministry received the competence for the European integration (ibid.: 141ff., 152).

Chancellor Adenauer gave priority to foreign and security policy. His position favored EEC which was supported by the influential Bundesverband der Deutschen Industrie (BDI), where German heavy industry was influential, with a positive attitude toward cartels (ibid.: 121; something the ordoliberal Erhard was opposed to). Lastly the BDI seems to have reached a hegemonic position among German industries as far as the 'small European integration approach' (ibid.: 126) was concerned. Furthermore, some of the industrialists wanted to avoid the impression that after having regained sovereignty, Western Germany was no more interested in European integration. Above all, the most powerful economy in Europe would not have to fear competition in the common market. Adenauer's economic advisor Hermann Josef Abs, however, seems to have been in line with Erhard in most or many economic issues critical of the EEC6 integration project (e.g. Rhenisch 1999: 97, 147).

Although Erhard failed to circumvent EEC6 integration, and was unable to determine the government position in this issue, the genesis between the preparatory 'Spaak-Report' of 1956 and the actual 'Treaty establishing the European Economic Community' (Treaty of Rome, signed in 1957) suggests that the lobbying of Erhard and fractions of German industry showed some success. An exemplary issue, from a development standpoint, was the institution of an 'investment fund'. The Spaak-Report's Section III.1. ('The Investment Funds') displayed a remarkable wording. Under heading two it reads:

> Common development of the less favoured areas, which exist in all the participating States, is a fundamental condition of the success of the common market. In the event of a sudden economic merging of territories of unequal economic development, cheaper labour and the greater productivity of investments do not automatically ensure more rapid progress of the initially less favoured territory and thereby harmonisation of the levels of the respective areas concerned. Indeed, as shown in the case of the unification of Italy after 1860 and the United States after the War of Secession, the disparity in development can go on increasing where fundamental conditions of production development are not initially created out of public funds, i.e. infrastructure of roads, ports, communications, facilities, the financing of schools and hospitals, drainage, irrigation and the improvement of soil productivity. Positive common action in this connection is beneficial not only to the territories it is desired to develop but also to those in a more favourable position, since the latter increasingly benefit from the greater activity resulting from that development and may in this way prevent relations with less favoured territories from jeopardising their wage levels and standard of living. (Intergovernmental Committee 1956: 65)

Erhard repudiated adjustment funds as proposed in the Spaak-Report, and wanted to accept general coordination of national economic policies only (Rhenisch 1999: 148). There was, moreover, broad resistance also among German industrialists against institutionalizing the investment funds. Parts of the industry aimed at watering down the provisions and treated them as preliminary (Rhenisch 1999: 108f.). The German mining industry saw investment funds useful to attract foreign capital to Europe but wanted to impede that it could be used to balance more and less advantaged areas—which was seen as working against the international division of labor (ibid.: 115). Similar arguments were brought forward by the German iron and steel industry (ibid.: 118). Moreover, Adenauer's economic advisor Abs also argued against maintaining common European investment funds: They would never be able to entirely replace international commercial loans.

> One takes care of strengthening confidence in the honesty of national governments as against foreign property and generally foreign rights, one struggles to keep currency and the economy stable then far more capital will be invested in foreign countries than can be achieved by the help of funds or other public subsidies. (Abs, quoted in Rhenisch 1999: 97)

What remained of the Spaak Report's investment fund appears to have been much more in line with liberal economic views. The Treaty of Rome envisaged the establishment of a European Investment Bank, the task of which was 'to contribute to a balanced and frictionless development of the Common Market in the interest of the Community' (EC EUR-Lex n.y.1: 67). Loans and loan guarantees for the capital market should enable projects (a) to make accessible 'less developed areas'; (b) 'to modernize or adapt companies or to create employment opportunities that arise from gradual formation of the Common Market, and which cannot—due to extent or manner—be completely financed by means of the single member states themselves'; (c) in the interest of several member states (ibid.: 67f.). Even if supranational regulations themselves were perceived by some being against radical liberal reasoning, the way the regulations were formulated followed radical liberal reasoning in the central issue of the liberal paradigm: competition. As we will see, EDS authors were very much aware of the fact that policies of industrial and regional development could be undermined simply by arguing violations of the competition principle. Furthermore, the Western German government safeguarded its liberal stance by managing to fill important positions at the community level: Walter Hallstein became first president of the European Commission, and Hans Groeben, a confidant of Ludwig Erhard from the ministry of economics, monitored the competition regulations as competition commissioner (Holland 1980: 13f.). Already in 1959, Groeben intervened in policies he perceived as 'unjustifiable levels of government aid in a problem sector—shipbuilding' (ibid.: 14). Other than the peripheral enlargement countries more than two decades later (see further down below), Italy and France at that time were able to dismiss such advances by the competition commissioner:

> The Italians in particular learned the lesson of this early experience of Commission liberalism, and thereafter simply refused to inform the Commission's competition division of the effective aid which they were giving to their new concentration of steel production in the South. (ibid.: 14)

It is important to see that the EEC/EU ideology had been economically liberal (ordo-or neoliberal) from the days when the integration model was founded. 'By seeking to give substance to every sub-clause in the Treaty', Holland (1980: 14) summarizes,

> as if nothing had really changed since Adam Smith, [the Commission] showed itself insensitive to real needs in basic industry, regional development and – thereby – the distribution of income and employment. It was not simply a problem of legalism on the part of some Commissioners at the time, trained as lawyers, reaching for the Treaty whenever they heard the words 'State aid'. It was the relevance of the liberal capitalist ideology of the Treaties, and especially the Rome Treaty, which was in question.

In the early decades, however, the founding member states were able to resist the ideology advanced by German governments. Although the six founding countries nominally shared the liberal capitalist ideology, the real economic policies diverged. Especially polarized Italy pursued

> policies through public enterprise which in northern Europe would have put it to the Left of the social democrats, [which] was not something which [the Commission] wished to rationalise, far less advertise. (ibid.)

The glue that held together the integration was something else. It was the anti-communist paradigm of the Cold War that also shaped the European integration process. Main protagonists of the integration process were politicians from Christian Democratic Parties, such as Robert Schuman, Konrad Adenauer, and Alcide De Gasperi (Haller 2009: 100ff.). 'Christian Democrats were […], by and large, the initial architects of European integration, and none of them were particularly enamoured with the notion of a national collective directly expressing a general will' (Müller 2012: 40). Such distrust against popular will formed an institutional structure of European integration between liberalism and a supra-national constitutionalism that gave power to unelected executive structures of integration and, by the same token, kept power at the national government level (Müller 2012: 43f.). 'At no point until—ostensibly—the British referendum of 1976 was there any real popular participation in the movement towards European unity' (Anderson 2011: 16).

5.2 From German Ordo- to International Neoliberalism: Anti-left Bias in the Enlargement Process

Patrick Ziltener (2000: 85ff.) offers an interpretation of European integration that consists of two modes of integration that correspond with two specific forms of statehood. He calls the first phase 'Monnet mode' of integration which lasted from the foundation days of the European Community (EC) to 1973 (which also marked the onset of the first global recession after World War II). In this integration regime, the EC played a supporting and complementary role. It strengthened statehood by invigorating the national state. The supranational level of the EC only gained momentum when statehood was to be transformed after the period of Fordism. Until then a Keynesian development model prevailed which was heavily regulated (monetary sector) and protected (farm sector). Industrial development of Western Europe caught up by using US-American technology ('catching up Fordism') and some protection against the world market. Companies from EC countries competed in the common market but again with some restrictions as far as the Agrarian sector was concerned. Corporatism, welfare state and economic growth secured political support. The crisis years of the 1970s brought a transition phase toward a 'competition state' mode of integration. It was established with the Single European Act in 1987 and gave momentum to the supranational organization of the EC. The European single market process was driven by a changed political environment that enforced neoliberal policies. Based on a new political consensus (flexibilization, deregulation, privatization, monetarism) capital fractions oriented on the world market (TNC, insurance groups, banks) together with other actors (central banks, governments, employers organizations) formed a power block that shaped a market-oriented development path of the European Union (Bieling and Steinhilber 2000: 15).

The change of paradigms from Keynes to neoliberal is well taken. It surely was driven by the restructuring process of capitalism in crisis. The more important denomination between the two models of European integration seems to be, however, the transition between two hegemonic models, from Pax Americana to Pax Germanica. Furthermore, the 'Monnet mode' of integration did not witness that much of a Keynesian development model in the most powerful European economy Western Germany, where a stiff controversy between advocates of Keynesian and ordoliberal approaches was taking place. Ordoliberal approaches found their ways into the early constitutive documents of the European Communities, with lasting influence on the room to maneuver in peripheral countries and regions as far as regional and industrial policies are concerned. The resistance against Keynesian economic policies was particularly strong in Ludwig Erhard's ministry of economics. But very generally, German industry was against any harmonization of social costs (wages, working hours, etc.) as proposed by the French negotiators. Such social costs were considered inappropriate ('Unkosten') with a strong potential of harming competition. Increasing labor costs toward the French level was a no-go for Erhard and German industry (Rhenisch 1999: e.g. 107, 120, 149ff.). Clearly Western Germany was able to mold integration policy from an early stage on. The Keynesian paradigma of early integration may have been the ability of EC nation states to resist German liberal advances. The model in itself was certainly economically liberal. With this privileged position within the integration model of capitalist Europe, Western Germany was able to pursue a neo-mercantilist economic policy:

> [R]ather than acting on an explicit statement, the choice of export-led growth must be seen as a-logical outcome of the choice of the German authorities to reach full employment by other than Keynesian means. That is to say, Keynesianism is seen as conducive to labor indiscipline, whereas sustaining aggregate demand indirectly through exports, and thereby necessitating price stability, is seen as conducive to labor discipline. The German preoccupation with the supply side should not be underestimated. [...] Relatively low wages were then seen as a safeguard against import penetration to discourage consumption of foreign goods associated with a higher standard of living [...]. More importantly, low wages implied a depressed domestic market, forcing firms to find external markets and thus generating an "export hypertrophy" [...]. All this considered, the trade surplus, a result of export-led growth and wage and domestic consumption compression, became the benchmark of a long-term advantage over competitors. In this respect, Germany can be considered a mercantilist country. (Cesaratto and Stirati 2010: 73)

Nurtured in Pax Americana, Western Germany gained room to maneuver when the US hegemony showed weaknesses in the 1970s. Prominent left authors argued an inner-imperialist competition between the United States and Western Europe (EC). Ernest Mandel (1967) considered it unlikely that 'European capitalists will accept their defeat as inevitable, and that they will not at least try to avert it' (ibid.: 29):

> [T]he growth of capital interpenetration inside the Common Market, the appearance of large amalgated banking and industrial units which are not mainly the property of any national capitalist class, represent the material infra-structure for the emergence of supra-national state power organs in the Common Market. (ibid.: 31).

Common market and efforts to create a common financial market reflected for Mandel (ibid.: 35) a 'tendency [...] of the legal superstructure adapting itself to changed property relationships, i.e. the appearance of a type of capitalist property having outgrown the limits of the old national state on the European continent'. He deemed a socialist solution possible:

> Both the tendencies of capital concentration and of obsolescence of the national state on the European continent are indicators of over-ripeness for socialist solutions: the need for a planned economy based upon collective ownership in the framework of a Socialist Federation of Europe (which would both be limited, of course, to the six Common Market countries). (ibid.: 37)

Nicos Poulantzas (2008: 255) saw in the argument of Mandel and others a 'decline being considered tendentially as the end of this hegemony'. He, in contrary, maintained that 'certain forms of this hegemony' were retreating, 'with Europe occupying the position of dependent or satellite imperialism': 'American hegemony has not ceased to be affirmed'. Giovanni Arrighi considered the hegemonial crisis of the United States in the 1970s a 'signal crisis' that marked the end of a period of material expansion and a caesura toward a period of financialization that also brought a temporal restoration of hegemony of the leading capitalist power (Arrighi 2010; Silver and Arrighi 2011). For Mandel (1967: 33), the 'main test [for the Common Market and its structures] will be a general recession in Western Europe'. And indeed the first global recession after World War II in the 1970s would turn out as a caesura also in Europe. But it looked more like a German than a European awakening. This awakening was safeguarded by limitations to democracy in Cold War Western Europe. Such shortcomings were most distinctive in Western Germany, argues Anderson (2012: 54),

> emerging from Nazism and confronting East Germany on the front line of the Cold War. There American influence was always strongest, and the battle cries of the Free World in its struggle against Totalitarianism rang loudest.

5.2.1 German Anti-communism and Western Integration

Also within the EADI-network, there was awareness of 'the political awakening of West Germany' (Duchêne 1982: 25). West Germany was 'the undisputed economic superpower of Western Europe', as Christian Deubner (1982: 43) put it, 'whose interests and policies exercise a dominating influence on the character of intra-EEC economic and political relations'. It supported a liberal political and economic doctrine to be enshrined into the treaties and regulations of Western European integration (cf. Chapters 5.1 and 5.2.2).

> On the political plane, West German forces are especially sensitive to any movements which endanger the principles of bourgeois parliamentary democracy and capitalism. This is accompanied by a rigid anti-communism, resulting partly from Soviet communism's role in the eastern part of a divided Germany, and partly from the West German ruling Social Democratic Party's (SDP's) very specific need to isolate its left wing from communist leanings. (Deubner 1982: 44)

Ingrained during fascism and cold war, as Duchêne (1982: 25) observed, the anti-communist sentiments in West German society were influencing the southern enlargement of the EC in the 1980s. Parties on the left that were critical of EC membership were marginalized.

> All parties in West Germany, and the government itself, have demonstrated an almost hysterical opposition to leftist alliances, including communists or other left-socialist forces, coming to power in the applicant countries. This attitude is the other side of the coin of close and cordial relations with the governments and Socialist Parties of the applicants. This close relationship

> is used to impress West German anti-communism and anti-leftism on the Socialist Parties and the governments in all too persuasive terms. It may for example be partly responsible for the immovable resistance of the Portuguese Socialists to an alliance with the local Communist Party. (Deubner 1982: 47)

West German support of transforming the Fascist Portuguese regime was one of soft intervention (above all, by organizations of the German Social Democratic Party, cf. Deubner 1982: 46ff.). After the 'Revolution of the Carnations' in 1974, however, the Portuguese socialists inherited a difficult economic situation and faced increasing resistance. The export-led growth strategy had 'led to a fourfold increase in foreign-trade deficits between 1964 and 1973' (Woodward 1983: 185), these 'deficits were compounded between 1974 and 1976 [...] by political retaliation against the revolution' (ibid.) of the bourgeoisie (in Portugal and abroad). In 1978, Portugal had to agree to an IMF sponsored austerity program, consequently in

> December 1979, the Socialist party was defeated in national elections, and less than six years after the revolution, government economic policy was growing progressively more conservative. (Woodward 1983: 186)

In Greece, Konstantinos Karamanlis, who had vehemently pursued Greek EEC accession before the dictatorship of the colonels (1967–1974), won the general elections of 1974 with the newly founded conservative Nea Dimokratia and pursued NATO- (1980) and EC membership (1981). In the year Greece entered the EC, ironically, Andreas Papandreou—leading the Panhellenic Socialist Movement (PASOK)—won absolute majority in the Greek Parliament. PASOK may have been the party in Europe, 'which has formulated a programme nearest to the concept of self-reliance', argued Heinz-Jürgen Axt (1985: 93). Papandreou had campaigned against EC membership and for disentangling the dependency on the United States. EC membership was seen as leading to further integration into the world economy in a subordinate position. Harsh realities of global economic crisis, and international and domestic resistance seems to have impaired PASOK's policies of self-reliance (Pollis 1985: 207ff.; cf. also Pollis 1983: 215ff.). Anti-communism and anti-leftism, summarized Deubner (1982: 47),

> blinds the German government and parties to the very important points made by [EC-critical left wing] parties, especially the Portuguese Communists and the Greek PASOK (which have both opposed their countries' applications for Community membership), against excessive optimism about the benefits of eventual membership, and of the exclusive orientation of their countries' economies towards the highly industrialised states of Western Europe which it probably implies.

5.2.2 *Pax Germanica Builds on Continuing Liberal Economic Paradigm*

The United States was able to establish a lasting stake in European integration by military and security means, because European integration had an overlap with NATO from the very beginning. Five of the inner six EU integration countries that formed the ECSC in 1951 (the cradle of today's EU), had also been founding members of NATO in 1949. The sixth member, (Western) Germany, that had been the European aggressor of World War II, joined NATO already in 1955, three years before the inner six founded the European Economic Community (EEC). Only six of 28 EU members (still including UK) today are not NATO members (Austria, Cyprus, Finland, Ireland, Malta, Sweden), all the others joined NATO before becoming EU members. The 'systematic affinity of West German foreign and economic policies to those of the United States' (Deubner 1982: 44f.), however, did not prevent West Germany to occupy political spaces where the United States did withdraw. 'West Germany is becoming a major force in the Mediterranean in her own name or through the Community', argues Duchêne (1982: 25f.):

> Hers is essentially a security policy to reinforce or replace waning American power in the area. In recent years she has given the impression of being the only West European state to have a systematic political strategy in Southern Europe and the means and determination to carry it through.

Pax Germanica started replacing, however, Pax Americana as hegemonic power in European integration. This includes the new role of the D-Mark as European anchor currency after the United States was not able to defend the Bretton Woods System any longer. The ordoliberal legacy of West Germany was seen as an advantage during the caesura to the global neoliberal paradigm: West Germany did not need to struggle to escape the neoliberal take-over, like the Mitterrand government in France (Duchêne 1982: 25).

The authors of the European dependency school recognized the confrontational make-up and the ideological bias of a European integration process rooted in the cold war period. Regulation and the laissez-faire principle coexisted in the founding years of European integration. The founders of the EC, as Dudley Seers (1982: 4) put it, intended an 'institutional laissez-faire system', which 'would make it difficult for any really left-wing government of the future to exercise controls and carry out far-reaching social changes'. Similar things were observed for the economic framework. Laissez-faire was seen as the 'appropriate doctrine' (Seers 1982: 1) for technological leaders. This 'would ensure that its industrial structures were made more efficient by exposure to competition, and contribute to the reestablishment of international free trade, which was an essential element in this neo-colonial scenario' (Seers 1982: 4). '[T]he core of the liberal capitalist ideology', wrote Holland (1980: 4),

> hungover from Smith and the eighteenth century still stood, incarnate, at the Treaties of the European Communities. And that theory served a major political end in cementing and legitimizing the capitalism which the United States had underpinned through Marshall Aid and the NATO since the postwar settlement. (ibid.: 4)

And this European integration was constructed irreversibly, which is why, argues Holland (1980: 6),

> so many internationalists are opposed to Community supranationalism. They question whether one model of the economy and society, such as that enshrined in the Community Treaties, is relevant to the changing structures of the economy and society over time.

The policy of competition was written as a fundamental ideology into the Treaty of Rome in 1958. It could always be used as an argument against regional and industrial policies that would 'distort' competition as soon as such policies would be communitarized. With a few specified exemptions, Article 92 (1) of the 'Treaty establishing the European Economic Community' codifies that

> any aid granted by a member State or through State resources in any form whatsoever which distorts or threatens to distort competition by favouring certain undertakings or the production of certain goods shall, insofar as it affects trade between member States, be deemed incompatible with the Common Market. (English translation by Holland: 1980: 12; original languages Dutch, French, German, Italian, cf. EC EUR-Lex [n.y.1])

Article numbers changed over the years and so did treaty reforms, but the content remained the same (cf. EC EUR-Lex [n.y.1]). The hands of the member governments were tied since exceptions to this regulations were decided upon by the Commission (Holland 1980: 12).

On the other hand, common agricultural policy (CAP) was characterized by high regulatory policies and subsidies, which made the Community increasingly autarchic (Seers 1982: 4). The distributive system of EC social and regional funds was judged insufficient; the rich club of the six original member states of the European Community (EC6) unwilling and unable to eliminate regional disparities. The idea that a 'trickle-down' principle would be able to solve regional problems was related to a possible disintegration, because within the EC '[t]he concentration of economic power now seems in some ways comparable to that in the Hapsburg Empire, where it was one of the causes of the latter's downfall' (Seers 1982: 10):

> Unemployment is especially high in peripheral areas. The Community's founders, being deeply conservative, did not see the need for a strong fiscal system, which might have been easier to wrest from member governments in the early, dynamic years. The tacit assumption was that the profits of growth would 'trickle down' sufficiently to solve regional problems, a proposition for the most part discredited in other continents, and obviously now in Western Europe too. (ibid.)

5.3 Integration of Unequal Partners

Authors writing in the EADI network (before and during the second enlargement) assessed the future of peripheral countries within Western European integration pretty soberly. The results of EC policies in overcoming the disparities within EC6 and then EC9 were considered meager, they were rather seen as increasing regional inequalities and perpetuating structural imbalances (Eßer et al. 1980: 61f.; Secchi 1982; Seers 1982: 10, cf. also Chapter 4). Interestingly, the analysis of statistical data by Marja-Liisa Kiljunen (1980: 212) suggested that the main reason for the absence of convergence was the increased divergence among national economies. The primary responsibility for development policies had been left with member states, the disparities within states did not change dramatically. That supports the thesis of a 'Keynesian integration model' up to the 1970s. The liberal make of the EC/EU, however, had been implemented in the Treaty of Rome (establishing the European Economic Community on January 1, 1958) already, carrying provisions that could be used when the Keynesian model lost momentum. Kiljunen (1980: 212f.) puts down what would later become a problematic aspect of the 'competitive region'-paradigm of the European Union that pushed back state intervention in regional development:

> [T]he underlying economic philosophy of free play of market forces, expressed in the Treaty (Article 3(f): 'competition shall not be distorted in the Common Market') is not easily compatible with policies which would involve public intervention in aid of weaker regions, both at national and Community levels. The member states were not and are not free to give whatever kind of financial assistance they might wish to regional development; the cases in which aid is compatible with the Common Market, including regional aid, are mentioned in Article 9.2. So that the aid does not 'distort competition', it is monitored by the Competition Policy rules which restrict the amounts of investment subsidies given to various regions. The Commission may, if necessary, call for withdrawal of state aid granted to particular firms to prevent any 'distortion of competition'.

In 1980, however, with the changes from Keynesian toward neoliberal paradigm still only proceeding, Kiljunen (1980: 213) could argue:

> As the free play of market forces has not reduced the gaps between Community regions, more exceptions to the principal rules have been made to tackle the problem of regional imbalance.

The EC took up initiatives for regional development only with the first enlargement in 1973 which coincided with the global economic crisis of the 1970s. The 'first enlargement in 1973 incorporated Ireland, which was hardly on par with the other member states of the EC, and the United Kingdom, which by then was beginning to be seen as a post-industrial society in the throes of decline' (Pollis 1983: 203). A regional development fund was created in 1975 (Kiljunen 1980: 213f.).

Britain seems to have pushed for such a fund due to adaptive difficulties of the industries in some of its regions: Staying in the Community, which it had joined only two years earlier, appeared too costly otherwise (Zingel 1976: 59). Similar to Yugoslavia, which had installed its regional development fund a decade earlier, measures to tackle regional disparities were implemented once the period of high economic growth was over (Weissenbacher 2005: 85ff.). If one takes the budgetary implications of 'cohesion' and 'integration', the EC Commission was aware of the redistributive task. It commissioned a study (MacDougall Report 1977), that calculated the funds necessary to reduce inequality. The MacDougall Report considered the 'redistributive power' of interregional transfers 100% 'if the effect of such transfers was completely to equalise regional or state per capita average incomes' (ibid.: 60). The average 'redistributive power' the core countries (studied for the report) used for their respective own domestic regions in 1975 amounted to 40%. If the European Community had applied similar measures in 1975 toward a 'redistributive power' of 40% in the EC, it would have spent 2% of the overall community GDP. This 'redistributive power'

> would have financed a large part or all of the current balance of payments deficits of the beneficiary states in the year in question. Thus very significant macroeconomic effects would have been achieved by expenditure amounting to about three times the actual size of the Community budget. (ibid.: 61)

The real 'redistributive power', the EC applied in 1975, however, had only 1%, 'i.e. one-fortieth of the average found in maturely integrated economies' (ibid.: 61). Of course, this was still the EC9 before the southern enlargement, when polarization of the integration model further increased: 'The receiving states would have been Italy, the United Kingdom and Ireland, the paying states being the remaining six member states' (ibid.: 60). Lastly, the overall budget of the EU commission never reached 2% (only 1%)! The MacDougall Report of 1977 (ibid.: 60ff.) called the situation of the EC pre-federal but strongly advised that even if the EC was not to be expected to spend redistributive measures comparable to a nation state of the core, it still needed to act because the southern enlargement would aggravate the situation. Deep integration and redistributive mechanisms both belonged to a successful integration model:

> Inter-regional redistribution produces a reasonably equitable sharing of both the cyclical and secular fortunes of an economic union, and thereby helps to maintain its political unity; it helps as far as possible attainment of comparable economic performance between regions; it compensates for the inability of regions or states to use trade or exchange rate policies in the management of their economies, and it limits the extent to which migration has to serve as part of the economic adjustment process. In all mature federal states, on the other hand, the counterpart of these powerful equalisation mechanisms is a mature political structure with a federal government and parliament and other federal agencies. (ibid.: 61)

Among the EDS authors, it was clear that the peripheral countries that entered the Western European integration with the second enlargement faced economic crisis and an increasingly liberal EC that was not much prepared to tackle yet more regional disparities. The EC structure changed from an institution with one and a half peripheral countries (Ireland and the Mezzogiorno) to one with four and a half (adding Greece, Portugal, Spain), increasing the population in peripheral countries from 10 to then 25% of the Community's population. '[A]ny serious policy commitment on equalisation of incomes [did require] transfers from north to south' (Duchêne 1982: 28). The European Commission, however, had been unable to tackle the existing uneven development of member states, let alone the task of such an 'enlargement of unequal partners'. It was aware that there was an integration problem but its policy consequences reflected the liberal construction of the EC and its institutions. The European Commission recommended, as Pollis (1983: 206) pointed out,

> aid be given to the three from the EC's social fund and from the European Regional Development Fund (ERDF), a recommendation that ignores the intense competition that already exists for these limited monies among the developing regions within the EC.

The European Commission was aware of the 'sharp differences in level of economic development between the three European Mediterranean countries and the core members' (ibid.: 1983: 205), but an ideological bias seems to have prevented it from deeper, more structural reforms. The commission was, as she called it (ibid.: 206), a 'technocratic decision-making organ [...] rooted in liberal economic thought, which provided in earlier centuries the philosophic rationale for emergent capitalism' (ibid.: 206). While there was widespread skepticism as far as growth and welfare for the new members were concerned, not only among EDS authors (Deubner 1982: 47), core country Germany would not be harmed by the enlargement. Other than in the cases of France and Italy, the accession of the Southern EC3 would bring no competition to its agrarian production. Its advanced industrial production, on the contrary, was rather likely to be a competitive problem for the EC3. Yet another story were the changes in the EC division of labor deemed necessary for sustainable integration of the EC3, and their cohesion with core countries:

> Much more important are the apprehensions of indirect affects harming West German economic interests as a result of changes in the EEC's internal and external trade and industrial policies which might become unavoidable. (Deubner 1982: 50)

Due to the genesis of its integration, the Western European integration model had been neglecting its uneven development and was institutionally unprepared for dealing with accessing peripheral countries. What made matters worse was the fact that the second enlargement was proceeding before the background of a political and economic crisis. At that point immediate consequences of the accession of EC3 were seen difficult to be isolated from overall economic processes.

The Western European integration process had started, as Stefan Musto (1982: 68) from the EADI network pointed out, as a rich club of industrialized countries in a time of economic growth and did

> not include the instruments required to protect a Community of countries at different levels of development against serious backwash effects or even a tendency towards disintegration at a time of relative economic stagnation. It is becoming more and more evident that existing and growing imbalances resulting from the dynamic impact of regional concentration and the structural economic disparities imply permanent structural crises.

Only in Spain, there were signs of deepening vertical integration in the manufacturing sector which set up favorable conditions for a modernization of the productive structure. Greece and Portugal were not able to establish a process of sustained industrialization. Moreover, they were caught in the trap of low wage production where already then countries of the global periphery were forcing their ways into the market. It was already clear that such tendencies would undermine the productive structure of peripheral Europe if the European division of labor remained unchanged. The structure of the production (small and medium sized companies) suggested a further deterioration if all protective measurements inside the Communities would be lifted after accession. The global recession brought a slowdown in economic growth and had resulted in a more hierarchical production structure in the EC9 with increasing regional disparities (cf. Chapter 4). Similar dynamics were being expected for the 1980s:

> Enlargement will not in itself cause this problems, but it will aggravate and accentuate them. In the present circumstances, it would seem difficult to lessen their effect, since the Community, being geared in every way to the needs of highly developed industrial countries, does not have sufficient structural policy instruments. [...] The strategic question is not how the negative consequences of enlargement should be offset with the present division of labour – using some kind of crisis management as it were – but what new forms of the division of labour are needed to eliminate the disintegrating effects of the structural imbalances in the Community. (Musto 1982: 70)

Although EC membership was an important step in the history of these countries, among EDS authors it was also seen within the general trend of integrative gravity the countries were drawn into, during the decades before:

> Economic growth had accelerated to fast rates long before the Community was founded. It was facilitated afterwards not merely by the continued expansion of the world economy but also by a heavy inflow of labourers from the Mediterranean area who took on unattractive jobs and helped restrain wage increases; they would have come to Western Europe anyway. (Seers 1982: 4)

Greece signed an association agreement with the EC in 1961 (as did Turkey in 1964), Portugal was a founding member of EFTA in 1960 (EFTA countries Great Britain and Denmark switched into the stronger model of integration EC in 1973), and 'Spain's overtures to the international economy after 1959 indicate a similar direction to accession' (Vaitsos 1982b: 244; cf. Holman 2002: 408). Alternatives to Western

European integration were not readily available. Greece's Western affiliation was decided upon immediately after World War II (Pollis 1985: 200).

Portugal and Spain, as Fascist dictatorships, were certainly not likely candidates for Comecon membership. Portugal, to be sure, did not pursue an option of a stronger orientation toward its former colonies (the last of which became independent only with the end of the Fascist regime), as economic area outside Europe. A non-allied affiliation would have brought the aura of third world-organization, furthermore the heterogeneous non-allied movement was too weak to offer a serious stance against core capitalist dynamics. Even Socialist Yugoslavia, one of the main protagonists and Greece's neighbor, could not escape the integration gravity of the Western European integration model (cf. Weissenbacher 2005). In the era of Cold War, the second enlargement was still a geopolitical project. The EC did shield peripheral countries from some turbulence of global structural imbalances but obviously not from the effects of the new international division of labor that shifted low wage production toward Asia.

The EC internalized the polarizing structure of international capitalist production, with consequences for the future of the integration process, as Constantine Vaitsos (1982b: 234ff.) from the EADI network pointed out.

> When addressing development issues, the theory of regional integration stresses the 'polarisation' or 'backwash' effects of market integration. The more unequal the initial development levels of prospective partners, the stronger tend to be the propensities to concentrate key activities and decisions in relatively more advanced areas. (Vaitsos 1980: 33)

Unsurprisingly, the structural imbalances increased to the extent to which peripheral countries/regions entered the EC. Consequently, a common (balancing) EC industrial policy ranked top on the agenda of dependency authors dealing with integration (as we will see in the following chapter). But a common industrial policy has remained a desideratum, indicating that 'community' ends where competition begins (cf. Deubner 1982: 52f.; Vaitsos 1980: 33).

Postwar boom and labor shortages in the core had fed some expectations in the possible arrival of modernization theorist promises. 'The apparent prosperity', writes Pollis (1983: 212), in Greece, Spain, and Portugal, the illusion of affluence, the availability and consumption of goods, and the increase in per capita income were all consequences of this overall worldwide prosperity emanating from the core.

But the underlying structural imbalances between core and periphery in Europe had remained unchanged and began to show more clearly with the crises of the 1970s and 1980s. 'At least prior to the socialist government in Greece', writes Pollis (1983: 210), it

is evident that both the EC and governments of the three Mediterranean countries [...] share the underlying economic and political premises regarding the desirability of enlargement as being beneficial to all in the long run.

5.4 The Absence of Common Industrial Policies

The German Development Institute (GDI) had pursued a variety of studies on the second enlargement of the European Community in general, and acceding countries in particular. The nature of industrial policies before the second enlargement, again, fits the analysis of single national policies in a 'Keynesian' development model. While GDI acknowledged successes in developing productive structures in France and the Netherlands, the Community performance as a whole was seen critical. The member states (EC 6) had not been willing to integrate their industries into a coherent production apparatus. As long as the postwar situation offered sufficient room to maneuver for economic expansion, this situation was seen unproblematic. With the crisis of the 1970s, however, disadvantages opposite to the United States and Japan became visible (Hillebrand 1978: 26ff.).

What has been said about EC regional policies is also true for industrial policies in the European Community:

The treaties of Rome make no reference to any common industrial policy. On the contrary, intervention in the industrial sector is qualified in negative terms as a policy intended to secure the removal of all types of constraints, barriers, and interventionist measures that could distort the conditions designed to ensure free competition within the Community. With the exception of the goods referred to in the European Coal and Steel Committee (ECSC) treaty, which are subject to regulation by Community

> authorities, and also the partial exception of new technologies and energy for which the Commission assumes a certain number of responsibilities in terms of coordination and funding, **the treaties prohibit in principle all types of measures or subsidies that could result in any distortion of competition, the fundamental ideology pursued by the Community's founding fathers** [highlighted by RW]. (Musto 1985: 87f.)

Again, this underlines the liberal-conservative nature of the Western European integration process that engraved competition into its founding treaties. As with the Community's regional policy, common industrial policy initiatives started with the first enlargement 1973 when distortions in the postwar accumulation regime were already being felt (Musto 1985: 85ff.). The First Summit Conference of the Enlarged Community in Paris 1972 declared that it intended to establish a common foundation for the Community's industry:

> Economic expansion which is not an end in itself must as a priority help to attenuate the disparities in living conditions. It must develop with the participation of both sides of industry. It must emerge in an improved quality as well as an improved standard of life. In the European spirit special attention will be paid to non-material values and wealth and to protection of the environment so that progress shall serve mankind. (European Council 1972: 15f.)

But member states seem to have been hesitant to follow the declaration of Paris (Hillebrand 1978: 34). The Mediterranean peripheral countries were not part of these discussions. It was clear for members of the European dependency school that the strong divergence in the industrial structures of the EC9 and the second enlargement EC3 were difficult to overcome, and that Community membership would reduce the ability of national policies at the periphery (confronted with competition from the core). In order to prevent social polarization, Community policies should 'extend social control over investment and distribution sufficiently to contain emerging contradiction' argued Bienefeld (1982: 109) from the EADI network. Two scenarios were being put forward by researchers from GDI (Musto 1982: 80ff.; Eßer et al. 1980: 62ff.). Either the Community would remain a club of core countries with decreasing room to maneuver and a kind of permanent crisis management, because regional polarization would increase with future accessions (cf. Eßer 1978b), or it pursued an internal development strategy that demanded an exceptional effort with a massive (not gradual) investment push in the periphery leading to a more decentralized production structure. If such a productive structure was not being established, more redistributive policies (than existing capacities) were seen necessary (due to growing disparities). At GDI, efforts to establish a balancing European industrial policy with 'the creation of comparable modern and effective industrial production structures in the various member states' (Musto 1981: 261f.; 1982: 76) were considered necessary, in order to maintain and improve the level of Community integration. Furthermore the implementation of such policies were considered more cost-efficient than increasing redistributive efforts (Eßer 1977: 65).

The industrial structure of the acceding countries of the second enlargement (EC3) was not large and not modern enough to face peripheral integration or economic crisis. Development, growth, and exports prospects of traditional labor intensive industries (like textiles, clothing, leather, and food processing) in terms of productivity, research, technology, and capital intensity were considered low. Yet such industries of Greece, Portugal, and Spain still represented important sectors and dominated some of their regions. As a share of overall industry they had 55% in Greece, 43% in Portugal, and 25% in Spain, in 1974. Such productive structures were seen as problematic in a global competitive context. Low wage production was more and more taken over by the global periphery in the new international division of labor. By the same token, these traditional sectors were not easily to be replaced for social reasons: Alternative industries were hard to implement in order to substitute employment and income. Furthermore these traditional industries belonged to a category of industries considered sensitive by the European Community (Musto 1982: 77f.). The GDI examined four sectors of sensitive Community industries: steel, shipbuilding, textiles and clothing, and synthetic fibers. The 1970s showed the contradiction between already established core country industries running into crisis and peripheral industries only being in the process of establishing such industrial sectors. While the Community used dirigiste and protective measures to deal with crisis prone over-production, the (future) acceding countries could still need expansive efforts, above all for the linkage-effects between steel and other industries. With the benefit of hindsight, the advice given by GDI sounds like wishful thinking:

> [I]t would [...] be appropriate for the Community to permit the acceding countries to continue industrialisation in these sectors to meet their own requirements and to provide active support for this process in so far as it makes for structural improvement of production. The expansion and modernisation of these sectors in Southern Europe can have very positive consequences for the competitiveness of the industries they supply. So semi-industrialised prospective new members should not refrain from expanding industry simply because the corresponding industry in neighbouring industrialised countries has been 'sensitive' for some time. (Musto 1982: 79f.)

GDI researchers (Eßer et al. 1980: 10) suggested a differentiated strategy:

> The industrial development of a partly industrialized country can be facilitated best by simultaneously opening the domestic market for development, import substitution, increasing and diversifying exports.

The EC should allow acceding countries to develop their young industries up to the level of self-sufficiency and waive own protectionist measures against their competitive export industries (Eußner 1983: 12). The advice to the European periphery by mainstream economics, namely following the comparative advantage principle—and thereby stimulating low-wage production for the European periphery—was seen particularly futile in the case of the European integration: Eßer (1977: 52ff.; Eßer et al. 1980: 63ff.) pointed at contradictions in policies suggested to European peripheral countries and the economic reality between core and peripheral countries within a future community on the one hand side, and between the community and the world market, on the other. The European periphery should not try and compete in the framework of the global division of labor, because an integrated Europe might then have to become (more) protectionist in favor of its periphery's low-tech production. Moreover, extreme levels of low wages in Europe, necessary for global competition, had only been achievable under dictatorship and not in a European integration model that boasted democratic values. Conflicting interests between core and periphery inside a future community were clearly envisaged because, as a matter of principle, industrialized countries supported free trade in order to gain new markets but were protective as far as their own critical sectors were concerned.

Protective measures that were judged ‘structurally conservative’ in such core country sectors were classified ‘relevant development policies’ in peripheral countries (cf. the sensitive sectors above).

Clearly the need of a common industrial policy was seen at GDI, a policy that envisaged planning of European productive structures in a way that developed the industrial structure of peripheral economies, and reduced development disparities in the EC (Table 5.1). Musto (1982: 85ff.) referred to a sideline of mainstream economic theory building that considered comparative advantage, free trade and competition not as a matter of principle beneficial in economic integration: ‘agreed specialization’ by Kiyoshi Kojima (1970).

Table 5.1 Dual strategy to reduce development disparities in the EC

	Goal category I: reduction of intra-community development disparities	*Goal category II: reduction of regional disparities in member states*
Community measures	Agreed specialization in modern growth industries	Replenishment of the regionally effective Community funds
	More intensive transfer of technology	More intensive promotion of peripheral regions
	Greater incorporation of the periphery in the establishment of integration industries	Promotion of small and medium industry in disadvantaged regions
	Tolerance vis-a-vis the vulnerable infant industries of the applicant countries	Development of Community criteria and new regional promotion instruments
	Change of industrial structure, modernization of potentially competitive branches of production	Employment-oriented industrialization in the disadvantaged regions
National measures taken by individual member states on the periphery	Intra-sectoral specialization for substitute (and not complementary) exchange of goods	Securing a minimum level of living in all regions
	Building up of infant industries for export	Improvement of the quality of live, establishment of social services
	Measures to protect the domestic market against third country imports	Agglomeration tax on non-priority industries in conurbations

Source Musto (1982: 86)

Kojima (1970: 316ff.) considered 'agreed specialization' of industries most promising between countries with similar productive and consumption structures (and more difficult to be agreed upon in cases where they are not) but Musto (1982: 86f.) saw it as a 'pre-condition—in spatial areas of economic integration—for the progressive removal of structural imbalances'. Economic integration without 'agreed specialization' would lead to agglomeration in particular areas (Kojima 1970: 310).

'Agreeing' on allocation of industry was possibly the only immanent hope—in a European community with a liberal institutional structure—to foster industrial development in the periphery. As we will see in this Chapter 5.5, planning was all but absent in capitalist Europe, it just happened inside transnational companies beyond democratic control. At GDI there were massive doubts that a policy of balancing industrial development would materialize (cf. Eßer 1977, 1978a). The obstacles to the goal of reaching a balanced European industrial structure, as pointed out by Musto (1982: 76), seem to have haunted European integration policy ever since. Other than the agricultural sector that was highly regulated, the Community followed very liberal industrial policies. The acceding countries were to close the gap to the core countries by themselves and depended on the industrial strategies they adopted. But they were to be in line with the principle of competition. Comparative advantage aiming at low-wage production was seen ineffectual as to compete in a European Community that aimed at no internal and very low external trade barriers, and a common EC competitive regime that would impair the room to maneuver for autonomous national (infant) industrial policies (Hillebrand 1978: 39). Conflicting interests as to how far the Community was willing to support efforts to modernize the production apparatus were clearly predicted:

> In this respect the short-term export interests of the present highly industrialised members will conflict with the long-term integration interests of the Community as a whole: the conquest of the applicant countries' markets by the core countries of the Community would jeopardise the further industrial development of these countries and therefore perpetuate the structural imbalance of an area seeking integration. (Musto 1982: 76)

Adamantia Pollis (1985: 209f.), writing in Musto's network, argues that the EC commission's proposal for an integrated Mediterranean program had already envisaged for Greece

> the strengthening of those very sectors that would preclude the future autonomous industrialization of Greece. Emphasis is placed on the expansion of the fishing industry [...]; expansion of agriculture by increasing productivity [...]; and last, the expansion of the tourist industry [...]. Little considerations was given to crop diversification, which would increase Greece's food self-sufficiency, as an alternative to continued specialization in a limited number of export crops that are in competition with similar products from other Mediterranean regions. The question of the development of Greece's industrial sector was largely ignored, undoubtedly premised on the doctrine of comparative advantage, since it is widely accepted that Community membership is destructive to Greece's non-competitive industries, albeit potentially beneficial to Europe's multinationals. In fact, the national bourgeoisie was opposed to membership for this very reason.

Without a coherent 'development and integration concept' (Eßer 1977: 65), peripheral countries within the European Union would face similar situations as countries in the global periphery. A laissez-fare industrial policy would be the 'appropriate doctrine' for the 'technological leaders' of the core, as pointed out by Seers (above), international free trade would wipe out the less efficient production structures in the periphery by competition, which was part of a 'neocolonial scenario'. It was obvious for GDI researchers that access to core markets had not brought and would not bear good chances for countries at the European periphery—such as Greece and Portugal—to increase industrial exports in order to earn enough foreign exchange to build up own industrial bases (Eßer 1977: 63). But also the question of Community funds for re-distribution of wealth gained by core countries was seen pessimistically. The status quo and the perspectives regarding development instruments, aid, and funds were perceived insufficient and ineffective (Musto 1982: 83ff.; Eßer 1977: 64f.). All in all GDI analyses led to intriguing conclusions, namely that

> enlargement will not pose any fundamentally new problems for the structure of the Community or its ability to function. But it will aggravate existing agricultural, industrial and regional problems [...]. Secondly, in a heterogeneous area seeking integration but involving unequal partners there will be a growing tendency for structural disparities to become consolidated or to worsen, resulting in increasing internal imbalance and external inflexibility. Thirdly, a new balance [...] can only be achieved

> through the improvement of structures in the weaker partner countries and thus the gradual elimination of the intra-Community development gap. Fourthly, such structural improvement cannot be effected either with the aid of rigid harmonisation arrangements [...] or through political abstinence on the part of the Community and a reference to free world trade. What is needed is greater scope for national policies to solve domestic structural problems [...]. Finally, this leads to a plea for the partial regionalisation and renationalisation of problem-solving mechanisms [...]. (Musto 1982: 87)

5.5 Corporate Integration and the European Division of Labor

We have seen that peripheral countries were not able to copy and reproduce core countries' capitalist development due to ever changing processes of global capitalism as a whole. Transnational companies (TNC) gained importance as players in global capitalism (cf. Chapters 2 and 4.2). World market developments had furthered the integration of many aspects of modern economics into the sovereignty of TNC, like input to production, internal market, decision-making, consumption, and cultural harmonization. Taxation belongs to the problems that arise from this kind of integration and internalization: Where is an input into production produced, and where is it accounted for? Where are profits being taxed? Where is the value being added (in a high or low-wage area)? Concentration and decision-making processes of corporate central planning can impair the ability of policy-making to counter polarization and backwash effects. Protection of company knowledge can also vanish hopes on spread effects of investments (Vaitsos 1980: 28ff.). Referring to the legal framework of the Treaty of Rome regarding competition and harmonization regulations (corporations, patents), Vaitsos (1982a: 137) argues that the EEC's industrial sector

> largely serves as a mechanism to provide freedom, facilitate and institutionalise the process of corporate internalisation. [...] [T]he functioning of the EEC is noted for the overwhelming absence of common commitments on locational and other key industrial policy matters. This is obviously a completely different situation from the spirit and practices of the CAP [Common Agricultural Policy, RW].

The distribution of power as regards such companies (and their countries of origin) was to the disadvantage of peripheral countries. In the European arena, the dominant core country Western Germany, again, seems to have been able to deal well with postwar difficulties:

> In spite of the massive inflows of foreign direct investment into West Germany in the last twenty years, the structural deformations experienced in other developed Western European countries have not occurred. With the notable, and significant, exceptions of oil and crucial production chains in electronics, West German industrial complexes have been competitive enough to keep up their market shares in oligopolist competition. In many cases, foreign corporations located in West Germany have become the R&D centres for the [TNC] network covering sister companies in Western Europe. This underlines the dominance of the Federal Republic in this respect, too. (Schlupp 1980: 189)

With structures of peripheral capitalism, the story was entirely different. Peripheral integration into TNC networks (United States and European) happened before actual European integration processes. Vaitsos (1982a: 143) indicates

> that Greece, Portugal, and Spain, before entering the EEC, registered levels of foreign penetration comparable with, and in many cases higher than, those of the existing EEC members. The transnationals have not been waiting for the entry of Southern Europe into the EEC to expand their operations in these three countries. Under existing international economic relations, the forces of corporate integration have already established significant inroads in the European economies whether or not formal regional integration took place.

Other members of the EADI network, and the Birmingham and Durham networks, respectively, came to similar conclusions: Transnational capital had influenced significantly the European peripheries' regional form of development. It penetrated Portugal from the late 1950s where it reinforced national monopoly structures without modernization of industries (Holland 1979: 142f.). Greece conceded TNC favorable conditions in taxation, for interest rates on bank credits, and on profit repatriation in 1953 (Pollis 1985: 204). In Spain 'industrial upgrading' of the national industry had 'created an industrial structure dependent on TNCs' (Muñoz et al. 1979: 166). The Spanish case seems to echo the analysis of Cardoso and Faletto: There was talk of a 'new dependence' as a price for the 'new vitality' foreign capital had 'injected' to Spanish capitalism (Muñoz et al. 1979: 166). Also the Spanish bourgeoisie was unable to fulfill the modernization theorists' visions:

> Given its obvious weakness, this system could only be upheld by increasingly strong doses of 'public order' and political authoritarianism. The State felt the need to compensate for the obvious weaknesses of the bourgeoisie and the limited success of industrialization. (Muñoz et al. 1979: 167)

Greek industrialization was especially

> characterized by an important inflow of foreign capital and technology since there was none to speak of in the country. Furthermore, planning which was formally introduced in the early 1960s has never played any important role, free market forces being the motor of the development process. (Nikolinakos 1985: 203)

Following Osvaldo Sunkel, Mary Evangelinides (1979: 185) argues for Greece a structural heterogeneity that according to Sunkel (1973: 300ff.) leads to a national disintegration by means of integration into transnational capitalism:

> [K]ey manufacturing sectors were left to foreign capital which, taking advantage of the enormous privileges granted by the Greek State, began to invade the Greek economy and invest in the key dynamic industries as well as penetrate other vital sectors like banking, insurance, construction, engineering and trade. (Evangelinides 1979: 185)

Drawing on the polarization theorist Gunnar Myrdal, Nikolinakos (1985: 197) argues that 'left to market forces, capital accumulation will almost inevitably lead to regional inequalities'. He concludes that

> Greek industry has in fact developed according to the laws governing its integration into the international division of labour, in particular undertaking the role Western European capital has ascribed to it. (Nikolinakos 1985: 205)

'For the countries of origin of European-based transnationals', argues Vaitsos (1982a: 146),

> their economic interest in Southern Europe lie significantly in the strengthening of a European industrial division of labour, which, as one of its central elements, includes the following characteristics: the European core through the operations of the TNEs strengthens and enhances its position as a supplier of a) capital goods, b) intermediate products intensive in highly skilled labor, c) technology, as well as marketing knowhow, and d) top level corporate management which is located in the European core but whose strategic decisions will affect the rest of the European structure.

In the periphery, foreign investments, above all in Greece and Spain, and to a lesser extend in Portugal, aimed at import-substitution. About 2/3 of Greece, Portugal, and Spain's imports came from EC9, a quarter to a half (depending on the sector) from Western Germany. Markedly Spanish policies of import-substitution had led to higher foreign corporate integration (Vaitsos 1982a: 147ff.). Export activities of Greece, Portugal, and Spain concentrated on EC9 (about half of the manufactured exports) but showed different features. Vaitsos (1980: 149f.) distinguishes between four categories:

> i) activities employing low-skilled, low-paid labour in repetitive operations which have a low level of energy consumption per man-hour of work, low capital intensity and a heavy reliance on imported parts – to be assembled locally – for export abroad;
> ii) local processing of resource-based products involving high capital intensity and energy consumption per man-hour of work, continuous industrial processes, semi-qualified or qualified personnel remunerated at levels generally much higher than the average local industrial wage averages;
> iii) assembly activities or standardised engineering operations employing semi-qualified and qualified personnel with relatively high productivity and wage levels [...], low capital intensity and reliable sources of [...] labour; and
> iv) activities related to specific final goods which involve 'traditional' products (basically in the textile, apparel and leather industries as well as parts of the food and beverages sector), and where some of the export requirements involve a semi-qualified, reliable labour force [...] while others need low wages as the main competitive tool [...].

Greece and Portugal are heavily involved in the fourth category, Spain had, due to its protectionist policy in the past, a more differentiated industrial structure. Only for the fourth category, argues Vaitsos

(1982a: 150), it does matter whether a country enters the Western European integration model or not. Particularly in times of crisis the EC could pose non-tariff barriers collectively to protect the sector.

> The other three activities are likely to be very little influenced by whether a country is or is not a member of the EEC [...]. Low wages for tasks requiring low skills, resource availabilities, a comparatively priced and reliable semi-skilled labour force as well as transport considerations are much more powerful factors in the international sourcing of TNEs in these areas than country membership in the EEC.

All in all, economic crisis and the dynamics of the new international division of labor were seen problematic for future prospects of EC3. TNCs had not waited for the Western European Integration process to start their investment strategies in the EC3.

> What is certain [...] is that the absence of an effective industrial policy in the EEC under a unified market, strengthens the bargaining power of the TNEs. Since they control decisions on the location of production, they will increasingly come to play off one government against another for subsidies and other facilities for new investment undertakings. (Vaitsos 1982a: 159)

5.6 Toward a Monetary Union: The European Monetary System (EMS)

The nature of the European monetary system (EMS) would have an important impact on core–periphery relations in Europe. Currency relations mirror power relations. Until the 1970s the postwar system was regulated and dominated by the United States. The US dollar was the key currency and fixed to the price of gold. The 'Nixon-Shock' of August 15, 1971 unilaterally terminated US dollar convertibility to gold (35 US dollar/1 ounce) and de facto ended the regulated postwar monetary system agreed upon in Bretton Woods 1944. Attempts to balance domestic inequalities (Lyndon B. Johnson's Great Society) and military spending to enforce hegemonic power (in Vietnam and elsewhere) had poured money into the global economic system. Stabilizing the Bretton Woods-System (BWS) meant holding US dollar reserves by US allies, the surplus producing EC6 and Japan, which increasingly became untenable. There was a struggle via interest rate policy, Germany, which wanted to raise interests, against the United States, which wanted to lower them. When the United States continued to refuse devaluing the US dollar, Germany (after some domestic discussion) revalued the German Mark (accompanied by the Dutch Guilder) in 1961 (Marsh 2011: 43f.). 1973 marks the official end of the BWS, European and the Japanese currencies began floating. The instability of the global system in the 1960s seems to have urged the EC6 toward more integration which put a European Monetary Union (EMU) on the agenda. Establishing an EMU was decided upon on the The Hague summit of 1969, a functioning monetary union was supposed to pave the way to a political union (Tsoukalis 1997: 139).

Prominent writers in the EADI network (Triffin 1980; Tsoukalis 1982) agree that the attempts to manage European currencies after the end of the BWS ('currency snake') failed and a European Monetary System (EMS) established in 1979 was a compromise that replaced for the time being the EMU (that was meant to be in place in 1980). With the EMS, a European Currency Unit (ECU) was to replace the function of the US dollar in the BWS. Any two national currencies were meant to fluctuate against each other no more than 2.25%, temporal exceptions allowing 6% (Triffin 1980: 225f.). 'The EMS is, in a sense', summarizes Tsoukalis (1982: 164),

> an attempt to reintroduce a more flexible Bretton Woods system within the Community and, at the same time, insulate intra-EEC exchanges from destabilising dollar speculation. It is no longer believed that the irrevocable fixity of exchange rates, complete liberalisation of capital movements and centralisation of monetary policies can be achieved in the foreseeable future. Periodic internal readjustments are an integral part of the system and a means of compensating for continuing divergence in inflation rates.

While the US dollar had been the key currency of the BWS, the D-Mark was to become the anchor currency of the EMS. Other than the United States, however, Germany has remained a trade surplus country ever since 1952 (Statistisches Bundesamt 2015). 'By the late 1980s, many European countries, either voluntarily, or with varying degrees of unwillingness, had effectively given up monetary autonomy to the Germans' (Marsh 2011: 15). The power play leading to the formation of the EMU was described by a couple of instructive accounts (i.e. Danescu 2013; Marsh 2011; Tsoukalis 1997), I will concentrate on the structural imbalances this formation created for core–periphery relations. It is very clear that the structural imbalances, as already obvious in the rich club EC6, were seen as problematic for the formation of a future EMU:

> The Heads of State and Government give top priority to correcting the structural and regional imbalances in the Community which could hinder the achievement of the Economic and Monetary Union. (European Council 1972: 18)

Basically there seem to have been two major approaches toward reaching a functional EMU, one was called 'monetarist' (not to be confused with adherents of Milton Friedman), the other 'economist' position:

> For the hard-currency countries — whose standard-bearers were Germany and the Netherlands — the priority had to be given to economic policy, the coordination of which should make it possible to strengthen the weaker economies, resulting eventually in less recourse [...] to monetary solidarity. They also supported broader powers for the Community institutions. The countries with weak currencies, on the other hand, with France in the lead, regarded monetary solidarity as fundamental. Monetary integration must entail economic integration, and convergence of the economies was no longer a preliminary to, but a consequence of, monetary union. (Danescu 2013: 32)

Belgium sided with France, and Italy seems to have been divided between the sides. Luxembourg moved more and more to the German side (Marsh 2011: 45). Economic convergence was being important for Germany but, as we have seen in previous chapters, this should not impair its competitive position and not lead to entitlements in Community legislation.

Emphasis on competition and laissez faire privileges the economic core. Industrial and regional policy basically remained national efforts. Consequently 'economists' were being opposed to setting up monetary institutions first (as demanded by monetarists) which they wanted to allow only after converging policies. They feared that balance of payment problems in a EMU without balanced economies would be paid for by European, especially German, reserves. In that sense, Germany and the other 'economists' would have postponed the EMU forever because they opposed any community policy that could have brought convergence in the first place. But if Germany was to agree to common institutions, they should not run against its institutional beliefs—as a future European

Central Bank was to follow the model of the German Bundesbank (Danescu 2013: 96ff.).

Writers in the EADI-network had a good grasp of the structural imbalances that would turn out to flaws in the making of the European integration. Again, the burden of adjustment would have to be shouldered by deficit countries alone. In Bretton Woods, the United States had decided against John M. Keynes' bancor plan which would have foreseen financial consequences for surplus and deficit countries alike. Also the EMS and later the EMU decisions fell against a balance between surplus and deficit countries. In times of liquidity such a system could increase imbalances (as in the 1970s or more recently in the EMU in the 2000s years):

> Even in systems with constrained exchange rates, such as the EMS, there are means of postponing the real effects of imbalances. The most obvious relies on the credit facilities which any trading system must provide to ensure the short-term solvency of trading partners, although the conditionality of such funds limits their use in a way. Other forms of capital flow may also balance trade deficits although their longer-term effects will vary widely. In extreme cases real adjustment may be postponed and certain costs externalised, by reckless borrowing. To do so, one must have reckless lenders, which implies that such possibilities will again arise only in situations like the current global disequilibrium. (Bienefeld 1980: 295)

Caught in the debt trap when the liquidity frenzy was over—as countries of the global periphery and state socialism after the Volcker-shock of 1979 or in the European periphery in the current crisis—the name of the game was austerity: '[T]he Community's most notable economic initiative in recent years, the EMS, could, like the gold standard, easily increase rather than reduce inequality, in the absence of policies to stop this happening' (Seers 1982: 10). Seers' account from 1980 on a possible future scenario seems familiar to readers from twenty-first-century Europe:

> Those [countries] in deficit [...] have to adopt deflationary policies. The more complete the degree of integration, the more serious this asymmetry is likely to be. If governments in an economic community have given up trade restrictions, foreign exchange control and even freedom to vary the exchange rate, then the only short-term weapons left to deal with a recession in exports (or rise in import prices) are fiscal and monetary policies that

> lower the level of employment – and wage controls to reduce costs and purchasing power. The effect is to make the governments of peripheral economies in an integrated system highly dependent on those of its core; if the latter give greater priority to curbing price inflation than to reducing unemployment, there is little the former can do but resign themselves to accepting this priority and shaping their own policies accordingly. (Seers 1980: 19)

Similarly Robert Baade and Jonathan Galloway (1983: 231) summarized:

> Full monetary integration means a sacrifice of monetary autonomy for Greece, Spain, and Portugal. Monetary policy will be determined jointly, and the collective policy will be more than likely less well suited to their needs. If monetary policy is conducted de facto by the area's reserve currency country, as was true in the case of the Bretton Woods system, what would be the implications? If Germany possesses the master currency, monetary policy for the three will be tighter than it has been. [...] Operating under the supposition that the deutsche mark will function as the reserve currency, the three Mediterranean countries may be forced to accept higher rates of unemployment, if a trade-off does indeed exist between inflation and unemployment.

What is being enforced on the European periphery today, above all, seems to be going back to the 'economist' position of Germany in the early days of discussions on the EMU in the 1960s. The Maastricht treaty (1993), argued Marsh (2011: 153),

> ensured that the Germans could introduce no further conditions for EMU, for example, on parallel establishment of 'political union'. This was an objective that both [chancellor Helmut] Kohl and the [German] Bundesbank said they wanted, in order to anchor German-style stability culture throughout Europe.

Meanwhile this 'stability culture' has been pushed forward even more by the Treaty on Stability, Coordination and Governance in the Economic and Monetary Union (2013, not signed by the Czech Republic and UK).

Greece, Portugal, and Spain had entered the European integration process with trade deficits. Important discussions on the future of the EMS were held when they were still governed by dictators. Post dictatorial aspirations for wealth wound up in austerity. Exiting the BWS, the currencies of all three countries were devalued against E6 (with the exception of Italy) in order to counter inflation differentials. Portugal 'was forced to accept the full rigour of IMF therapy' (Tsoukalis 1982: 167) in 1977/78 (IMF, n.y.) that improved the balance of payments 'at the expense of economic growth, employment and price stability' (Tsoukalis 1982: 167). Without counteracting mechanisms to balance the integration of 'unequal partners', the existing asymmetry would continue being translated into the monetary system. Cohesion and redistribution activities by the Community, beginning with the Single European Act 1987, were still considered low but annual transfers reached more than 3% of GDP in Portugal and Greece and more than 2% in Ireland and Spain (Tsoukalis 1997: 199ff. and 221).

> On the other hand, stronger demand for investment goods also means more imports. Between 30 and 40 per cent of the total amounts transferred to cohesion countries through the Structural Funds is being translated into imports from the other more developed countries of the EU [...]. (Tsoukalis 1997: 203f.)

In the case of Greece, moreover, 50% of the funds went into infrastructural investments. Generally, the negotiation power seems to have determined the grade of influence the EU Commission was able to apply, and e.g. led to manifest differences how the EU Commission interfered in Greece in the 1980s and later in Germany post unification (Tsoukalis 1997: 207).

Basically, this asymmetry can be observed from the early post-BWS ('snake') in the 1970s into EMS and then EMU. Governments of peripheral countries (and Italy, for that matter) could fight domestic inflation by high short-term interest rates, which would also attract foreign capital. On the other hand such policies would progressively overvalue currencies, impair competitiveness in foreign trade (and increase core low interest countries' competitiveness), which again would widen imbalances. Liberal doctrines furthered deregulation of financial markets and forfeited capital controls. The main adjustment burden, however, was on the shoulders of weaker currencies. The increasing role of the D-mark as international reserve currency led to a division of labor between the German Bundesbank that intervened mostly 'outside' the EMS, mostly against the US dollar, and the other central banks that adjusted internally (Tsoukalis 1997: 152ff.). As with common industrial policies,

> strong preference for the status quo [...] has enormously strengthened the negotiation power of Germany, thus enabling it in most cases to impose its own terms with respect to the transition and the contents of the final stage of the EMU. The arrangements for the final stage are very much along German lines, even though Germany would have liked even more strict rules with respect to the excessive deficit procedure. Not surprisingly, German representatives have been pushing in this direction subsequent to the ratification of the Maastricht treaty. The convergence criteria also strongly reflect German preferences. Although arguably they may make little economic sense, they will help to restrict, at least for some time, the number of countries allowed into the final stage [...]. A monetary union without Germany makes no sense; and Germany will not have a monetary union unless it is on its own terms. (Tsoukalis 1997: 171)

Peripheral countries had to shoulder the burden of adjustment from day one entering the European integration process. When, in the 1970s, a Pax Germanica began replacing the Pax Americana in Europe, Germany could secure its version of a monetary institutional setup. The consequences of which are being felt in Europe today.

5.7 'True' Integration or a 'Sort of Colonial System'? A Puerto Rico Scenario?

Members of the European Dependency School were skeptical of future integration prospects. Trends for future developments had been set before Mediterranean countries entered the scene. The rich club EC6 never seems to have intended or been able to bring the Community to converge peripheral areas to the level of the core. Moreover, the internal structural problems of EC6 and then EC9 countries were seen unresolved.

> Yet if there are no major reforms in the Community, there will be, after the enlargement, serious dualism, indeed a sort of colonial system. In the poorer group which already suffers whenever a government of the core adopts financially restrictive policies, the effects could be more severe if they give up the possibility of adopting measures to protect their national economy. (Seers 1982: 11, cf. also Seers 1979: 27)

Past integration processes had brought about more open or subtle forms of economic domination, argues Constantine Vaitsos (1982b: 244f.).

In the Western European case, the two least developed countries Greece and Portugal, could become economic variants of Puerto Rico in Europe. But also a Puerto Rico scenario would bring about instability due to extreme polarization. Therefore the most extreme forms of polarization needed to be countered.

'An immensely important choice', as Seers (1979: 29) put it, 'is emerging for the core governments of Europe. Enlargement seems impossible: yet it simultaneously appears inevitable'. The alternative scenario, Seers (1982: 11ff.) indicated, was one of 'true' integration. True integration would need more capital for the reconstruction of peripheral industrial and agricultural sectors. It could aim at a 'Community self-reliance' as a counterpart to the collective self-reliance in South-South cooperation which was being promoted at the time. A more homogeneous Europe could build the base for the EMS and the ECU to challenge the US dollar in world trade. Seers also seems to have perceived possible a kind of control how and where TNC would engage in business and therefore reduce harm in the global South.

> Perhaps the most constructive European policy in the 1980s would be increasingly to allow the countries of the Third World to solve their own problems – in sharp contrast to the paternalistic self-interest of European Third World policy in the past three decades. One of the most significant implications of the second enlargement is that it permits, and may compel, a degree of disengagement. (Seers 1982: 13)

Vaitsos (1982b: 244ff.) talks of his second scenario as a 'truly integrated Europe' that was to 'be achieved on the basis of conscious and direct measures to reduce the present contrasts in the level of productive activity and per capita income among its constituent parts'. Since spatial polarization had already grown among the EC Nine, distributional efforts remained too small, and common industrial policies were absent, Vaitsos was pessimistic about the likeliness of the 'true' integration scenario. The Community was not a transfer union, transfers to the periphery were more than equalized by increasing trade income flowing to the core (which again worsened the periphery's trade deficit, leading to balance of payment constraints and finally to the pressure to implement deflationary and austerity policies). Also Manfred Bienefeld (1980: 303ff.), a writer in the EADI network, considered a progressive integration necessary for a functioning Community. But he as well had major doubts because the Community would not be able to externalize development issues the way Western Germany did. Reaching an German style export surplus was unrealistic, and a balanced (industrial) production and trade structure was not in sight.

The European reality of the 1980s seems to have pointed toward a fortress Europe, as Wolfgang Hager (1985: 75) wrote in Musto's network: France proposed 'less national protectionism within the Community in return for more protectionism at Community level' and there would be 'no German agreement to the French bargain unless the implied notion of Community preference is extended to the EFTA partners with which Germany has such close trading and investment links' (ibid.). 'The Commission's real preference', argues Hager (1985: 75),

> is not the fortress but the tank: the element of protection balanced by the capacity to attack. In tune with most member governments, all elements of economic policy are put in the service of a medium-term-oriented strategy that is neo-mercantilist in inspiration.

Structural adjustment and austerity already seem to have been envisaged in such a concept:

> In the guise of preaching adjustment to international market forces, the strategy requires adjustment, in terms of basic socioeconomic priorities, to "best international practice." Tolerance of large-scale unemployment, reduction of government budgets to free resources for industry, and redirection of government spending to industry-relevant purposes are the hallmark of this strategy. (Hager 1985: 75f.)

The situation within the fortress or tank Europe was not unlike the core–periphery relations in the global context. As long as peripheral countries fail to show unity against the core, the polarization is not to be stopped. What would make the situation more difficult for the Southern periphery was the integration of Comecon countries. One periphery could be played off against the other. As long as they were the major peripheral insiders, Portugal, Greece, and Spain could negotiate their consent to a deepening of the Economics and Monetary Union (EMU) in monetary terms, argues Otto Holman (2002: 417): Spain alone received with 43 billion Ecu more than 6 times the amount of the entire region of Central and Eastern Europe from the structural and cohesion funds between 1994 and 1999. But overall, as Costis Hadjimichalis (1994: 27) pointed out, the 'southern fringes have lost one important political parameter in their negotiations to avoid disintegrative effects': '[W]e must notice that German capitalists now have plenty of cheap and well-educated labour from ex-socialist countries in situ, and new immigrants are filling blue-collar jobs held by southern Europeans during the 1960s and 1970s. [...] This means that Germans and other central Europeans are no longer willing to pay for the reproduction of cheap labour in the south'.

References

Anderson, Perry. 2011 [2009]. *The New Old World*. London and Brooklyn: Verso.

Anderson, Perry. 2012. After the Event. *New Left Review* 73, 49–61.

Arrighi, Giovanni. 2010. Postscript to the Second Edition of the Long Twentieth Century. In *The Long Twentieth Century: Money, Power, and the Origins of Our Times*, 371–386. London and New York: Verso.

Axt, Heinz-Jürgen. 1985. Self-Reliance and Reality in Greece. In *Endogenous Development: A Myth or a Path? Problems of Economic Self-Reliance in the European Periphery*, ed. Stefan Musto, 41–71. Tilburg: EADI.

Baade, Robert, and Jonathan Galloway. 1983. Monetary Integration in a 12-Member European Community: The Implications for Greece, Portugal, and Spain. In *The Contemporary Mediterranean World*, ed. Carl Pinkele and Adamantia Pollis, 221–236. New York: Praeger.

Bieling, Hans-Jürgen, and Jochen Steinhilber. 2000. Einleitung. In *Die Konfiguration Europas. Dimensionen einer kritischen Integrationstheorie*, ed. Hans-Jürgen Bieling and Jochen Steinhilber, 7–22. Münster.

Bienefeld, Manfred. 1980. Externalising Problems in a Future EEC. In *Integration and the Unequal Development: The Experience of the EEC*, ed. Dudley Seers and Constantine Vaitsos with the assistance of Marja-Liisa Kiljunen, 291–306. London and Basingstoke: Macmillan (=Studies in the Integration of Western Europe 1).

Bienefeld, Manfred. 1982. Impact on Industry. In *The Second Enlargement of the EEC: The Integration of Unequal Partners*, ed. Dudley Seers and Constantine Vaitsos with the assistance of Marja-Liisa Kiljunen, 109–135. London and Basingstoke: Macmillan (=Studies in the Integration of Western Europe 2).

Cesaratto, Sergio, and Antonella Stirati. 2010. Germany and the European and Global Crises. *International Journal of Political Economy* 39 (4): 56–86.

Czichon, Eberhard. 1995. *Die Bank und die Macht. Hermann Josef Abs, die deutsche Bank und die Politik*. Köln.

Danescu, Elena Rodica. 2013. *A Rereading of the Werner Report of 8 October 1970 in the Light of the Pierre Werner Family Archives—A Detailed Study.* Sanem: Centre Virtuel de la Connaissance sur l'Europe.

Deubner, Christian. 1982. West German Attitudes. In *The Second Enlargement of the EEC: The Integration of Unequal Partners*, ed. Dudley Seers and Constantine Vaitsos with the assistance of Marja-Liisa Kiljunen, 43–56. London and Basingstoke: Macmillan (=Studies in the Integration of Western Europe 2).

Duchêne, Francois. 1982. Community Attitudes. In *The Second Enlargement of the EEC: The Integration of Unequal Partners*, ed. Dudley Seers and Constantine Vaitsos with the assistance of Marja-Liisa Kiljunen, 25–42. London and Basingstoke: Macmillan (=Studies in the Integration of Western Europe 2).

Eßer, Klaus. 1977. Integration zwischen Industrie- und teilindustrialisierten Ländern – Portugal in der EG. In *Zur Erweiterung der Europäischen Gemeinschaft in Südeuropa*, ed. Claus Burghard et al. Berlin (=Schriften des Deutschen Instituts für Entwicklungspolitik (DIE) 52).

Eßer, Klaus. 1978a. Industrie- und teilindustrialisierte Länder in der Europäischen Gemeinschaft. In *Europäische Gemeinschaft und südeuropäische Beitrittsländer*, ed. Klaus Eßer et al., 47–72. Berlin (=Schriften des Deutschen Instituts für Entwicklungspolitik (DIE) 54).

Eßer, Klaus. 1978b. Tendenzen regionaler Entwicklung in den Beitrittsländern. In *Europäische Gemeinschaft und südeuropäische Beitrittsländer*, ed. Klaus Eßer et al., 147–166. Berlin (=Schriften des Deutschen Instituts für Entwicklungspolitik (DIE) 54).

Eßer, Klaus, et al. 1980. *Überlegungen zur portugiesischen Industriepolitik angesichts des Beitritts zur EG.* Berlin (=Schriften des Deutschen Instituts für Entwicklungspolitik (DIE) 60).

Eußner, Ansgar. 1983. *Industriepolitik und Süderweiterung der EG am Beispiel der Werftindustrie.* Berlin (=Schriften des Deutschen Instituts für Entwicklungspolitik (DIE) 72).

European Council (ed.). 1972. Meetings of the Heads of State or Government: The First Summit Conference of the Enlarged Community. Paris, 19–21 October 1972. Bulletin of the European Communities, No. 10. Reproduced by Archive of European Integration (AEI), University of Pittsburgh.

Evangelinides, Mary. 1979. Core-Periphery Relations in the Greek Case. In *Underdeveloped Europe: Studies in Core-Periphery Relations*, ed. Dudley Seers, Bernard Schaffer, and Marja-Liisa Kiljunen, 177–195. Sussex: Humanities Press (=Harvester Studies in Development 1).

GFP—German Foreign Policy. 2019. Reparationsabwehr aus der Trickkiste. https://www.german-foreign-policy.com/news/detail/7959/ (June 6, 2019).

Hadjimichalis, Costis. 1994. The Fringes of Europe and EU Integration: A View from the South. *European Urban and Regional Studies* 1 (1): 19–29.

Hager, Wolfgang. 1985. Fortress Europe: A Model? In *Europe at the Crossroads: Agendas of the Crisis*, ed. Stefan Musto and Carl Pinkele, 65–84. New York et al.: Praeger.

Haller, Max. 2009. *Die Europäische Union als Elitenprozess. Das Ende eines Traums?* Wiesbaden.

Harvey, David. 2004. Die Geographie des 'neuen' Imperialismus: Akkumulation durch Enteignung. In *Die globale Enteignungsökonomie*, ed. Christian Zeller, 183–215. Münster: Westphälisches Dampfboot.

Hilberg, Raul. 1990 [1961]. *Die Vernichtung der europäischen Juden*. Band 3. Frankfurt/Main.

Hillebrand, Wolfgang. 1978. Hypothesen zur zukünftigen Entwicklung der Industriepolitik der Gemeinschaft. In *Europäische Gemeinschaft und südeuropäische Beitrittsländer*, ed. Klaus Eßer et al., 25–46. Berlin (=Schriften des Deutschen Instituts für Entwicklungspolitik (DIE) 54).

Hobsbawm, Eric. 1996. *The Age of the Extremes: A History of the World 1914–1991*. New York: Vintage.

Holland, Stuart. 1979. Dependent Development: Portugal as Periphery. In *Underdeveloped Europe: Studies in Core-Periphery Relations*, ed. Dudley Seers, Bernard Schaffer, and Marja-Liisa Kiljunen, 139–160. Sussex: Humanities Press (=Harvester Studies in Development 1).

Holland, Stuart. 1980. *The UnCommon Market*. London and Basingstoke: Macmillan.

Holman, Otto. 2002. Die Neue Europäische Peripherie. Ost- und Süderweiterung der Europäischen Union im Vergleich. *Prokla* 32 (2): 399–420.

Intergovernmental Committee of the Messina Conference. 1956. Report by the Heads of Delegations to the Foreign Ministers. Brussels, April 21. In University of Luxembourg (ed.), http://www.cvce.eu/obj/report_of_the_heads_of_delegation_to_the_foreign_ministers_brussels_21_april_1956-en-4dd69921-433b-4bc0-acec-808f72fec9ae.html (February 25, 2018).

International Monetary Fund (IMF). n.y. Portugal: Fast Facts, http://www.imf.org/external/np/exr/countryfacts/prt/ (May 27, 2015).

James, Harold. 2001. *The Deutsche Bank and the Nazi Economic War Against the Jews*. Cambridge: Cambridge University Press.

James, Harold. 2004. *The Nazi Dictatorship and the Deutsche Bank*. Cambridge, MA: Cambridge University Press.

Kiljunen, Marja-Liisa. 1980. Regional Disparities and Policy in the EEC. In *Integration and the Unequal Development: The Experience of the EEC*, ed. Dudley Seers and Constantine Vaitsos with the assistance of Marja-Liisa Kiljunen, 199–222. London and Basingstoke: Macmillan (=Studies in the Integration of Western Europe 1).

Kojima, Kiyoshi. 1970. Towards a Theory of Agreed Specialization: The Economics of Integration. In *Induction, Growth and Trade: Essays in Honour of Roy Harrod*, ed. Walter Eltis et al., 305–324. Oxford: Clarendon Press.

Leonard, Dick. 1992. *Guide to the European Community*. London: Economist.
Luif, Paul. 1988. Die Europäische Gemeinschaft. In *Der un-heimliche Anschluss. Österreich und die EG*, ed. Inge Morawetz and Margit Scherb, 1–18. Wien: Verlag für Gesellschaftskritik.
Mandel, Ernest. 1967. International Capitalism and "Supra-Nationality". In *Socialist Register 1967: A Survey of Movements and Ideas*, ed. Ralph Miliband and John Saville, 27–41. London: Merlin Press.
Marsh, David. 2011. *The Euro: The Battle for the New Global Currency*, New Edition. New Haven and London: Yale University Press.
Moravcsik, Andrew. 1998. *The Choice for Europe: Social Purpose and State Power from Messina to Maastricht*. Ithaca: Cornell University Press.
Müller, Jan-Werner. 2012. Beyond Militant Democracy? *New Left Review* 73: 39–47.
Muñoz, Juan, Santiago Roldán, and Angel Serrano. 1979. The Growing Dependence of Spanish Industrialization on Foreign Investment. In *Underdeveloped Europe: Studies in Core-Periphery Relations*, ed. Dudley Seers, Bernard Schaffer, and Marja-Liisa Kiljunen, 161–175. Sussex: Humanities Press (=Harvester Studies in Development 1).
Musto, Stefan. 1981. Die Süderweiterung der Europäischen Gemeinschaft. *Kyklos* 34 (2): 242–273.
Musto, Stefan. 1982. Structural Implications. In *The Second Enlargement of the EEC: The Integration of Unequal Partners*, ed. Dudley Seers and Constantine Vaitsos with the assistance of Marja-Liisa Kiljunen, 67–91. London and Basingstoke: Macmillan (=Studies in the Integration of Western Europe 2).
Musto, Stefan. 1985. The Loss of Hegemony: Sensitive Industries and Industrial Policies in the European Community. In *Europe at the Crossroads: Agendas of the Crisis*, ed. Stefan Musto and Carl Pinkele, 85–102. New York et al.: Praeger.
Nikolinakos, Marios. 1985. Transnationalization of Production, Location of Industry and the Deformation of Regional Development in Peripheral Countries: The Case of Greece. In *Uneven development in Southern Europe: Studies of Accumulation, Class, Migration and the State*, ed. Ray Hudson and Jim Lewis, 192–210. London and New York: Methuen.
Oberndorfer, Lukas. 2012a. Hegemoniekrise in Europa – Auf dem Weg zu einem autoritären Wettbewerbsetatismus? In *Die EU in der Krise. Zwischen autoritärem Etatismus und europäischen Frühling*, ed. Forschungsgruppe 'Staatsprojekt Europa', 49–71. Münster: Westfälisches Dampfboot.
Oberndorfer, Lukas. 2012b. Die Renaissance des autoritären Liberalismus? Carl Schmitt und der deutsche Neoliberalismus vor dem Hintergrund des Eintritts der "Massen" in die europäische Politik. *Prokla* 42 (3): 413–431.
Panitch, Leo, and Sam Gindin. 2012. *The Making of Global Capitalism: The Political Economy of American Empire*. London and New York: Verso.

Plehwe, Dieter. 1998. Ludwig Erhards D-Mark. Kontinuitätslinien des Rechtsliberalismus. In *Fünfzig Jahre Deutsche Mark*, ed. LAKS Hessen, 16–27. Berlin: Elefanten Press.

Pollis, Adamantia. 1983. The Southern European Semiperiphery and the European Community. In *The Contemporary Mediterranean World*, ed. Carl Pinkele and Adamantia Pollis, 202–220. New York: Praeger.

Pollis, Adamantia. 1985. International and Domestic Constraints on Socialist Transformation in Greece. In *Europe at the Crossroads: Agendas of the Crisis*, ed. Stefan Musto and Carl Pinkele, 197–217. New York et al.: Praeger.

Poulantzas, Nicos. 2008 [1979]. Interview with Nicos Poulantzas. In *The Poulantzas Reader: Marxism, Law and the State*, ed. James Martin, 387–402. London and New York: Verso.

Ptak, Ralf. 2004. Vom Ordoliberalismus zur sozialen Marktwirtschaft: Stationen des Neoliberalismus in Deutschland. Opladen: Leske + Budrich.

Rhenisch, Thomas. 1999. *Europäische Integration und industrielles Interesse. Die deutsche Industrie und die Gründung der Europäischen Wirtschaftsgemeinschaft*. Stuttgart: Franz Steiner (=VSWG Beihefte 152).

Ritschl, Albrecht. 2012. Germany, Greece and the Marshall Plan. *The Economist*. http://www.economist.com/blogs/freeexchange/2012/06/economic-history (March 18, 2015).

Roth, Karl Heinz. 1998. Das Ende eines Mythos. Ludwig Erhard und der Übergang der deutschen Wirtschaft von der Annexions- zur Nachkriegsplanung (1939 bis 1945). Teil II: 1943 bis 1945. *1999, Zeitschrift für Sozialgeschichte des 20. und 21. Jahrhunderts* 13 (1): 92–123.

Roth, Karl Heinz. 1999a. Das Ende eines Mythos. Ludwig Erhard und der Übergang der deutschen Wirtschaft von der Annexions- zur Nachkriegsplanung (1939 bis 1945). Teil II: 1943 bis 1945. Fortsetzung und Schluß. *1999, Zeitschrift für Sozialgeschichte des 20. und 21. Jahrhunderts* 14 (1): 73–91.

Roth, Karl Heinz. 1999b. Replik. *1999, Zeitschrift für Sozialgeschichte des 20. und 21. Jahrhunderts* 14 (1): 207f.

Roth, Karl Heinz. 2001. Klienten des Leviathan: Die Mont Pèlerin Society und das Bundeswirtschaftsministerium in den fünfziger Jahren. *1999, Zeitschrift für Sozialgeschichte des 20. und 21. Jahrhunderts* 16 (2): 13–41.

Roth, Karl Heinz, and Hartmut Rübner. 2017. *Reparationsschuld. Hypotheken der deutschen Besatzungsherrschaft in Griechenland und Europa*. Berlin: Metropol.

Scherb, Margit. 1988. Die Europäische Gemeinschaft – Objekt österreichischer Begierden. In *Der un-heimliche Anschluss. Österreich und die EG*. ed. Inge Morawetz and Margit Scherb, 47–72. Wien: Verlag für Gesellschaftskritik.

Scheuerman, William. 1997. The Unholy Alliance of Carl Schmitt and Friedrich A. Hayek. *Constellations* 4 (2): 172–188.

Schlupp, Frieder. 1980. Federal Republic of Germany. In *Integration and the Unequal Development: The Experience of the EEC*, ed. Dudley Seers and Constantine Vaitsos (with the assistance of Marja-Liisa Kiljunen), 176–198. London and Basingstoke: Macmillan (=Studies in the Integration of Western Europe 1).

Schwartz, Thomas Alan. 1990. Die Begnadigung deutscher Kriegsverbrecher. John J. McCloy und die Häftlinge von Landsberg. *Vierteljahrshefte für Zeitgeschichte* 38 (3): 375–414.

Secchi, Carlo. 1982. Impact on the Less Developed Regions of the EEC. In *The Second Enlargement of the EEC: The Integration of Unequal Partners*, ed. Dudley Seers and Constantine Vaitsos with the assistance of Marja-Liisa Kiljunen, 176–189. London and Basingstoke: Macmillan (=Studies in the Integration of Western Europe 2).

Seers, Dudley. 1979. The Periphery of Europe. In *Underdeveloped Europe: Studies in Core-Periphery Relations*, ed. Dudley Seers, Bernard Schaffer, and Marja-Liisa Kiljunen, 3–34. Sussex: Harvester Press (=Harvester Studies in Development 1).

Seers, Dudley. 1980. Theoretical Aspects of Unequal Development at Different Spatial Levels. In *Integration and the Unequal Development: The Experience of the EEC*, ed. Dudley Seers and Constantine Vaitsos with the assistance of Marja-Liisa Kiljunen, 9–23. London and Basingstoke: Macmillan (=Studies in the Integration of Western Europe 1).

Seers, Dudley. 1982. Introduction: The Second Enlargement in Historical Perspective. In *The Second Enlargement of the EEC: The Integration of Unequal Partners*, ed. Dudley Seers and Constantine Vaitsos with the assistance of Marja-Liisa Kiljunen, 1–21. London and Basingstoke: Macmillan (=Studies in the Integration of Western Europe 2).

Silver, Beverly, and Giovanni Arrighi. 2011. The End of the Long Twentieth Century. In *The Roots of Global Financial Meltdown*, ed. Craig Calhoun and Georgi Derluguian, 53–68. London and New York: New York University Press.

Statistisches Bundesamt (ed.). 2015. *Foreign Trade: Overall Development in Foreign Trade Since 1950*. Wiesbaden.

Sunkel, Osvaldo. 1973. Transnational Capitalism and National Disintegration in Latin America. *Social and Economic Studies* 22 (1): 132–176 (Based on earlier works in 1968, see FN 2).

Teichova, Alice. 1988. *Kleinstaaten im Spannungsfeld der Großmächte. Wirtschaft und Politik in Mittel und Südosteuropa in der Zwischenkriegszeit*. Wien (=Sozial- und wirtschaftshistorische Studien 18).

The MacDougall Report. 1977. *Study Group on the Role of Public Finance in European Integration*, vol. I. Brussels: Commission of the European Communities. http://ec.europa.eu/economy_finance/emu_history/

documentation/chapter8/19770401en73macdougallrepvol1.pdf (June 27, 2017).

Triffin, Robert. 1980. The European Monetary System. In *Integration and Unequal Development: The Experience of the EEC*, ed. Dudley Seers and Constantine Vaitsos with the assistance of Marja-Liisa Kiljunen, 223–233. London and Basingstoke: Macmillan (=Studies in the Integration of Western Europe 1).

Tsoukalis, Loukas. 1982. Impact on the European Monetary System (EMS). In *The Second Enlargement of the EEC: The Integration of Unequal Partners*, ed. Dudley Seers and Constantine Vaitsos with the assistance of Marja-Liisa Kiljunen, 163–175. London and Basingstoke: Macmillan (=Studies in the Integration of Western Europe 2).

Tsoukalis, Loukas. 1997. *The New European Economy Revisited*. Oxford et al.: Oxford University Press.

Vaitsos, Constantine. 1980. Corporate Integration in World Production and Trade. In *Integration and Unequal Development: The Experience of the EEC*, ed. Dudley Seers, and Constantine Vaitsos with the assistance of Marja-Liisa Kiljunen, 24–45. London and Basingstoke: Macmillan (=Studies in the Integration of Western Europe 1).

Vaitsos, Constantine. 1982a. Transnational Corporate Behaviour and the Enlargement. In *The Second Enlargement of the EEC: The Integration of Unequal Partners*, ed. Dudley Seers and Constantine Vaitsos with the assistance of Marja-Liisa Kiljunen, 137–162. London and Basingstoke: Macmillan (=Studies in the Integration of Western Europe 2).

Vaitsos, Constantine. 1982b. Conclusions: Economic Effects of the Second Enlargement. In *The Second Enlargement of the EEC: The Integration of Unequal Partners*, ed. Dudley Seers and Constantine Vaitsos with the assistance of Marja-Liisa Kiljunen, 243–268. London and Basingstoke: Macmillan (=Studies in the Integration of Western Europe 2).

Weissenbacher, Rudy. 2005. *Jugoslawien. Politische Ökonomie einer Desintegration*. Wien: Promedia.

Weissenbacher, Rudy. 2007. Historical Considerations of Uneven Development in East Central Europe. In *Dollarization, Euroization and Financial Instability: Central and Eastern European Countries Between Stagnation and Financial Crisis?* ed. Joachim Becker and Rudy Weissenbacher, 35–83. Marburg: Metropolis.

Woodward, Susan. 1983. Political Changes in the European Mediterranean Arena: An Overview of Considerations for Policy Makers. In *The Contemporary Mediterranean World*, ed. Carl Pinkele and Adamantia Pollis, 175–201. New York: Praeger.

Wünsche, Horst Friedrich. 1999. Ludwig Erhard und die Grundlegung der Sozialen Marktwirtschaft 1943/44. *1999, Zeitschrift für Sozialgeschichte des 20. und 21. Jahrhunderts* 14 (1): 200–207.

Ziltener, Patrick. 2000. Die Veränderung von Staatlichkeit in Europa – regulations- und staatstheoretische Überlegungen. In *Die Konfiguration Europas: Dimensionen einer kritischen Integrationstheorie*, ed. Hans-Jürgen Bieling and Jochen Steinhilber, 73–101. Münster.

Zingel, Wolfgang-Peter. 1976. Grundsätzliche Fragen einer europäischen Regionalpolitik. In *Möglichkeiten und Grenzen einer Europäischen Union. Band 2. Verteilung der wirtschaftlichen Kräfte im Raum*, ed. Hans von der Groeben and Hans Möller, 33–69. Baden-Baden.

CHAPTER 6

Alternative Strategies in the 'European Dependency School'

6.1 Toward a New Development Paradigm 'from Below'

With the collapse of the traditional paradigms, also non-Marxist social scientists like Dieter Nohlen and Walter Stöhr from the European Dependency School formulated theoretical and policy alternatives using the dependency framework. The old paradigms had brought 'growth without development' in the best case but mostly aggravated existing structural imbalances (Nohlen and Schultze 1985: 19). Nohlen (1985: 12) called his concept region-centered development and 'periphery up and inward development' strategy. It was to be oriented on the history of the respective societies rather than a theoretical model. Critical and emancipatory epistemological approaches should focus on development (growth, employment, equality, justice, participation, political, and economic autonomy) (Nohlen and Schultze 1985: 48). Political decisions should not follow functional integration but be led by the needs of regional population.

A region-centered approach resulted from the thesis of uneven development and structural dependency of peripheral from core regions. It was inspired by Latin American dependency approaches but did not directly adopt them. Using the dependency paradigm aimed at overcoming traditional economic and structural policy that was oriented on the interests of the central state. Questions of democratic participation and power politics are of immediate importance in this concept that urges to integrate political, economic, and cultural factors and perspectives (Nohlen 1985: 12ff.). Dependency analysis considers

R. Weissenbacher, *The Core-Periphery Divide in the European Union*,
https://doi.org/10.1007/978-3-030-28211-0_6

differences in development levels as exogenously caused and based on structural imbalances, as a result of industrial-capitalist production and division of labor. A complete new start, a new paradigm, and processes of change are perceived as inescapable. Dependency and underdevelopment of peripheral region can be changed only if the prevailing subordination under the core determined functional integration can be removed (Nohlen and Schultze 1985: 20ff. and 42f.). The concept suggested by Friedmann and Weaver (1979) involved

> a territorial as opposed to a functional development strategy [...]. This latter concept juxtaposes the principle of functionality with its orientation towards a world-wide division of labour, hierarchical structures and therefore polarisation, and the principle of territoriality, which looks to the common interests of a given region, decentralisation, selective dissociation and self-reliance. (Musto 1985: 4)

Room to maneuver for a region-centered policy is dependent on 'the vicious circle of advanced capitalism':

> We cannot achieve more democratic participation without a prior change in social inequality and in consciousness, but we cannot achieve the changes in social inequality and consciousness without a prior increase in democratic participation. (Macpherson 1977: 100, quoted in Nohlen and Schultze 1985: 50)

Nohlen and Schultze (1985: 51f.) offer hypotheses for a new start of regional policy: (a) decentralist rather than centralized political systems; (b) forms of participation; (c) no sudden change or complete decoupling but a gradual transformation; (d) resistance of the political core can be overcome if issues of alternative regional policies can be made part of an overall political change in the countries collectively.

Referring to Friedmann and Weaver (1979), Nohlen and Schultze (1985: 61ff.) argue that a 'selective territorial closure' was necessary for a paradigmatic new beginning. But such a policy would not suffice. The authors point at what they perceive as a weak spot in dependency theory, the discrepancy between structuralist analysis of the causes of uneven development, and the capability to counter dependencies politically. Strategies for change were voluntaristic and suggested a room to maneuver that would not exist in a dependency perspective—if it assumed an external control of political decision-making (Nohlen and Schultze 1985: 63ff.).

The development paradigm 'from above' as argued by Walter Stöhr perceived economic and development policies biased in favor of countries of the core, too. An alternative paradigm had to overcome the economistic preoccupation that focused on new markets, low wage production, low-cost resources. The application of technology was subjugated to such a bias as well. Unsurprisingly he as well focused on development as integral process that included interaction of economic, sociocultural, political, and environmental factors (Stöhr 1983b: 124; 1981: 39f.). Shaping a new development model had to be an interdisciplinary process (Stöhr 1981: 40).

An alternative development strategy had to gradually reduce polarizing backwash effects and selectively control positive spread effects. As with the concept of Nohlen and Schultze, a transfer of decision-making—in a participatory democratic way—to the regional level is deemed important. Such a move would also help people in the regions to regain self-confidence which was lost under the prevailing development model (Stöhr 1983b: 124). But the development paradigm 'from below' was more than that, it

> implies alternative criteria for factor allocation (going from the present principle of maximizing return for selected factors to one of maximizing integral resource mobilization); different criteria for commodity exchange (going from the presently dominating principle of comparative advantage to one of equalizing benefits from trade); specific forms of social and economic organization (emphasizing territorial rather than mainly functional organization [...]) and a change in the basic concept of development (going from the present monolithic concept defined by economic criteria, competitive behaviour, external motivation, and large-scale redistributive mechanisms to diversified concepts defined by broader societal goals, by collaborative behaviour and by endogenous motivation). (Stöhr 1981: 39)

Stöhr (1985: 231ff.) argues for a concept of 'selective self-reliance', which follows the dependency school's conception of 'self-reliance' (Galtung 1983). He assumes that each region has an endogenous development potential with ecological, human, sociocultural, and institutional resources. He calls self-determined (but not self-reliant) regions that can appropriate resources of other regions and therefore increase their own development potential (most core regions). A self-reliant development means a self-determined development based on own resources. Therefore core regions needed to concentrate on their own resources, and reduce the exploitation of peripheral regions' resources. In a global system of interactive nature, however, such self-reliance was deemed possible only as 'selective'. This concept can be used axiomatically on a local, regional, or national scale, Stöhr emphasizes a

> self-reliant mobilization of endogenous development potential [...] against trans-territorial penetration where this is detrimental to the sustained development of these communities [...]. Such a strategy I have [...] called development 'from below' or a strategy of 'selective spatial closure. (Stöhr 1985: 232, cf. also: Stöhr 1981: 45, in more detail: Stöhr and Tödtling 1979: 152ff.)

Importantly, Stöhr (1983b: 125) argues that a development strategy must try reducing dependencies but should neither strive for economic autarchy nor full political autonomy. A certain level of 'selective spatial closure', however, was necessary

> to inhibit transfers to and from regions or countries which reduce their potential for self-reliant development. This could be done by control of raw material or commodity transfers which contribute to negative terms of trade and/or by control of factor transfers (capital, technology), and by the retention of decision making powers on commodity and factor transfers in order to avoid the underemployment or idleness of other regional production factors, or major external dependence. Instead of maximizing return of selected production factors on an international scale, the objective would be to increase the over-all efficiency of all production factors of the economically less-developed region in an integrated fashion. (Stöhr 1981: 45)

Stöhr (1981: 61) does not object to economic growth but places it in the context of satisfaction of regional needs. John Friedman (1967: 9) early distinguished growth from development. 'Growth', he (ibid.) argued in his 'General Study of Polarized Development'

> may be conceptually distinguished from "development". The former refers to the expansion of a system in one or more dimensions without structural change; the latter refers to a change in the structure of a system that may or may not be expanding

Stöhr 1981: 46 refers to Albert Hirschman by distinguishing between the advantages of more integration (with less sovereignty but more technology and organizational innovation), and advantages of more dissociation with more sovereignty regarding a selective self-reliance. He considers, however, historically grown dependencies difficult to overcome. A development strategy from below

> might be particularly suitable for the many areas which in the near future cannot expect to benefit from traditional 'center-down' development strategies. At the very least it can be used as a transitional strategy while competitiveness with the world economic system is improved [...]. (Stöhr 1981: 63)

There are no recipes for a development 'from below' but Stöhr (1981: 64f.; 1983a: 11ff.; 1983b: 125ff.; 1985: 233ff.) formulates a set of principles for a policy of 'selective self-reliance':

- Priority for sectoral and functional diversification with a higher level of resilience to external shocks and emphasis on inter-sectoral development;
- Empowerment of decentralized and endogenous power structures with egalitarian decision-making between social groups/classes and regional units (in order to prevent concentration of surplus, wealth, and power); broad access to scarce resources (land, natural resources), internalization of development costs;
- Priority for mobilization of endogenous resources;
- Priority for regional need satisfaction (food, housing, basic needs) and facilitation for self-sufficiency in times of crisis;
- Promotion of multi-level technology development (including capital-intensive production in addition to labor intensive production);
- Promotion of territorial self-regulation and mechanisms of adjustment; increasing the autonomous regional innovation potential;
- Setup of exchange and accumulation conditions similar to those of core regions (for example regional development banks that finance regional production);
- Shift away from big export projects in favor of regional companies and set-up of a regional service sector;
- Evaluation of projects and investments according to their regional (multiplier) effects and value added;

- Restructuring and development of public transportation systems within the regions (regional accessibility instead of external connections);
- Mobilizing of regional energy resources;
- Improvement of regional environmental quality (responsibility toward future generations);
- Strengthening education and training;
- Limitation of external aid and assistance to projects that facilitate selective self-reliance.

Stöhr and Nohlen seem to have taken up Cardoso and Faletto's 'methodology for the analysis of concrete situations of dependency' as they argue for an individual treatment of the respective regions in analysis and policy conclusions. This seems also true for Seers (1981) and Bienefeld (1981) who also argued for analyses of special situations, and emphasized that differences between peripheral countries very much mattered. Size, resources (especially food and oil), access to technology, power status in international political economy, and vicinity to a global power set the framework of each single government's room to maneuver.

6.2 Between Reform and Utopia: Policy Considerations of Such a New Paradigm

While the mainstream approaches 'from above' perceive (regional) 'problems of development' being endogenous and attribute them to modernization deficits or lack of factor endowment, the dependency school points at external dependencies as the roots of problems. Therefore remedies cannot come from prevailing (dominant) external sources but need to be endogenous. A self-reliant development needs to fight trans-territorial penetration. Because international interrelations are powerful, such self-reliance is envisioned as 'selective' in nature, employing a 'selective spatial closure'. No standard recipes are being given, nature, history, geography, resources, and size influence development policies. Stöhr's (1983b: 125) 'selective self-reliance' does not go as far as economic autarchy or full political autonomy, Seers (1979: 28) argues that 'reducing dependency does not necessarily mean aiming at autarchy' but stresses (like Stöhr) that such a development strategy 'is not to break all links, which would almost anywhere be socially damaging and politically unworkable, but to adopt a selective approach to external influences of all types'. Their experiences seem to have brought European authors from the ECLA tradition to suggest anti-capitalist solutions, but their way to change societies and counter dependencies was one of gradual transformation and had to count in one way or the other on the support of national elites.

I can see four key pillars in the thinking of the European Dependency School:

1. Transnational capitalism and its private (TNC) and public (development) institutions are harmful to regional/national development;
2. The traditional economic paradigm ('development from above') has failed in formulating viable development strategies and policies; it postulates internal problems and suggests external solutions;
3. Transnational capitalism is too powerful to be overcome in short term;
4. In order to counter harmful penetration by TNC, regions and countries need to apply a Plan B. Regional policies need to follow a paradigm of 'development from below' or 'selective self-reliance' (with a very broad and not exclusively economic understanding of development) and to introduce socialist policies (at times not explicitly called socialist), in any case a policy of 'selective spatial closure' to minimize harmful external effects. Endogenous policies are seen important because problems of development are externally induced and require domestic remedies.

European dependency theorists were no revolutionaries. Palma (1981: 59) categorizes authors from the EADI-dependency group (i.e. Dudley Seers and others) as advancers and developers of the ECLA tradition. If we classify the ECLA tradition as more reformist and pragmatic (than the more revolutionary stance of the 'theory of underdevelopment' group), then this will seem true as well for most of the other non-Marxist protagonists from the 'European dependency school' like Stöhr or Nohlen. But having visionary concepts without presenting models how to achieve such ends garnered criticism. Edward Soja called the non-Marxist regionalists of the group 'overly romantic and utopian' (cf. Chapter 3.1). John Friedmann, again, argued that many Marxists were more interested in revolution and system transformation and 'generally disinterested in policy prescription [so that] they have failed to articulate the practical implications of their work' (Friedmann 1983: 149).

But Marxists were also a heterogenous group. Marxists from the EADI-network (from Eastern and Western Europe) were skeptical in their assessment of the dependency paradigm and self-reliance. Tamás Szentes (1983: 108), a Hungarian member of EADI, demanded precision from and in the variants of the dependency school, otherwise it would remain a mere 'ideological concept without practical implications':

> [I]t may even turn into an apologetics, namely in defence of the domestic ruling leadership, the local ruling and exploiting classes, exempted from any responsibility. A progressive policy needs not only a progressive theory but also some guiding principles for practical implementation, an advise on the priorities and about the feasible alternatives, and an expertise of how to assess the latter.

The Greek economist Marios Nikolinakos (1985), writing within Musto's EADI-network, delivered an angry response to the self-reliance concept (of Galtung, Amin, Stöhr and others): '[A]utonomous development, self-reliance, and so forth is characterized by an almost bucolic wish to return to idyllic conditions prevailing before World War II or in some cases, even before the capitalist era' (ibid.: 327). While it remains unclear why pre-World War II (or pre-capitalism) had been idyllic, Nikolinakos (1985: 328) emphasizes that the

> main argument presented here is that in face of an increasing tendency toward transnationalization of the production process, the idea of autonomous development or self-reliance is groundless and anachronistic; worse, it may be dangerous.

Although delivered in a very harsh manner, some of Nikolinakos' critical points carry some truth that still seem pertinent today. We will take some of them up again in the concluding discussion. But many of the authors of the European Dependency School were not that starry-eyed. Since the import substitution industrialization (ISI) favored by ECLA had failed (the technology and capital goods import—for the export industry—even tended to increase imports and cost more than imports of such products would have cost, cf. Bienefeld 1982: 47), the role of TNC in providing necessary volumes of technology and capital goods was acknowledged (Seers 1983: 53). An autonomous capitalist development was seen impossible which is why 'a socialist path offers the only escape for peripheral societies' (Bienefeld and Godfrey 1982: 5). And

Nikolinakos' account appears contradictory as well: He denounces the naivety of self-reliance authors, arguing that 'economic problems are political, not moral problems; hence solutions must be politically operational and not dependent on a moral doctrine' (ibid.: 339).

> According to self-reliance strategists, autonomy will be restored if one sets one's own goals and realizes them through one's own forces, and so forth. This model does not exist anymore; the production process has been internationalized, mainly through modern technology, irrespective of the economic and political dependencies, so that the national economy tends to disappear, while the national state is more and more incapable of influencing the endogenous variables and tends to be anachronistic. Even a government representing the people's interest that makes its own decisions is constrained by the fact that these decisions are dependent on genuinely factual, not political, conditions objectively determined outside the system. (ibid.: 335)

He holds self-reliance politically dangerous, because it is 'hardly conceived to be compatible with democratic procedures': He claims that democracy would not allow to implement self-reliance due to a lengthy process of convincing people, and therefore only a Stalinist-type of dictatorship would enable self-reliance, despite the fact that 'participation and self-management of the people are preconditions of self-reliance' (ibid.: 336). For a social scientist positively relating to Karl Marx, Nikolinakos seems to downplay actors and to over-emphasize structures and objective laws ('law of the increasing transnationalization'). But he, neither, offers a modus operandi to achieve an alternative, despite the fact that 'the solutions will be necessarily global or there will be no solutions' (ibid.: 339):

> The lesson of history is that if no realistic solutions can be found to change through the intervention of human will the objective factors that make out of the prevailing capitalist model of development an inhuman system, then history will apply its own law of finding solutions through wars, riots social disturbance, and so forth. (ibid.: 328f.)

Nikolinakos rejects any considerations (as being put forward in the self-reliance concept) that offer long term solutions incorporating reconsiderations of overall consumption patterns (for environmental and resources reasons): Only saturated scientist would count qualitative standards (of the core) against quantitative standards (of the poor in the periphery still lacking basic needs): 'self-reliance requires that the people consciously renounce the wish for the present and retain only the hope for long-run solution' (ibid.:332).

> Besides, how many of the citizens in the highly industrialized countries would be willing to sacrifice the material standard they have reached so far for the sake of some quality of life? Quality of life is accepted generally but not when it means, for example, renunciation of the private car – and it is exactly here where the irrelevance of every self-reliance theory becomes apparent. (ibid.: 332).

To be sure, there was critical assessment also within the European Dependency School. Manfred Bienefeld (1981: 81), working together with Seers at IDS, joined the criticism of a dependency thinking that elevates nationally oriented polices to an absolute level:

> The consequence is a use of the concept of 'self-reliance', as if that conformed to the principle of 'the more the better', and a use of the notion of 'delinking' which implies that this is an end in itself, rather than a means to an end. A further consequence of these fallacies is to induce a concern with internal structures and price relativities, without significant regard for changing external circumstances. This is, of course, the antithesis of the dependency perspective.

Above all, self-reliance was a concept in progress (cf. Chapter 2.6) that meant aiming at a post-capitalist society. For some that meant 'socialism' but even then regional requirements as how to tackle capitalist penetration differed. José Villamil (1977: 58) from the EADI network and developer of the ECLA tradition in Palma's (1981: 59) categories, referred to the self-reliance concept—arguing with Samir Amin—as a strategy for transition from capitalism to socialism in peripheral countries (cf. Amin 1981: 535). 'In some cases', argues Villamil (1977: 60), 'the priorities may lie in the establishment of a national cultural policy aimed at creating a "feeling of nationhood", as Myrdal has called it'. Lacking a promising strategy to change 'external circumstances' (at least in short term), Bienefeld argued not to be too strict in what to expect from, or how to determine, a socialist alternative to capitalism. Is socialism only possible when the productive forces have been developed sufficiently? What are the minimum requirements for 'socialism'? Bienefeld (1981: 86) offers a pragmatic 'defensible version of dependency' which

> is based on the more plausible and less restrictive assumption that socialism could be regarded as a potentially desirable object of immediate political struggle in the context of many developing countries, not because it held out the promise of an immediate transformation to an ideal type of socialism, but because it raised the possibility that in spite of political weaknesses and obstacles a substantial increase in the social control exercised over the economic process could prove to be progressive [...]. In an international context this control would, of course, initially be exercised through the agency of the state, and its orientation would necessarily be based on some definition of a national interest. [...] [In the debate about 'the transition to socialism' the question should be asked] whether or not a greater degree of social control can be imposed on the development process through the mechanism of the state, and whether this control can be (or is being) exercised in the interests (short- or long-term) of the great majority of the members of that society.

Stöhr and Nohlen did not argue for socialist societies, although their approaches had certainly—as we have seen—anti-capitalist or post-capitalist elements, i.e. in opposition to many familiar notions of a capitalist mode of production, in terms of ownership, participation, distribution, allocation, competition, economic democracy, free trade, control of resources, planning of production, and the treatment of the natural environment. A transformation of the global or at least European (capitalist) mode of production seems to have been the ultimate aim of the European dependency school. In the absence of an immediate prospect of such a change, alternative national or regional development was their focus. A plan B suggests using the regional and national institutional framework to strive for an alternative development from below. The question is how to use regional room for maneuver politically and with what substance. The presented approaches of a 'European dependency school' suggest egalitarian (anti-racist) strategies: 'A self-reliant society is an inclusive, non-hierarchical society that stresses cooperation over competition, harmony with nature over exploitation, and social needs over unlimited personal desire. It represents the one best chance for the survival of the human race' (Friedmann 1986: 205). But how can such a self-reliant society be established? Only a few authors from the 'European dependency school' presented in this book did inquire into state theory or theory of democracy. Friedmann talked of subordinating the destructive 'economic space' to the 'life space' which would make necessary a reordering of values:

> Speaking practically, this means subordinating economic space to the political authority of the State. It means protecting the historical life space of cities, regions, and the nation from the blind incursions of capital. To extend this protection, the State must have control over the basic conditions of livelihood within a given territory, and exercise this power in the interests of the people as a whole. A State so inclined would have to rest on a very different base of power than at present. It would have to rest directly on the power of the people mobilised for a life in common in both their life space and their place of work. [...] If the State is to respond effectively to their needs, people must first reclaim their sovereign power by revitalising the political communities in which they live. Implied is a restructuring of institutions in the direction of self-management and greater local authority. (Friedmann 1983: 156)

Friedmann (1986: 205) distinguished, similar to Stöhr (see above), between 'endogenous or self-directed development' and 'self-reliant development', which he presupposed a radical political practice. The former was applicable only in regions 'at the crossroads of the global economy [...] based on large cities that function as world centers of control, production, and capital accumulation'. For peripheral regions, however, he (Friedmann 1986: 211f.) considered

> the route to an endogenous development within the mainstream of economic policy [...] virtually closed. It is a viable option only for world city regions that can use their countervailing power to negotiate with global capital and with the state for arrangements favourable to themselves or, to be more precise, to their political and economic elites. For world city regions, an endogenous development may be viewed as a resultant in the struggle between territorial and functional interests, with the latter in dominance. In this sense, it is a far cry from what some of its proponents mean when they speak of a development "from below"

Peripheral regions only had the alternative of self-reliant development: 'self-reliance does not appear as a question concerning the use of policy instruments by the state but as a form of radical social practice originating within civil society' (ibid.: 205), and 'which is thus much "from below"'. Hadjimichalis (1983: 137f.) envisaged social movements arising from the 'objective conditions of uneven regional development and subjective conditions of rising regional consciousness'.

Seers surely hoped for an electoral success of progressive parties who than should apply pragmatic policies. But he did not go into detail how such a success could be accomplished. Nohlen and Schultze (1985: 63cc.) perceived as an overall weakness of dependency theory the discrepancy between structuralist analysis of the causes of uneven development, and the capability to counter dependencies politically. Strategies for change were voluntaristic and suggested a room to maneuver that would not exist in a dependency perspective (if it assumed an external control of political decision-making). They draw on Macpherson (1977: 100, quoted in Nohlen and Schultze 1985: 50) when arguing a 'vicious circle of advanced capitalism': 'We cannot achieve more democratic participation without a prior change in social inequality and in consciousness, but we cannot achieve the changes in social inequality and consciousness without a prior increase in democratic participation'. Nohlen and Schultze (1985: 51c.) offer hypotheses for a new start of regional policy: (a) decentralist rather than centralized political systems; (b) forms of participation; (c) no sudden change or complete decoupling but a gradual transformation; (d) resistance of the political core can be overcome if issues of alternative regional policies can be made part of an overall political change in the countries collectively:

> The chance to implement regional centered policies depends on concept, form, and degree of participation. In order to realize them, traditional forms of political participation (representative democracy) do not suffice and neither does direct-democratic pure activism ["direktdemokratischer Aktionismus"]. Required are a double strategy in patterns of participation, participation as means and ends, as stake and social participation, conventional and unconventional forms, within and outside the institutional structure of politics. (Nohlen and Schultze 1985: 51)

Authors following the state theory of Nicos Poulantzas (as Hadjimichalis 1983, 1984) came to similar conclusions. Coming from the opposite of the political spectrum as Nohlen, Poulantzas criticized both the liberal parliamentary democracy and what he considered a Soviet-type parallel state:

> The essential problem of the democratic road to socialism, of democratic socialism, must be posed in a different way: how is it possible radically to transform the State in such a manner that the extension and deepening of political freedoms and the institutions of representative democracy (which were also a conquest of the popular masses) are combined with the unfurling of forms of direct democracy and the mushrooming of self-management bodies? (Poulantzas 2014: 256)

It is obvious that the European dependency school has provided rather defensive visions to counter transnational capitalism. Such alternative plans mostly focused on what was to be achieved and not how this was to be achieved. An inward looking policy was confronted with the problem of how to deal with regional or national elite that might see its own interest impaired in the wake of an overall egalitarian policy. Returning to academia from operational development work after almost a decade, Dudley Seers (1979 [1977]: 28) asked:

> Why should the elites be any more willing to co-operate in this sort of 'development', which would also deprive them of many of the goods and services they consider essential to being part of the modern world? Basically, the answer is that such a programme may appeal to what seems in many countries to be stronger than social conscience – nationalism. This may be more likely to outweigh short-term material interests, as is shown by wartime experience in many countries.

In his last book, Dudley Seers (1983) reissued a collection of essays he found most important under the title *The Political Economy of Nationalism*. What might seem like a strange title for a twenty-first- century framework (and probably sounded odd when the 'age of globalization'—a euphemism for TNC capitalism—was getting off) bears a couple of interesting considerations that could serve as departures for contemporary alternative policies. They also seem to fit into Edward Sojas conception of a 'combination and articulation of a horizontal (periphery vs. center) and vertical (working class vs. bourgeoisie) class struggle', we have talked about earlier.

We need to be aware, however, that Seers was writing in a Cold War-world, and that he was critical of both neoclassical liberal capitalism (including Keynesian capitalism that he considered a version of it), and state socialism. In the wake of an overwhelming transnational capitalism with increasing differentials in productivity, TNC retaliation was to be expected against regional or national policies that curbed TNC interest (Seers 1983: 59). Seers (1983: 55ff.) considered, however, nationalism as a way to react against an internationalism, as propagated by the superpowers United States and Soviet Union, that does harm to regional development. Since a government would not be able to simply opt out, he talks of 'room to maneuver' of a government, an 'area within which policy can be varied without the government incurring costs that are excessive in relation to the potential benefits' (Seers 1983: 55). Facing an international reality that a single government would not be able to change, Seers focused on a progressive and pragmatic approach to government policies which should intend to move to the left and to the south (toward or in the N-E quadrant) in Fig. 6.1. How far could it go without risking retaliation a country was not able to bear (which might lead to a coup d'état that would do physical harm to politicians and activists), or risking that the costs of alternatives would become excessive. Such pragmatic considerations address the gap between wishful electoral promises and the harsh reality of a limited room to maneuver. The available options are being assessed differently:

> [B]ureaucrats, for example, tend to exclude all possible policies outside a narrow range, whereas many academics assume policy to be largely or totally unconstrained. Differences over what governments should do are often really about what they can do. (Seers 1983: 56)

As can be seen in Fig. 6.1, Dudley Seers (1983: 47f.) offers an 'ideological map' that 'shall help us assess political information and theoretical developments, and tell friend from foe'. He goes beyond the conventional political left–right distinction (presented here on a horizontal axis between egalitarian and anti-egalitarian policies) and introduces a vertical axis of policies between nationalist and anti-nationalist. The ideology of the top right hand quadrant (AN-AE)

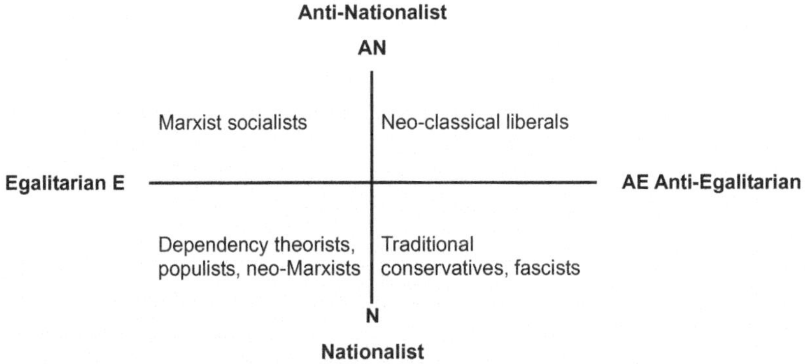

Fig. 6.1 Ideological map (*Source* Seers 1983: 48)

> is broadly compatible with the interests of the TNCs. It also suits local capitalists who are associated with them, and a small 'labour aristocracy' which is provided with relatively high wages and fringe benefits by capital-intensive technology. These classes have come to depend on the governments of the United States or Western Europe for military support and technological and cultural inspiration, and also slogans to legitimate their policy. Economic liberalism still serves this purpose. (Seers 1983: 48)

Seers (1983: 48) acknowledges currents of nationalism and elitism in socialist countries, however, '[i]n the Soviet bloc, Marxism still holds out to Communist parties and their sympathizers the goal of a socialist world order' (quadrant AN-E). In the bottom left (N-E) quadrant, Seers places Western European labor movements that are no longer convinced of Marxism but still are concerned with the inequalities produced by the Capitalist system. Dependency theorists also belong to this quadrant, as well as

> peasant movements [that] are better suited by something that is not only egalitarian but draws on national roots, like the forms of populism common overseas, especially in Latin America [...]. The 'social incentives' which are heavily emphasized by Marxist governments, in non-European countries (such as China and Cuba), can be interpreted as largely national incentives. (Seers 1983: 48f.)

Other programs of (especially large) non-European countries are being placed in the bottom right quadrant (N-AE) because

> a government may, in fact, not bother much in its day-to-day business about reducing inequality. Landowners and indigenous capitalists naturally prefer an anti-egalitarian ideology, but [...] not one that is internationalist. Significant parts of the bureaucracy and the armed forces also support ideologies in the same quadrant, together with some extremist religious groups, such as the Muslim Brotherhood. Like Fascist ideologists, despite egalitarian rhetoric they are basically hierarchical. (Seers 1983: 49)

Seers gives examples for alliances of parties or within parties that run counter the traditional search of coalitions in the immediate ideological neighborhood but the traditional left–right axis is not necessarily void as it was shown in the coalition against Chile's Allende government, consisting of the bottom and the top right quadrant. (Seers 1983: 187, endnote 2 of Chapter 2)

A section of Seers' book is dedicated to the constraints of nationalism (economic, political, social, and demographic realities, and the question of resources and technology). Liabilities are seen in a small population, serious ethnic division, geographic vicinity to a superpower, few natural resources, culturally subverted bureaucracy, high consumer expectations, and a narrow technological base. The economical neoclassic's ignorance toward food self-reliance (and using an alleged comparative advantage in the production of cash crops) is being seen particularly problematic. A declining demand for cash crops can lead to immediate problems in financing food imports. The current discussions on food sovereignty appear to be in the tradition of the dependency school arguments for food self-sufficiency as part of development planning (Seers 1983: 116). Further constraints of regional political economy are seen in energy policy and technology:

> Dependence on foreign investment and technology are among the main constraints on a government's room to manoeuvre. This need not be very damaging if they are carefully screened as part of a strategy of industrialization that reflects national interests and if the most appropriate technologies are drawn from the most appropriate sources. [...] Indeed, the initiative in technology transfer should lie with the host government. They should know what they want and where to get it – as Japanese officials did in the early stages of their highly professional industrial strategy: foreign businessmen with the presumption to take the initiative in Tokyo have faced the prospect of being delicately but forcefully snubbed. (Seers 1983: 81)

Seers considers careful planning of the industrial structure as essential for a development policy, incentives to attract technology might be costly. He sees strong dependence on TNC problematic because they have their own agenda, limit trade flexibility, and impair options of a national industrialization model according to the Japanese model. Technology in Seers' analysis is also important for military capabilities and a proxy for cultural dependency. As a classification for countries, Seers suggests using profiles of dependence instead of developed, centrally planned, and developing (Table 6.1).

Self-reliance is the priority in Dudley Seers' strategy for a nationalist political economy. It includes military considerations in order to be able to counter external threats. The room to maneuver is seen small but every government has policy options and needs to pursue a pragmatic policy. Establishing a unity in government (eliminating potential

Table 6.1 Illustrative profiles of dependence on key inputs (ca. 1980)

	Oil	*Cereals*	*Technology*[a]
Least Dependent			
(one I, two Es)			
United States	I	E	E
Soviet Union	E	I	E
Moderately Dependent			
(one I, one E)			
East Germany	I	O	E
West Germany	I	O	E
Britain	O	I	E
Argentina	O	E	I
Heavily Dependent			
(two Is)			
Japan	I	I	E
Kuwait	E	I	I
Nigeria	E	I	I
Thailand	I	E	I
China	O[b]	I	I
Most Dependent			
(three Is)			
Brazil	I	I	I
Cuba	I	I	I
Poland	I	I	I
Portugal	I	I	I
I = significant chronic imports;			
E = significant chronic exports;			
O = very roughly self-sufficient;			

Notes [a]Potentially a significant exporter
[b]Dependence on technology is sometimes measured by purchases of patents. However, a country with a high indigenous technological capacity (notably Japan) can, for that very reason, be a heavy purchaser of patents without losing its economic independence: technological capacity includes the ability to select whatever foreign inventions or innovations appear useful and to decide whether to buy patents. Here technological dependence is measured by net trade in machinery, transport equipment, and arms
Source Seers (1983: 83) (further classificatory remarks: 84ff.)

struggles between ministries) is essential as well as integrated development strategies. Especially left-wing governments need strict budgetary rules in order to avoid a deepening of dependencies (Seers 1983: 92f., 113 and 120ff.). Clearly Dudley Seers' indicators for 'profiles of dependence' needed to be adjusted to present day circumstances. The indicators seem to reflect Seers' writing in late 'Fordist' times, however, he made clear the importance of indebtedness for a country's dependence and room to maneuver, in the age of financialization an indicator reflecting financial dependence seems appropriate.

References

Amin, Samir. 1981. Some Thoughts of Self-Reliant Development, Collective Self-Reliance and the New International Economic Order. In *The World Economic Order: Past and Prospects*, ed. Sven Grassman and Erik Lundberg, 534–552. London and Basingstoke: Macmillan.

Bienefeld, Manfred. 1981. Dependency and the Newly Industrialising Countries (NICs): Towards a Reappraisal. In *Dependency Theory: A Critical Reassessment*, ed. Dudley Seers, 79–96. London: Pinter.

Bienefeld, Manfred. 1982. The International Context of National Development Strategies: Constraints and Opportunities in a Changing World. In *The Struggle for Development: National Strategies in an International Context*, ed. Manfred Bienefeld and Martin Godfrey, 25–64. Chichester et al.: Wiley.

Bienefeld, Manfred, and Martin Godfrey. 1982. Introduction. In *The Struggle for Development: National Strategies in an International Context*, ed. Manfred Bienefeld and Martin Godfrey, 1–24. Chichester et al.: Wiley.

Friedmann, John. 1967. *A General Theory of Polarized Development*. Santiago: The Ford Foundation: Urban and Regional Advisory Program in Chile.

Friedmann, John. 1983. Life Space and Economic Space: Contradictions in Regional Development. In *The Crises of the European Regions*, ed. Dudley Seers and Kjell Öström, 148–162. London and Basingstoke: Palgrave Macmillan.

Friedmann, John. 1986. Regional Development in Industrialised Countries: Endogenous or Self-Reliant? In *Self-Reliant Development in Europe: Theory, Problems, Actions*, ed. Michel Bassand, Ernst Brugger, John Bryden, John Friedmann, and Barbara Stuckey, 203–216. Aldershot: Gower.

Friedmann, John, and Clyde Weaver. 1979. *Territory and Function: The Evolution of Regional Planning*. London: Edward Arnold.

Galtung, Johan. 1983. *Self-Reliance. Beiträge zu einer alternativen Entwicklungsstrategie*, ed. Mir Ferdowsi. München: Minerva.

Hadjimichalis, Costis. 1983. Regional Crisis: The State and Regional Social Movements in Southern Europe. In *The Crisis of the European Regions*, ed. Dudley Seers and Kjell Öström, 127–147. London and Basingstoke: Palgrave Macmillan.

Hadjimichalis, Costis. 1984. The Geographical Transfer of Value: Notes on the Spatiality of Capitalism. *Environment and Planning D: Society and Space* 2 (3): 329–345.

Musto, Stefan. 1985. In Search of a New Paradigm. In *Endogenous Development: A Myth or a Path? Problems of Economic Self-Reliance in the European Periphery*, ed. Stefan Musto, 1–13. Tilburg: EADI (=European Association of Development Research and Training Institutes: EADI Book Series 5).

Nikolinakos, Marios. 1985. The Impossibility of Self-Reliance. In *Europe at the Crossroads: Agendas of the Crisis*, ed. Stefan Musto, and Carl Pinkele, 327–342. New York et al.: Praeger.

Nohlen, Dieter. 1985. Ungleiche Entwicklung und Regionalpolitik in Südeuropa (Italien, Spanien, Portugal). Eine Einführung. In *Ungleiche Entwicklung und Regionalpolitik in Südeuropa: Italien, Spanien, Portugal*, ed. Dieter Nohlen und Rainer-Olaf Schultze unter Mitwirkung von Wolfgang Merkel, 9–15. Bochum (=Politikwissenschaftliche Paperbacks 6).

Nohlen, Dieter, and Rainer-Olaf Schultze. 1985. Ungleiche Entwicklung und Regionalpolitik in Südeuropa. Externe Verursachungsdfaktoren und endogene Entwicklungschancen. In *Ungleiche Entwicklung und Regionalpolitik in Südeuropa: Italien, Spanien, Portugal*, ed. Dieter Nohlen and Rainer-Olaf Schultze unter Mitwirkung von Wolfgang Merkel, 17–73. Bochum (=Politikwissenschaftliche Paperbacks 6).

Palma, Gabriel. 1981. Dependency and Development: A Critical Overview. In *Dependency Theory: A Critical Reassessment*, ed. Dudley Seers, 20–78. London: Pinter.

Poulantzas, Nicos. 2014 [1978]. *State, Power, Socialism*. London and New York: Verso.

Seers, Dudley. 1979 [1977]. The Meaning of Development. With a Post Script. In *Development Theory: Four Critical Studies*, ed. David Lehmann, 9–30. London: Frank Cass.

Seers, Dudley. 1981. Development Options: The Strengths and Weaknesses of Dependency Theories in Explaining a Government's Room to Manoeuvre. In *Dependency Theory: A Critical Reassessment*, ed. Dudley Seers, 135–149. London: Pinter.

Seers, Dudley. 1983. *The Political Economy of Nationalism*. London et al.: Oxford University Press.

Stöhr, Walter. 1981. Development from Below: The Bottom-Up and Periphery-Inward Development Paradigm. In *Development from Above or Below? The Dialectics of Regional Planning in Developing Countries*, ed. Walter Stöhr and Fraser Taylor, 39–72. Chichester et al.: Wiley.

Stöhr, Walter. 1983a. Alternative Strategies for Integrated Regional Development. In *The Crisis of the European Regions*, ed. Dudley Seers and Kjell Öström, 6–14. London and Basingstoke: Palgrave Macmillan.

Stöhr, Walter. 1983b. Alternative räumliche Entwicklungsstrategien endogener 'selektiver Eigenständigkeit'. *Österreichische Zeitschrift Für Soziologie* 8 (3): 117–134.

Stöhr, Walter. 1985. Selective Self-Reliance and Endogenous Regional Development—Pre-conditions and Constraints. In *Ungleiche Entwicklung und Regionalpolitik in Südeuropa: Italien, Spanien, Portugal*, ed. Dieter Nohlen and Rainer-Olaf Schultze unter Mitwirkung von Wolfgang Merkel, 229–249. Bochum (=Politikwissenschaftliche Paperbacks 6).

Stöhr, Walter, and Franz Tödtling. 1979. Spatial Equity: Some Anti-thesis to Current Regional Development Doctrine. In *Spatial Inequalities and Regional Development*, ed. Hendrik Folmer and Jan Oosterhaven, 133–160. Boston, The Hague, and London: Nijhoff.

Szentes, Tamás. 1983. The TNC Issue: Naive Illusions or Exorcism and Lip-Service. In *Emerging Development Patterns: European Contributions*, ed. István Dobozi and Péter Mándi, 97–118. Selected Papers of the 3rd General Conference of EADI. Budapest (=EADI Book Series 1).

Villamil, José. 1977. Development Planning and Dependence. *IDS Bulletin* 9 (1): 57–61.

CHAPTER 7

Paradigm Lost? 'Endogenous Development' Replaces 'Selective Self-Reliance'

The European dependency school formulated progressive alternatives to hegemonic paradigms in development studies and economics. The dynamics of the era ending the bipolar world would turn, however, in a different direction, which captivated dependency authors but also left of center political parties. Already in 1994, Panitch (1994: 81f.) pointed out that most mainstream center-left parties subscribed to the (neoliberal) competitiveness paradigm by advancing 'a more progressive form' that, however, did 'not constitute much of an alternative':

> For a considerable period through the 1970s and well into the mid-1980s, a large part of the Left refused to acknowledge that the crisis of the Keynesian/welfare state was a structural one, pertaining to the very nature of capitalism and the contradictions it generates in our time. [...] But rather than allow bourgeois economists calling the tune with their neo-liberal logic of deregulation, free markets, privatization and austerity to dictate the terms of the race, a "progressive competitiveness" strategy is advanced by intellectuals on the Left (from social democratic to left-liberal to a good many erstwhile marxists) whereby labour and the state are urged to take the initiative and seize the hand of business in making the running toward competitive success.

This account is only partially true for the 'European dependency school'. As I have shown, authors form this school clearly challenged the structural crisis of capitalism in their Keynesian and neoliberal expression.

R. Weissenbacher, *The Core-Periphery Divide in the European Union*,
https://doi.org/10.1007/978-3-030-28211-0_7

They also formulated alternatives but defensively and skeptically. Since, in social science, a scientific revolution is rather consequence of a real life revolution, neoliberal counterrevolution succeeded Keynesianism and efforts of the dependency school were consequently forgotten. As for their further scientific work, the 'era of globalization' did not leave many of the European dependency scholars unimpressed. But this was true also among the Latin Americans.

'Globalization' was the name established for the 'new' dynamic that for many first also carried hope for progress. In this new era, a prominent member of the Latin American dependency school, Fernando Henrique Cardoso, argued, *all* the old theories and political concepts were useless. He broke with his critical past and entered a (successful) election campaign for the Brazilian presidency in 1994 (Fischer et al. 1999: 9). 'Globalization' led, however, to 'globalization crisis', the 'new' dynamic was increasingly seen critically and therefore often nicknamed '*neoliberal* globalization' (cf. Panitch et al. 2004, a very instructive compilation of critical essays on globalization published in the Socialist Register during the 1990s). Today any euphoria is gone, 'globalization crisis' belongs to the past, what is left of 'neoliberal globalization' is (neoliberal) capitalism with inherent crises.

As far as the 'European dependency school' is concerned, authors of the Binghamton network, subscribing to world-systems theory, had certainly no 'developmentalist illusions' and seemed better prepared to face a radicalization of the liberal paradigm in the 1990s. Scholars working with Arrighi's network connected directly to the Binghamton network in the 1980s and theorized the paradigmatic change as 'sudden change in the "rules of the game" [that] would play a key role in reconstituting the rattled foundations of the North-South wealth divide' (Arrighi et al. 2003: 20). Arrighi et al. (2003: 23ff.) did not adapt to the paradigmatic changes but theorized them (cf. also Arrighi et al. 1996). 'Structural mechanism did not operate in an ideological void' (ibid.: 23) they argued:

> Rather, they were shaped by beliefs and theories about the pursuit of national wealth in a global economy that channeled Third World development efforts in particular directions. These beliefs and theories were fundamentally contradictory because they reflected the hegemonic power's attempt to do two incompatible things – to accommodate Third countries' aspirations to catch up with the standards of wealth of First World countries, and to preserve standards of oligarchic wealth for itself and for its closest allies. From this point of view, the main difference between the

> pre-1980 and the post-1980 periods is that, while in the earlier period the need to accommodate Third World aspirations was predominant, in the latter period the need to preserve oligarchic wealth gained the upper hand. (ibid.: 23f.)

The concept of 'oligarchic wealth' in contrast to 'democratic wealth' was borrowed from Roy Harrod (1958):

> Democratic wealth is the kind of command over resources that, in principle, all can attain in direct relation to the intensity and efficiency of their efforts. Oligarchic wealth, in contrast, bears no relation to the intensity and efficiency of its recipients' efforts, and is never available to all because generalized attempts to attain it raise costs and reduce benefits for all actors involved. (Arrighi et al. 2003: 19)

The intense competition among peripheral and semiperipheral countries did prevent them from achieving similar wealth as in core countries (cf. the theoretical explanation in Chapter 3) but also undermined the industrial foundations of core countries (deindustrialization).

Overall the research networks of the 'European dependency school' seem to have discontinued their activities related to the dependency paradigm in the 1980s. Only single authors continued publishing critical accounts. I use again the two threads of the European dependency school, the more state level oriented EADI and the 'regionalists', in order to briefly—by using only a few examples—approximate what seems to have happened to researchers from these networks afterwards. The most prominent figure of the EADI branch of the 'European dependency school', Dudley Seers, had died in 1983. He had criticized international penetration and presumably would have been also a critic of 'globalization'. More than a decade later, in 1996, EADI was in the midst of the globalization discourse, holding its 8th conference (in Vienna) under the title: 'Globalisation, Competitiveness and Human Security: Challenges for Development Policy and Institutional Change'. In the following year, a selection of conference papers was being published in the European Journal of Development Research which had an eminent researcher of the Latin American dependency school as an editor: Cristóbal Kay (1997, cf. 1989). Regionalism was being newly defined. In the European Dependency school, the penetrating 'development from above' had been perceived as either coming from the state or interregional companies against peripheral (domestic) regions, or being directed from core states into peripheral states. Neatly fitting into the globalization discourse, Björn Hettne (1997: 83) from the EADI network, now argued 'that development theory as a state centric concern lacks relevance'. In order to regain explanatory relevance, development theory was to merge with International Political Economy (IPE). This should enable a compromise in the 'political rationality' between the fading Westphalian and the post-Westphalian world order in the making: 'A "post-Westphalian" logic rests on the [...] assumption that the nation state has lost its usefulness, and that solutions to emerging problems must increasingly be found in transnational structures' (Hettne 1997: 84). 'In terms of development principles', Hettne sees—adapting Friedmann and Weaver (1979)—a compromise between territory and function. Hettne calls these compromises 'new regionalism'. Many in the European dependency school had identified TNC as main actors penetrating peripheral regions or states, Friedmann and Weaver (1979: 171) saw them 'gaining in this contest for dominion'. In the globalization discourse, however, anonymous globalization often seems to have replaced actors responsible for the fact that function prevailed over territory. The attention shifted toward global governance necessary to counter negative effects. On the regional level 'a large number of different institutions, organizations, and movements'—and no longer states—are seen as 'actors behind regionalist projects' (Hettne 1997: 85). How these objectives were to be achieved, remained unexplained. Presumably drawing on his earlier work in the EADI network (cf. Hettne 1985), Hettne (1997: 85ff., 100ff.) uses elements from the European dependency school for the new regionalism such as 'from below' and the notion of some form of spatial closure ('similar to mercantilism'): 'Self-reliance is an old development goal which rarely proved viable on the national level. Yet it may be a feasible development strategy at the regional level if defined not as autarky but as coordination of production' (Hettne 1997: 100). While these concepts originally meant to counter penetration from TNC, international institutions, and state level government with an alternative paradigm, they were now being presented as remedy against 'globalization'. TNC could, therefore, be part of the solution, which opened the way for the 'competitive region'.

At the very same EADI conference, however, the 'decentralization discourse' that thought of the nation state as loosing importance, had been vehemently criticized by Frans Schuurman (1997): Decentralization had been put forward, he argued, as part of the attack against the Fordist state which aimed at deregulation of central governments and was spread to the periphery by what is today called Washington Consensus. However, some of the political left saw decentralization as a progressive political project (including municipal democracy and local government) which would counter negative effects of liberalism. Schuurman questions the 'decentralization euphoria', arguing that further fragmentation would make regions more vulnerable for international capital penetration. '[A]s long as the decentralization discourse contributes to hollowing out the state, and as long as there is no institutionalized social contract at the global and/or local level [as compared to the nation state], it is rather premature to parade decentralization as the Post-Fordist paradigm' (Schuurman 1997: 166). Already a couple of years earlier, Manfred Bienefeld (1994: 107) had deconstructed left-liberal notions of globalization. Like an echo of Dudley Seers' last book, he made the case for a 'positive nationalism':

> Competition cannot lead to true and sustained efficiency unless it is embedded in a social and political matrix that is capable of restraining the struggle for economic efficiency sufficiently, to allow society to make genuine choices trading off economic efficiency against other objectives like environmental protection, social cohesion, political stability or the ability to maintain full employment. But such choices can only be made within political entities with sufficient sovereignty to enforce them. Such entities are termed 'generic nation states' for the purposes of this discussion and they are an essential prerequisite for the efficient functioning of markets.

Also in the German Development Institute (GDI), the change in discourse was being reflected in the 1990s. In a study by GDI—'Global competition and national room for maneuver' (Eßer et al. 1996)—one of the key researchers who had done critical studies on European peripheral states and integration in the 1970s and 1980s (e.g. Eßer 1978a, b), now discussed globalization and competition (Eßer 1996). He observed a tendency toward globalization that put pressure on national actors but by the same token he refers to the ambivalence in interpretation (e.g. that critics perceived globalization short of being a myth). Eßer (1996: 1) recognizes 'not only a drive towards globalization. Rather, globalization, regionalization, transformation of the nation state and localization are interdependent and mutually reinforcing'. Most interesting, however, for our understanding of the remains of the European dependency school, is Eßer's (1996: 1) following statement: 'The national room for maneuver – to implement system alternatives to the general pattern "market economy and liberal democratic political order", or even a fundamentally different development of societies, is shriveled, probably not even longer existing'. Consequently he explores the options of states, which he considers still the most important level in decision-making, in the global competition.

Changing the old development paradigm and the capitalist mode of production had belonged to the agenda of the European dependency school. What is striking, however, is how the prevailing paradigm was being organized into a 'new competition paradigm'. Some elements of this new competition paradigm seem to echo dependency notions. The presentation of new concepts in international competitiveness by Hurtienne and Messner (1996) (cf. 39–59, as part of the GDI study) may help to explain why neoliberal concepts could attract heterodox economists and actors on the political left. First of all, 'one-dimensional and static neoclassical viewpoints of factor-based competitiveness and comparative advantages' had been given up in favor of 'a new dynamic and integrative perspective, that explained competitiveness by specific economic, social, cultural, and institutional circumstances of a country and understood development of competitive advantages as historical process' (Hurtienne and Messner 1996: 39). This approach was to be found in Michael Porter's classic of the genre ('The Competitive Advantage of Nations', 1990), which originated in his work for US president Ronald Reagan's 'President's Commission on Industrial Competitiveness' (1983–1985), and drew on experiences of *industrial districts* of the 'Third Italy' (Hurtienne and Messner 1996: 39).

Secondly, increasing competition had a polarizing effect, TNC privileged some national locations, and less attractive states were confronted with disintegrative tendencies. The answer was seen in regional agglomerations and clusters, they were to create 'virtuous circles of interaction between accumulation of physical capital, qualification of labor, technical accumulation and competitiveness of companies' (Hurtienne and Messner 1996: 52). The national production was to be shielded from globalization processes. State policy should provide cross-links between companies in order to avoid ruinous (international) competition. With such an economics of agglomeration, small companies could provide each other with the advantages big companies used internally.

Thirdly, small and medium enterprises were seen as new dynamic actors if they used 'economies of agglomeration' within regional clusters or industrial districts. Some authors even heralded the end of TNC. Having said that, the state was seen unable to create such competitive structures (only companies themselves could achieve that) but it could foster general conditions. Fourthly, sociocultural, noneconomic factors became important which respected different local actors: Such a 'cultural superstructure' creates social cohesion and a socioeconomic milieu that allows for a productive mix of cooperation and competition, and market and regulation. In the *districts*, company decisions become possible that need not obey short-term profit logics, but could also follow long-term interests of a region' (Hurtienne and Messner 1996: 58f.). In terms of industrial planning, fifthly, industrial districts were being presented as third way of regulation between market liberalism and state industrial policies. The magic concept seems to have been 'network structures'. The state receives the role as stimulator, coordinator, and moderator in a location policy oriented on dialogue. Local actors from companies, unions, and science are included in the decision-making process in order to spread relevant information and develop visions for the region. Companies in a cluster compete *and* cooperate: 'This *new competition* in networks is based on partnership, loyalty, common values and mutual trust, elements that seemed overcome in capitalism, but are of importance for the stabilization of flexible arrangements among companies in a cluster' (Hurtienne and Messner 1996: 59).

The 'regionalist' Walter Stöhr (2001: 37ff.), however, distinguishes between clusters and networks. Also referring to Porter—seemingly for the first time in his writings—as initiator of the cluster idea, Stöhr (2001: 38) assesses clusters as further development of the growth-center theory (which formerly had belonged to the development from 'above' paradigm and would increase polarization). 'Networks, in contrast, are not necessarily spatially determined' (ibid.), Stöhr as well presents them as harmonic and cooperative. 'Development from below' seems to have undergone a transformation from 'self-reliance', a more self-conscious and antagonistic alternative approach from the dependency school, to networks, an allegedly harmonic version of capitalism.

Originally, 'development from below' had been a broad alternative to (regional) development from above (and outside) that included competition, outside demand, and technological dependence. Selective self-reliance was seen to break existing patterns, with certain limitations as to a trade-off between sovereignty and technology and innovation—due to technological dependence (Stöhr 1981: 46).

Later Stöhr seems to have reformulated his development concepts 'from below', which, as he concedes, had been challenged regarding feasibility 'under present international conditions' (Stöhr 1990b: 22). The more radical development alternative 'self-reliance' seems to have disappeared from his texts during the 1980s. But 'endogenous development' prevailed as the pragmatic concept when regions needed to adapt to the international restructuring crisis starting in the 1970s. National governments, the OECD and the European Commission—which in his earlier work would have represented development institutions 'from above', now promoted 'endogenous development' themselves. Most often local initiatives were employment initiatives (Stöhr 1990c: 45ff.). It goes beyond the scope of this brief delineation as to clarify where the differences in the findings of Porter (1990: 155, 422) and Stöhr (1985: 22; 1987: 174) lie, who simultaneously drew for their analysis on the same research on the industrial districts of the *Third Italy*. Hadjimichalis (1994: 21) from the EADI network counts Stöhr to the 'proponents of the Third Italy model [that] follow two more or less clear political views of regional development'. Next to the neoliberal view, there is, 'for some radicals who appreciate many of the [...] neo-liberal points, a Proudhonian vision of successful craft production in SMEs providing jobs in non-hierarchical artisan groups'. Stöhr (1990a: 3), indeed, envisaged the social entrepreneur as actor for a regional resilience, as further elaborated by Johannison (1990: 61ff.) in the same volume: The social entrepreneur 'considers the development of the community as a primary personal goal', is perceived to belong to Friedmann's territorial strategy and aims at sustainability using 'economies of scope'. The 'autonomous entrepreneur' on the other hand 'considers the community as a means to personal goals', is part of the functional strategy, and aims at profitability using 'economies of scale'. Having said that, the language is reminiscent of the 'new regionalism' using the competition principle on regions (competitiveness) which was so aptly criticized by Gillian Bristow (2005, 2010). The quest for an alternative is being replaced by empowerment for self-assertion in competition. Stöhr (2001: 41) searches for 'comparative advantages of action at the local/regional level' (Stöhr 2001: 41). The development paradigm 'from above' is now 'central regional policy', the development paradigm 'from below' is now called 'local development action' (Stöhr 2001: 35f.). Selective self-reliance had disappeared from his analysis. The motive (why) for production (basic needs and self-reliance) was given up in favor of the organization (how) of production. Implicitly this production is export production, a regional 'bottom-up' development is being supported by national or supranational agencies (Stöhr 2001: 43f.)—which in the past had been seen as triggering 'development from above'. The key element of self-reliance, a selective spatial closure, seems now being replaced by subsidiarity, a social system structured from below:

> In practice, there are at least two interpretations of this concept: one maintains that each social level should take care of what it can do best, but at the same time, in a spirit of solidarity, it can rely on help "from above" if it cannot solve a problem [...]; and the other is more related to neoliberal thinking, and maintains that each individual and the lower social levels should fend for themselves, and the state and higher levels should exercise only a minimum of functions. [...] In the European context, it has been derived from catholic social philosophy [...]. (Stöhr 2001: 39)

The Maastricht Treaty had been criticized for being too centralist, bureaucratic, and distant from citizens, and therefore motivated widespread discussions of implementing the subsidiarity principle. Stöhr (2001: 40) seems to have sensed, however, that the EU applied the principle only where it wanted to avoid uniform standards.

Using concepts such as 'competitiveness' and 'comparative advantage', and counting on 'help from above' indicates that Stöhr belonged to those who had arrived in the mainstream of regional development. Lastly, it had been an idealized version of (regional) capitalism that seems to have built the case of networks and clusters. With the benefit of hindsight, the traps of the 'long' globalization decade seem easy to discern. But there were authors within the discussed networks that were early aware of false promises and paradigmatic changes: next to (the already discussed) Schuurman (1997), Bienefeld (1994), Friedmann (1986), and particularly Costis Hadjimichalis should be mentioned. '[S]ince the mid 1980s', Hadjimichalis and Papamichos (1990: 181, 184, and 187) argued (referring to Stöhr, Musto and others),

> the combination of 'development-from-below' theories with certain success stories of local capitalist development, have generated widespread beliefs that alternative policies promoting indigenous local development based on SMEs would diffuse growth potentials like those in Third Italy all over southern Europe [...]. 'Local development' thus became the new

> catch phrase, a new kind of development doctrine during a period of great financial difficulties on the part of the central state. As in the past with other catchy ideas, 'local development' has rapidly spread among technocrats, politicians and local authorities as a new doctrine of development. The emphasis, however, was still on industrialization, which now will take place via SMEs in rural areas or in small and medium towns. These 'local areas' will take advantage of existing local skills and networks and, if properly helped and guided, will develop following a different path from known big scale industrial projects in growth poles. In this growing euphoria, very few are interested what 'local' really means or how autonomous an industrial sector can be in a EC competitive framework.

Hadjimichalis and Papamichos (1990: 189, 203) are particularly critical of the widespread use of the experience of the Third Italy as a model for other Southern European regions. A criticism, Hadjimichalis (2006: 82f.) later advanced more: He was puzzled that 'radical theorists and researchers', who had discovered in industrial districts 'a localized development model, which permits regions to again become global players', did 'succumb to the charms of grand narratives, even when they strongly argue for the need to pay attention to differences and to local processes'. Using 'Third Italy' as example, his account reads as deconstruction of the industrial district as a (general) model. He puts emphasis on specific forms of workers' expropriation (e.g. working and safety conditions, low payment, working hours, informal sector) in the industrial districts as part of the international division of labor (competition) and global production chains (subcontracting) supported by the state (tax legislation, protectionism). What had been there in economic success deteriorated in the 2000s due to world recession (before the crisis that began 2007/8!), monetary union (which ended the option of depreciating currencies), and expiration of multi-fiber agreement (ended core protectionism in textile sector). While Italian companies shifted their production abroad, (formal and informal) immigrants took over employment in the low wage and informal sectors (cf. also Hadjimichalis and Hudson 2014). Hadjimichalis and Papamichos (1990: 204), however, early sensed the danger of an alternative development vision being turned into a liberal strategy (of a competitive region):

> Above all, local development seems to be of high priority among neo-liberals in the EC inspired by Thatcherite policies [...]. [T]hey prefer "local areas" to compete freely among themselves for resources, investment, jobs

and prosperity, as individual firms do in the "free" market. It seems therefore, that European integration will strengthen such views among rightist governments, and what today appears as a trivial development alternative could be developed to an offensive rightist strategy in a few years.

The neoliberal concept of the 'competitive region' could therefore embed fragments of the European dependency school that in its political conclusion had envisaged a regional alternative to global/European capitalism. Lastly, such neoliberal policies also advanced the European disintegration process, as Hadjimichalis (1994: 26f.) argues: Policy-makers from Germany, the Netherlands, and the UK resisted a 'proposal for the Integration Fund' for 'interregional transfer payments in order to alleviate persistent and new regional disparities. Instead, they preferred 'local areas' to compete freely among themselves'.

References

Arrighi, Giovanni, Beverly Silver, and Benjamin Brewer. 2003. Industrial Convergence, Globalization, and the Persistence of the North–South Divide. *Studies in Comparative International Development* 38 (1): 3–31.

Arrighi, Giovanni, Roberto Korzeniewicz, David Consiglio, and Timothy Moran. 1996. Modeling Zones of the World Economy: A Polynomial Regression Analysis (1964–1994). Paper Presented at the 1996 Annual Meeting of the American Sociological Association, New York, NY.

Bienefeld, Manfred. 1994. Capitalism and the Nation State in the Dog Days of the Twentieth Century. *Socialist Register 1994: Between Globalism and Nationalism*, ed. Ralph Miliband and Leo Panitch, 94–129. London: Merlin.

Bristow, Gillian. 2005. Everyone's a 'Winner': Problematising the Discourse of Regional Competitiveness. *Journal of Economic Geography* 5 (3): 285–304.

Bristow, Gillian. 2010. *Critical Reflections on Regional Competitiveness: Theory, Policy and Practice*. London et al.: Routledge (=Routledge Studies in Human Geography 31).

Eßer, Klaus. 1978a. Industrie- und teilindustrialisierte Länder in der Europäischen Gemeinschaft. In *Europäische Gemeinschaft und südeuropäische Beitrittsländer*, ed. Klaus Eßer et al. Berlin, 47–72 (=Schriften des Deutschen Instituts für Entwicklungspolitik (DIE) 54).

Eßer, Klaus. 1978b. Tendenzen regionaler Entwicklung in den Beitrittsländern. In *Europäische Gemeinschaft und südeuropäische Beitrittsländer*, ed. Eßer, Klaus et al. Berlin, 147–166 (=Schriften des Deutschen Instituts für Entwicklungspolitik (DIE) 54).

Eßer, Klaus. 1996. Nationaler Handlungsspielraum durch systematische Wettbewerbsfähigkeit. Einleitung. In *Globaler Wettbewerb und nationaler Handlungsspielraum: Neue Anforderungen an Wirtschaft, Staat und Gesellschaft*, ed. Klaus Eßer et al., 1–28. Köln: Weltforum.

Eßer, Klaus, et al. (eds.). 1996. *Globaler Wettbewerb und nationaler Handlungsspielraum: neue Anforderungen an Wirtschaft, Staat und Gesellschaft*. Köln: Weltforum.

Fischer, Karin, Andreas Novy, and Christof Parnreiter. 1999. Globalisierung und Peripherie. In *Globalisierung und Peripherie*, ed. Karin Fischer, Andreas Novy, and Christof Parnreiter, 9–33. Frankfurt/Main: Brandes & Apsel and Südwind, (=Historische Sozialkunde 14).

Friedmann, John. 1967. *A General Theory of Polarized Development*. The Ford Foundation: Urban and Regional Advisory Program in Chile. Santiago.

Friedmann, John. 1986. Regional Development in Industrialised Countries: Endogenous or Self-Reliant? In *Self-Reliant Development in Europe: Theory, Problems, Actions*, ed. Michel Bassand, Ernst Brugger, John Bryden, John Friedmann, and Barbara Stuckey, 203–216. Aldershot: Gower.

Friedmann, John, and Clyde Weaver. 1979. *Territory and Function: The Evolution of Regional Planning*. London: Edward Arnold.

Hadjimichalis, Costis. 1994. The Fringes of Europe and EU Integration: A View from the South. *European Urban and Regional Studies* 1 (1): 19–29.

Hadjimichalis, Costis. 2006. The End of Third Italy as We Knew It? *Antipode* 38 (1): 82–106.

Hadjimichalis, Costis, and Nicos Papamichos. 1990. 'Local' Development in Southern Europe: Towards a New Mythology. *Antipode* 22 (3): 181–210.

Hadjimichalis, Costis, and Ray Hudson. 2014. Contemporary Crisis Across Europe and the Crisis of Regional Development Theories. *Regional Studies* 48 (1): 208–218.

Harrod, Roy. 1958. The Possibility of Economic Satiety—Use of Economic Growth for Improving the Quality of Education and Leisure. In *Problems of United States Economic Development*, ed. Committee for Economic Development, vol. 1, 207–213. New York: Committee for Economic Development.

Hettne, Björn. 1985. Development Theory and the European Crisis. In *Endogenous Development: A Myth or a Path? Problems of Economic Self-Reliance in the European Periphery*, ed. Stefan Musto, 41–71. Tilburg: EADI.

Hettne, Björn. 1997. Development, Security and World Order: A Regionalist Approach. In *European Journal of Development Studies* 9 (1): 83–106.

Hurtienne, Thomas, and Dirk Messner. 1996. Neue Konzepte internationaler Wettbewerbsfähigkeit in Industrie- und Entwicklungsländern. In *Globaler Wettbewerb und nationaler Handlungsspielraum: neue Anforderungen an Wirtschaft, Staat und Gesellschaft*, ed. Klaus Eßer et al., 39–72. Köln: Weltforum.

Johannison, Bengt. 1990. The Nordic Perspective: Self-Reliant Local Development in Four Scandinavian Countries. In *Global Challenge and Local Response: Initiatives for Economic Regeneration in Contemporary Europe*, ed. Walter Stöhr, 57–89. London, New York, and Tokyo: Mansell Publishing and United Nations University.

Kay, Cristóbal. 1989. *Latin American Theories of Development and Underdevelopment*. London and New York: Routledge.

Kay, Cristóbal. 1997. Introduction: Globalisation, Competitiveness and Human Security. *European Journal of Development Studies* 9 (1): 1–6.

Panitch, Leo. 1994. Globalisation and the State. In *Socialist Register 1994. Between Globalism and Nationalism*, ed. Ralph Miliband, and Leo Panitch, 60–93. London: Merlin.

Panitch, Leo, et al. (eds.). 2004. *The Globalization Decade: A Critical Reader*. London: Merlin.

Porter, Michael. 1990. *The Competitive Advantage of Nations*. London et al.: Macmillan.

Schuurman, Frans. 1997. The Decentralisation Discourse: Post-Fordist Paradigm or Neo-liberal Cul-de-Sac? *European Journal of Development Research* 9 (1): 150–166.

Stöhr, Walter. 1981. Development from Below: The Bottom-Up and Periphery-Inward Development Paradigm. In *Development from Above or Below? The Dialectics of Regional Planning in Developing Countries*, ed. Walter Stöhr and Fraser Taylor, 39–72. Chichester et al.: Wiley.

Stöhr, Walter. 1985. Industrial Structural Change and Regional Development Strategies. Towards a Conceptual Framework. Paper presented at the joint UNIDO/IGU Symposium on Regional Development Processes/Policies and the Changing International Division of Labour, Vienna, August 20–24, 1984. Wien (=IIR Discussion 21).

Stöhr, Walter. 1987. Regional Development Strategies and the Spatial Division of Labour. In *International Economic Restructuring and the Regional Community*, ed. Herman Muegge and Walter Stöhr with Paul Hesp and Barbara Stuckey, 167–179. Aldershot et al.: Avebury.

Stöhr, Walter. 1990a. Synthesis. In *Global Challenge and Local Response: Initiatives for Economic Regeneration in Contemporary Europe*, ed. Walter Stöhr, 1–19. London, New York, and Tokyo: Mansell Publishing and United Nations University.

Stöhr, Walter. 1990b. Introduction. In *Global Challenge and Local Response: Initiatives for Economic Regeneration in Contemporary Europe*, ed. Walter Stöhr, 20–34. London, New York, and Tokyo: Mansell Publishing and United Nations University.

Stöhr, Walter. 1990c. On the Theory and Practice of Local Development in Europe. In *Global Challenge and Local Response: Initiatives for Economic*

Regeneration in Contemporary Europe, ed. Walter Stöhr, 35–45. London, New York, and Tokyo: Mansell Publishing and United Nations University.

Stöhr, Walter. 2001. Subsidiarity: A Key Concept for Regional Development Policy. In *New Regional Development Paradigms. Vol. 3. Decentralization, Governance, and the New Planning for Local-Level Development*, ed. Walter Stöhr, Josefa Edralin, and Devyani Mani, 35–51. Westport: Greenwood Press in cooperation with the United Nations Centre for Regional Development (=Contributions in Economics and Economic History 225).

CHAPTER 8

Persistent Core–Periphery Divide in the EU

While the globalization decade steamrolled the European dependency school, enlargements of what became the European Union (EU) added to existing polarization in the European integration process. Already in 1990, the German Democratic Republic (GDR) was the first country of Eastern enlargement, when the former Eastern European core country experienced a peripheral integration into the Federal Republic of Germany (FRG) as workbench for West German companies. The other Central and Eastern European Comecon States lived through a transformation crisis and entered the EU at the peripheral end of the hierarchy in 2004 and 2007, similarly the former Yugoslav republics of Slovenia and Croatia entered the EU in 2004 and 2013. The small island states Malta and Cyprus entered the EU in 2004 and became special places in the EU financial markets. Already in 1995, core countries Austria, Finland, and Sweden had left the European Free Trade Association (EFTA) in order to join the EU.

In this chapter, I am going to suggest a core–semiperiphery–periphery typology for the contemporary EU from a dependency perspective. If one compares recent estimates of regional inequality in the EU by Eurostat (2018a, n.y.3) with the incomplete egg of core regions in Europe by Dudley Seers in 1979 (Chapter 3.4), then one can see that the egg shape was depleted or deformed. Much of France and (Southern) England lies below the average EU-28 level of GDP per capita at PPS (cf. Fig. 8.1) and most of the new member regions that entered the EU in the 2000s remain far behind outside (Eurostat, n.y.3). The extreme outliers are the

R. Weissenbacher, *The Core-Periphery Divide in the European Union*,
https://doi.org/10.1007/978-3-030-28211-0_8

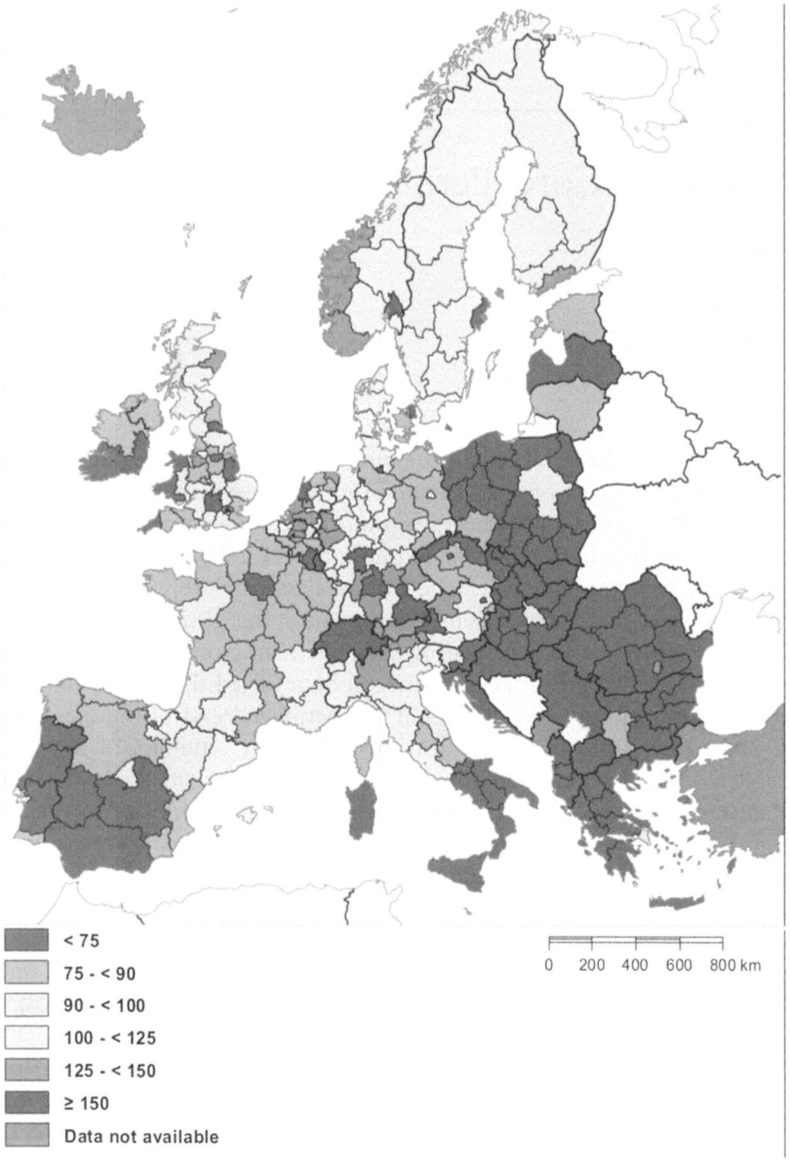

Fig. 8.1 GDP per inhabitant 2016, based on data in purchasing power standards (PPS) in relation to the EU-28 average, EU-28 = 100), NUTS 2 regions (*Source* Eurostat, n.y.3)

regions Severozapaden in Bulgaria with 29% of the EU28 average and Inner London in the United Kingdom with 611% in 2016 (Eurostat 2018a). While Fig. 8.1 displays a category larger than 150% of the EU28 average, however, the category 'smaller than 75%' of EU28 average does not tell the whole story of polarization toward the bottom: 21 of the EU regions even remain underneath the 50% margin, Bulgaria reaches 49% as a country average, Romania 58%, and Croatia 60% (ibid.). The inquiry in the next subchapters aims at a more systematic analysis of core–periphery relations in the contemporary EU.

8.1 Core–Semiperiphery–Periphery in the Contemporary European Union

This inquiry into a typology of current EU core–periphery relations follows the considerations of EDS authors outlined in Chapter 3. I will stick to a narrow set of economic indicators that are economistic compared to the broader discussions on social and development indicators in the 1970s and 1980s. Such economic indicators are closer connected, however, to the mode of discussions in recent decades, and may offer a view on EU fragmentation by traditional means. They will certainly challenge approaches that see remedy in industrial policies without questioning the mode of production.

In a conventional way, economic convergence is measured by beta- and sigma-convergence. The former tries to capture whether there is a 'catching-up' process between low- and high-income countries by means of higher economic growth, while the latter 'refers to a reduction in the dispersion of income levels across economies' (ECB 2015: 31). The ECB (2015: 31) argues that 'real convergence mainly pertains to the [beta]-dimension of convergence, with [sigma]-convergence being a by-product; sustainable convergence is the key precondition for economies that are catching up to be resilient to shocks'. Other authors stress the importance of Sigma-convergence 'because it speaks directly as to whether the distribution of income across economies is becoming more equitable' (Young et al. 2008: 1084) and 'that the concept of Sigma-convergence is more revealing of the reality as it directly describes the distribution of income across economies without relying on the estimation of a particular model' (Monfort 2008: 5). Calculations that use Sigma-convergence usually observe statistical variations among the EU28 or EU15 groups; EuroStat presents data that refer to EU28 = 100 (cf. Fig. 8.1) or EU15 = 100.

For my presentation of a typology, I will also use a model of income distribution across economies. Consequently, I am not interested in estimating the actual living situation of people in the core and periphery of the EU, but the (relative) relations between core and periphery and their change over time. Furthermore, I am interested in the level of industrialization in these economies. I will follow the methodical and theoretical model of Arrighi and Drangel (1986) and Arrighi et al. (2003), which I have outlined in Chapter 3.3, in the attempt to estimate core–periphery relations in the EU at the country level. Other than typical data presentations that relate countries to the average of a sample, I will, therefore, relate EU countries to the EU core.

While Arrighi et al. (2003) used the OECD 'convergence club' as the core proxy, they relate the periphery and the semiperiphery to, I will use the undisputed core country of Europe, Germany, as the sole EU core reference (Germany = 100). Germany certainly has core characteristics different from the United States, and therefore the interpretation in terms of industrialization will differ somewhat. The main argument of deindustrialization, however, seems to hold for both Germany and the United States, according to the data I used. If one takes 1960 = 100 as base line, then the share of manufacturing industry in all branches (gross value added) as proxy for industrialization will start to show declining values no later than the 1970s (Tables 8.1 and 8.2). It will not be a surprise that these data suggest a lead by Transnational Companies (TNC) from the United States—as compared to those from Germany—in the outsourcing process toward the (semi)periphery. The widening of the gap between the United States and Germany slowed down in the 1990s, when the German economy was faced with the integration of Eastern Germany.

Table 8.1 Share of manufacturing industry (UVGM) in all branches (UVG0)—gross value added at current prices, ECU/Euro, for the United States and Germany (1960 = 100)

	1960–1969	*1970–1979*	*1980–1989*	*1990–1999*	*2000–2009*	*2010s**
Germany#	99	93	84	67	61	63
USA	99	86	72	63	51	47

Germany#: before 1991: Western Germany
2010s*: Germany: 2010–2016, USA: 2010–2014; Averages over decades, for detailed information on data and sources see Table 8.8

Table 8.2 Share of manufacturing industry (UVGM) in all branches (UVG0)—Gross value added at current prices, ECU/Euro, for the United States and Germany (Germany = 100)

	1960–1969	*1970–1979*	*1980–1989*	*1990–1999*	*2000–2009*	*2010s**
Germany#	100	100	100	100	100	100
USA	74	68	64	70	60	55

Germany#: before 1991: Western Germany
2010s*: Germany: 2010–2016, USA: 2010–2014; Averages over decades, for detailed information on data and sources, see Table 8.8

However, the German 'wage-dumping policy' (Flassbeck and Spiecker 2011), which brought the German economy a significant competitive edge, seems to have stopped deindustrialization. One could read the confrontational protectionist policies by the Trump administration as a reaction to a weakening of US control of global TNC capitalism, with its commodity chains (CC). The obvious difference between the United States and Germany (in the data presented) is the higher share of industrialization of the smaller and more export-oriented German economy in all available data.

The main objectives in this chapter are, however, to find a working classification of the core–periphery system in the EU, and the importance of industrial policies for convergence and cohesion if the logic of TNC capitalism remains unaltered. I will suggest a contemporary core–periphery system of the EU at the national level. The GNI per capita (PPS) considers income from residents of one country that is earned in other countries and subtracts domestic income by nationals from other countries. PPS is an artificial common currency that respects countries' different price levels (cf. Eurostat, n.y.1&2). I used the data on GNI per capita (PPS) provided by the AMECO database (EU Commission, n.y.). Data for EU15 are available from 1960 and data for EU28 from 1990. I related the data to Germany = 100 and used an average over each available decade (cf. Table 8.3).

Arrighi and Drangel (1986) worked within the world system and CC. Their assessment aimed at a working scheme for the global level. Following the dependency paradigm and staying geographically in Europe, particularly the EU, I was interested whether there could be a three-tier system observed in the EU as well. As we have seen

Table 8.3 Gross national income (GNI) at current prices per capita (PPS) Germany = 100 (average over decades)

Country	1960-1969	1970-1979	1980-1989	1990-1999	2000-2009	2010-2018
Bulgaria*	...	...	...	22	30	37
Romania	...	...	...	21	29	44
Croatia*	...	...	...	36	46	46
Latvia	...	...	...	28	40	50
Poland**	...	...	...	32	42	52
Hungary****	...	...	...	38	47	52
Lithuania***	...	...	...	28	42	56
Estonia****	...	...	...	28	45	57
Greece	56	77	69	68	77	57
Slovakia****	...	...	...	38	49	60
Portugal	38	46	46	61	67	60
Czech Rep.	...	...	...	57	63	64
Slovenia	...	...	...	58	70	65
Cyprus	...	...	...	68	75	67
Malta**	...	...	...	59	65	68
Spain	56	64	59	69	82	72
Italy	73	79	83	92	93	78
UK	90	79	73	84	97	85
France	76	83	82	89	95	86
Finland	67	73	79	82	98	90
Belgium	81	87	86	96	102	95
Germany#	**100**	**100**	**100**	**100**	**100**	**100**
Ireland	57	58	55	73	101	101
Austria	79	87	88	99	105	101
Sweden	104	100	94	95	107	101
Denmark	92	89	85	93	104	103
Netherlands	95	96	87	99	115	104
Luxembourg	99	102	115	154	166	143

Source Own calculations based on data from the AMECO database: http://ec.europa.eu/economy_finance/ameco/user/serie/SelectSerie.cfm
Data sorted by last decade, Germany = 100; # Before 1991: Western Germany
Grey: Enlargements from EU15 to EU28
*1990–1999: Average of 1995–1999, **1990–1999: Average of 1991–1999, ***1990–1999 Average of 1993 and 1995–1999, ****1990–1999: Average of 1993–1999

in Chapter 3.3, Arrighi and Drangel (1986) actually suggest a three-tier system, plus a perimeter of the periphery and a perimeter of the core. There would be candidates for Arrighi and Drangel's (1986) perimeters (of the periphery and of the core) also in the EU (Slovakia and the Czech Republic in the 1990s/2000s, and Ireland and Finland [1990s] or Spain and Italy [2000s], respectively). With a much more limited data set than Arrighi and Drangel (1986) and Arrighi et al. (2003), however,

Table 8.4 EU28 core–semiperiphery–periphery in the 1990s (GNI per capita)

Core	Austria, Belgium, Denmark, Finland, France, Germany, Italy, Luxembourg, Netherlands, Sweden, UK
Semiperiphery	Czech Republic, Cyprus, Greece, Ireland, Malta, Portugal, Slovenia, Spain
Periphery	Bulgaria, Croatia, Estonia, Latvia, Lithuania, Hungary, Poland, Romania, Slovakia

Table 8.5 EU28 core–semiperiphery–periphery in the 2000s (GNI per capita)

Core	Austria, Belgium, Denmark, Finland, France, Germany, Ireland, Italy, Luxembourg, Netherlands, Sweden, UK
Semiperiphery	Czech Republic, Cyprus, Greece, Malta, Portugal, Slovenia, Spain
Periphery	Bulgaria, Croatia, Estonia, Latvia, Lithuania, Hungary, Poland, Romania, Slovakia

Table 8.6 EU28 core–semiperiphery–periphery in the 2010s (GNI per capita)

Core	Austria, Belgium, Denmark, Finland, France, Germany, Ireland, Luxembourg, Netherlands, Sweden, UK
Semiperiphery	Czech Republic, Cyprus, Italy, Malta, Slovenia, Spain
Periphery	Bulgaria, Croatia, Estonia, Greece, Latvia, Lithuania, Hungary, Poland, Portugal, Romania, Slovakia

I intend to stick to a three-tier system between EU core and EU periphery and try to explain some of the special cases. The data, indeed, suggest a three-tier system in the EU. I use the upper three quintiles of GNI per capita (100=Germany) to approximate core=81–100, semiperiphery=61–80, and periphery=41–60 (For data basis in Tables 8.4, 8.5, and 8.6; see Table 8.3).

For the 1960s, this three-tier system seems very pronounced among EU15 (Table 8.3, Fig. 8.2: squares). The core countries group in the top of the top quintile: Sweden (ahead)–Germany–Luxembourg–the Netherlands–Denmark–UK. Finland, Italy, France, Austria, Belgium seem to form a semiperipheral group (Belgium already looming into the core area). Portugal (far behind), Greece, Spain, and Ireland pool in the third quintile (cf. the historical data with Tables 3.1, 3.2, and 3.3 in Chapter 3).

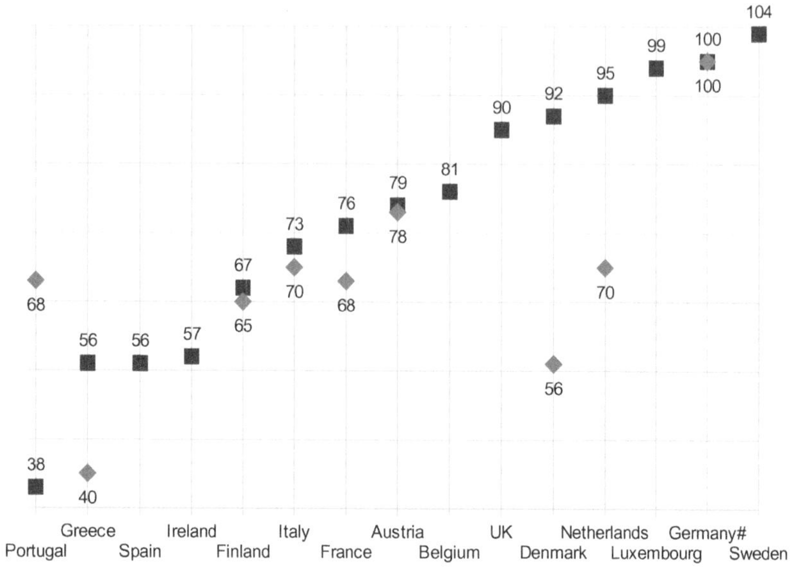

Fig. 8.2 GNI per capita (squares) and manufacturing industry (diamonds), 1960–1969 (Germany = 100) (*Sources and data information* for GNI per capita see Table 8.3, and for the share of manufacturing see Table 8.8. #: Western Germany, no data (diamonds) for Belgium, Ireland, Luxembourg, Spain, Sweden, UK)

In the 1970s, more countries join the top quintile (Table 8.3, Fig. 8.3: squares). The core group consists of a 'hard core' with Luxembourg, Sweden, Germany, possibly the Netherlands, plus behind: Denmark, Belgium, Austria, and barely: France. UK declined to the semiperiphery (fitting Seers' observation in Chapter 3). Italy, in this context, had not yet but almost reached core status, followed by Greece (surprisingly) and Finland. Spain could be counted to the semiperiphery in a strict quintile system but seemed still closer to the periphery: Ireland, and still far behind: Portugal.

In the 1980s, Luxembourg went through the roof and starts distorting the charts. It is not displayed in Fig. 8.4 (but cf. Table 8.3). ECB (2015: 32) is arguing its decision to exclude Luxembourg 'because GDP per capita computations are distorted by the high number of cross-border workers'. But one could add that Luxembourg controls a disproportionately high share of global/European CC and certainly has a most

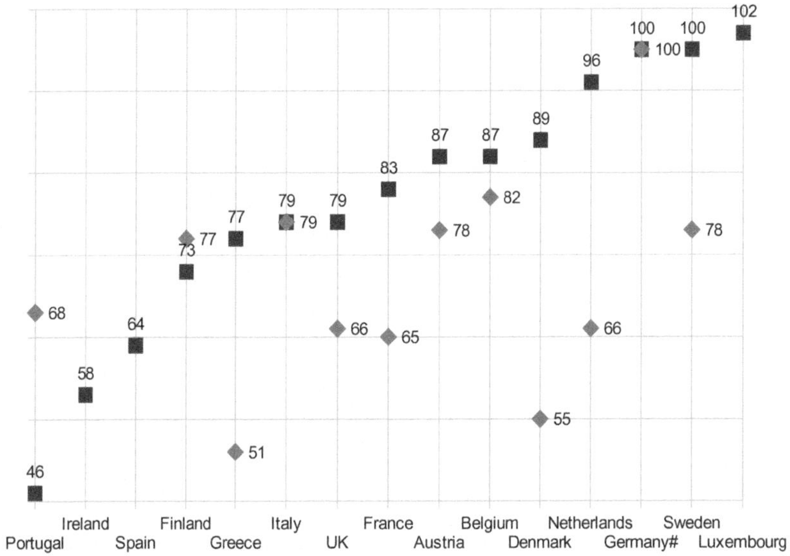

Fig. 8.3 GNI per capita (squares) and manufacturing industry (diamonds), 1970–1979 (Germany = 100) (*Sources and data information* for GNI per capita see Table 8.3, and for the share of manufacturing see Table 8.8. #: Western Germany, no data (diamonds) for Ireland, Luxembourg and Spain)

pronounced financial industry which also might contribute to that high number. I will return to that question later. With the exceptions of the special case Luxembourg, newly arrived core member Italy, and Austria, the core countries lost against the German position in the 1980s. In the semiperiphery, UK further lost ground, and Greece declined again. Only Finland gained momentum. Spain returned as a 'true' member to the peripheral group.

While the 1960s had been the last decade of the postwar boom, and the 1970s and 1980s saw the first two global recessions after World War II, the **1990s** were the decade of transformation and transition in the countries of the former integration model COMECON and Yugoslavia. Germany's political economy had to digest the integration of Eastern Germany which was also the first Eastern Enlargement of the EC/EU. The relative weakness of the German political economy sent Luxembourg

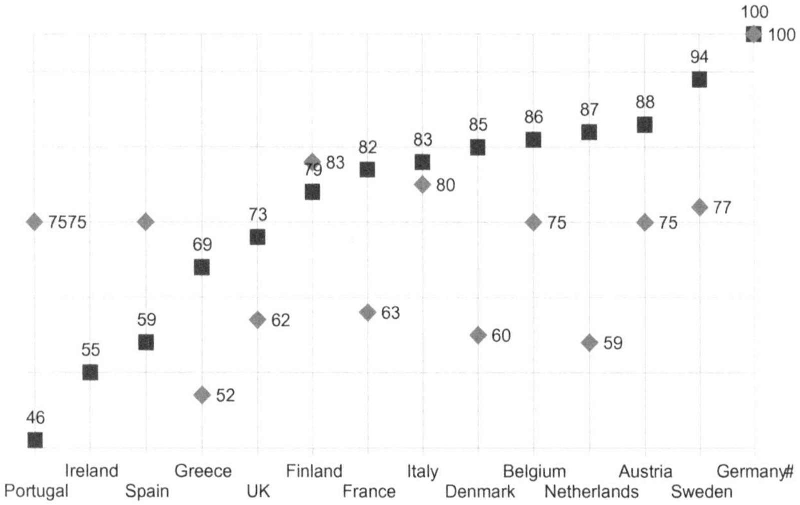

Fig. 8.4 GNI per capita (squares) and manufacturing industry (diamonds), 1980–1989 (Germany = 100) (*Sources and data information* for GNI per capita see Table 8.3, and for the share of manufacturing see Table 8.8. #: Western Germany, no data (diamonds) for Ireland, Luxembourg: not displayed, because of extreme data (squares: 115, diamonds: 68))

further through the ceiling of Fig. 8.5 (squares) and is therefore invisible (but cf. Table 8.3). Furthermore the hard core came close to Germany (The Netherlands, Austria, Belgium and Sweden). The core quintile (81–100, Germany=100) was very heterogeneously stretched, Finland making it into the group and the UK returned. France and Italy gained ground to the Scandinavian and Central European hard core.

Strictly adhering to the quintile system, the periphery of EU15 made it to the semiperiphery but with Portugal only looming into the group and lagging behind. With the available data for the EU28 group, however, the picture changes considerably, mirroring the transformation depression. The Czech Republic and Slovenia are the only two from the former COMECON/YU group that 'entered' Western integration in the upper level of the 41–60 periphery group. They are, however, much closer to the laggard of the semiperiphery (Portugal) than the far behind rest of the group: The transformation depression seems to have produced a new periphery, below the periphery quintile of EU15.

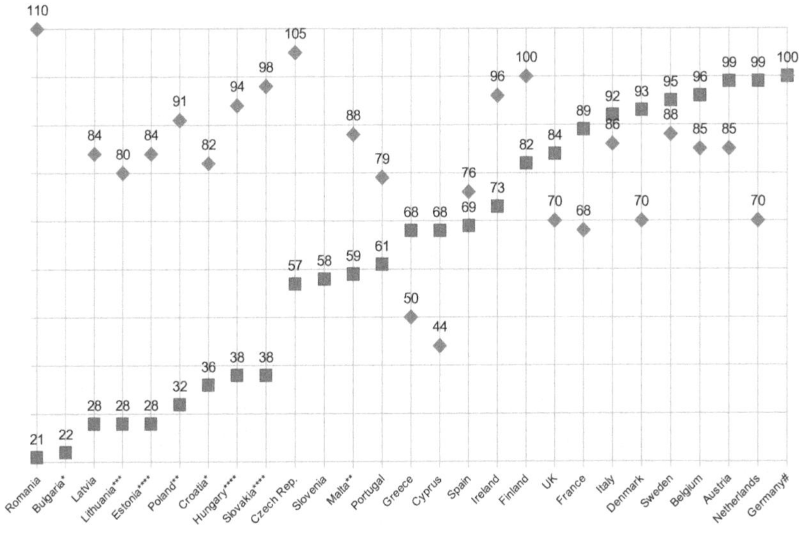

Fig. 8.5 GNI per capita (squares) and manufacturing industry (diamonds), 1990–1999 (Germany = 100) (*Sources and data information* for GNI per capita see Table 8.3, and for share of manufacturing see Table 8.8. #: before 1991 Western Germany, Luxembourg: not displayed, because of extreme data (squares: 154, diamonds: 57))

I interpret the better position of the Czech Republic and Slovenia by their histories as industrial centers of other integrations models, Habsburg, COMECON, Yugoslavia (cf. Seers in Chapter 3.7, Weissenbacher 2005, 2007). Malta and Cyprus—Mediterranean islands, former British protectorates, parts of the British Commonwealth, and special places for the EU financial markets, are grouped between Portugal and Slovenia, and with Greece, respectively (cf. Fig. 8.5).

Figure 8.6 (squares) displays a distinct three-tier system for EU28 in the **2000s years**, with two countries (Bulgaria and Romania) lagging far behind. Again, Luxembourg is not visible (extreme data) and also the Netherlands seem to follow suit. The hard core had overtaken Germany, followed by Ireland, the case of which we need to explain later. Finland and UK come close to Germany followed by France and Italy. There is a large gap between Italy and Spain, which could, with a strict adherence

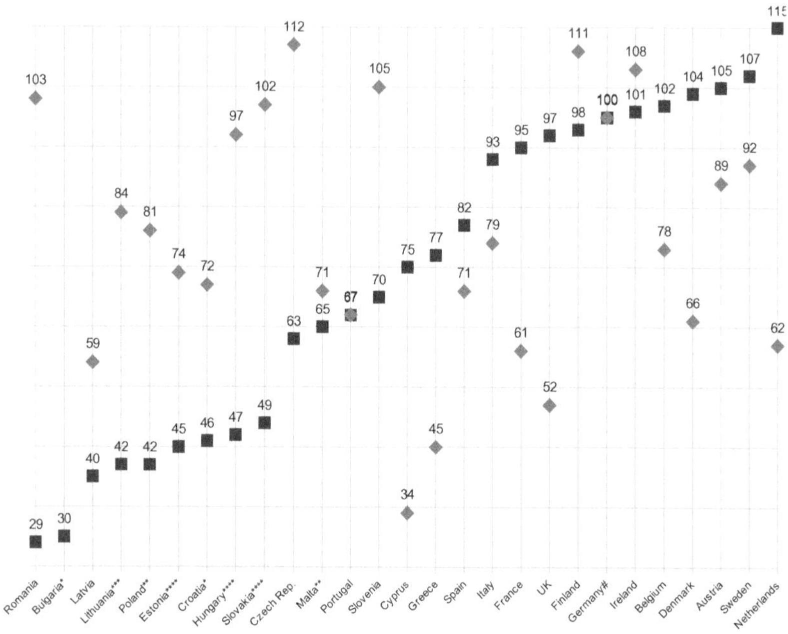

Fig. 8.6 GNI per capita (squares) and manufacturing industry (diamonds), 2000–2009 (Germany = 100) (*Sources and data information* for GNI per capita see Table 8.3, and for share of manufacturing see Table 8.8. Luxembourg: not displayed, because of extreme data (squares: 166, diamonds: 40))

to the quintile system, be counted to the core but seems to lead the semiperipheral group, followed by Greece down to the Czech Republic. There is also a large gap between the Czech Republic and Slovakia, which leads the peripheral group. If Spain is counted toward the semiperipheral group, only special case Ireland marks a change to the decade before (Figs. 8.5, 8.6 and 8.7).

In the **current decade**, the consistent hard core countries (except Belgium) plus Ireland still score higher than Germany (cf. Tables 8.3 and 8.7). Belgium has lost ground, and so did Finland, France, and the UK. Italy even dropped to the semiperiphery, which it leads followed by Spain down to the Czech Republic. Portugal lost and Slovakia gained, both appear as a crossover (perimeter?) between semiperiphery and periphery,

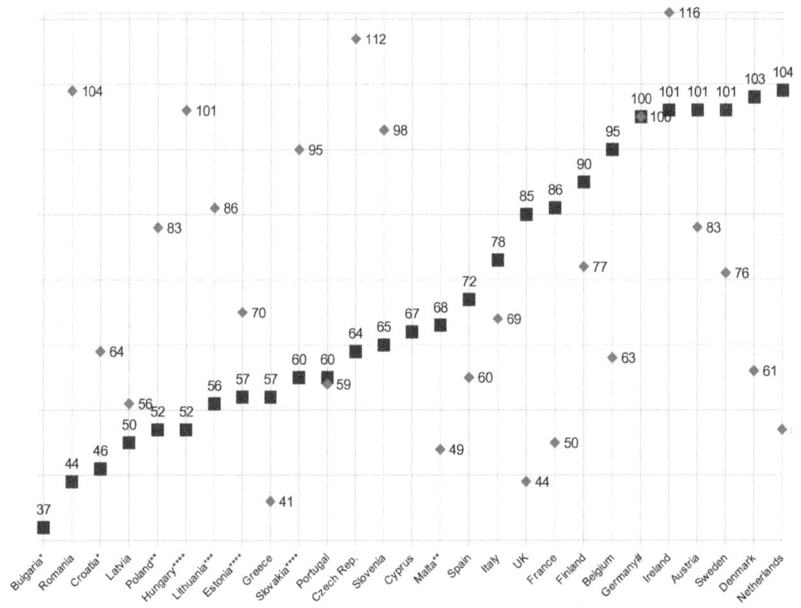

Fig. 8.7 GNI per capita (squares) and manufacturing industry (diamonds), 2010–2016/18 (Germany = 100) (*Sources and data information* for GNI per capita see Table 8.3 and for share of manufacturing see Table 8.8. Luxembourg: not displayed, because of extreme data (squares: 143, diamonds: 24))

which is led by Greece and Estonia (which have declined from their previous positions) down to Romania and far behind: Bulgaria. Tables 8.3 and 8.7 offer a synopsis. Most of the countries are 'organic members' as Arrighi and Drangel (1986) put it, of their group during the observation period, and therefore their overall classification fits their historical record. According to the AMECO data, Greece started as a periphery and wound up as a peripheral country, again. The GNI per capita increase that suggested a rise to semiperiphery (of EU15/EU28) seem somewhat a surprise, especially if we look at the share of manufacturing in total gross value added over the entire observation period (Table 8.8). I ranked Greece therefore as periphery. Slovakia has risen to the threshold between periphery and semiperiphery but if it really advances to the semiperiphery, remains to be seen. The historical data suggest an overall

Table 8.7 Core–semiperiphery–periphery typology for EU28

Country	1960-1969	1970-1979	1980-1989	1990-1999	2000-2009	2010-2018	Total
Bulgaria	x	x	x	P	P	P	P
Romania	x	x	x	P	P	P	P
Croatia	x	x	x	P	P	P	P
Latvia	x	x	x	P	P	P	P
Poland	x	x	x	P	P	P	P
Hungary	x	x	x	P	P	P	P
Lithuania	x	x	x	P	P	P	P
Estonia	x	x	x	P	P	P	P
Greece	P	SP	SP	SP	SP	P	**P**
Slovakia	x	x	x	P	P	**P**	P
Portugal	P	P	P	SP	SP	**P**	**P**
Czech Rep.	x	x	x	**SP**	SP	SP	SP
Slovenia	x	x	x	**SP**	SP	SP	SP
Cyprus	x	x	x	SP	SP	SP	SP
Malta	x	x	x	**SP**	SP	SP	SP
Spain	P	**P**	P	SP	**SP**	SP	SP
Italy	SP	SP	C	C	C	SP	**SP**
UK	C	SP	SP	C	C	C	**C**
France	SP	C	C	C	C	C	C
Finland	SP	SP	SP	C	C	C	C
Belgium	**SP**	C	C	C	C	C	C
Germany	C	C	C	C	C	C	C
Ireland	P	P	P	SP	C	C	**C**
Austria	SP	C	C	C	C	C	C
Sweden	C	C	C	C	C	C	C
Denmark	C	C	C	C	C	C	C
Netherlands	C	C	C	C	C	C	C
Luxembourg	C	C	C	C	C	C	C

Countries sorted by last decade, Germany = 100 (cf. Table 8.3); before 1991: Western Germany; Grey: enlargements countries post EU15; Bold letters: Czech Republic, Slovenia, and Malta could be counted to the periphery in 1990–1999 as could Belgium to the core in 1960–1969, but this would not change the overall assessment. For all the other bold letters see explanations above

peripheral classification. Similarly I ranked Portugal, which reached the threshold by a recent decline, as a peripheral country. Spain had loomed into the core before it declined. A treatment as semiperiphery seems justified. Italy remains the commuter between core and semiperiphery, the perimeter of the core. Recent tendencies in the Italian political economy suggest a characterization as semiperiphery for the time being. UK seems to have had recovered from semiperipheral status but recent developments also suggest a decline. I will keep UK in the core group although there is reason to believe that this might change in a not too distant future. We will return to the Irish case in the following chapter.

Table 8.8 Share of manufacturing industry (UVGM) in all branches (UVG0)—Gross value added at current prices, ECU/Euro (Germany=100)

Country	1960-1969	1970-1979	1980-1989	1990-1999	2000-2009	2010-2016
Cyprus5	...	...	...	44	34	22
Luxembourg3	...	...	68	57	40	24
Greece	40	51	52	50	45	41
UK	...	66	62	70	52	44
Malta5	...	...	...	88	71	49
France	68	65	63	68	61	50
Netherlands1	70	66	59	70	62	52
Latvia6	...	...	...	84	59	56
Portugal	68	68	75	79	67	59
Spain	...	...	75	76	71	60
Denmark2	56	55	60	70	66	61
Belgium8	...	82	75	85	78	63
Croatia5	...	...	...	82	72	64
Italy8	70	79	80	86	79	69
Estonia4	...	...	...	84	74	70
Sweden	...	78	77	88	92	76
Finland	65	77	83	100	111	77
Austria	78	78	75	85	89	83
Poland6	...	...	...	91	81	83
Lithuania5	...	...	...	80	84	86
Slovakia4	...	...	...	98	102	95
Slovenia7	...	...	...	118	105	98
Germany*	**100**	**100**	**100**	**100**	**100**	**100**
Hungary7	...	...	...	94	97	101
Romania9	...	...	...	110	103	104
Czech Rep.	...	...	...	105	112	112
Ireland	...	...	...	96	108	116

Source Own calculations based on data from the AMECO database: http://ec.europa.eu/economy_finance/ameco/user/serie/SelectSerie.cfm

*Before 1991: Western Germany; data sorted by last decade; grey: enlargements countries post EU15. Strictly adhering to a three-tier system (upper three quintiles of Germany = 100), the middle frame distinguishes a typology of industrialization: countries with a high level of industrialization (higher than 80), medium level (61–80), and low level (60 and lower)

Data limitations: 1: 1960s = 1969, 2: 1966–1969, 3: 1985–1989, 4: 1993–1999, 5: 1995–1999, 6: 1992–1999, 7: 1991–1999, 8: 2010–2015, 9: 1995–1999, 2010–2014; No data for Bulgaria

Gross value added equals output valued at basic prices less intermediate consumption at purchasers' prices. Gross value added includes consumption of fixed capital. Manufacturing industry: Nace Rev. 1 D

8.2 A Ladder Without Upper Rungs: Commodity Chains and the Confusion of Industrial Development with Development

Following Arrighi and Drangel (1986), as we have seen in Chapter 3.3, industrial production lost its core characteristics in the 1960s. This is pretty much in line with the ever more pronounced 'new international division of labor' that brought an outsourcing and reorganization of production from the core to the (semi)periphery, especially with the crisis of the 1970s. Consequently, TNC strategy has changed the focus from organizing production (industrialization) in the territories/jurisdictions of the countries of their home bases to controlling (production in) the CC. It is important to remember that it is not territories and their governments or jurisdictions that control CC but core TNC. If I use the spatial expression of control by core countries, it will be used as proxy for the symbiosis the core TNC developed with core territories/jurisdictions they use as home bases. Historical experience saw a rather persistent divide between core and periphery which is also reflected in the dataset for the EU. Furthermore, research by UNCTAD (2013: 122) suggests that 80% of world trade is organized by TNC in CC, and about 60% of global trade consists of intermediate goods and services. Beginning with the millennium, 'global trade and FDI have both grown exponentially, significantly outpacing global GDP growth, reflecting the rapid expansion of international production in TNC-coordinated networks' (ibid.). As far as the core–periphery distribution of such activity in commodity chains is concerned, the predominant share of investments still stems from what UNCTAD considers 'developed world'. Judged by the global invested stock (FDI outward stock in Million US dollar), 79.15% of total 23,592,739 million US dollar originated in the developed world (41.69% EU, 22% USA) in 2012. In order to get an idea of the EU situation: out of the total EU FDI outward stock of 9,836,857 million US dollar, 0.44% originated in Greece, 0.72% in Portugal, 6.38% in Spain, and 15.73% in Germany in 2012. Also high shares in global FDI inward stock suggest that much of commodity chain activity still is a core countries' agenda: 62.34% (UNCTAD 2013: 217).

These data seem to confirm the thesis by Arrighi's research groups that it is the control of commodity chains and not the geographical place of the production that matters. The TNC-core region symbiosis makes sure that 'brain activities' are being concentrated in core states, while the 'muscle-and-nerve activities' are predominantly reserved for (semi) peripheral states (cf. Chapter 3.3). Upgrading a state's position appears difficult, Arrighi talked of a 'developmentalist illusion'. Arrighi et al. (2003) related changes in (semi)peripheral industrial production and income levels to a core OECD 'convergence club' and found that there was convergence in industrial production while the 'North-South divide' persisted.

In my inquiry, I use the undisputed European core country Germany as reference for changes in industrial production and income levels per capita. With the latter, we have already seen that there were some fluctuations. During the observation period, however, the three-tier system showed remarkable persistence against the pretense of the overall core integration model of EU28, which is convergence and cohesion. The matter of industrialization directly concerns the political economy of the EU and immediate economic policy. Can reindustrialization or more industrialization (more industrial production) in the EU (semi)periphery bring development or convergence? The findings of the Arrighi research groups suggest that even if one called climbing the ladder in this hierarchy development such 'development' was unlikely.

In order to numerically estimate the EU situation in terms of industrialization, I used the share of manufacturing industry in all branches (gross value added) at current prices (expressed in ECU/Euro) as proxy for industrial development or level of industrialization, and related each country to Germany (=100, cf. Table 8.8). I averaged the yearly data (where available from the AMECO database) over decades. The interpretation of the findings necessarily varies from Arrighi et al. (2003). They used the OECD convergence club and marked the deindustrialization of these core countries as an important reduction in the industrialization gap: the core deindustrialized and the (semi)periphery industrialized. I do not treat groups of countries but rather single countries, and the reference country is Germany, the industrial export champion. But the deindustrialization process of core countries can still be reproduced with these data. If we take the core countries of Table 8.7 plus Italy (and without Ireland, which will be explained later) than we will get the following picture (in Table 8.8): Luxembourg deindustrializes from the 1980s (no earlier data) to the 2010s. Belgium, Denmark, France, Italy, the Netherlands, and UK deindustrialize vis-à-vis Germany from the 1960s to the 2010s (UK data: from 1970s), with one important exception: the 1990s. I interpret the 1990s as the decade which statistically reflects the integration of the former GDR into the Federal Republic (first eastern enlargement of the EC/EU), a process which temporarily weakened the German economy. For Austria, Finland, and Sweden, this comparative recovery of industrial production vis-à-vis Germany lasted into the 2000s.

In the Southern EU (semi)periphery, Greece and Portugal did participate in the industrialization process of the overall (semi)periphery, according to these data, until the 1980s, but the accession to the EC/EU as 'unequal partners' stopped the process, unsurprisingly so if one follows the analysis of authors from the European dependency school. Data for Spain start in the accession decade, and if one takes the 1990s as the German decade of 'weakness', then we can see immediate deindustrialization.

The data for the EU28 start with the 1990s. If one compares Tables 8.3 and 8.8, the difference is striking. While in Table 8.3, which represents a proxy for hierarchies of wealth, the grey rows (enlargement countries after EU15) are grouped at the 'peripheral' side, the tendency in Table 8.8, with a proxy for industrialization, shows a different story. These countries are grouped with the core country, Germany. Furthermore, if we assume, for the sake of the argument, a strict three-tier system following these industrialization data (a three-tier system of the three upper quintiles of Germany = 100, sorted from bottom to top, cf. Table 8.8), then the current decade would find this typology: **countries with high levels of industrialization** (higher than 80) are Austria, Poland, Lithuania, Slovakia, Slovenia, Germany, Hungary, Romania, Czech Republic, Ireland; **countries with medium levels of industrialization** (61–80): Denmark, Belgium, Croatia, Italy, Estonia, Sweden, Finland; **countries with low levels of industrialization**: (60 and lower): Cyprus, Luxembourg, Greece, UK, Malta, France, the Netherlands, Latvia, Portugal, Spain.

The strong industrialization data of the former COMECON countries and Slovenia arguably could look back at a legacy of industrial production in a different integration model and 'started' in Western statistics with high levels of industrialization. Slovenia, the Czech Republic, and even Romania enter the AMECO data in the 1990s with shares of manufacturing production in overall gross value added that lie above the German level (cf. Fig. 8.5: diamonds). But these countries entered Western European integration after a political-economic shock, the waves of which are felt until today. Before the transformation depression, Arrighi and Drangel (1986: 70) list Hungary, Romania, the USSR, and Yugoslavia among the global semiperiphery in the 1960s, and between 1975 and 83, respectively, alongside with Greece. As far as the European political-economic relations are concerned, Dudley Seers had sketched, as we have seen in Chapter 3.7, a core–periphery system for the Eastern integration model in Europe. Similar to Britain, Finland, and Italy, he perceived Czechoslovakia, Hungary, and Poland in an intermediate position even if (as he observed) social conditions and income showed more similarities with the periphery of Western Europe. Also, Seers considered Bulgaria and Romania more peripheral in their economic structure, income level, and social conditions already in the Eastern integration model. Basically, further research would have to focus on the different core–periphery systems and their effects on countries, and their consequences for transition and transformation. This would have to include revisiting the investigation on the nature of the state socialist countries as indicated in Chapter 2.5. For our purpose, the analysis of the integration model EU, one could assume that without the transformation depression the wealth gap between the Southern European (semi)periphery and the new (semi)periphery might not have been so severe (cf. Fig. 8.5). The existing industrial structure seems to have partly survived and was integrated into the Western (European) commodity chains.

Unsurprisingly, the countries Stöllinger (2016) calls the 'Central European (CE) manufacturing core' (Germany, Austria and the Viségrad countries Czech Republic, Hungary, Poland, and Slovakia) are among the 'countries with a high level of industrialization' in our typology. It also indicates the Austrian dependence on Germany. Austria's FDI stocks balance had only turned positive recently, due to its engagement in the production networks with the regional EU enlargement countries which joined in 2004 (Table 8.11, cf. Becker et al. 2015). Stöllinger (2016: 803) starts, however, with general assumptions that the Arrighi research groups (discussed above) had rejected for core countries (and accepted for semiperipheral and peripheral countries only): '[We] will consider a decline in the value added share of the manufacturing sector as an adverse structural shift for an economy'. Stöllinger (2016: 804) is here drawing, however, on literature which was written in a time when industrial production was still considered a 'core activity' by the Arrighi research group:

> Closely related to our work is Chenery (1960) who links manufacturing value added per capita, i.e. manufacturing intensity in several manufacturing industries to domestic supply and demand conditions which are proxied by income per capita. He finds a positive relationship between manufacturing intensity and income per capita for all industries. (Stöllinger 2016: 804)

For Arrighi's research groups, industrial production had ceased to be the characteristic core activity (in core territories) in the 1960s, and upward shifts by industrialization processes were seen as being possible, afterwards, above all within the group of peripheral and semiperipheral countries. Stöllinger (2016: 806f.) presents literature that considers consequences of CC participation as possible in either direction, catching-up or increasing uneven development. 'Offshoring' of production from the core is on Stöllinger's (2016: 805) radar, but he does not focus on explaining why it is possible for countries to maintain their core status despite the fact that the

> flip side of this agglomeration of manufacturing activities in the CE manufacturing core is a significant decline in the share of EU manufacturing value added exports in other EU Member States, in particular in high-income countries including the Nordic and the Benelux countries and above all France and the United Kingdom. (Stöllinger 2016: 814)

The evidence presented in this book suggests that the observations of the Arrighi research groups for the capitalist world system are also true for the EU, namely that it is the ability to control TNC commodity chains that enables a core status to prevail, or, in other words, that 'core activity' goes well beyond organizing manufactured production on countries' own territories. For all (semi)peripheral countries except Greece, the convergence in industrial production is much more pronounced than the income situation (for Portugal, the situation seems more balanced). The situation of the semiperipheral countries Cyprus, Malta, Italy, and Spain will be explained below. For all core countries except the special case of Ireland, the situation is the other way round, as convergence in industrial production is well below the income situation. Ireland is an example of the phenomenon of extreme financialization, part of which was a domestic loan expansion due to cheap credit, made possible by Ireland's entry to the Eurozone. Mortgage debt more than trebled from 2002 (47.2 billion euro) to the onset of the crisis of 2008 (139.8 billion euro) (Wickham 2012: 66ff.). As far as manufacturing production is concerned, the dependence of the Irish economy on TNC is seen as a weakness, part of which 'is the practice of transfer pricing whereby the foreign-owned companies tend to inflate the value of their output in the Irish economy in order to avail of the state's low tax on manufacturing profits' (Kirby 2010: 22). Irish data for manufacturing in the AMECO database start with the 1990s, with an already high percentage that would overtake the German level in the following decade. The 2010s seem to surpass the industrial success story of Finland, but not as pronounced regarding the income situation. Italy's progress in manufacturing industry (according to these data) does not show such massive jumps and also loses out in the 2000s. Italy has never reached the per capita income levels of Finland and Ireland (compared to Germany = 100) and loses massively in the 2010s. For our purpose, the success stories and the upward shift to the core are particularly interesting. Following the model of Arrighi's research groups, industrialization ceased to be a characteristic of core countries in the second half of the 1960s. If this is true also for the EU (the overall core integration model), we would therefore expect that additional efforts in industrialization would—in optimal cases—lead to upward movement among peripheral and semiperipheral countries, but not to the shift of a semiperipheral country to the core. If we take the core countries of the 1970s, namely Austria, Belgium, Denmark, France, Germany, Luxembourg, The Netherlands and Sweden, and compare them to the core countries of the 2010s, then there are three countries that have entered the core zone: Finland from the semiperiphery, UK reentering from the semiperiphery, and, surprisingly, Ireland marching through from the periphery. Additionally, we will keep Italy on the radar, because it seems to have reached the perimeter of the core, and then the core, by 'traditional' core means, namely industrialization.

The striking issue (but not a surprise following Arrighi's working groups) is that, with a few exceptions, the 'convergence' to the German level (Germany = 100) on part of the (semi)peripheral countries is higher, in many cases very much higher, in terms of industrial production (Table 8.8), than the 'convergence' in the income level (Table 8.3). The exceptions are Greece and Cyprus, Malta in the 2000s, and Spain, beginning with the 2000s. I interpret the Spanish situation with the 'pseudo boom' that poured foreign capital into the economy's non-tradable sector (cf. Becker and Weissenbacher 2014). All in all, there is a trend that supports the Arrighian notions: (a) industrial production ceased to be a core characteristic; (b) the core countries keep the core status by controlling the global (European) commodity chains; (c) core TNC are able to control and exploit manufacturing production in the periphery and semiperiphery. We will discuss these aspects in a moment.

8.3 State Governments and TNC

In order to further establish this argument, I suggest using additional indicators. I use—taking from the OECD database on outward activities of TNC (OECD, cf. Table 8.9)—(a) the figures of TNC in the manufacturing sector (of all available country data) in the EU28 area, and (b) the turnover of these TNC in the EU28 area in 2014. I use these data (cf. Table 8.9, Figs. 8.8 and 8.9) as a proxy for the extent of control of European commodity chains. I took into account the size of countries and therefore calculated a TNC per capita amount and a TNC turnover per capita amount (Euro millions at current prices). In order to make these data comparable with the data of GNI per capita and share of manufacturing industry, I, again, related them to Germany (=100), therefore they do not represent absolute numbers.

These data seem to confirm the Arrighian thesis of control of European commodity chains versus productive activity in the manufacturing sector (Figs. 8.8 and 8.9). For most core countries, the number of TNC with outward activities in the EU28, as well as their turnover (both per capita), are above or at least around the level of GNI income per capita (compared to Germany=100), while the share of manufacturing production lies below the comparative income level. Some countries are extreme (top: Luxembourg with 1012 TNC per capita and a TNC turnover per capita of 1966, both compared to Germany=100). Only Ireland, Italy (which has lost its core position), and the UK (which might again lose its core position again) are exceptions to this overall core trend. The opposite is true for (semi-)peripheral EU countries. The GNI income per capita is below the share of manufacturing production (with the exceptions mentioned above), but above the number of TNC per capita, as well as their turnover per capita levels. These data paint an intense picture of the core–(semi)periphery situation in the EU. The status of the core means the control of TNC and European commodity chains. This is very clear in the cases of the hard core (Austria, Belgium, Denmark, Germany, Sweden) and also Finland. It seems to explain the persistent role of France despite its weaker GNI per capita positions. But what about Ireland? And the seemingly weakened Italy and UK? Also, the Netherlands are not included (no data). And we need to explain more the—at first glance—somewhat surprising positions of Cyprus and Malta (which may be historically explained by their British legacy).

Table 8.9 Outward activities in manufacturing of TNC in the EU28 area by available country in 2014, number of companies and turnover in Euro millions at current prices (Germany = 100)

Country	TNC per capita	TNC Turnover per capita	2010-2018 GNI/capita	2010-2016 share of manufacturing industry
Latvia	26	...	50	56
Estonia	138	...	57	70
Slovakia2	40	3	60	95
Greece	17	5	57	41
Czech Republic3,4	23	5	64	112
Poland4	12	8	52	83
Slovenia	108	9	65	98
Spain	24	11	72	60
Portugal1	30	13	60	59
Hungary4	6	19	52	101
Italy	142	39	78	69
United Kingdom4	76	64	85	44
Ireland	101	88	101	116
Germany	**100**	**100**	**100**	**100**
Belgium	186	105	95	63
France	185	125	86	50
Austria	261	157	101	83
Finland	436	195	90	77
Denmark4	381	198	103	61
Sweden4	733	225	101	76
Luxembourg	1012	1966	143	24

Sorted by TNC turnover per capita

1 Average of 2013 and 2014 in the columns TNC per capita and TNC Turnover (very divergent data)

2 TNC per capita: average of 2013 and 2014 (very divergent data)

3 Turnover: average of 2013 and 2014 (very divergent data)

4 Average exchange rate to the Euro 2014: Zloty: 4.1843, Swedish Krona: 9.0985, Pound Sterling: 0.80612, Forint: 308.71, DK Krone: 7.4548, Czech Koruna: 27.536

Years for population data: 2015: Latvia; 2014: France, Ireland, Slovenia, Spain, UK; 2013: Austria, Estonia, Finland, Germany, Hungary, Italy, Portugal, Slovakia, Sweden; 2012: Luxembourg

Source OECD database, http://stats.oecd.org, outward activity of multinationals by country of location—ISIC Rev. 4, and population. Population data for Latvia are from the Latvian Statistical Office, http://www.csb.lv for September 2015. The Exchange rates are from ECB Statistical Data Warehouse, http://sdw.ecb.europe.eu

Let us have a look at TNC home countries as yet another proxy for the amount of power in the global political economy. Among the 100 largest global nonfinancial TNC in 2016 (as presented by UNCTAD 2017b), exactly one half was considered to have an EU country as its home base. (To be sure, there are also other European TNC among the top 100, i.e. from Switzerland.) 15 TNC are considered to have the UK

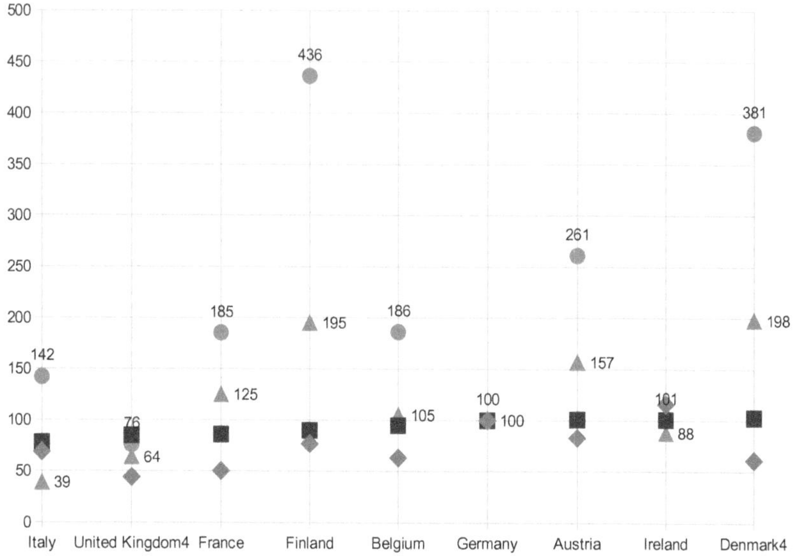

Fig. 8.8 Selected core countries plus Italy: outward activities of TNC (manufacturing) in the EU28 Area 2014 (sorted by squares). Circles: Number of TNC per capita (Germany = 100); Triangles: TNC turnover per capita (Euro millions at current prices, Germany = 100); Squares: GNI per capita (Germany = 100, cf. Fig. 8.7); Diamonds: Share of manufacturing industry in all branches (Germany = 100, cf. Fig. 8.7); Not displayed, because of extreme data: Luxembourg (circle: 1012, triangle: 1966), Sweden: (circle: 733, triangle: 225); (4 Average exchange rate to the Euro 2014: Pound Sterling: 0.80612, Swedish Krona: 9.0985, DK Krone: 7.4548 Years for population data: 2014: France, Ireland, UK; 2013: Austria, Finland, Germany, Italia, Sweden; 2012: Luxembourg [*Source* OECD database, http://stats.oecd.org, outward activity of multinationals by country of location—ISIC Rev. 4, and population. The Exchange rates are from ECB Statistical Data Warehouse, http://sdw.ecb.europe.eu])

as their 'home economy', 11 from France and also 11 from Germany, three from Spain, two each from Ireland and Italy, and one each from Belgium, Denmark, Finland, Luxembourg, the Netherlands, and Sweden (Table 8.10). From this perspective, it seems clear why the UK can preserve its position as a core country. The level of France's TNC control in the top 100 seems also in line with its persistent role as core country,

Table 8.10 Share of EU TNC among 100 largest global nonfinancial TNC

	Number of TNC in top 100	*Foreign assets %*	*Foreign sales %*	*Employees abroad %*
Belgium	1	3	1	2
Denmark	1	0	1	1
Finland	1	1	1	1
France	11	10	9	9
Germany	11	11	15	13
Ireland	2	2	0	0
Italy	2	3	2	0
Luxembourg	1	1	1	1
The Netherlands	1	1	0	1
Spain	3	3	2	2
Sweden	1	0	1	1
United Kingdom	15	17	15	12
United States	22	21	24	27

Source UNCTAD (2017b): Table 24, own calculations

despite weakening GNI per capita levels. Semiperipheral Italy (in GNI per capita terms) controls 3% of foreign assets in this top 100 list, and also semiperipheral Spain. With the exception of Austria, all the smaller countries of the hard core control one TNC in the top 100 list. Ireland is listed as homebase for two TNCs, but with a low share of foreign sales and employment.

Another proxy I suggest for regional/country 'control' of TNC is Foreign Direct Investments (FDI). There is an entire data set available for FDI outward stock in Millions of (current) US dollar (UNCTAD 2016, 2017a). These data indicate the extent TNC control investments abroad, but not specifically in the EU28 area and not for the manufacturing sector in particular (as with the OECD data above). Table 8.11 shows the differences in political-economic power in numbers. I calculated averages over decades for the FDI net (outward and inward) stock and averages of country populations over the respective decades (population data from Eurostat or national sources) to receive FDI stocks per capita for each decade. In order to make the data comparable to the data we used so far, I again calculated a relation to Germany (=100). Table 8.11 presents absolute figures and the relation to Germany (=100), respectively. The core–(semi)periphery divide is again apparent.

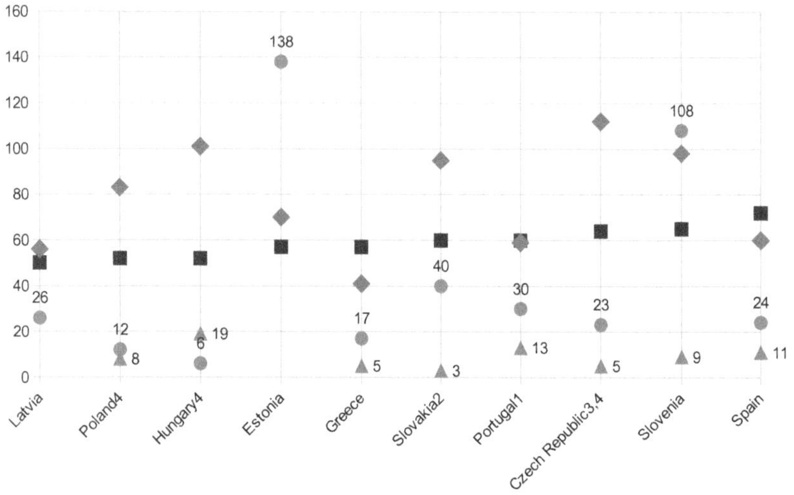

Fig. 8.9 Semi(peripheral) EU countries: outward activities of TNC (manufacturing) in the EU28 Area 2014, where data available, cf. Table 8.9 (sorted by squares); Circles: Number of TNC per capita (Germany = 100); Triangles: TNC turnover per capita (Euro millions at current prices, Germany = 100); Squares: GNI per capita (Germany = 100, cf. Fig. 8.7); Diamonds: Share of manufacturing industry in all branches (Germany = 100, cf. Fig. 8.7); (1 Average of 2013: 63/2473 and 2014: 176/6545 (very divergent data) 2 Number of companies: average of 2013: 54 and 2014: 113 (very divergent data) 3 Turnover: average of 2013: 26318 and 2014: 64875 (both Koruna: very divergent data) 4 Average exchange rate to the Euro 2014: Zloty: 4.1843, Forint: 308.71, Czech Koruna: 27.536 Years for population data: 2015: Latvia; 2014: Slovenia, Spain; 2013: Estonia, Hungary, Portugal, Slovakia [*Source* OECD database, http://stats.oecd.org, outward activity of multinationals by country of location—ISIC Rev. 4, and population. Population data for Latvia are from the Latvian Statistical Office, http://www.csb.lv for September 2015. The Exchange rates are from ECB Statistical Data Warehouse, http://sdw.ecb.europe.eu])

The demarcation line of net FDI stocks runs between Spain and Italy, which might indicate the better position of Italy in the hierarchy. Very generally, the (semi)peripheral countries do have negative values in net FDI stocks, which means they import more FDI than they export. The situation is reversed in the core countries.

Table 8.11 Net FDI stock, average over decades in millions of current US Dollar and per capita (Germany = 100)

	1990-1999	2000-2009	2010-2016	FDI_PC 1990-1999 Germany = 100	FDI_PC 2000-2009 Germany = 100	FDI_PC 2010-2016 Germany = 100	GNI_PC 2010-2018 Germany = 100
Bulgaria	**-595.24**	**-19056.63**	**-43345.96**	**-3**	**-116**	**-94**	37
Romania	**-1423.14**	**-31590.49**	**-72085.86**	**-3**	**-69**	**-57**	44
Croatia	**-262.50**	**-14337.67**	**-23913.29**	**-3**	**-156**	**-89**	46
Latvia	**-458.11**	**-5597.61**	**-12578.15**	**-8**	**-116**	**-98**	50
Hungary	**-10154.44**	**-52034.75**	**-60952.14**	**-43**	**-242**	**-97**	52
Poland	**-8534.47**	**-90845.12**	**-170623.57**	**-10**	**-112**	**-71**	52
Lithuania	**-637.04**	**-7246.16**	**-12473.87**	**-8**	**-102**	**-66**	56
Estonia	**-666.34**	**-6952.50**	**-12806.53**	**-20**	**-240**	**-153**	57
Greece	**-7423.81**	**-10170.25**	9612.03	**-31**	**-44**	14	57
Portugal	**-14320.44**	**-32534.04**	**-57807.89**	**-63**	**-147**	**-87**	60
Slovakia	**-1459.03**	**-28161.84**	**-46512.01**	**-12**	**-247**	**-136**	60
Czech Rep.	**-6755.58**	**-62795.21**	**-107341.74**	**-29**	**-288**	**-161**	64
Slovenia	**-1463.79**	**-3108.21**	**-5075.04**	**-32**	**-73**	**-39**	65
Cyprus	20.62	**-6708.76**	**-5359.88**	1	**-430**	**-100**	67
Malta	**-719.35**	**-22528.09**	**-92523.92**	**-85**	**-2649**	**-3444**	68
Spain	**-56565.26**	**-51117.99**	**-31076.89**	**-63**	**-56**	**-11**	72
Italy	35121.94	43683.87	148084.58	27	36	39	78
UK	101842.27	575667.92	310964.46	78	450	77	85
France	96530.24	280272.64	567068.56	74	217	142	86
Finland	8184.80	29257.22	40365.78	71	263	117	90
Belgium	ND	**-16182.21**	**-10206.43**	ND	**-73**	**-14**	95
Germany	183788.03	174897.44	513821.46	100	100	100	100
Austria	**-5708.61**	**-3849.20**	40069.82	**-32**	**-22**	74	101
Ireland	**-30192.18**	**-68977.77**	66824.28	**-370**	**-789**	228	101
Sweden	37129.34	37989.00	57957.92	187	198	95	101
Denmark	2259.21	15081.68	78419.82	19	131	220	103
Netherlands	54800.11	152340.07	380215.60	158	442	357	104
Luxembourg	ND	**-5384.47**	**-4847.05**	ND	**-551**	**-141**	143

Sources FDI data from: UNCTAD: World Investment Report, http://unctad.org/en/Pages/DIAE/FDI%20Statistics/World-Investment-Report-(WIR)-Annex-Tables.aspx. Population data from: Eurostat: population main table, http://ec.europa.eu/eurostat/web/population-demography-migration-projections/population-data/main-tables; last decade: 2010–2017 France: population for mainland plus Corsica, average of 2010–2013; Grey: EU enlargements post EU15. Own calculations. Sorted by GNI per capita 2010–2018 (for GNI data, cf. Table 8.3)

The most striking exceptions in the sphere of semiperipheral countries are Cyprus and Malta. The explosion of their inward and outward FDI stock in the decade of EU accession seems to indicate that these two countries are being used as bridgeheads into the EU, but also as nodes of tax avoidance. Cyprus was by far the top 'investor economy' in 'transition countries' (Russian Federation etc.) in 2009 and 2014 but also the largest recipient of FDI stocks from the Russian Federation (UNCTAD

2016: 57, 60) before 2015. In one episode, Cyprus appears as the location for money laundering in the court case against former Lega Nord boss Umberto Bossi (and his treasurer) who recycled 56 Million euro of public money for the use of the Bossi family (Fatto Quotidiano 2017). Malta, again, made it into the news when the journalist Daphne Caruana Galizia, who investigated the involvement of top politicians into corruption and money laundering (Panama papers) was murdered in a car bombing in October 2017. Recent research at the University of Amsterdam (Garcia-Bernardo et al. 2017) inquired into transnational ownership structures of TNC and into global ownership relations between company affiliates in order to construct country chains. Garcia-Bernardo et al. (2017: 2) identified Malta and Cyprus as sink offshore centers (OFCs), which 'are countries that attract and retain foreign capital – territories in this category are usually characterized as tax havens [...]. Most sink-OFCs have small domestic economies and large values of foreign assets, which are attracted through low or zero corporate taxes'. Among the 24 OFCs the authors identify, Malta and Cyprus belong to the 18 countries (¾ of total !!) that 'were under British sovereignty in the past or are still UK dependencies' (Majiti 2017).

However, there are also cases in core countries that merit our attention. There is, above all, Luxembourg boasting exorbitant FDI inward and outward stock data (Table 8.12), which indicates a special TNC network country (with special tax regulations). Among the core countries, Luxembourg is followed by Ireland, also with striking data for inward and outward FDI stocks. There is reason to believe that it is this special privileged situation of Ireland that enabled the quick rise from periphery to core. Among the hard core countries, Belgium and the Netherlands show extreme data as well. Their data reflect the ability of TNC to transfer prices to and evade taxes in the most preferred jurisdiction. 'Ireland and the Netherlands led the rise in FDI outflows from Europe, corporate inversion deals were largely responsible for this performance, as large United States [TNC] became affiliates of newly created parent companies in these economies [...]' (UNCTAD 2016: 68). Possibly the reverse of net FDI stock from negative to positive (cf. Table 8.11) is related to such policies. In the study by Garcia-Bernardo et al. (2017), core country Luxembourg is being counted sink OFC alongside semiperipheral Cyprus and Malta. But also the other special cases in our data, Ireland and the Netherlands (plus UK which had been able to defend its core status) seem to be reflected in the findings of Garcia-Bernardo et al. (2017).

Table 8.12 Outward and inward FDI stock per capita (millions of current US Dollar, Germany = 100)

	Outward FDI stock per capita 1990-1999	Inward FDI stock per capita 1990-1999	Outward FDI stock per capita 2000-2009	Inward FDI stock per capita 2000-2009	Outward FDI stock per capita 2010-2016	Inward FDI stock per capita 2010-2016	2010-2018 GNI_PC
Romania	0	2	0	18	0	32	44
Bulgaria	0	2	1	30	2	56	37
Latvia	2	8	2	31	3	61	50
Poland	0	7	1	29	3	45	52
Slovakia	1	9	3	65	4	82	60
Lithuania	0	5	2	28	5	45	56
Croatia	2	6	6	46	7	60	46
Czech Rep.	1	20	5	78	9	105	64
Hungary	1	30	9	72	18	83	52
Greece	5	29	17	32	19	22	57
Slovenia	5	29	19	43	19	52	65
Estonia	1	15	19	84	26	126	57
Portugal	8	54	39	85	32	99	60
Italy	34	38	46	49	47	52	78
Spain	18	71	76	109	71	116	72
Germany	**100**	**100**	**100**	**100**	**100**	**100**	**100**
France	108	130	107	79	113	97	86
Finland	57	48	156	129	134	144	90
Austria	25	62	100	130	137	172	101
UK	102	119	208	147	147	186	85
Denmark	83	124	181	194	179	156	103
Sweden	137	104	247	259	236	315	101
Belgium	ND	ND	395	511	309	490	95
Netherlands	189	210	376	359	364	368	104
Ireland	85	385	263	526	694	956	101
Malta	3	62	603	1417	932	3389	68
Cyprus	3	4	470	695	1239	1991	67
Luxembourg	ND	ND	1442	1941	2012	3220	143

Sources FDI data from: UNCTAD: World Investment Report, http://unctad.org/en/Pages/DIAE/FDI%20Statistics/World-Investment-Report-(WIR)-Annex-Tables.aspx. Population data from: Eurostat: population main table, http://ec.europa.eu/eurostat/web/population-demography-migration-projections/population-data/main-tables; last decade: 2010–2017; France: population for mainland plus Corsica, average of 2010–2013; Grey: EU enlargements post EU15. Own calculations. Due to rounding inward stock per capita may appear higher over a decade even if net stock is displayed positive in Table 8.11 (cf. Cyprus in the 1990s).
Sorted by Outward FDI Stock per capita 2010–2016

They show that 'the majority of investment from and to sink OFCs occurs through only five jurisdictions [...]: The Netherlands, the United Kingdom, Switzerland, Ireland and Singapore' (ibid.: 9). These five countries are called conduit offshore financial centers which 'facilitate the movement of capital between sink-OFCs and other countries' (ibid.: 6):

> Conduit-OFCs typically have low or zero taxes imposed on the transfer of capital to other countries, either via interest payments, royalties, dividends or profit repatriation. In addition, such jurisdictions have highly developed legal systems that are able to cater to the needs of multinational corporations. Conduits play a key role in the global corporate ownership network by allowing the transfer of capital without taxation. In this way, profit from one country can be re-invested in another part of the world paying no or little taxes. Countries such as the Netherlands and Ireland have been criticized for these types of activities. (ibid.: 2)

Furthermore the authors 'find a clear geographical specialization in the offshore financial network', and a sectoral distinction:

> [T]he Netherlands is the conduit between European companies and Luxembourg. The United Kingdom is the conduit between European countries and former members of the British Empire, such as Hong Kong, Jersey, Guernsey or Bermuda. Hong Kong and Luxembourg, being themselves sink-OFCs, also serve as the main countries in the route to typical tax havens (British Virgin Islands, Cayman Islands and Bermuda). The specialization is not only geographical, but also present at the sector level. For instance, the Netherlands is specialized in holding companies, the United Kingdom in head offices and fund management, Ireland is prominent in financial leasing and head offices, Luxembourg in support activities, Hong Kong and Switzerland are characterized under the "Other financial activities category", which encompasses commodity dealing, financial intermediation and derivatives dealing. Companies choose to centralize their investment apparatus in specific jurisdictions according to the tax regulations of the jurisdiction, its bilateral tax treaties, and its sectoral advantages. (ibid.: 9)

Among the core countries, Ireland might surely be considered having shaky foundations, because it seems to depend on the integration into two core structures, the US and the EU core, for upholding its position in the global commodity chains. 'Until 2008 Ireland was the poster boy of neoliberal politicians', writes Wickham (2012: 59), but

> [a] socio-economic crisis which was produced by Ireland's almost pathological commitment to the priorities of Anglo-American capitalism has ended up moving Ireland closer to the United States than to the European Union. (ibid.: 75)

In UNCTAD's (2016: 64) 'developed world', the Netherlands, Ireland, and Germany are among the top 5 FDI home countries and the top 10 investor countries. An Arrighian 'core activity' must clearly be seen in the ability to participate substantially in the organization of TNC' FDI networks. In some core countries, outward FDI income make a substantial contribution to GDP. The EU28 countries among the 25 countries' outward FDI incomes relative to GDP, UNCTAD (2016: 22) presents, are: Luxembourg 114.4%, Ireland 24.3%, the Netherlands 17.6%, Belgium 4.9%, UK 3.3%, Austria 2.8%, Sweden 2.7%, Spain 1.5%, Germany 0.8%, France 0.6%. Italy is not listed among these countries but the small but continuing positive net FDI stocks position seems to add to the impression that Italy's ability to maintain some TNC control counters the devastating recent industrial development. FDI data in Tables 8.11 and 8.12 further support the impression that control of TNC networks is what keeps UK and France among core countries. Similar things can be said about Finland. Belgium's negative FDI stocks data may be explained by a history of dependent industrialization (with FDI from France and Germany). Similarly the Austrian case is dependent on the industrial links to Germany. Only recently the Austrian FDI stocks balance turned positive due to the engagement into the production networks with the regional enlargement countries of 2004 (cf. Becker et al. 2015).

Figures 8.10, 8.11 and 8.12 display the data of Tables 8.11 and 8.12 graphically. The squares represent the GNI per capita, the diamonds value added in manufacturing as a share of overall value added, and the triangles net FDI stocks. I left out Ireland as single runaway number for net FDI in Fig. 8.10: 1990–1999 (and for Belgium and Luxembourg no data were provided). Although I left out runaway data for Malta, Ireland and Luxembourg in Fig. 8.11 (2000–2009), increasing numbers of FDI stocks compress squares (GNI) and diamonds (value-added data). In Fig. 8.12 (2010–2016) only Malta was omitted as outlier. The general picture for the periphery and semiperiphery shows the diamonds over the squares, indicating industrial convergence without income convergence, and triangles below the zero line, indicating FDI inward stocks. The general situation for core countries is different. The diamonds tend to be below the squares, indicating that manufacturing within the own jurisdiction is not necessary for holding a core status (squares). The picture is completed by FDI stocks above the zero line and often above the squares. The outliers have been described. Those core countries showing extreme high net levels of FDI inward stocks also have outward stocks much higher than Germany's.

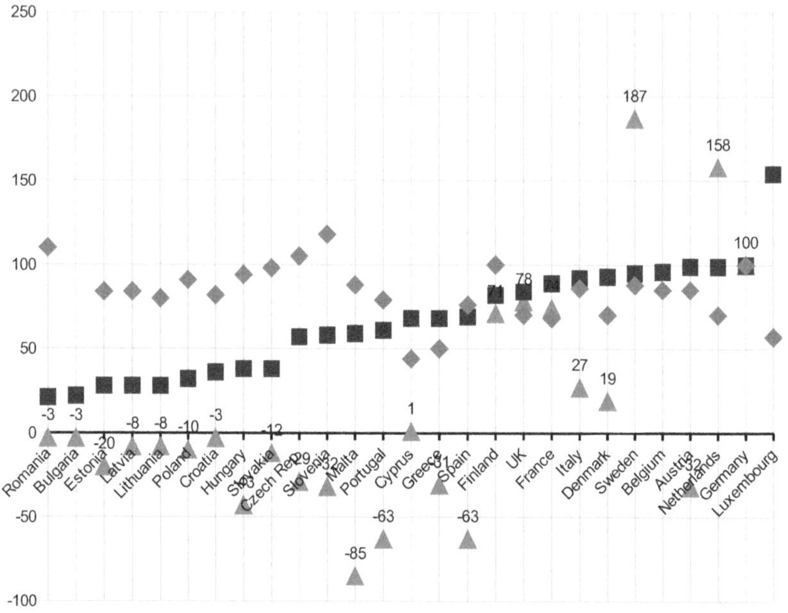

Fig. 8.10 FDI net stock per capita (millions of current US Dollar)—1990–1999, Germany = 100; Triangles: FDI net stock per capita; Squares: GNI per capita (Germany = 100, cf. Fig. 8.7); Diamonds: Share of manufacturing industry in all branches (Germany = 100, cf. Fig. 8.7); Sorted by Squares (*Sources and information*, cf. Tables 8.11 and 8.12. No data for Belgium and Luxembourg, Not displayed, because of extreme data: Ireland (-370))

8.4 The Core–Periphery System in the EU: A Persistent Structure

Contrary to the narrative of convergence and cohesion in the EU, only few countries were able to move their positions in the international division of labor. Italy had succeeded by means of spurring industrial development in the postwar boom, entering the core following our GNI data in the 1980s. Finland's postwar industrial development enabled the formation of a TNC that would temporarily become the world's leading telecommunication company (Nokia). According to our GNI data, Finland entered the core in the 1990s and surpassed Italy in the 2000s. Both countries declined afterwards but Italy has never recovered from the restructuring toward a financialized economy (Weissenbacher 2019). Our interpretation suggests that catching-up development paths like the Italian were closed in the second half of the 1960s. Successes in industrial development appeared as dependent industrialization in the sense that countries entered European or global commodity chains at a peripheral or semiperipheral position. This reduced options for independent development and limited countries' rooms to maneuver in improving their positions in the chains (which are controlled by core TNC). The reason why Ireland was able to enter the realm of the EU core was—as we have seen—due to its privileged position in the global financialized capitalism. Our GNI data suggest a characterization of Ireland as periphery in the 1980s, semiperiphery in the 1990s, and core

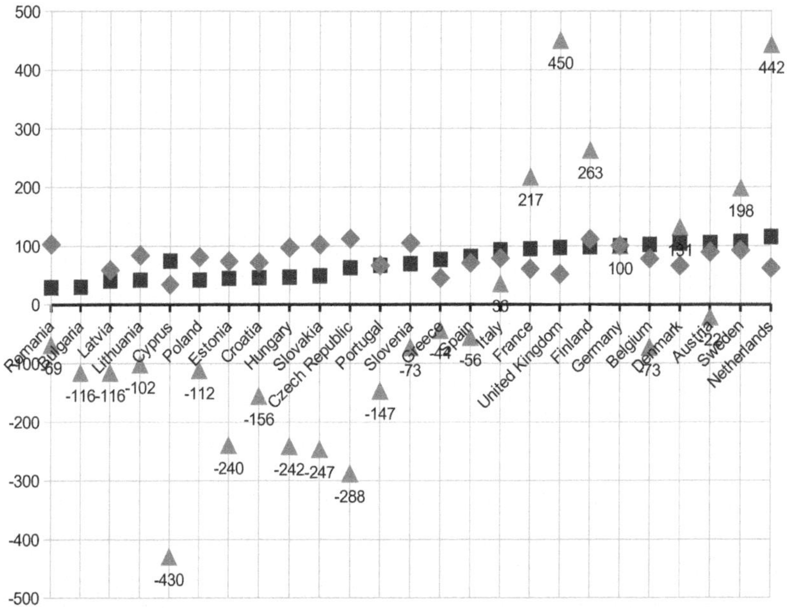

Fig. 8.11 FDI net stock per capita (millions of current US Dollar)—2000–2009, Germany = 100; Triangles: FDI net stock per capita; Squares: GNI per capita (Germany = 100, cf. Fig. 8.7); Diamonds: Share of manufacturing industry in all branches (Germany = 100, cf. Fig. 8.7); Sorted by Squares (*Sources and information*, cf. Tables 8.11 and 8.12. Not displayed, because of extreme data: Ireland (-789), Luxembourg (-551), and Malta (-2649))

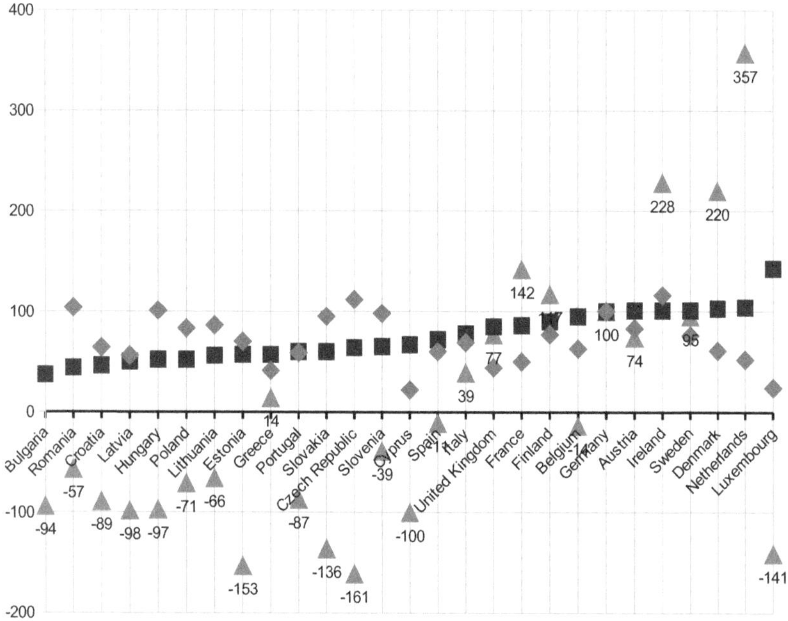

Fig. 8.12 FDI net stock per capita (millions of current US Dollar)—2010s Germany=100; Not displayed, because of extreme data: Malta (-3444). Triangles: FDI net stock per capita; Squares: GNI per capita (Germany = 100, cf. Fig. 8.7); Diamonds: Share of manufacturing industry in all branches (Germany = 100, cf. Fig. 8.7); Sorted by Squares (*Sources and information* cf. Tables 8.11 and 8.12)

(above Germany) in the 2000s. Having said that, Ireland ran into troubles no later than with the global crisis of 2008. And also the discussion in the UK, whether or not the country shall leave the EU, may be related to the UK's declining role in EU capitalism.

Before I approach the question whether we are currently in a transition process toward a new era (that may again change the characteristics of how core countries can defend their position), I would like to summarize and qualify the status quo in core–periphery relations in the EU (with recent available data, not averages). Table 8.15 once more presents the data for net FDI stocks per capita (column 3) and outward activities of manufacturing TNC per capita in the EU28 area (compared to

Germany = 100). Typically, peripheral and semiperipheral countries display higher FDI imports than exports, either for their industrial production or in the financialized sector, e.g. banks, financial institutions (cf. Becker et al., forthcoming). An extreme example for the latter appears to be Malta, whereas Italy's positive FDI stock balance points toward its perimeter position. Only few core countries have a negative balance in FDI stocks, Ireland and Luxembourg with their particularly financialized economies and Belgium. (We have seen that Austria's FDI position changed with the enlargement of the EU by the CEE countries, which improved its situation in the Central European commodity chains.) We have also established the argument for high levels of outward activities of manufacturing TNC per capita as core activity. Table 8.13 displays the matrix, we have outlined in Chapter 8.2: the core–periphery system combined with the level of manufacturing production in a country's economy.

In a further step, I qualify the manufacturing production and try to take into account the dependence on financialization and public debt. Tables 8.14, 8.15, 8.16, 8.17, and 8.18 provide data for this qualification. (These data are more a snapshot than the data I used before, because they focus on one recent year.) A clear core–periphery divide can be reproduced with the data from the manufacturing sector as well. The median hourly wage level (euro, manufacturing sector) in column 7 of Table 8.17 offers one intermediate country between low and high wage countries in the EU (the quintile of 61–80, Germany = 100), and that is Italy. Also interesting, for all such defined low wage countries, column 8 (median hourly wages in purchasing power parities—PPS which reflect price levels), displays a higher value than column 7 (and vice versa for Italy and the core).

I use manufacturing of machinery and equipment as a proxy for the ability to produce and provide the machinery that is used to produce actual consumer commodities. I follow the hypothesis that such an ability is necessary to 'control' the commodity chains and therefore can be regarded as 'core characteristic'. Table 8.17 provides data for this qualification. Although I do offer data on employment in this subsector as well, I use the subsector's (= manufacturing of machinery and equipment) share of value added in manufacturing total (column 3), in order to qualify manufacturing in Table 8.14. I assume that in such sectors productivity gains will lead to a reduction of workers. Having said that, only in the case of the Czech Republic, high employment numbers in that subsector

Table 8.13 Core-Periphery Typology and Level of Industrialization

	Core	*Semiperiphery*	*Periphery*
Low level of industrialization	France, Luxembourg, the Netherlands, UK	Cyprus, Malta, Spain	Greece, Latvia, Portugal,
Medium level of industrialization	Belgium, Denmark, Finland, Sweden	Italy	Croatia, Estonia
High level of industrialization	Austria, Germany, Ireland	Czech Republic, Slovenia	Bulgaria, Hungary, Lithuania, Poland, Slovakia, Romania

(columns 5 and 6, the latter as a share of an already high level of manufacturing employees: higher than Germany, cf. column 4) would lead to a status of medium level of industrialization instead of low level (as suggested by column 3).

As far as core countries are concerned, such a qualification does nothing to change the positions of France and UK. For Luxembourg a MQM (Table 8.14) may not be able to raise its position, due to a very low level of industrialization to begin with. Ireland's data on comparative industrialization seem doubtful, because of its level of dependent financialization. Considering the LQM, Ireland is in the corner with the HI countries of CEE that are dependently industrialized within the European commodity chains (cf. Table 8.14). Belgium appears in a dependent position similar to Spain.

Clearly Germany (and connected with it Austria) form a qualitative industrial core which is followed by Denmark, Finland, and Sweden, and perimeter Italy, respectively. As for the semiperiphery, data for Italy once more support the country's affinity to the core (perimeter) despite the enormous difficulties (e.g. deindustrialization) of the country in recent decades (Weissenbacher 2019). Commodity chain research on Italy suggests that companies from the Italian North have joined the European commodity chains as suppliers (ibid.: 64), the present data point in the direction that this happened at a higher level in the chains. Furthermore, the data on the automotive manufacturing sector (Table 8.18) suggest that recent restructuring of the Italian flagship FIAT (ibid.) has led to a decreasing dependency on the automotive sector.

Semiperipheral Czech Republic touches the zone of medium level industrialization by these qualifications but is still far away from HQM.

Table 8.14 Qualification of industrialization in the EU

Germany = 100	Low level of qualified manufacturing (LQM, ≤ 60)	Medium level of qualified manufacturing (MQM, 61-80)	High level of qualified manufacturing (HQM, > 80)
Low level of industrialization (LI, ≤ 60)	Core: France, UK Semiperiphery: Cyprus, Malta Periphery: Greece, Latvia, Portugal	Core: Luxembourg	Core: the Netherlands
Medium level of industrialization (MI, 61-80)	Core: Belgium Semiperiphery: Spain Periphery: Croatia, Estonia		Core: Denmark (GHG), Finland, Sweden (GHG/HMV) Semiperiphery: Italy
High level of industrialization (HI, > 80)	Core: Ireland Semiperiphery: Czech Republic (HMV), Slovenia (GHG) Periphery: Bulgaria (GHG/HMV), Hungary (GHG/HMV), Lithuania, Poland, Slovakia (HMV), Romania (GHG/HMV)		Core: Austria, Germany (HMV)

Data from Table 8.17: Level of industrialization: column 2 (Bulgaria: column 4), level of qualified manufacturing: column 3 (Malta: no data, estimate); Grey: Net export of FDI stocks (Table 8.16, column 3)
High level of dependence on motor vehicle manufacturing (HMV)
Comparatively low output of greenhouse gases from manufacturing (GHG)

The negative net FDI stocks, however, point in the direction of a dependent industrialization of the Czech Republic, Slovakia, Hungary. Furthermore, the high dependence on the motor vehicle sector may be seen as additional structural weakness: a very high dependence on manufacturing in a saturated market of environmentally troublesome transportation means (which is also true for Romania, the manufacturing core Germany, and to a lesser extent Sweden). As far as greenhouse gas pollution in the manufacturing sector is concerned, a few countries have a relatively low output for their productive status: Denmark and Sweden from the core, Slovenia from the semiperiphery, and Hungary and Romania from the periphery.

Table 8.15 A classification of financialization for EU core and periphery

Germany = 100	Low level of financialization (LF, ≤ 110)	Medium level of financialization (MF, 111-130)	High level of financialization (HF, > 130)
Low level of public debt (LD, ≤ 110)	Core: Germany Periphery: Bulgaria, Czech Republic Estonia, Hungary, Latvia, Lithuania, Poland, Slovakia, Slovenia, Romania	Semiperiphery: Malta	Core: Denmark, Finland, Ireland, Luxembourg, the Netherlands, Sweden
Medium level of public debt (MD, 111-130)	Periphery: Croatia	Core: Austria	
High level of public debt (HD, > 130)	Semiperiphery: Italy	Periphery: Greece	Core: Belgium, France, UK Semiperiphery: Cyprus Periphery: Portugal, Spain

Data from Table 8.16: level of public debt: column 2, level of financialization: column 1; Grey: Net export of FDI stocks (Table 8.16, column 3)

As far as financialization is concerned, I use as a proxy private debt as a percentage of GDP (Table 8.16, column 1, cf. Becker et al., forthcoming). Germany is the least financialized core country in this respect, which does not mean that it lacks a substantially financialized economy: German financialization is strongly export-oriented (ibid.). I will further qualify that indicator by (a) public debt (column 2) in order to proxy the room to maneuver governments have, and (b) FDI net balance of stocks which signals dependence on FDI import (ibid.).

The former state socialist countries from CEE (except Estonia and Latvia) and Slovenia are HI and LQM as far as manufacturing is concerned, and also have—except Estonia—levels of private debt/GDP lower than Germany. Furthermore, Hungary (together with Slovenia and Croatia) are the exceptions to a (partially much) lower public indebtedness. The financialization process in these countries started later than in Western Europe (cf. Tables 8.14, 8.15, 8.16). All core countries have higher levels of financialization than Germany, some of them are exorbitant.

Malta has an LD/MF position but its exorbitant FDI/capita balance would justify a ranking in the HF category as well. Core countries France

Table 8.16 Core–periphery indicators for EU 28 (Germany = 100, except columns 6 & 7: Croatia = 100)

	1	2	3	4	5	6	7	8
Bulgaria	100	40	-77	x	4	85	35	38
Croatia	98	121	-75	x	17	**100**	**100**	45
Romania	51	55	-50	x	3	92	103	46
Latvia	83	63	-90	x	25	101	69	52
Hungary	71	115	-74	19	21	61	25	53
Poland	76	79	-59	8	18	51	42	53
Greece	116	276	-2	5	4	5	46	54
Lithuania	56	62	-55	x	28	119	146	58
Estonia	106	14	-134	x	50	47	56	58
Portugal	162	195	-83	13	9	x	28	60
Slovakia	96	80	-99	3	30	31	6	61
Cyprus	315	150	-25	x	159	75	12	63
Slovenia	76	116	-47	9	39	10	44	65
Czech Repub.	67	54	-126	5	29	40	5	66
Malta	118	80	-3332	x	99	26	21	71
Spain	139	154	-12	11	27	x	17	73
Italy	110	205	26	39	13	10	17	76
UK	171	137	52	64	58	x	18	84
France	148	154	116	125	43	1	36	85
Finland	146	96	99	195	131	x	17	87
Belgium	187	162	-27	105	71	4	25	93
Germany	**100**	**100**	**100**	**100**	**100**	0	12	**100**
Austria	122	123	70	157	116	13	16	100
Sweden	194	64	130	225	302	22	20	100
Netherlands	252	89	370	x	104	3	27	100
Denmark	200	56	196	198	174	x	24	102
Ireland	243	107	-20	88	123	x	63	118
Luxembourg	316	36	-370	1996	240	39	35	139

Sorted by Column 8, grey: enlargement countries after 1995, dark frame: semiperiphery as explained for Table 8.7

1 Private sector debt, consolidated—percentage of gross domestic product (GDP) 2017, Germany = 100. *Source* Eurostat, https://ec.europa.eu/eurostat/tgm/table.do?tab=table&init=1&plugin=1&language=en&pcode=tipspd20, own calculations. The private sector debt is the stock of liabilities held by the sectors Nonfinancial corporations and Households and Nonprofit institutions serving households. The instruments that are taken into account to compile private sector debt are Debt securities and Loans. Data are presented in consolidated terms, i.e. not taking into account transactions within the same sector, and expressed in % of GDP and millions of national currency

2 General government consolidated gross debt, Percentage of gross domestic product (GDP) 2017, Germany = 100. *Source* Eurostat [gov_10dd_edpt1]

3 FDI net stock (Million US Dollar per capita) 2016, Germany = 100. *Source* UNCTAD: World Investment Report, http://unctad.org/en/Pages/DIAE/FDI%20Statistics/World-Investment-Report-(WIR)-Annex-Tables.aspx, own calculations

4 Outward Activities in Manufacturing of TNC in the EU28 Area, Turnover in Euro millions at current prices per capita in 2014, Germany = 100. Czech Republic and Portugal: average of 2013 and 2014 (very divergent data), no data for Bulgaria, Croatia, Estonia, Latvia, Lithuania, Malta, Cyprus, the Netherlands, Romania. *Source* OECD, cf. Table 8.9

5 Outbound tourism expenditure 2017 (UK: 2013) "for leisure or with family and friends" (1 night or over), Thousand euro per capita, Germany = 100. *Source* Eurostat: Expenditure [tour_dem_extot]

Table 8.16 (continued)

6 Remittances from EU 28 in 2017 (Netherlands: 2016), Croatia = 100: Secondary income: Personal transfers (Current transfers between resident and non resident households), Million euro per capita. *Source* Eurostat [bop_rem6], own calculations. Croatia is chosen as a benchmark because Germany would have distorted results, and Eurostat estimated Croatia as the most dependent EU28 country as far as remittances/GDP is concerned (Eurostat 2018b)

7 Emigration by citizenship 2017 (Germany: 2015), Reporting country number/population, Croatia = 100 (see explanation above). *Source* Eurostat, Emigration [migr_emi1ctz], own calculations. Definition: 'Emigration: the action by which a person, having previously been usually resident in the territory of a Member State, ceases to have his or her usual residence in that Member State for a period that is, or is expected to be, of at least 12 months'

8 Gross national income at current prices (PPS) per head of population (HVGNP): 2016, Germany = 100. *Source* Ameco database

and UK are placed in the HD/HF corner but they are the only ones in that corner that boast an FDI stock export position which possibly gives their economies some room to maneuver. Austria has a middle position in both public and private debt. The LD/HF countries have a comparable low public debt but still there is a distinctive hierarchy: Luxembourg has three times, Denmark and Sweden twice the private debt indicator of Germany but only a third, half, and 2/3 of the public debt. The Netherlands (1.5), Ireland and Finland (both about 2.5) are higher in private debt than Germany but also show similar levels in public debt, Finland even higher than Germany's. Italy in the HD/LF corner has a private debt level comparatively close to the German level but its public debt is twice as high. Having said that, Italy still boasts a positive FDI stock balance.

The structural qualification of core–periphery relations support the impression of a unique position of Germany on basis of qualitative manufacturing and financialization. Having said that, the export-oriented financialization can face a crisis if the creditors run into difficulties as happened in the crisis of 2008. Also, the persistence on outdated and environmentally problematic industries (motor vehicle industries) constitutes a structural weakness of Germany, increasingly difficult to defend. Austria is closely integrated into and dependent on the German industrial production process. Denmark, Finland, and Sweden seem to have kept manufacturing abilities which may be an advantage if international financialization should lose dynamics. The Netherlands have sustained manufacturing but do also have characteristics of Ireland and Luxembourg that appear to be substantially dependent on the privileges and workings of global financialization. This may to a lesser extent also be true for Belgium. Financialized economies are also important features

Table 8.17 EU 28 core and periphery and qualified manufacturing sector (Germany = 100)

	1	2	3	4	5	6	7	8	9	10
Malta	**71**	**38**	**x**	**57**	**x**	**x**	**43**	**54**	**3**	**56**
Cyprus	**63**	**22**	**14**	**40**	**4**	**11**	**35**	**40**	**90**	**53**
Greece	54	43	15	28	6	21	36	43	59	57
Ireland	118	162	17	51	18	39	101	84	66	86
Latvia	52	55	19	61	12	20	17	25	32	30
Lithuania	58	84	21	82	16	19	16	27	92	29
Portugal	60	60	26	77	16	22	23	28	80	33
Estonia	58	70	26	97	23	24	26	34	95	40
Poland	53	90	28	72	24	32	21	38	79	41
Croatia	45	67	31	70	20	30	24	36	50	36
Spain	**73**	**63**	**36**	**44**	**16**	**37**	**56**	**62**	**82**	**70**
France	85	49	38	47	18	39	81	76	64	74
Romania	46	103	38	73	20	28	10	19	58	22
Belgium	93	63	40	43	18	42	93	87	144	100
Bulgaria	38	x	41	87	33	39	8	17	48	21
Slovenia	**65**	**105**	**48**	**x**	**x**	**46**	**36**	**45**	**53**	**56**
UK	84	43	49	45	21	47	85	71	54	75
Czech Rep.	**66**	**120**	**58**	**129**	**88**	**65**	**24**	**38**	**81**	**42**
Hungary	53	106	59	84	47	55	18	32	56	34
Slovakia	61	101	60	94	60	60	23	35	149	37
Luxembourg	139	24	77	69	54	81	94	79	121	81
Sweden	100	73	81	62	50	82	105	85	64	85
Austria	100	83	84	80	68	85	82	79	151	92
Netherlands	100	53	85	42	34	78	88	81	128	94
Finland	87	73	86	63	59	95	101	84	102	90
Italy	**76**	**69**	**97**	**52**	**47**	**83**	**64**	**63**	**70**	**74**
Denmark	102	69	99	57	68	118	149	109	49	98
Germany	100	100	100	100	100	100	100	100	100	100

Sorted by column 3, grey: enlargement countries after 1995, bold: semiperiphery as defined for Table 8.7

Population data: Eurostat database, Population change—Demographic balance and crude rates at national level [demo_gind]

1 Gross national income at current prices (PPS) per head of population (HVGNP): 2016. *Source* Ameco database

2 Share of manufacturing industry (UVGM) in total all branches (UVG0)—Gross value added at current prices: 2016. *Source* Ameco database. *Note* Ireland had a value of 91 in 2014!

3 Manufacturing of machinery and equipment: share of value added in manufacturing total (%): 2016 (Ireland: 2014). *Source* Eurostat: [sbs_na_ind_r2]

4 Employees in manufacturing (full-time equivalents) per capita: 2016. *Source* Eurostat: [sbs_na_ind_r2]

5 Employees in manufacturing of machinery and equipment (full-time equivalents) per capita: 2016 (Ireland: 2014). *Source* Eurostat: [sbs_na_ind_r2]

6 Manufacturing of machinery and equipment: Share of employment in manufacturing total (%): 2016 (Ireland: 2014). *Source* Eurostat: [sbs_na_ind_r2]

7 Median hourly earnings in euro, 2014, all employees (excluding apprentices) in companies of 10 employees or more, manufacturing sector. *Source* Eurostat: [earn_ses_pub2n]

8 Median hourly earnings in PPS, 2014, all employees (excluding apprentices) in companies of 10 employees or more, manufacturing sector. *Source* Eurostat: [earn_ses_pub2n]

9 Greenhouse gases (CO_2, N_2O in CO_2 equivalent, CH_4 in CO_2 equivalent) from Manufacturing sector in 2017, tons/population. *Source* Eurostat: Air emissions accounts by NACE Rev. 2 activity [env_ac_ainah_r2]

Table 8.18 EU 28 and the automotive core: manufacture of motor vehicles, trailers and semi-trailers in 2016

	1	**2**	**3**	**4**	**5**	**6**	**7**
Luxembourg	x	x	x	x	x	24	139
Malta	x	x	x	x	x	38	71
Ireland	4	1 954	1,4	0,3	0,1	162	118
Greece	1	1 373	0,6	0,2	0,3	43	54
Cyprus	1	126	0,5	0,4	0,5	22	63
Croatia	6	2 370	0,9	0,9	0,9	67	45
Denmark	6	3 618	1,3	0,9	1,0	69	102
Finland	12	6 406	2,1	1,4	1,6	73	87
Lithuania	17	4 888	2,3	1,7	2,4	84	58
Latvia	9	1 755	1,6	2,0	2,5	55	52
Netherlands	11	19 641	3,1	3,8	3,1	53	100
Estonia	23	3 010	2,8	2,9	3,4	70	58
Bulgaria	30	21 936	4,0	3,4	3,4	x	38
Belgium	21	23 783	5,7	6,1	3,9	63	93
Italy	21	130 733	4,4	8,4	5,3	69	76
Portugal	32	33 153	4,9	8,8	5,6	60	60
Austria	35	30 999	5,1	8,6	6,1	83	100
Slovenia	x	x	6,4	10,4	7,4	105	65
France	29	197 439	7,3	13,0	8,4	49	85
Poland	47	181 214	7,3	11,9	9,9	90	53
Spain	31	146 883	8,3	14,9	10,2	63	73
UK	24	158 063	6,2	13,2	10,4	43	84
Sweden	64	64 155	12,4	20,1	13,8	73	100
Germany	**100**	833 945	11,6	23,0	18,5	**100**	**100**
Romania	87	173 919	14,4	22,2	20,3	103	46
Hungary	92	92 125	12,6	25,4	20,4	106	53
Czech Repub.	154	164 890	13,0	27,9	21,4	120	66
Slovakia	127	69 739	14,7	35,9	22,3	101	61

Grey: Enlargement countries after 1995, sorted by column 5, x: no data

1 Employees in full-time equivalent units—number per capita, Germany = 100

2 Employees in full-time equivalent units—number

3 Share of employment in manufacturing total—percentage

4 Share of turnover in manufacturing total—percentage

5 Share of value added in manufacturing total—percentage

Source Eurostat: Annual detailed enterprise statistics for industry (NACE Rev. 2, B-E) [sbs_na_ind_r2], own calculations

6 Share of manufacturing industry (UVGM) in total all branches (UVG0)—Gross value added at current prices: 2016, Germany = 100. *Source* Ameco database, own calculations. *Note* Rapid increase in Irish data, value of 91 in 2014!

7 Gross national income at current prices (PPS) per head of population (HVGNP): 2016, *Source* Ameco database, own calculations

of France and UK. The data available in this book suggest, however, that their financial centers manage to play active roles in the (as of now prevailing) financialized global economy. Their industrial capabilities seem to have been severely affected.

In the realm of the semiperiphery, Malta and Cyprus have financialized economies very much dependent on international financialization and its regional privileges. Italy is still connected to the core. It has, despite severe difficulties and deindustrialization processes, defended an important sector of industrial production. Spain has a better position in the European commodity chains than Portugal and Greece but the recent boom and bust have shown the vulnerability of its dependent financialization. Based on their industrial heritage, Slovenia and the Czech Republic were able to lift their position from the CEE periphery. Still they are integrated into the dependent industrial relations of European commodity chains. Due to their late integration, the CEE countries have no severe dependent financialization as the peripheral countries of the EU south, Greece and Portugal. Greece and Portugal have lived through the early integration of 'unequal partners', experienced deindustrialization and were drawn into the dangerous relations of dependent financialization by temporary low-cost capital import.

References

Arrighi, Giovanni, and Jessica Drangel. 1986. The Stratification of the World-Economy: An Exploration of the Semiperipheral Zone. *Review* 10 (1): 9–74 (=Anniversary Issue: The Work of the Fernand Braudel Center).

Arrighi, Giovanni, Beverly Silver, and Benjamin Brewer. 2003. Industrial Convergence, Globalization, and the Persistence of the North-South Divide. *Studies in Comparative International Development* 38 (1): 3–31.

Becker, Joachim, and Rudy Weissenbacher. 2014. Berlin Consensus and Disintegration: Monetary Regime and Uneven Development in the EU. In *The Deepening Crisis of the European Union: The Case for Radical Change: Analysis and Proposals from EuroMemo Group*, ed. Włodzimierz Dymarski, Marica Frangakis, and Jeremy Leaman, 5–32. Poznań: Poznań University of Economics Press.

Becker, Joachim, Franziska Disslbacher, and Rudy Weissenbacher. 2015. Zwischen Deutschland und Osteuropa: Österreichs neue Mittellage. In *Politische Ökonomie Österreichs. Kontinuitäten und Veränderungen seit dem EU-Beitritt*, ed. Beigewum, 132–155. Wien: Mandelbaum.

Becker, Joachim, Rudy Weissenbacher, and Johannes Jäger. Forthcoming. Uneven Development in the EU: Processes of Core-Periphery Relations. In *The Routledge Handbook of Critical European Studies*, ed. Yannis Stivachtis et al. London: Routledge.

Chenery, Hollis. 1960. Patterns of Industrial Growth. *American Economic Review* 50 (4): 624–654.

ECB—European Central Bank. 2015. Real Convergence in the Euro Area: Evidence, Theory and Policy Implications. *ECB Economic Bulletin* 5: 30–45.

EU Commission (ed.). n.y. AMECO Database. http://ec.europa.eu/economy_finance/ameco/user/serie/SelectSerie.cfm (September 8, 2017).

Eurostat. 2018a. Regional GDP per Capita Ranged from 29% to 611% of the EU Average in 2016. Eurostat Newsrelease 33/2018. Brussels, February 28, https://ec.europa.eu/eurostat/documents/2995521/8700651/1-28022018-BP-EN/15f5fd90-ce8b-4927-9a3b-07dc255dc42a (November 7, 2018).

Eurostat. 2018b. Croatia and Latvia Are Most Dependent from International Remittances in the EU. https://ec.europa.eu/eurostat/statistics-explained/index.php/Personal_remittances_statistics#Croatia_and_Latvia_are_most_dependent_from_international_remittances_in_the_EU (April 12, 2019).

Eurostat (ed.). n.y.1. Glossary: Purchasing Power Standard (PPS). Brussels. http://ec.europa.eu/eurostat/statistics-explained/index.php/Glossary:Purchasing_power_standard_(PPS) (September 8, 2017).

Eurostat (ed.). n.y.2. Glossary: Purchasing Power Parities (PPPs). Brussels. http://ec.europa.eu/eurostat/statistics-explained/index.php/Glossary:Purchasing_power_parities_(PPPs) (September 8, 2017).

Eurostat (ed.). n.y.3. GDP at Regional Level. Brussels. https://ec.europa.eu/eurostat/statistics-explained/index.php/GDP_at_regional_level (November 7, 2018).

Fatto Quotidiano, Il. 2017. Nuova condanna per Umberto Bossi: due anni e mezzo per truffa allo Stato. Confiscati 48 milioni di euro al Carroccio. July 24. http://www.ilfattoquotidiano.it/2017/07/24/lega-nord-nuova-condanna-per-bossi-due-anni-e-mezzo-per-truffa-allo-stato-confiscati-48-milioni-di-euro-al-carroccio/3750650/ (October 18, 2017).

Flassbeck, Heiner, and Friederike Spiecker. 2011. The Euro—Story of Misunderstanding. *Intereconomics* 46 (4): 180–187.

Garcia-Bernardo, Javier, Jan Fichtner, Frank W. Takes, and Eelke M. Heemskerk. 2017. Uncovering Offshore Financial Centers: Conduits and Sinks in the Global Corporate Ownership Network. *Scientific Reports* 7 (1): 6246. https://doi.org/10.1038/s41598-017-06322-9.

Kirby, Peader. 2010. *Celtic Tiger in Collapse. Explaining the Weaknesses of the Irish Model*, Second Edition. Basingstoke and New York: Palgrave Macmillan.

Monfort, Philippe. 2008. *Convergence of EU Regions: Measures and Evolution*. Brussels: European Union (=Directorate-General for Regional Policy 1/2008).

Stöllinger, Roman. 2016. Structural Change and Global Value Chains in the EU. *Empirica* 43 (4): 801–829.

UNCTAD (ed.). 2013. World Investment Report 2013. Global Value Chains: Investment and Trade for Development. New York and Geneva.

UNCTAD (ed.). 2016. World Investment Report 2016. Investor Nationality: Policy Challenges. New York and Geneva.

UNCTAD (ed.). 2017a. World Investment Report 2017. Investment and the Digital Economy. New York and Geneva.

UNCTAD (ed.). 2017b. World Investment Report 2017: Annex Tables. http://unctad.org/en/Pages/DIAE/World%20Investment%20Report/Annex-Tables.aspx (October 13, 2017).

Weissenbacher, Rudy. 2005. *Jugoslawien. Politische Ökonomie einer Desintegration.* Wien: Promedia.

Weissenbacher, Rudy. 2007. Historical Considerations of Uneven Development in East Central Europe. In *Dollarization, Euroization and Financial Instability: Central and Eastern European Countries Between Stagnation and Financial Crisis?*, ed. Joachim Becker and Rudy Weissenbacher, 35–83. Marburg: Metropolis.

Weissenbacher, Rudy. 2019. „In wenigen Monaten wird nichts mehr wie früher sein“: Die gelb-grüne Regierung und der Abstieg Italiens im europäischen Kapitalismus. *Kurswechsel* 24 (1): 62–71.

Wickham, James. 2012. After the Party's Over: The Irish Employment Model and the Paradoxes of Non-learning. In *A Triumph of Failed Ideas European Models of Capitalism in the Crisis*, ed. Steffen Lehndorff, 59–77. Brussels: ETUI.

Young, Andrew, Matthew Higgins, and Daniel Levy. 2008. Sigma Convergence Versus Beta Convergence: Evidence from U.S. County-Level Data. *Journal of Money, Credit and Banking* 40 (5): 1083–1093.

CHAPTER 9

Capitalism and Beyond?

This final section will lead us from the global crisis of the 1970s to the global crisis that reached Europe in 2008. While the former marked a crisis of Keynesian capitalism, the latter is one of financialized capitalism. I will summarize the main arguments by the European dependency school and then briefly sketch the transformation of capitalism toward financialization. I will use Giovanni Arrighi's theoretical model of these changes, from what he calls 'signal crisis' to 'terminal crisis'. I will, furthermore, present in a nutshell the main strand of financialized capitalism's paradigm, neoliberalism, that helped restoring 'development from above' before I shall try to use elements of EDS suggestions to sketch an alternative political economy in the wake of recent developments.

We have so far put emphasis on the caesura of capitalism in the 1970s that had influenced EDS writing. EDS authors had included that crisis and its consequences in their analysis (Chapter 4), they were aware of the fact that (postwar) boom-related economic growth did nothing to reduce dependencies ('growth without development', 'industrialization without development') in most quarters (Italy might count toward a temporary exception). They were also aware of some of the systemic attempts to counter the crisis of global capitalism, which drew the global periphery more in the realm of core TNC's commodity (production) chains ('new international division of labor'). Although EDS authors had recognized the caesura, they were not concerned with that period being transformational in terms of forms of capitalism, and therefore did not recognize that it was financialization that surmounted the system crisis.

R. Weissenbacher, *The Core-Periphery Divide in the European Union*,
https://doi.org/10.1007/978-3-030-28211-0_9

There was, however, awareness of this transformation among other social scientists, for example German political economists. Elmar Altvater (1983: 234ff.), Kurt Hübner (1983: 210ff.), Alexander Schubert (1985: 58ff.) are examples of authors who understood the trend they had observed in a decade of crisis, namely that falling profit rates in the productive sector translated into a higher mass of profits seeking utilization in the financial sector. As Jörg Goldberg (1983: 156) put it: 'The downside of structural over-accumulation of capital in the reproductive sector [...] is a supremacy of the credit and finance sectors that increasingly limit investment and utilization of reproductive capital'. Accumulation and social reproduction in this form of capitalism (that would be dubbed 'financialized') still depends on the productive sector but the high 'returns of investments in the monetary sector [...] lead to increasing expectations on the level of profit rates in real investments, and to a reallocation of profits toward the financial sector, respectively. [...] The allocations battle between the monetary and the producing sector takes a dramatic shape in the light of the high interest policy' (Hickel 1983: 72).

9.1 Capitalist Crisis of the 1970s and Financialized Restoration

When global capitalism entered yet another crisis period in 2007/8, it was thus characterized crisis of financialized capitalism (Lapavitsas 2013: 2). This phase of 'financialization', however, was by no means the first one, as Giovanni Arrighi (2010a, b) and Silver and Arrighi (2011) argued. They proposed a historical cycle in capitalist history with two alternating phases, a productive phase wearing out, which is then followed by a phase of financialized capitalism. A phase of materialized capitalism was then reorganized at a higher structural level. In four cycles (Genoese-Spanish—Dutch—British, and the US-American in the twentieth century) profitability in the material accumulation turned sluggish and shifted investments toward financial markets. Difficulties in material production were accompanied by a 'signal crisis' of the hegemonic power. The hegemonic power was able to restore power temporarily (in a period called 'belle epoque') before a 'terminal crisis' made way for a new productive cycle with a new hegemonic power. Hegemony was organized on an ever-higher level, as far as the territory was concerned but also structural complexity (with decreasing dependencies for the hegemonic power). While Genoa had relied on Spain for its defense, the Netherlands had internalized the costs of security. The Dutch, again, still relied 'on others for most of the agro-industrial production' (Arrighi 2010a: 376) but were able to organize their own defense, which was 'internalized' into their hegemonic system. The British then organized the material production themselves (in addition to the defense).

> Finally, the United States was a continental military-industrial complex with the power to provide effective protection for itself and its allies and to make credible threats of economic strangulation or military annihilation towards its enemies. This power, combined with the size, insularity, and natural wealth of the United States, enabled its capitalist class to internalize not just protection and production costs – as the British capitalist class had already done – but transaction costs as well, that is to say, the markets on which the self-expansion of its capital depended. (ibid.)

The signal crisis of US hegemony came with the 1970s, and financialization can be seen as a strategy to restore US power. Altvater (1983) and Schubert (1985) belong to the authors who early emphasized the devastating effects of US monetary policy with an high interest policy for the indebtedness of the global periphery. Arrighi (2010b [1994]) analyzed the breathtaking story of changes in the world economy from the 1970s into the 1980s in great detail. It comprises the attempts to counter hegemonic weakness by the US government and the development of offshore dollar markets beyond the control of the US federal reserve. Low interest rates in the 1970s, new technologies that enabled quicker transfers, economic crisis that curtailed real in favor of financial investments, and the increasing oil price rents fed an ever increasing global financial market. This liquidity provided 'US business with additional pecuniary means and incentives to outbid competitors in the appropriation of the world's energy supplies and in the transnationalization of processes of production and exchange' (Arrighi 2010b: 323). It appears typical for a situation of exhausted material production that incentives of monetary policy to stimulate production are overall to no avail because investments seek more profitable options in the financial sector. The US government tried in vain to stimulate the productive economy by low interest rates up to the end of the 1970s. In the end, the situation was neither beneficial for the US government nor the US banks. An abundant private dollar supply, offered at low interest, freed

> an increasingly larger group of countries […] from balance of payments constraints in the competitive struggle over the world's markets and resources, and thereby undermined the seignorage privileges of the US government. On the other hand, the expansion of the public supply of dollars, fed off shore money markets with more liquidity than could possibly be recycled safely and profitably. It thereby forced the members of the US-led confraternity of banks that controlled the Eurocurrency business to compete fiercely with one another in pushing money on countries deemed creditworthy, and indeed in lowering the standards by which countries were deemed creditworthy. If pushed too far, this competition could easily result in the common financial ruin of the US government and of US business. (Arrighi 2010b: 324)

The recovery of US hegemony was thus an alliance of the state and financial capital that restored the value of the dollar and tightened international money supply. For our purpose, it is interesting to see how this US policy of drawing liquidity into the US ('recentralization of purchasing power', Arrighi 2010b: 334) curtailed exports from the periphery, laid the ground for austerity programs, and thereby paralyzed any challenges from the global periphery. Abundant global liquidity in the 1970s changed to a fundamental credit crisis in the 1980s. What made matters worse was that international lending practices in the 1970s had changed from fixed toward flexible interest rates which made existing credits more expensive when interest rates rose:

> As if by magic, the wheel had turned. From then on, it would no longer be First World bankers begging Third World states to borrow their overabundant capital; it would be Third World states begging First World governments and bankers to grant them the credit needed to stay afloat in an increasingly integrated, competitive, and shrinking world market. To make things worse for the South and better for the West, Third World states were soon joined in their cut-throat competition for mobile capital by Second World states. (ibid.)

It is important to see that signal crisis and restoration of hegemony had an impact on core countries as well. Over-accumulation led to crisis in the old industrial regions and to the outsourcing strategies in the framework of the 'new international division of labor'. Shutting down, reorganization, and relocation of constant capital was accompanied by labor policies ('variable capital'): low-wage production in the global periphery and real wage decline and union push back in core countries. Keynesianism, the postwar economic paradigm in core countries was swept away and undermined social democratic parties which had supported it as a key pillar (Altvater 1983: 245). Global economic crisis and the mechanisms to overcome it (outsourcing and new international division of labor) contributed to an increase of TNC power in financialized capitalism. The transformation from Keynesian to financialized capitalism was also one of changing characteristics as regards core activities discussed in Chapter 8. While EDS authors were writing at the beginning of the cycle of financialization, this cycle currently has entered a phase of crisis. Before I will turn to the current crisis of financialized capitalism and Arrighi's explanation of the 'terminal crisis', I will summarize the EDS authors arguments concerning crisis and alternatives, and then present in a nutshell the main strand of financialized capitalism's paradigm, neoliberalism.

9.2 Capitalism, Crisis, and the Dependency Paradigm

Authors of the Latin American Dependency School emphasized in the 1960s that the integration of countries in the global capitalist system led to national (social and regional) disintegration. This school drew conclusions from the unsuccessful attempt of Latin American structuralism to decrease dependencies and further development in a broad sense, despite sparking industrial development in some countries by import-substituting industrialization. Idealized perceptions of economic convergence or reproducible paths of historical developments ('modernization') were considered unrealistic. Transnational companies (TNC) were regarded as the powerful actors in the formation of a new dependency of the periphery from the core. They represented impediments to national and regional alternatives difficult to overcome. TNC were predominantly based in core states, which enabled them to pursue a neomercantilist policy. Arrighi and Drangel (1986), who followed the dependency paradigm in their world-systems approach, would later talk of the symbiosis of a common development of core states and core TNC. For them, the 1960s ended the era when industrial production was considered a (sole) core characteristic ('industrial countries') which coincided with Arrighi's 'signal crisis' that would lead to the advance of financialization as predominant form of capitalism (due to US policies seeking to consolidate their hegemony). The control of transnational commodity chains was becoming more important for core countries to maintain their core positions than to organize industrial production within their own jurisdictions. Development via industrial development was a 'ladder without upper rungs' in the hierarchy of commodity chains. Arrighi called the idea that industrial development could lead to 'development' in capitalism 'developmentalist illusion'. Such reasoning connected directly to dependency thinking: Industrial development was not to be mistaken as development in a broader societal sense. As we have seen, Cardoso and Faletto (1976) emphasized that they meant development of productive forces when talking of dependent development in the periphery. They explicitly did not expect from or in capitalism a 'more egalitarian or more just society', neither in the core countries nor (and especially not) in the periphery. What had 'to be discussed as an alternative is not the consolidation of the state and the fulfillment of "autonomous capitalism", but how to supersede them. The important question, then, is how to construct paths toward socialism' (see Chapter 2).

In the first two global economic crisis after World War II in the 1970s and 1980s, many old industrial regions of core countries experienced peripheralizing tendencies. But already in the 1960s, core states began coordinating and financing measurements to reduce over-capacities, modernize infrastructure and regain competitiveness but were unable to prevent accelerating de-industrialization processes (cf. Carney 1980). As we have seen, TNC found their strategic solution to the 'Keynesian' accumulation crisis in a global restructuring of production that consisted of outsourcing toward the (semi-)periphery and led to what became known as 'new international division of labor'. Even for many peripheral regions of the core, the crisis of the 1970s ended a period that had brought economic 'growth without development' or 'industrialization without development'.

As the Latin American dependency school a decade earlier, the EDS began formulating alternatives to the dominant paradigms in the 1970s. It critisized liberal currents in economic theory (neoclassical economics, Keynesianism) and modernization theory. EDS authors applied findings from critical development studies to Europe. I identified two groups in this heterogeneous school of EDS. Authors that focused on the nation state level viewed the European integration process critically and treated the accession of peripheral countries as an integration of 'unequal partners'. Southern enlargement of the EC occurred in times of economic crisis. Neither the EC, whose countries reacted to the crisis with protectionist measures, nor the accession countries were prepared for such an 'unequal' integration. In order to avoid further polarization that could lead to a neocolonial scenario between core and periphery, two sets of measures were suggested, (a) a balanced industrial policy or (b) a more pronounced financial redistribution from core to periphery, comparable to national states' internal adjustments. The latter measure was seen as possible alleviation not structural improvement. Neither of the measurements, however, materialized. Establishing a monetary union under such conditions was considered fatal.

The second group engaged with aspects of regional development. The prevailing development models were judged as 'development from above' or 'development from the outside'. These development models treated regions as functional entities without geography or history. They observed endogenous modernization deficits that were to be countered by exogenous remedies (capital flows, technology import, state investments into infrastructure, etc.). But economic convergence did not occur in boom phases: Positive effects that were to spread or trickle down from core to periphery were smaller than negative backwash effects from the core. The crisis of the 1970s then struck away the 'crutches' of Keynesian regional policy that was meant to keep running the neoclassical model (Stöhr and Tödtling 1979: 138).

EDS authors viewed the functional integration of regions into the national and international division of labor critically. For them, selective decoupling (selective spatial closure) was a necessary step toward alternative development. They argued for more endogenous, region-centered policies. 'Self-reliance' was the term originating with the dependency school but they articulated it as 'selective self-reliance'. Penetrating influences from outside should be reduced. They suggested 'development from below' as alternative paradigm. Empowerment and participation in decentralized, egalitarian decision-making structures would ensure that scarce resources and land, and regionally produced wealth would be used for the benefit of all and not concentrated among few. The production of use value would have priority to exchange value in order to satisfy food supply, accommodation, and other basic needs. Regions should increase their resilience to economic crisis. Important catch phrases were mobilization of endogenous resources and internalization of development costs. Technological progress and innovation should serve the development of societies and not be subordinated to the competition paradigm. Regional development banks would stimulate regional production, counter dependence on the core, and reduce external debt. Large export projects should be replaced by regional enterprises with a regional service sector. A regional multiplier effect would be criteria for evaluation. Transport infrastructure should increase regional accessibility and networks and not be reduced to the needs of the export industry. Regional resources should be mobilized for the energy needs of the region. Environmental and education policies were to anchor responsibilities toward future generations.

This wish list of development studies by EDS authors sounds equally radical and hopeful. It presupposes dissolving the capitalist mode of production and then replace it. (The authors argued gradual changes.) The reality was and is, however, capitalism and the capitalist mode of production. We have seen that Edward Soja had criticized authors of the 'new territorialism' (to whom he counted some of the EDS authors) for being overly romantic and utopian. They were obscuring the history of capitalist development. Indeed, the later work of some of them seemed to fit well into the neoliberal paradigm whose wave steamrolled many alternative approaches in the 1990s, the 'globalization decade'. The competition among companies was applied to territories and gave birth to the competitive region. In their idealized version of capitalism, benevolent small entrepreneurs collaborate in networks of flat hierarchies and create a competitive advantage (cf. Chapter 7). Hadjimichalis und Papamichos (1990) early sensed that such trivial notions would become popular among right-wing governments. Consequently, the relations of production survived, while the fetish of productive forces keeps feeding the idea that technological progress and innovation can cure the harm done by capitalist production, in social and environmental terms.

What were the perspectives of transforming the mode of production? In the Latin American dependency school, such a political change and an implementation of development alternatives had a revolutionary component that was missing in most cases in the EDS. Dudley Seers seems to have expected that left-wing governments would/could be elected in conventional liberal electoral systems. What participation in socio-economic processes could look like was not detailed, neither how an alternative political system could prevail against a capitalist state or international environment. Some made clear, however, that progressive changes and transformation were not to be expected in actual existing bourgeois democracies. It seems coherent that Nohlen and Schultze (1985: 50f.) drew on the Canadian political scientist Crawford Macpherson who tried

> to work out a revision of liberal-democratic theory, a revision which clearly owes a great deal to Marx, in the hope of making that theory more democratic while rescuing that valuable part of the liberal tradition which is submerged when liberalism is identified with capitalist market relations. (Macpherson quoted in Morrice 1994: 646)

Macpherson considered a vicious circle of advanced capitalism that more democratic participation presupposed a change in social inequality and in consciousness which in turn could not be changed without an increase in democratic participation (Nohlen and Schultze, cf. Chapter 6.2). Where democratic legitimacy displayed particular deficits, changes could be initiated by small and incremental steps, argue Nohlen and Schultze (1985: 51). Some of the EDS authors perceived social movements a key to break up blockades in bourgeois democracy. John Friedmann (1986: 205) saw in self-reliance the only alternative for peripheral regions, 'self-reliance does not appear as a question concerning the use of policy instruments by the state but as a form of radical social practice originating within civil society'. For Hadjimichalis (1983: 137f.) social movements arose from the 'objective conditions of uneven regional development and subjective conditions of rising regional consciousness'. A region-centered policy relies on a high quality of participation, wrote Nohlen and Schultze (1985: 50). Traditional representative democracy would not suffice, and neither would direct-democratic participation as in social movements: 'Required are a double strategy in patterns of participation, participation as means and ends, as stake and social participation, conventional and unconventional forms, within and outside the institutional structure of politics' (Nohlen and Schultze 1985: 51). Authors following the state theory of Nicos Poulantzas (as Hadjimichalis 1983, 1984) came to similar conclusions. Coming from the opposite of the political spectrum of Nohlen, Poulantzas (2014: 256) criticized both the liberal parliamentary democracy and what he considered a Soviet type parallel state. He posed the question as to how the state could be transformed by deepening representative democracy but in combination with forms of direct democracy and worker's self-management.

This question remained unanswered. Instead of a transformation of the capitalist state toward socialism, the capitalist state transformed toward a more authoritarian rule. This was in line with parts of Poulantzas theory, namely the 'authoritarian state' that reduced democratic participation due to the necessity of intervening ever more in an increasingly complex and crisis-prone TNC capitalism (cf. Chapter 3.1). The relative autonomy of the state declined, and so did the ability of the state to function as embodiment of the general interest of society, but no 'hegemonic organization of the working class' materialized that would conquer the state. Poulantzas defended representative democracy but by the same time acknowledged the role of dominant parties (Christian and Social Democrats) that tended 'to function as a single mass party of the bourgeoisie, in spite of the differences that might exist between them' (Poulantzas 2008: 400; cf. Narr 1977). Poulantzas did not spell out how the transformation of a 'real existing' representative democracy (based on 'popular parties' that are essential for the functioning of the capitalist state) toward a socialist state might work. The revolutionary party was still the important organizational form,

> it has a central role as long as it [!] believes that politics has a central role, and as long as the state has a central role. But then as long as we need some type of organization, we must have a type of centralism or a type of homogenization of differentiations if we must make this articulation between representative democracy and direct democracy. (Poulantzas 2008: 401)

While in the past, the party itself played such a centralizing role, Poulantzas seems to have envisaged the future mediation between representative and direct democracy in two ways. First, state representative organs should be transformed, 'some aspects of this [centralizing] role must be transferred from the party itself to the representative organs where many parties can play their own role. We must have this differentiation and non-identification between party and the state' (Poulantzas 2008: 401). The Yugoslav socialist experiment had reflected such attempts to overcome 'democratic centralism' and combine it with a form of 'direct democracy' in a model of 'self-management bodies'. The problems of representation, participation, and ownership, however, remained unsolved (cf. Weissenbacher 2005). Furthermore, the Yugoslav system was not a 'pluralist' type (but a democracy with a one party system). In a pluralist system of a capitalist state, the 'articulation between representative democracy and direct democracy' appears even more difficult. It seems unlikely that the 'bloc in power', the capitalist state and its parties, would consider constitutional changes advanced by a revolutionary party.

The second suggestion, Poulantzas made, aims at restructuring the party itself. The party shall open itself toward social movements. Poulantzas (2008: 401) was

> not sure that a political party is the best form of organizing even, in their differences, the new forms of social movements. For example, I am not sure at all that we must ask a revolutionary political party to take under consideration the ecological problem, the feminist problem and so on. So the problem is not only to have a party so good that it is not only going to be political but take up every sphere of social life and economic life. I think that this conception of the party as the unique centralizer, even if it is a very subtle centralization, is not necessarily the best solution. I think more and more that we must have autonomous social movements whose type of organization cannot be the same as that of a political party organization. There must be a feminist movement outside the most ideal possible party because the most ideal party cannot include such types of social movements even if we insist that the revolutionary party must have certain conceptions of the woman question.

One could argue that the becoming of the green parties in the 1980s had been a version of collaboration between social movements and representation in the parliamentary democracy, in order to achieve transformation of the capitalist mode of production. Whatever there might have been in ideas of radical change in green parties, it also had lost momentum.

9.3 Restoration of the Development Paradigm 'from Above': Authoritarian Liberalism in a Hayekian Universe

The global crisis of the 1970s and 1980s brought to an end the postwar form of capitalism, and consequently also the prevailing interpretation of how capitalism would or should function, above all Keynesianism. The Latin American or European challengers of that development paradigm from the dependency schools were unable to fill the paradigmatic void. Instead, a more radical liberal economic doctrine than Keynesianism succeeded: neoliberalism. This doctrine has been closest connected to Friedrich Hayek and the Mont Pèlerin-Society (MPS, n.y.), whose founding president Hayek had been. The crisis of the 1970s brought the doctrine's breakthrough, by the end of the decade it was spread also as government doctrine by core countries. Nicos Poulantzas died in 1979, about half a year after Margarete Thatcher had taken office as UK prime minister, and she as well as Ronald Reagan adopted a neoliberalist stance (Thatcherism, Reaganomics). These governments could argue their anti-labor policy with ingredients of Hayek's universe:

> [I]f there is to be any hope of a return to a free economy, the question of how the powers of trade-unions can be appropriately de-limited in law as well as in fact is one of the most important of all the questions to which we must give our attention. (Hayek 1958: 126)

The fundamental de-democratization was most devastating. Hayek's principles have been guiding ever since. Other than the simplistic idea of a rational individual that participates in the market with 'perfect' information (as put forward by neoclassical economics), the Hayekian (1958: 15) edifice was more subtle. The classical writers (in part reference for the economic neoclassic) had been wrongly interpreted as 'of having extolled selfishness'. Hayek corrected the 'argument in simple language': by 'people are and ought to be guided in their actions by their interests and desires [...] we mean [...] that they ought to be allowed to strive for whatever *they* think desirable'. Does the individual know his or her interest best? '[N]obody can know who knows best and [...] the only way by which we can find out is through a social process in which everybody is allowed to try and see what he can do'. There is an 'unlimited variety of human gifts and skills' but also the 'consequent ignorance of any single individual of most of what is known to all the other members of society taken together'. Consequently, 'no man is qualified to pass final judgment on the capacities which another possesses or is to be allowed to exercise'.

'[T]he theory of individualism', as put forward by Hayek (1958: 22), contributes 'to the technique of constructing a suitable legal framework and of improving the institutions which have grown up spontaneously'. The conservativism of Hayek is obvious: It is a small and familiar world that has evolved and builds the nucleus of his liberal society:

> [T]rue individualism affirms the value of the family and all the common efforts of the small community and group, [...] it believes in local autonomy and voluntary associations, and [...] indeed its case rests largely on the contention that much for which the coercive action of the state is usually invoked can be done better by voluntary collaboration. (Hayek 1958: 23)

It was nothing short of replacing the role of religion in society, what Hayek's social order meant to achieve:

> Though the declining influence of religion is undoubtedly one major cause of our present lack of intellectual and moral orientation, its revival would not much lessen the need for a generally accepted principle of social order. We still should require a political philosophy which goes beyond the fundamental but general precepts which religion or morals provide. (Hayek 1958: 2)

The market is the important adjustor between the small 'part of our social order which can or ought to be made a conscious product of human reason' (Hayek 1958: 22) and the complex reality of society:

> What the economists understood for the first time was that the market as it had grown up was an effective way of making man take part in a process more complex and extended than he could comprehend and that it was through the market that he was made to contribute "to ends which were no part of his purpose". (Hayek 1958: 14f.)

Possibly, Hayek was the 'organic intellectual' to succeed Talcott Parsons in the attempt to defend capitalist hegemony in ideological terms (Arrighi 2010b: 29ff.). Parsons had been the connector between Max Weber (the protestant ethics as base for the ideology of the American dream—from rags to riches) and modernization theory (US type mass consumption for all societies). Both of these fading ideological narratives had a character conserving the status quo of societies. The illusion that participating in a mass consumption society was possible for all posed an ideological incentive to postpone contemporary political action (cf. Weissenbacher 2012a). The crisis of the 1970s brought disillusion in all quarters. Arrighi (2010a, Silver and Arrighi 2011) had perceived it as 'signal crisis' of US hegemony. In an obviously unequal and polarizing world, Hayek's ersatz-religious order could not provide an illusion for all but it made responsibilities clear for miseries (and helped justifying the wealth of the rich): Those who failed to respect the (market) rules, be it union leaders or politicians. The state could intervene for group interests (e.g. workers, unions), limit the liberties of private property and hence curtail the prospect for social development. Hayek's state was consequently a small one with limited influence:

> [T]he state, the embodiment of deliberately organized and consciously directed power, ought to be only a small part of the much richer organism which we call "society," and that the former ought to provide merely a framework within which free (and therefore not "consciously directed") collaboration of men has the maximum of scope. (Hayek 1958: 22)

The idea of leaving responsibilities to the market helped concealing the reality of late TNC capitalism (as described e.g. by Adorno or Poulantzas above, or Agnoli 1995 [1978]): The state was increasingly necessary to manage complex and crisis-prone accumulation and reproduction processes but it became more authoritarian by defending the mode of production. What Hayek claimed to be a state characteristic ('deliberately organized and consciously directed power') became true evermore for TNC. In the 1970s, 'the march into neoliberalism began, as a rebellion of capital against Keynesianism, with the aim of enthroning the Hayekian model in its place' (Streeck 2016: 22). Sheltered by the market ideology, technocrats received ever more power to steer societies, neoliberals described as too complex to understand for the average individual. 'Hayekian democracy serves', as Streeck (2016: 188) put it,

> the function of making a capitalist market society appear to be "the people's choice" even though it has long been removed from democratic control. What I refer to as a technocratic-authoritarian market dictatorship is a political-economic regime that delegates decisions on the distribution of people's life chances to the "free play" of market forces or, which is the same, concentrates them in the hands of executive agencies that supposedly command the technical knowledge necessary to organize such markets so that they perform best.

Hayek's organizational principles for societies had a priority for 'liberty' and the 'rule of law' and not universal suffrage. Drawing on Greek antiquity, Hayek saw no problems in keeping major parts of the population from voting which he did not perceive contradictory to liberty and the rule of law: 'It is also no longer possible to deny the existence of freedom in ancient Athens by the assertion that its economic system was "based" on slavery, since recent research has clearly shown that it was comparatively unimportant' (Hayek 2011 [1960]: 238, FN 10). There is a certain construction, Hayek needs for his arguments. Obviously one has to ask: liberty for whom? It is not the liberty of the slave but still freedom exists for the elite. Liberty, freedom, and equality before the law seem to be synonyms in the Hayekian universe.

> Equality before the law leads to the demand that all men should also have the same share in making the law. This is the point where traditional liberalism and the democratic movement meet. Their main concerns are nevertheless different. Liberalism (in the European nineteenth-century meaning of the word, to which we shall adhere throughout this chapter) is concerned mainly with limiting the coercive powers of all government, whether democratic or not, whereas the dogmatic democrat knows only one limit to government – current majority opinion. The difference between the two ideals stands out most clearly if we name their opposites: for democracy it is authoritarian government; for liberalism it is totalitarianism. Neither of the two systems necessarily excludes the opposite of the other: a democracy may well wield totalitarian powers, and it is conceivable that an authoritarian government may act on liberal principles. (Hayek 2011 [1960]: 166)

If one prefers to secure (economic) liberties for some at the expense of democracy, this can be called 'authoritarian liberalism', a phrase Hermann Heller (1933) used, discussing the 'autoritarian state' of the German Franz Papen cabinet of 1932 and the ideology of the right-wing state theorist Carl Schmitt. In Fig. 9.1, I have attempted to sketch a Hayekian ideological map following the one by Dudley Seers (Chapter 6). The space in which a Hayekian society can be organized democratically (L-D quarter) does not seem to be very populated. Consequently, he argues:

> It can scarcely be said that equality before the law necessarily requires that all adults should have the vote; the principle would operate if the same impersonal rule applied to all. If only persons over forty, or only income-earners, or only heads of households, or only literate persons were given the vote, this would scarcely be more of an infringement of the principle than the restrictions which are generally accepted. It is also possible for reasonable people to argue that the ideals of democracy would be better served if, say, all the servants of government or all recipients of public charity were excluded from the vote. (Hayek 2011 [1960]: 169)

Furthermore, he adds a footnote to these sentences, published in 1960:

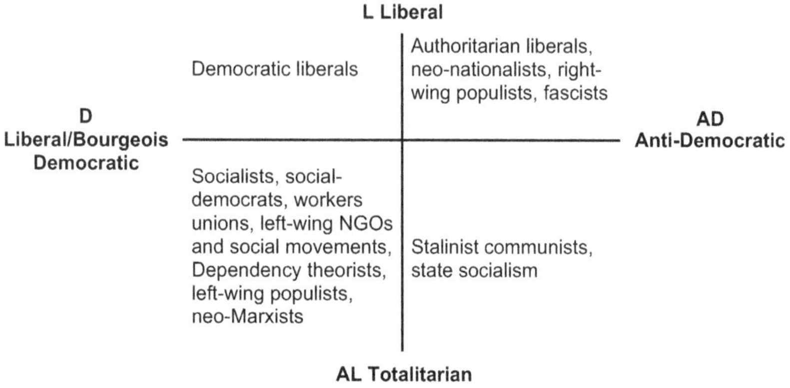

Fig. 9.1 Ideological map in a Hayekian Universe (*Source* Own presentation following Seers 1983: 48 [cf. Fig. 6.1])

> It is useful to remember that in the oldest and most successful of European democracies, Switzerland, women are still excluded from the vote and apparently with the approval of the majority of them. (footnote 4, in Switzerland women gained the right to vote – on the federal level, not yet in all cantons – in 1971, RW)

Almost two decades later, Hayek (1981 [1979]: 113f.) spelled out his idea for a model of a legislative assembly. The 45 year olds would 'once in their lives [...] select from their midst representatives to serve for fifteen years'. This would assure that 'only people who have already proved themselves in the ordinary business of life should be elected'. Thus one-fifteenth of the assembly 'would be replaced every year'. It looks as if Hayek had changed the voting restrictions from voting rights to eligibility (e.g. people who had 'served' in party organizations should not be eligible for the legislative assembly).

Hayek seems to have preferred liberal democracies but also been willing to accept fascist regimes that intended to respect the liberties of private property (if in pluralist societies he perceived such liberties being endangered). There is a line of arguments from the 'unholy alliance' (Scheuerman 1997: 183) between Hayek and Carl Schmitt, who had become 'the leading theorist of the Nazi-state' (Wistrich

1983: 243) after joining the NSDAP on May 1, 1933, and Hayek's support of Augusto Pinochet in Chile (Farrant and McPhail 2014). 'Notwithstanding Hayek's anxieties about the growth of discretionary state authority in our century', argues Scheuerman (1997: 183),

> he ultimately seems to have surprisingly few qualms about defending a rather worrisome political alternative to contemporary liberal democracy. Why? Like Schmitt, Hayek ultimately sees the interventionist welfare state as a "revolutionary" threat to a political universe dominated, to use one of Schmitt's favorite expressions, by those with "property and education" (Besitz und Bildung). Given the welfare state's purportedly revolutionary character, both theorists are ready to unlease a rather disturbing array of political instruments against it.

Santiago de Chile had been an important center of the Latin American dependency school and also hosted EDS authors. 'I don't know of any totalitarian governments in Latin America. The only one was Chile under Allende', Hayek is quoted (Farrant and McPhail 2014: 334) as saying about the democratically elected government. The coup d'etat against the Allende government in Chile had also a negative impact on the dependency school and was the beginning of a neoliberal experiment in Latin America.

Hayek's faith puts the property order first. The freedom of the property classes and the defense of what is perceived as 'free' market is rated higher than democratically elected governments that might curtail it. Consequently, fascist bureaucracies seem to be acceptable means to protect or (re-)establish such freedoms. In democratic societies, the religious function of liberalism appears important to keeping up appearances. Hayek's pretense of a liberal society that could benefit all but in reality secured the liberty of the few may otherwise be hard to digest. So far the formal economic power and informal political power of TNC have very much depended on the state. Neoliberal states, so far, have not given companies the right to issue their own currencies, although for Hayek (1978: 22) it was the question

> whether it would not be [...] desirable to do away altogether with the monopoly of government supplying and to allow private enterprise to supply the public with other media of exchange it may prefer.

For him, free competing currencies were preferable to

> the utopian scheme of introducing a new European currency, which would ultimately only have the effect of more deeply entrenching the source and root of all monetary evil, the government monopoly of the issue and control of money. (ibid.: 19)

The pragmatic neoliberal policy framework of the EU is to cut out the state and state institutions from accessing public money directly via central banks. The ECB was empowered and regulated in a way that it only was allowed to lend money to private banks. They, again, are able to lend money to the government. Consequently, the ECB could play—by tightening the supply of Euros—an important role in narrowing the room to maneuver of the Greek government trying to resist austerity measurements. Generally, the workings of the 'troika' against Southern European euro member states appear as a recent example of neocolonial rule. Technocratic bureaucracies of the IMF, the ECB and the EU Commission applied conventional neoliberal wisdom to the EU periphery, irrespective the positions of elected democratic bodies or stakeholders in these countries. The interviews conducted by Harald Schumann for a documentary (Schumann and Bondy 2015) are a rare occasion of making visible the core economic interest behind the ideological bureaucracy language. In terms of the European dependency school, this paradigm by Hayek can be called just another development from above or outside, constructed by authors from the core, helping to frame another neocolonial relationship.

9.4 The Terminal Crisis of the Twenty-First Century

Neoliberal ideology has been able to frame financialized capitalism for a while but the structural problems of capitalist accumulation have only been postponed. '[W]hile the party for the Third and Second Worlds was over', writes Arrighi (2010b: 334f.),

> the bourgeoisie of the West came to enjoy a belle époque in many ways reminiscent of the "wonderful moment" of the European bourgeoisie eighty years earlier. The most striking similarity between the two belles époques has been the almost complete lack of realization on the part of their beneficiaries that the sudden and unprecedented prosperity that they

> had come to enjoy did not rest on a resolution of the crisis of accumulation that had preceded the beautiful times. On the contrary, the newly found prosperity rested on a shift of the crisis from one set of relations to another set of relations. It was only a question of time before the crisis would reemerge in more troublesome forms.

Financialized capitalism, however, has restructured core societies as well. The productive system in core countries had come under additional pressure as profit rates are being measured primarily by the profit rates in the financial sector. The consequences were yet more outsourcing toward low-wage countries. Furthermore wages declined or stagnated, spending for social security and pension funds were reduced. Public assets that were socially built up over generations were incorporated into the realm of private financial accumulation by commodification: public transportation, health systems, insurance systems, pension systems, water supply and other public utilities, and educational systems. David Harvey called this process 'accumulation by dispossession' (cf. Weissenbacher 2008: 102). It has long been evident that financialized capitalism was even less sustainable or viable than its predecessor, socially, and ecologically. The appeasement of the working class in the core during the 'Keynesian' postwar period was secured by higher living standards. In financialized capitalism, consumption levels—and therefore social peace—was upheld, despite wage cuts and increasing unemployment, by private indebtedness. Such massive claims on future earnings were dubbed 'colonizing the future' (Reuten 2011: 53f.). Dramatic for core—periphery relations is the 'imported' stability via low import prices and inflation. Low-wage production was outsourced and left to regulatory systems out of sight of the consumers in core countries (Weissenbacher 2008: 106f.). It reopened the discussions on a complicity of core workers with core capitalists in global uneven development (cf. Fischer and Weissenbacher 2016). Last but not least, climate debts and fruits of economic systems based upon carbon energy production and transportation have been unevenly distributed.

We have seen that there is an evolutionary process built in the conception of Arrighi. Hegemony is being restructured at a higher level, both in terms of territory (from the city-state to the 'military-industrial complex of continental size') as well as the increase in power and complexity. This evolutionary process, however, has reached its limits because 'the state- and war-making capabilities of the traditional power centers of the capitalist West have gone so far that they can increase further only through the formation of a truly global world empire' (Arrighi 2010b: 368). Consequently, there are no direct conclusions possible from the historical experiences to the phase after the US hegemony. With the division of economic (East Asia) and Military Power (USA), for the first time in history of capitalism, a critical anomaly had occurred: the military power (USA) was in debt in East Asia, an 'unprecedented bifurcation of financial and military power' (Arrighi 2010a: 372). In 1994, Arrighi (2010b: 379) had argued the following three situations after the terminal crisis of US hegemony: (1) A new hegemonic regime would have a government organization that would come closer to a world state 'and most important, the new regime would internalize the costs of reproducing both human life and nature, which the US regime has tended to externalize'. Such a regime would consist of the US and its European allies. In case this 'first truly global empire in world history' (Arrighi 2010a: 381) would not come into existence that was able 'to use their military superiority to extract a "protection payment" from the emerging capitalist centers of East Asia' (Arrighi 2010a: 381), (2) the 'formation of a non-capitalist economy' (Arrighi 2010b: 372) might occur, 'over time East Asia might [...] become the center of a world market society buttressed, not by superior military power as in the past, but by the mutual respect of the world's cultures and civilizations' (Arrighi 2010a: 381). Or (3) 'a situation of endless systemic chaos' (Arrighi 2010b: 372) may occur. The 'belle epoche' of US hegemony had rested

> on the synergy of two conditions: the US capacity to present itself as performing the global functions of market of last resort and indispensable political-military power; and the capacity and willingness of the rest of the world to provide the US with the capital it needed to continue to perform those two functions on an every-expanding scale. (Arrighi 2008: 194)

The terminal crisis of US hegemony in Arrighi's interpretation had come already before the global economic crisis of 2007/8, it was marked by the 'bursting of the "new economy" bubble in 2000–2001, in combination with the failure of the neoconservative response to September 11' (Arrighi 2010a: 384):

> [T]he occupation of Iraq has jeopardized the credibility of US military might, further undermined the centrality of the US and its currency in the global political economy, and strengthened the tendency toward the emergence of China as an alternative to US leadership in East Asia and beyond. (Arrighi 2008: 209)

'Dominance without hegemony', Arrighi (2010a: 384; 2008: Chapter 7) calls the situation after the terminal crisis of US hegemony. He held, however, all three original scenarios possible (Arrighi 2010a: 385). To be sure, not all authors from the dependency school subscribed to the idea that US domination of global capitalism had been a hegemony (e.g. Amin 2017). Clearly, the restoration of global US dominance was based on the largest military and armament industry in the world (Serfati 2004). US dominance was, therefore, called imperialism instead (Hirsch 2001; Harvey 2003). Giovanni Arrighi died in 2009 and did not live to interpret the US administration of Donald Trump. From what one can tell so far, the Trump administration does not show interest in 'more favorable conditions for the emergence of a collective Western project' (Arrighi 2010a: 385). The sweeping blows of the US government include their allies and suggest that it considers gone the times when the US could enforce its interests as one of the greater good: hegemony. China is arguably the main target of US' confrontational stance in trade disputes. The US government seems to perceive as peril Arrighi's second scenario, 'an East Asian-centered world market society [that] appears today a far more likely outcome of present transformations of the global political economy than it did fifteen years ago' (ibid.). Consequently, the US administration of Donald Trump can abandon the Hayekian faith openly. Furthermore, it makes clear that it would no longer accept trade tariffs it considered unfair. It has started to use threats as means of trade disputes and no longer seems to trust its strength within the institutional framework of the World Trade Organisation (WTO). The 'America First'-Policy by the Trump administration seems to be an indicator for a change in the core—periphery system regarding the control of commodity chains (as described in Chapter 8) by the main core country US.

The confrontational stance in global political economy makes urgently needed international arrangements (e.g. policies countering climate change) difficult. The EU in 2019 is a player with severe limitations and deficits. Neither does it represent a system alternative, nor has the leading EU power Germany been willing to present policies toward a unification of member states under a hegemonic umbrella. 'Germany first' seems to have been always the guiding principle but Germany (its TNC and banks, respectively) managed to become the main exporter and a main creditor within the EU. Becker and Weissenbacher (2014: 16) called this situation an 'imbalanced Union in crisis'. It is part of the weakness of the European Union that Germany was able to defend its interest at the expense of the European periphery. While in the US debts stimulated global imports, in the EU German credits stimulated German exports. When austerity policies and credit stagnation curtailed imports of peripheral countries, German exporters increased their exports to 'third countries' outside the EU, which was facilitated by a low exchange rate of the euro (ibid.: 26). Obviously, this lopsided model is frail as well. While the social polarization in the US backed support for Donald Trump's presidency, social polarization in the EU brought electoral success for neonationalist parties (cf. Becker 2018). Pax Germanica was a hegemony only as far as the German governments were able to hide their interests behind the EU rhetoric of peace, prosperity (cohesion and convergence), and solidarity. The German stance against Greece to push through austerity in order to save (among others) German banks brought to the fore the dividing line in Europe and sent a clear signal to supporters of an alternative European Union. The European dividing line has also geopolitical implications. EU member countries from the (semi-)periphery belong to those who turn to China for parts of their infrastructure investments which may have created new dependencies. Hungary and Greece seem to have toned down EU decisions which meant to be critical of China (Kynge and Peel 2017: 7). 'We see the world economy's center of gravity shifting from the Atlantic region to the Pacific region', Victor Orban, the Hungarian prime minister, was quoted as saying (ibid.). The collaboration of Central, Eastern, and Southeastern European countries with China was institutionalized as 16 + 1 group, 'China builds a group around the EU's newer and poorer members' (ibid.). In 2019, the main unifying element within the EU appears to be a strong anti-migration stance while underlying EU responsibilities in producing migration (geopolitical and economic) are basically ignored or sidelined. Migration and asylum issues divert popular attention from the ongoing liberal economic agenda. Such policies largely continue to prioritize national economic competition and growth against environmental issues.

The strongest opposition against EU regulations on part of governments comes from the extreme European right (partially turning moderate right parties extremist, partially including parties from the extreme right, or both): the Visegrád Group states upfront, supported by Austria, Italy, and the German constituent state of Bavaria. Liberal, national-liberal, and fascist parties that currently gain ground in Europe do not have an agenda of transforming the mode of production and consequently the ownership structures in societies. In line with Hayek's position, neonationalist parties would rather relinquish democracy than the defense of private property (cf. Becker and Weissenbacher 2016, for a typology of neonationalist parties cf. Becker 2018). Therefore, different capital fractions can support pro-systemic parties of various natures according to their perception of the degree the relations of productions are being threatened. Such parties include, to be sure, conformist social democratic parties, which had led some authors to consider the Western German democracy as on its way to a one party state (Narr 1977).

Historically it is not a new situation that fractions of capital turn to the radical right in order to secure a mass base for the capitalist mode of production (cf. the arguments in the 'Deutsche Führerbriefe', an information bulletin for about 1200 members of German monopoly capital, before the NSDAP won a majority in the Reichstag, e.g. Sohn-Rethel 1973). In June 2018, however, major organizations of 'the' German business ('Die deutsche Wirtschaft') positioned themselves in favor of chancellor Angela Merkel of the conservative CDU against its Bavarian sister party CSU, which had radicalized the migration and asylum issue along the lines of the Hungarian, Austrian, and Italian governments. The common open letter (Kramer et al. 2018) to the German government by BDA (Bundesvereinigung der Deutschen Arbeitgeberverbände, the German employer's organization), BDI (Bundesverband der Deutschen Industrie, German Industrialists), DIHK (Deutscher Industrie- und Handelskammertag, the umbrella organization of German chambers of industry and trade), and the Zentralverband des Deutschen Handwerks (the umbrella organization of German craft's chambers and associations) used an old CDU slogan as heading: 'for Germany and Europe' (cf. Adenauer 1954; CDU 1995). 'Politics and society must not grow distant from each other', these organizations appealed. They argued with the interests of the export industry, applied EU mythology and pointed out that European integration had brought Germany/German industry ('us') prosperity:

> Our country processes 60 per cent of its trade volume within the EU. German business is convinced that national solo attempts cause more harm than good. Re-nationalization as a response to global challenges is ineffective. The European Union today is the largest democratic space of freedom, peace, economy and wealth – without precedent in history. Europe is part of our identity. The European integration process was a success story. The idea of peace and freedom, market economy and social balance has always been the criterion for political action. It has provided us a life in democracy and prosperity. (Kramer et al. 2018)

It seems as if it was the association of family businesses ('Familienunternehmer') among which one can find the main capital fractions in support of the fascist party AfD ('Alternative für Deutschland') that radicalizes the Bavarian CSU even more toward extremist positions (GFP 2018). This by no means indicates that these fractions are against export orientation. Rather, this conflict seems to rekindle the conflict between Adenauer's and Erhard's position (cf. Chapter 5). The 'Familienunternehmer' (2018: 6), who refer to the common struggle together with Ludwig Erhard in the 1950s, seem to favor a Erhardian position of European integration without any institutional responsibility (cf. GFP 2018).

Endeavors of strategical reorganization in the light of geopolitical struggles have started. In this process, competition principles are being readapted and newly interpreted. The 'National Industrial Strategy 2030 Strategic guidelines for a German and European industrial policy' by the German 'Federal Ministry for Economic Affairs and Energy' (GFM EA&E 2019) point toward a caesura. No longer, German companies appear as—the privileged—natural technological leaders that can self-confidentially insist on rules of competition. China and the USA are portrayed as locations of new dynamic global corporations, especially state-led industrial strategy in China is given credit for its dynamics. Under geopolitical pressure, according to the new strategy, German and EU competition principles should be revised.

> Free and open markets require comparable framework conditions for all market players and competitors (level playing field). They are not created automatically especially as some states do not play according to existing rules. In the interests of its economy, Germany must therefore work intensively on eliminating existing inequalities and disadvantages. (ibid.: 14)

What may historically have helped peripheral EU countries in supporting their industries against predominant German industries, namely national plans to protect their own industries, shall now back German industrial and strategic interest: 'The long-term success and the survival of such enterprises' as 'Siemens, Thyssen-Krupp, automotive manufacturers or Deutsche Bank [that] have existed for 100 years'

> is in the national political and economic interest because they make a substantial contribution to value added and in many cases are also jointly responsible for the excellent image enjoyed by the German economy and industry throughout the world. (ibid.: 12)

With the fear of losing the dominant export position, the lamentation indicates that environmental and social issues are no genuine interest of economic policy makers and TNC.

> In recent decades, [...] framework conditions [for industrial production in Germany] have altered considerably in part through state intervention such as for reasons of environmental protection, climate protection, energy transition, and social policy. This has worsened the costs and therefore the competitive position compared with countries in which this is not the case. (ibid.: 13)

From the perspective of development studies, however, current development responsibilities of industrial production would needed to be complemented by historical and path-dependent responsibilities: Economic reasoning most often disregards centuries of historical and geographical dependencies that have led to privileges and helped constituting competitive positions, e.g. the history of externalizing environmental pollution, or the extraction of resources to the advantage of industries in the global north (with all the human casualties). From a global or systemic or environmental logic, externalities and extractions are severe drawbacks of industrialization and should be treated as 'internal' systemic responsibilities (cf. Poma 2018). Geopolitical considerations of competition are in variance with development issues (e.g. following a global 'Buen Convivir' (ibid.: 253), a living together in a good life for all). In the current Arrighi situation, however, (geopolitical) competition is escalating, and core industries of core country Germany seem to try to improve their position by turning toward a strategic industrial policy:

1. The general public shall pay for 'higher ranking political reasons' (but subsidies shall not be termed as such):

   > Where the state compensates for interventions necessary for higher ranking political reasons in terms of their damaging effects on competition, this is not subsidising but restoring comparability in competition. This must be possible in line with EU law. (GFM EA&E 2019: 13)

2. EU regulation shall be changed (in the coincidence to the EU Commission's decision to prohibit Siemens' proposed acquisition of the French Alstom corporation, in February 2019): The report urges a revision of competition laws:

   > German or European mergers which are useful and necessary with a view to the global market frequently fail due to the focus on national and regional markets in prevailing law. European and German competition law must be reviewed and changed where applicable so that international competition "at eye level" remains possible for German and European companies. (ibid.: 11)

3. The German state shall make foreign takeovers more difficult. The German state may prohibit 'company takeovers by foreign competitors' in case 'this is necessary to defend against risks to national security, including the area of critical infrastructures' (ibid.: 12). As far as 'takeover attempts concern technological and innovation leadership rather than primarily following the state interest in security', the German state 'can provide encouragement and support' for the German private sector seen responsible 'to prevent such takeovers by suitable bids'. The fear that such strategic endeavors could open the door to public ownership discussions is obvious:

   > Only in very important cases should the state be able to act as buyer of shares for a restricted period of time. All in all, the stake held by the state may not increase in the long term, however, which is why the creation of a national participation facility comes into consideration with the requirement of reporting to parliament on a regular basis about the extent of any participation. Taking-over of new stakes must in principle be balanced by the privatisation of others. (ibid.: 12)

Furthermore: 'The state may never encroach upon business decisions of individual companies' (ibid.: 13).

4. Re-industrialization policies are urgent, and EU commodity chains shall be reconstructed under the control of German industries. Industrial production of Germany shall reach a share of 25% in total value added. Such a task is deemed

   > considerably more difficult for the EU as a whole because the process of de-industrialisation is still in full swing in many countries. A trend reversal is in the German economic interest, however, as important momentum for all countries is to be expected from an industrial renaissance in Europe. In perspective, the industrial share in the EU as a whole should therefore increase to 20 per cent by 2030. (ibid.: 10)

Furthermore, the control of entire commodity chains (from bottom to top production levels) within the EU is perceived to be an important pillar to succeed in global competition. Catching-up in certain technologies and repairing disintegrated chains seem important elements of geostrategic considerations:

> Maintaining closed value added chains is highly important: if all parts of the value added chain exist in an economic area from the production of basic materials, through finishing and processing, to distribution, services, research and development, the individual links in the chain will be more resistant, and it becomes more probable that a competitive lead can be achieved or extended. This is why we need a holistic approach and analysis as to where former value added chains have already been broken or are endangered as well as an agreement on suitable measures to prevent or reverse further erosion. We must extend existing strengths and at the same time launch a catching-up process in areas in which we are better than the others. Experience has shown that once "lost" to other competitors, industrial areas are very difficult to regain. This is why we must fight for every industrial job. It is misguided to make the wrong distinction between "old and dirty" industries and "clean new ones". (ibid.: 11)

This may sound ironic if one looks at the policies in the EU during the last decades, in part discussed in this book. In geopolitical terms these advances can be seen as attempts to close the ranks with the EU states turning toward China and Russia because the current EU policy was marked by austerity and geopolitical ignorance. German economic policy seems to intend a reorganization of its neo-mercantilism at the EU level (cf. the 'Franco-German Manifesto for a European industrial policy fit for the twenty-first century', Government of France 2019).

9.5 The Puzzle of System Change with Pieces from EDS?

In this concluding chapter, I will consider an alternative political economy, drawing on elements and ideas from EDS concepts. In the realm of the crisis decade between the 1970s and 1980s, the recommendations of EDS were in opposition to the prevailing mode of production but remained rather defensive. However, even the suggestions for alternatives within the current mode of production, like a balanced industrial policy for the EU, were incompatible with EU economic realpolitik.

The European Central Bank (ECB 2015: 31) has expressed its disappointment of the degree of convergence within the EU/EMU between 1999 and 2014 and identified the key elements of economic growth and convergence (still) as 'technology', 'innovation', and 'research and development'. The ECB (2015: 38ff.) acknowledges the difficulty of neoclassical theory in explaining technological progress that 'appeared like manna from heaven' (Maier et al. 2006: 57). Drawing on the externalities or endogenous growth model (cf. ibid.: 96ff.), the ECB (2015: 40) suggests that an 'alternative way' is necessary 'to endogenously create growth, and for convergence to be explained in a theoretical model, innovation must be 'produced' in a separate sector of the economy'. This seems to leave responsibilities for financing and producing technology and innovation up to the public sector. Therefore, it may be no surprise that '[c]ountries that spend more on R&D tend to exhibit higher income levels' (ECB 2015: 42). Within the prevailing logic, that furthers polarization.

EDS authors had also discussed re-distributive funding, not as convergence policy but an alleviating instrument to calm tensions from uneven development. Already today, EU funding takes an important part of some peripheral countries' budgets, and 34% of the entire EU budget is spent for economic, social, and territorial cohesion. Having said that, the overall amounts are limited by the relatively small budget of the EU. In 2017, the budget (commitments) of the EU (with some

500 million inhabitants) amounted to 157.86 billion euro (EU Council, n.y.), not quite twice the Austrian budget of 82.14 billion euro with some 8 million inhabitants in the same year (BMF 2016). Additionally, the current attitude toward the EU among member governments is one of budgetary restraints, rather than expansion (e.g. the Austrian government that had taken over the EU council chair in 2018 defied an expansive budget plan by the EU Commission, cf. Der Standard 2018). The Hayekian universe of a liberal paradigm (and its implications in a postmodern capitalist context, cf. Weissenbacher 2008) had been engrained deeply in societies, so that even left authors seem to have difficulties to leave it behind (cf. Weissenbacher 2014). European neo-nationalists have been able to fill the void of eroding liberal ideology with competition on the national level: Fears of social decline lead to voting support for parties defending the mode of production (cf. Weissenbacher 2012b, 2018b). Among the neonational right, the impasse of mainstream economic policies has led to mixed approaches, and acceptance of policies closer to Keynesian policies (Becker and Weissenbacher 2016; Weissenbacher 2015, 2019).

The crisis of 2008 has brought a reawakening of awareness also among social democrats (formerly key actors of Keynesianism) in what harm TNC capitalism is doing (cf. the report coordinated by Joseph Stiglitz et al. (2019), which was facilitated by the Foundation for European Progressive Studies, the 'intellectual crossroads between social democracy and the European project').

> Without adequate regulation and an appropriate role for government, society will experience massive collateral damage. For example, there will be too much pollution, too many risky financial products, hordes of overpaid executives, insufficient expenditures on basic research, and too little dissemination of innovation. (Stiglitz et al. 2019: 76)

For Stiglitz et al. (ibid.), it is necessary 'to make European markets work as they are supposed to, with competitive companies striving to improve societal well-being, through better corporate governance, which includes better executive compensation schemes'. From what we have seen in Chapter 7, such hopes in the benevolent capitalist entrepreneurs may even be more futile than the idea that the egoistic behavior of entrepreneurs will lead to societal improvements. Some hope rests on the idea that a 'European' industrial policy could be a cure for the impasse of the EU economic situation (cf. Lucchese et al. 2016). The solutions are to be found 'beyond the magic of the market' (Dosi 2016), the state needs to take up a strategic function again, for accumulation, cohesion, development of peripheral areas, and geopolitical reasons. Guarascio and Simonazzi (2016: 318) suggest even returning to an old development policy: 'A policy of "import substitution" (targeting for instance imported inputs) could be effective in strengthening existing industries, removing bottlenecks, filling gaps in the productive structure and supporting firms' upgrading and participation in high-value chains'. Furthermore, '[r]egional policy must not be a side action to, but must be an integral part of National policies on industry, infrastructure, welfare, research and innovation' (ibid.: 317). Lundvall (2016: 270) agrees with the need of transformational policies in Europe that, above all, emphasize the needs of the European periphery but cautions that the German-led EU response to the crisis ('each single country should become competitive through austerity policies') and the 'refugee crisis' that 'added a new kind of popular nationalism' made a 'revival of the idea of European-wide policies' unlikely. For Italy he suggested—due to a European lock-in situation—an Italian 'national plan for economic transformation that gives priority to specified social needs, promotes specific new technologies and emphasizes that the South of Italy requires a boost in terms of knowledge based manufacturing' (ibid.). Aiginger (2019), finally, argues that necessary environmental and social policies should be prioritized against traditional industrial policies.

All such suggestions appear radical in the neoliberal context of EU policies during recent decades that treated strategic state investments and industrial planning as curtailing the efficient workings of market forces. However, even if the current distribution of power between popular classes and TNC allowed a dramatic change—e.g. a new regulatory framework of national banks and the ECB in terms of financing industrial policies, the contradictions of the mode of production would not disappear. From an EDS perspective, a post-capitalist paradigm needs to be established. As long as the motive for production remains profit, a reorganization of production, consumption, and distribution will be difficult. It is not only persistent uneven development and socio-spatial polarization that call for more radical alternative policies. The consequences of capitalist production on the environment and the earth's climate system have been sidelined for decades. What has been formulated as 'selective self-reliance' and 'development from below' are conceptional references that can tie in with contemporary frameworks inclined to tackle both, socio-spatial polarization and the causes of climate change. Capitalist production externalizes real costs of resources, human labor, transportation and the consequences of production (e.g. green house gases). In a price competition that does not reflect such externalities a regional production often cannot survive. Such harmful consequences of the prevailing competition principle have led to suggestions of defining competitiveness as the ability of a region to achieve societal goals (Aiginger 2019: 104). The idea of self-reliance, however, goes well beyond that and replaces competition with cooperation. It aims at avoiding penetration from others *and* penetrating others.

More than four decades after the first report to the Club of Rome (Meadows 1972) and the Cocoyoc Declaration (1974), what the latter termed the inner (social) and outer (environmental) limits of the global economy have been continuously ignored. The challenge that cannot be ignored, however, is climate change. Surely, peripheral countries have less means to prepare for and counter the consequences of global warming but people in all countries will face the consequences. The earth's atmosphere cannot be substituted and abandoning earth is an unlikely scenario, even for the super-rich.

Immediate measurements to counter an increase in global warming can tie into self-reliance thinking, namely decentralizing production of renewable energy, food, and durables. Consequently, transportation (and the implications of energy use and pollution) would decrease. Use value would gain importance in such an economy combined with reusing, recycling, and repairing of products ('repair economy', 'circular economy') and the implications for regional production (longer product life cycles, regional linkages) and a growing service sector. Infrastructure investments would also serve regional linkages and not support export industries (quick import of pre-products and intermediates, export of production). Technology would focus on (regional) societal needs, Galtung talked of re-inventing existing technology in order to learn important techniques and procedures regionally and increase independence from outside owners of technologies. Educational institutions, schools, and universities, would provide a basis for regionally adapted technologies. Their interregional and international networking could be seen as the antennae for innovation and technology. Last but not least, production and consumption must be reorganized. EDS authors called for democratic and participatory economic systems. Clearly that touches property relations, e.g. the need to prevent single regional or national economic actors to gain roles of monopolistic producers or monopsonist buyers as a consequence of cutting dependencies to the outside. Calibrating a mixture of publicly owned companies (strategic industries, e.g. large energy producers), and companies owned by workers (self-management) or private individuals will belong to the most difficult endeavors. Large financial institutions (development funds, development banks) are among strategic industries which support regional development endeavors.

Such basic strategical elements of an alternative political economy shall not imply that there was a recipe for self-reliance. Regions and states do have a variety of different development paths and dependencies. All of them face, however, the challenge of pursuing an alternative non- or post-capitalist development path in a capitalist EU surrounding. In order to reduce the grip of functional integration into international division of labor ('function') on the development of a society ('territory'), the actual spatial entity of alternative activities may vary but will mostly depend on historically grown experiences. In emergency cases (like the consequences of the EU/Troika policy toward Greece), spontaneous alternatives decoupled, from grown political-administrative structures, will have to fill the void of disintegrating state functions. Often, the existing democratic structures need to be defended and expanded, which make nation states and regions with some political-administrative structures and jurisdiction likely candidates for larger alternative endeavors. Alternative regional governments, however, may be restricted in their room to maneuver if the national governments and parliaments are in opposition to alternative policies. National governments that break new grounds will face all kind of systemic pressure. Seers had pointed out that European integration from the very beginning was constructed to avoid transformational systemic changes by left governments. To a certain extent, member governments may be able to use their voting in the European Council, today, as a leverage to pursue alternative development paths. Having said that, alternative governments will most likely be in a position of weakness. Seers had already warned left governments of foreign indebtedness which could work as an outside leverage against alternative policies. The situation has worsened ever since. It is the bitter irony that the accumulated foreign public debt in many countries is (a) a systemic debt due to crisis policy-making ('safe the banking sector'), and (b) will hardly ever come close to the Maastricht criteria (for Italy cf. Weissenbacher 2019). If a country is member of the Euro zone, the leverage is particularly strong, as the case of the Syriza government's attempt of a Greek deviation from EU regulation had shown. Depleting a country of currency in circulation will bring it to the verge of collapse. Issuing a parallel currency (government certificates for circulation: IOU) may be one emergency measure that presumably had to be accompanied by a nationalization of strategic industries (energy, public transportation, water supply, banks, …). Already these aspects of a transformation shock will pressure a government. Only huge popular support that goes well into a country's elite may give it necessary backing by the state bureaucracy. For all 'antisystemic movements' different class interests (national and transnational) will constitute major challenges which Poulantzas or Latin American dependency thinkers (e.g. Cardoso and Faletto, Sunkel) had tried to grasp. Soja emphasized a horizontal and vertical class struggle.

The Syriza government of Greece had received no solidarity by other EU governments. The signal was clear and may have paved the way to a Greek diversification of foreign (economic) policy (e.g. the 16+1 group, cf. Chapter 9.4). Dependency authors had called collective self-reliance a solidarity and collaboration of antisystemic governments that would imply a balanced division of labor in terms of industrial production. Seers formulated a vision of a kind of Community self-reliance that might lead to a European alternative to the capitalist world economy. A national government acting alone, however, will certainly have to set its sights lower and have to pursue a more defensive project (even more so a regional government). While EDS concepts have never aimed at autarky but a preferential use of regional resources and human abilities, such policies of 'selective spatial closure' meant to reduce socially and environmentally destructive products and services may be preceded (or swept away) by a transformation shock. Import dependency and a dependent position of a country's productive sector in the European commodity chain may lead to bottlenecks in supply. Consequently, EDS approaches emphasized a gradual transformation.

Having said that, from an alternative EDS perspective, system transformation would need to go beyond betting on convincing TNC to accept environmental and social priorities. It'll be important for popular classes in societies to regain empowerment regarding planning and public property in one way or another. It seems essential to shake off the ideological shackles of the Hayekian past that leave planning and controlling economic endeavors to the realm of TNC's (virtual) space. First of all, it seems unlikely that the current state of media concentration and lobbying would easily allow the implementation of 'rational' policies. This touches the issue of private ownership and decartelization but also democratic policies of citizens' participation. Distribution of information should be (democratically and participatory) organized via a public infrastructure, e.g. citizens and companies would use publicly owned and controlled networks instead of Facebook and others. Having said that, participation will remain a buzzword if citizens do not have the opportunity (e.g. participatory budgeting) and time to participate. Participation needs to be learned and practiced. Such participatory systems need to go beyond the practice of sending members or followers of political parties into the realm of public companies. Friedmann's 'life space' needs to be recovered from domination by the 'economic space', participation enabled by reorganization of work/activities and wage labor. Systemic industries and services, however, need to be in public, democratically organized, ownership in order to secure standards and prevent commodification and private monopolies that can pressure societies: public transportation, public utilities (energy and electrical power supply, water supply, garbage collection systems, etc.), hospitals, and education. To be sure, public ownership of such industries is neither unusual nor new, it belongs to the success story of neoliberal ideology to spread the notion that public ownership was inefficient. Having said that, public ownership does not mean alternative policies as long as the mindset of the mode of production remains unchanged (e.g. national oil and gas industries that are not supportive of a clean energy transition, cf. Pollin 2018: 19f.). Last but not least, the entire system of financial services and banks needs to be (again: democratically and participatory) reorganized under the premises of societal and systemic considerations.

Secondly, the overall prevailing logic of production for profit (ignoring externalities) builds on the idea that anything may be produced as long as it reaches sufficient exchange value and demand on world markets. Even if one peripheral country found a niche for export production, that would not solve its overall problems, and moreover could hardly work as a blueprint for all peripheral countries. Alternatively, social and environmental concerns would have priority in a reorganization of production, consumption, and distribution patterns. A reconsideration of production motives would shift the emphasis from exchange value toward use value. The 'external' parts of the costs of production and consumption—transportation, resource inputs, pollution, energy use, and all social costs—would be internalized. If these aspects could be reflected in a price mechanism, it may be one pillar of changing consumption behavior in the core with immediate consequences for people in the periphery. (To be sure, such a caesura of traditional economic relations will have short-term negative effects—the reconfiguration of trade patterns with the disintegration of commodity chains, which is why compensation seems even more important, see further below.)

However, emphasis on much longer life cycles of products in a combination with a repair economy would expand regional production, employment and 'linkages', and serve also environmental goals. Aspects of such a new economic model have been introduced with the model of a 'circular economy' (meant to replace the traditional 'linear economy'). It is difficult to see, however, how a model that would revolutionize production and consumption patterns and culture in such a way can be pursued within the logic of a prevailing capitalist mode of production. One prominent author of the circular economy, Walter Stahel (2019), seems to assume inherent change was possible, despite the fact that in a mature circular industrial economy 'the use value [would replace] the exchange value as the central economic value' (ibid.: 16).

Thirdly, historical privileges for the core need to be acknowledged, from expropriation of labor (e.g. compensation of wartime slave labor in Europe or today's working situation in the global south) to the extraction of resources and the historical 'climate debt' of polluting the natural environment). Compensation funds and democratic sharing of technology could support self-reliant development in the periphery, alongside distributional efforts within core societies as well. Fourthly, the high productivity of TNC capitalism has led to fractions within waged work employees. A handful of workers-experts are needed to run a high-tech production factory in modern steel industry, and only partially jobs are transformed into back office and infrastructure service jobs (cf. Becker et al. 2018: 7). 'Increasing productivity must not be achieved primarily through higher labor productivity, but by promoting resource and energy productivity when unemployment is already high', argues Aiginger (2019: 105), and adds: 'That may sound dirigistic because it might require information that the state does not have'. Or anyone else, one might add. Meanwhile 'the state' in TNC capitalism makes all kind of decisions. Where large low-wage service sectors are politically created, like in Germany and Austria, socio-spatial frictions and polarization are the consequence. The contradiction of capitalist production are obvious: fewer people can actually produce commodities but the distributional reality makes it increasingly difficult for many to participate in consuming them. For the time being, frictions in core countries have been postponed, because real wage reduction and austerity has been shouldered by workers in the European or global periphery who produce, under conditions largely ignored by core consumers, low price commodities, and therefore stability in core countries (cf. Weissenbacher 2008). Furthermore, real working time reduction has long been reality in core countries, it is called precarious or involuntary part-time work. Distributional solutions need to follow, in a first step, the societal employment reality, and pay full wages for reduced working hours. Consequently the entire edifice of employment/wage labor versus work needs to be negotiated anew, in order to free personal resources for participatory societal, community, and family activities (cf. Haug 2014). Such changes could reduce socio-spatial rivalry (in the absence of external powers that wanted to defeat such a solidarity system).

What seems to have lacked in the past was the ability to enable and participate in a political process of implementation and transformation. EDS scholars were not successful in the sense of Johan Galtung's (1977: 64) philosophy of science: 'Empirical analysis is indispensable but should be seen as highly truncated'. Galtung rejects 'empiricism alone, as carrier of the definition of scientific activity'. 'A good theory' goes beyond accounting 'for empirical reality, but [...] leads to the realization of a preferred potential reality'. 'Action research' in his definition was belonging to normal scientific routine:

> Science is not only critical and/or theoretical reflection on reality [...]; nor speculation on potential realities axiologically or theoretically defined and how to get there. Science is all this, but also the practice of changing reality, of creating new reality. Action is needed, and if this action involves a power component, then political action is needed. (ibid.)

The odds against transforming the mode of production have not improved. The level of centralization of control of capital and the over-centralization of surplus generalized by monopolies/oligopolies produce an unbearable situation for the majority of humanity, argued Samir Amin (2017), one of the dependency gang of four (Amin, Arrighi, Frank, Wallerstein). 'Capitalism cannot walk out of capitalism', Amin (ibid.) summarized the contradictions, but no revolutions were in sight. 'Revolutionary advances' were necessary, however, to build capacities. Such advances he considered less and less realistic in the global north: 'revolutionary advances will happen in the periphery' (ibid.). EDS authors who formulated concepts of 'development from below' or 'selective self-reliance' were equally assuming that such concepts were pertinent for regions less in the clutch of core based commodity chains. Such peripheral regions are disconnected from the privileges of the core, have less to lose and are less important for the maintenance of the overall system. The more decoupled a region was, the stronger an organizational structure of 'self-reliance' could become a strategic necessity (cf. Stöhr 1981: 3; Friedmann 1986: 205).

Yet neither in core nor in peripheral countries, revolutionary changes are very likely. In peripheral countries and regions, they can be seen as a defensive strategy, but the global context cannot be disregarded. EDS authors had expressed the limitations of the established democratic electoral systems in order to initiate a transformation (of the mode of production). Elements of direct democracy, work place democracy, and social movements were seen as important. Today work place democracy will have to be organized within a broader context of restructuring production and consumption. High productivity in core and semiperipheral countries shifts employees into service sectors (e.g. care 'industry') or precarious employment relations. Chronic under- or unemployment in the periphery leaves many outside the formal employment sector.

Dudley Seers had put his hope in electoral successes of left-wing parties that might enable alternative developments, and construct something like community self-reliance of a 'true' integration. But liberal party democracy has been incapable to respond adequately to social and environmental challenges. With the changes in contemporary capitalism, transformation movements need go beyond workers' movements and also challenge the party system. World-systems theorists had talked of antisystemic movements (e.g. Arrighi et al. 1989). Gaining legislative power in an electoral process is an important but not sufficient task. Wainwright (2016: 82) talks of 'transformative power [...] distinct from (not opposed to) electoral politics': movements outside a party (therefore also extra-parliamentary movements) need to keep their own and essential role. Radical parties using 'power as transformative capacity' need to pose and answer systemic questions that seem familiar from the EDS context: 'Production for what purpose? With what technology?

With what environmental and social consequences? And drawing on whose knowledge, with what relations to its workers and users (ibid.: 98)?' 'The contradictions for any radical government', write Panitch and Gindin (2016: 54), 'will include responsibilities for managing a capitalist economy that is likely in crisis while simultaneously trying to satisfy popular expectations for the promised relief, and yet also embarking on the longer-term commitment to transform the state, i.e. not pushing the latter off to an indefinite future'. A possible way to prepare and develop such transformative capacity sounds like an echo from the EDS: A 'revolutionary gradualism' (Wainwright 2016: 99) shall start at the community or regional level in order to improve skills to organize political-economic systems and participatory self-management skills (ibid.; Panitch and Gindin 2016: 55). After neoliberal rehierarchization, a complete restart will be necessary (one example: universities). Participatory budgeting at the communal or district level may belong to such efforts as do transition initiatives. The international movement Attac advocates in its 'transformation paths for a "good life for all"' (Strickner et al. 2017: 249ff.) more democracy in economy, society, and the political system. Concepts of workers' self-management (Wolff 2017) or participatory economics (Albert 2014) focus on alternatives to hierarchical economic decision-making.

Possible traps along the way must be discussed (Gindin 2016) and studied (e.g. the Yugoslav case, Weissenbacher 2005). The immediate confrontation will be with TNC that have gained more power since the days of the dependency schools. 'In many countries, self-reliance would also involve increasing national ownership and control, especially of subsoil assets, and improving national capacity for negotiating with transnational corporations', Dudley Seers (1979 [1977]: 27) had argued in 1977. Today, the necessity to take up this challenge is again acknowledged. 'Breaking the power of corporations', writes the authors collective of Attac (AutorInnenkollektiv 2016: 248), ultimately means replacing the capitalist economy with another'. 'Ultimately' means in the European context also building a new and alternative European integration (cf. Attac 2017). Among EDS authors it had been clear that the European integration was not a construction fault but result of a power struggle that engrained liberal structures into the regulatory framework, making it an 'institutional *laissez-faire* system', which 'would make it difficult for any really left-wing government of the future to exercise controls and carry out far-reaching social changes' (Seers 1982: 4). The alternative

'Community self-reliance' (Seers 1982: 12) that would establish solidarity among the people of Europe and beyond seems far away. The politics of the Troika was more reminiscent of what Constantine Vaitsos (1982, 244f.) predicted if the mode of integration was not changed: a neocolonial Porto Rico-scenario for Greece and Portugal. Meanwhile, the Arrighi situation creates new dynamics. It is more and more difficult for Germany to mime the benevolent industrialist and present German interest as beneficial for the entire EU. Neonational governments break away from the political consensus while German industrial interests seem to swap German neomercantilism against an EU neomercantilism under German leadership. The German position seems to shift further from hegemony toward domination, which would not increase the room to maneuver in peripheral countries. Increasing indisposition with this situation may open, however, leeway to re-format European integration toward a Community self-reliant project. After the lost decades of EU development, the Community self-reliance needs to be more radical than envisaged by EDS scholars, initiating a socio-ecological transformation.

References

Adenauer, Konrad. 1954. *Freiheit, Wohlfahrt, Sicherheit für Deutschland und Europa. Regierungserklärung von Bundeskanzler Dr. Adenauer zur deutschen Außenpolitik vor dem Deutschen Bundestag am 15. Dez. 1954.* Bonn: Presse-uInformationsamt d Bundesregierung.

Agnoli, Johannes. 1995 [1978]. Der Staat des Kapitals. „Zivilgesellschaft" oder bürgerliche Gesellschaft? In Johannes Agnoli: *Der Staat des Kapitals und weitere Schriften zur Kritik der Politik.* Freiburg i. Br.: Ça ira, 21–89 (=Gesammelte Schriften 2).

Aiginger, Karl. 2019. Industriepolitik mit gesellschaftlichen Zielen verbinden – systemischer Ansatz statt Uraltkontroverse. *Wirtschaftsdienst* 99 (2): 101–105.

Albert, Michael. 2014. Partizipative Ökonomie – Eine Alternative zur Dauerkrise. Interview in Kontext. TV, 07.02. http://www.kontext-tv.de/de/sendungen/partizipative-oekonomie-eine-alternative-zur-dauerkrise (February 2,2018).

Altvater, Elmar. 1983. Bruch und Formwandel eines Entwicklungsmodells. Die gegenwärtige Krise ist ein Prozess gesellschaftlicher Transformation. In *Überproduktion, Unterkonsumtion, Depression. Analysen und Kontroversen zur Krisentheorie*, ed. Jürgen Hoffmann, 217–252. Hamburg: VSA.

Amin, Samir. 2017. Talk Given at the Plenary Session of the Conference 'Capitalist Development in Hostile Environments', June 6–8, June 6. Università della Calabria, Rende/Cosenza.

Arrighi, Giovanni. 2008 [2007]. *Adam Smith in Beijing: Lineages of the Twenty-First Century*. London and New York: Verso.
Arrighi, Giovanni. 2010a. Postscript to the Second Edition of the Long Twentieth Century. In *The Long Twentieth Century: Money, Power, and the Origins of Our Times*, 371–386. London and New York: Verso.
Arrighi, Giovanni. 2010b [1994]. *The Long Twentieth Century: Money, Power, and the Origins of Our Times*, 2nd ed. London and New York: Verso.
Arrighi, Giovanni, and Jessica Drangel. 1986. The Stratification of the World-Economy: An Exploration of the Semiperipheral Zone. *Review* 10 (1): 9–74 (=Anniversary Issue: The Work of the Fernand Braudel Center).
Arrighi, Giovanni, Terence Hopkins, and Immanuel Wallerstein. 1989. *Antisystemic Movements*. London and New York: Verso.
Attac, (ed.). 2017. *Entzauberte Union*. Wien: Mandelbaum.
AutorInnenkollektiv. 2016. Konzernmacht brechen – Zivilgesellschaftliche Ansätze und Strategien. In *Konzernmacht brechen!: von der Herrschaft des Kapitals zum guten Leben für alle*, Hg. Attac, 248–276. Wien: Mandelbaum.
Becker, Joachim. 2018. *Neo-Nationalismus in der EU: sozio-ökonomische Programmatik und Praxis*. Wien: AK (=Materialien zu Wirtschaft und Gesellschaft 179). https://emedien.arbeiterkammer.at/viewer/ppnresolver?id=AC15181468 (November 12, 2018).
Becker, Joachim, Christina Plank, and Weissenbacher, Rudy. 2018. Editorial. *Kurswechsel* 23 (2): 3–13.
Becker, Joachim, and Rudy Weissenbacher. 2014. Berlin Consensus and Disintegration: Monetary Regime and Uneven Development in the EU. In *The Deepening Crisis of the European Union: The Case for Radical Change: Analysis and Proposals from EuroMemo Group*, ed. Włodzimierz Dymarski, Marica Frangakis, and Jeremy Leaman, 5–32. Poznań: Poznań University of Economics Press.
Becker, Joachim, and Rudy Weissenbacher. 2016. Heterodoxy from the Right: Economic Policy Concepts of the Nationalist Right in Europe. Euro Memo Group: 22nd Conference on Alternative Economic Policy in Europe, Coimbra, Portugal, 15.9.–17.9. http://www2.euromemorandum.eu/uploads/becker_heterodoxy_from_the_right.pdf (February 2, 2018).
BMF—Bundesministerium für Finanzen. 2016. *Budgetbericht 2017*. Wien. https://www.bmf.gv.at/budget/das-budget/Budgetbericht_2017.pdf?67runp (November 12, 2018).
Cardoso, Fernando Henrique, and Enzo Faletto. 1976. *Abhängigkeit und Entwicklung in Lateinamerika*. Frankfurt/Main: Suhrkamp.
Carney, John. 1980. Regions in Crisis: Accumulation, Regional Problems and Crisis Formation. In *Regions in Crisis: New Perspectives in European Regional Theory*, ed. John Carney, Ray Hudson and Jim Lewis, 28–59. London: Croom Helm.

CDU—Christlich-Demokratische Union. 1995. Verantwortung für Deutschland und Europa. 50 Jahre CDU. UiD Extra 20/1995. Konrad Adenauer Stiftung. http://www.kas.de/wf/doc/kas_27628-544-1-30.pdf?110826092800 (July 3, 2018).

Cocoyoc Declaration, The. 1974. Adopted by the Participants in the United Nations Environmental Program (UNEP) and United Nations Conference on Trade and Development (UNCTAD) Symposium on 'Patterns of Resource Use, Environment and Development Strategies', October 8–12. Cocoyoc, Mexico.

Der Standard. 2018. Kommission will höheres EU-Budget: Kurz lehnt Vorschlag als inakzeptabel ab, May 2. http://www.derstandard.at/2000079034573/Bruessel-will-hoeheres-EU-Budget-1-11-Prozent-der-Wirtschaftsleistung (November 12, 2018).

Dosi, Giovanni. 2016. Beyond the 'Magic of the Market': The Slow Return of Industrial Policy (But Not yet in Italy). *Economia e Politica Industriale* 43 (3): 261–264.

ECB—European Central Bank. 2015. Real Convergence in the Euro Area: Evidence, Theory and Policy Implications. *ECB Economic Bulletin* 5: 30–45.

EU Council. n.y. https://www.consilium.europa.eu/en/policies/eu-annual-budget/2017/ (November 12, 2018).

Familienunternehmer, Die. 2018. *Satzung. Stand 13*, April 2018. https://www.familienunternehmer.eu/fileadmin/intranet/infothek/intern/satzung/satzung.pdf (July 3, 2018).

Farrant, Andrew, and Edward McPhail. 2014. Can a Dictator Turn a Constitution into a Can-Opener? F.A. Hayek and the Alchemy of Transitional Dictatorship in Chile. *Review of Political Economy* 26 (3): 331–348.

Fischer, Karin, and Rudy Weissenbacher. 2016. Ungleicher Tausch – Grundannahmen, Widersprüche und aktuelle Bedeutung eines umstrittenen Theorems. *Z. Zeitschrift Marxistische Erneuerung* 27 (105): 140–157.

Friedmann, John. 1986. Regional Development in Industrialised Countries: Endogenous or Self-Reliant? In *Self-Reliant Development in Europe: Theory, Problems, Actions*, ed. Michel Bassand, Ernst Brugger, John Bryden, John Friedmann, and Barbara Stuckey, 203–216. Aldershot: Gower.

Galtung, Johan. 1977. *Methodology and Ideology: Essays in Methodology*, vol. 1. Copenhagen: Christian Ejlers.

GFM EA&E. 2019. German Federal Ministry for Economic Affairs and Energy. 2019. National Industrial Strategy 2030. Strategic Guidelines for a German and European Industrial Policy. Berlin. https://www.bmwi.de/Redaktion/EN/Publikationen/Industry/national-industry-strategy-2030.html (June 13, 2019).

GFP—German Foreign Policy. 2018. *Europas Achsen*, July 3. https://www.german-foreign-policy.com/news/detail/7658/ (July 3, 2018).

Gindin, Sam. 2016. Chasing Utopia. *Jacobin*, October 3. https://www.jacobinmag.com/2016/03/workers-control-coops-wright-wolff-alperovitz (November 13, 2019).

Goldberg, Jörg. 1983. Uberakkumulation von Kapital als Regulierungsproblem. In *Überproduktion, Unterkonsumtion, Depression. Analysen und Kontroversen zur Krisentheorie*, ed. Jürgen Hoffmann, 167–183. Hamburg: VSA.

Government of France. 2019. A Franco-German Manifesto for a European Industrial Policy Fit for the 21st Century. N°1043, February 19. Paris. https://www.gouvernement.fr/en/a-franco-german-manifesto-for-a-european-industrial-policy-fit-for-the-21st-century (May 10, 2019).

Guarascio, Dario, and Annamaria Simonazzi. 2016. A Polarized Country in a Polarized Europe: An Industrial Policy for Italy's Renaissance. *Economia a Politica Industriale* 43 (3): 315–322.

Hadjimichalis, Costis. 1983. Regional Crisis: The State and Regional Social Movements in Southern Europe. In *The Crisis of the European Regions*, ed. Dudley Seers and Kjell Öström, 127–147. London and Basingstoke: Palgrave Macmillan.

Hadjimichalis, Costis. 1984. The Geographical Transfer of Value: Notes on the Spatiality of Capitalism. *Environment and Planning D: Society and Space* 2 (3): 329–345.

Hadjimichalis, Costis, and Nicos Papamichos. 1990. 'Local' Development in Southern Europe: Towards a New Mythology. *Antipode* 22 (3): 181–210.

Harvey, David. 2003. *The New Imperialism*. New York: Oxford University Press.

Haug, Frigga. 2014. Die Transformation muss am Herrschaftsknoten ansetzen. In *Futuring. Perspektiven der Transformation im Kapitalismus über ihn hinaus*, Hg. Michael Brie, 178–193. Münster: Westfälisches Dampfboot.

Hayek, Friedrich. 1958 [1948]. *Individualism and Economic Order*. London and Chicago: The University of Chicago Press.

Hayek, Friedrich. 1978. *Denationalisation of Money—The Argument Refined: An Analysis of the Theory and Practice of Concurrent Currencies*, 2nd ed., rev. and enlarged, n.p. London: The Institute of Economic Affairs.

Hayek, Friedrich. 1981 [1979]. *Law, Legislation and Liberty: Vol. 3: The Political Order of a Free People*. London and Chicago: The University of Chicago Press.

Hayek, Friedrich. 2011 [1960]. *The Constitution of Liberty: The Definitive Edition*, ed. Ronald Hamowy. Chicago and London: Chicago University Press.

Heller, Hermann. 1933. Autoritärer Liberalismus? In Hermann Heller. 1992. *Gesammelte Schriften*, ed. Christoph Müller. Zweiter Band. Recht, Staat, Macht, 2nd and rev. ed., Extented with an Epilog, 643–653. Tübingen: Mohr.

Hickel, Rudolf. 1983. Ökonomische Ursachen- und Politikprobleme der Massenarbeitslosigkeit. In *Überproduktion, Unterkonsumtion, Depression. Analysen und Kontroversen zur Krisentheorie*, ed. Jürgen Hoffmann, 55–88. Hamburg: VSA.

Hirsch, Joachim. 2001. Die Internationalisierung des Staates. Anmerkungen zu einigen aktuellen Fragen der Staatstheorie. In Joachim Hirsch, Bob Jessop, und Nicos Poulantzas: *Die Zukunft des Staates*, 101–138. Hamburg: VSA.

Hübner, Kurt. 1983. Warum dauert die Krise so lange? Anmerkungen zum Verhältnis von Zyklus und Trend. In *Überproduktion, Unterkonsumtion, Depression, Analysen und Kontroversen zur Krisentheorie*, ed. Jürgen Hoffmann, 185–216. Hamburg: VSA.

Kramer, Ingo, Dieter Kempf, Eric Schweitzer, and Hans Peter Wollseifer. 2018. Aus Verantwortung für Deutschland und Europa. Gemeinsamer Appell der deutschen Wirtschaft, 29. Juni 2018. Bundesverband der deutschen Industrie (BDI). https://bdi.eu/#/publikation/news/gemeinsamer-appell-der-deutschen-wirtschaft/ (July 3, 2018).

Kynge, James, and Michael Peel. 2017. Eastern Europe's China Pivot. *Financial Times*, November 28, p. 7.

Lapavitsas, Costas. 2013. *Profiting Without Producing: How Finance Exploits Us All*. London and New York: Verso.

Lucchese, Matteo, Leopoldo Nascia, and Mario Pianta. 2016. Industrial Policy and Technology in Italy. *Economic e Politica Industriale* 43 (3): 233–260.

Lundvall, Bengt-Åke. 2016. From Manufacturing Nostalgia to a Strategy for Economic Transformation. *Economia e Politica Industriale* 43 (3): 265–271.

Maier, Gunther, Franz Tödtling, and Michaela Trippl. 2006. *Regional- und Stadtökonomik, Vol. 2. Regionalentwicklung und Regionalpolitik*. Wien/New York: Springer.

Meadows, Donella. 1972. *The Limits to Growth: A Report for the Club of Rome's Project on the Predicament of Mankind*. New York: Universe.

Mont Pèlerin-Society (MPS n.y.) F. A. Hayek. https://www.montpelerin.org/f-a-hayek/ (November 13, 2019).

Morrice, David. 1994. C. B. Macpherson's Critique of Liberal Democracy and Capitalism. *Political Studies* 42 (4): 646–661.

Narr, Wolf-Dieter (ed.). 1977. *Auf dem Weg zum Einparteienstaat*. Opladen: Westdeutscher.

Nohlen, Dieter, and Rainer-Olaf Schultze. 1985. Ungleiche Entwicklung und Regionalpolitik in Südeuropa. Externe Verursachungsdfaktoren und endogene Entwicklungschancen. In *Ungleiche Entwicklung und Regionalpolitik in Südeuropa: Italien, Spanien, Portugal*, Hg. Dieter Nohlen und Rainer-Olaf Schultze unter Mitwirkung von Wolfgang Merkel, 17–73. Bochum (= Politikwissenschaftliche Paperbacks 6).

Panitch, Leo, and Sam Gindin. 2016. Class, Party and the Challenge of State Transformation. In *Socialist Register 2017: Rethinking Revolution*, ed. Leo Panitch and Greg Albo, 35–58. London: Merlin.

Pollin, Robert. 2018. De-Growth vs A Green New Deal. *New Left Review* 112, 5–25.

Poma, Muruchi. 2018. Buen (Con)Vivir, das gute Leben für alle. Über die Prinzipien des guten Zusammenlebens und das Paradox von Entwicklung. In *Anders wachsen! Von der Krise der kapitalistischen Wachstumsgesellschaft und Ansätzen einer Transformation*, ed. Maximilian Becker and Mathilda Reinicke, 241–264. München: oekom.

Poulantzas, Nicos. 2008 [1979]. Interview with Nicos Poulantzas. In *The Poulantzas Reader: Marxism, Law and the State*, ed. James Martin, 387–402. London and New York: Verso.

Poulantzas, Nicos. 2014 [1978]. *State, Power, Socialism.* London and New York: Verso.

Reuten, Geert. 2011. Economic Stagnation Postponed. Background of the 2008 Financial-Economic Crisis in the European Union and the United States. *International Journal of Political Economy* 40 (3): 50–58.

Schubert, Alexander. 1985. *Die internationale Verschuldung. Die Dritte Welt und das Transnationale Bankensystem.* Frankfurt/Main: Suhrkamp.

Scheuerman, William. 1997. The Unholy Alliance of Carl Schmitt and Friedrich A. Hayek. *Constellations* 4 (2): 172–188.

Schumann, Harald, and Árpád Bondy. 2015. *The Trail of the Troika.* RBB/ARTE. https://www.youtube.com/watch?v=BLB3uu1IXM0 (June 13, 2018).

Seers, Dudley. 1979 [1977]. The Meaning of Development. With a Post Script. In *Development Theory. Four Critical Studies*, ed. David Lehmann, 9–30. London: Frank Cass.

Seers, Dudley. 1982. Introduction: The Second Enlargement in Historical Perspective. In *The Second Enlargement of the EEC: The Integration of Unequal Partners*, ed. Dudley Seers and Constantine Vaitsos (with the assistance of Marja-Liisa Kiljunen), 1–21. London and Basingstoke: Macmillan (=Studies in the Integration of Western Europe 2).

Seers, Dudley. 1983. *The Political Economy of Nationalism.* London et al.: Oxford University Press.

Serfati, Claude. 2004. Militarismus: der bewaffnete Arm der Globalisierung. In *Die globale Enteignungsökonomie*, ed. Christian Zeller, 21–59. Münster: Westphälisches Dapfboot.

Silver, Beverly, and Giovanni Arrighi. 2011. The End of the Long Twentieth Century. In *The Roots of Global Financial Meltdown*, ed. Craig Calhoun and Georgi Derluguian, 53–68. London and New York: New York University Press.

Sohn-Rethel, Alfred. 1973. *Ökonomie und Klassenstruktur des deutschen Faschismus. Aufzeichnungen und Analysen.* Frankfurt/Main: Suhrkamp.

Stahel, Walter. 2019. *The Circular Economy. A User's Guide.* London and New York: Routledge.

Stiglitz, Joseph et al. 2019. *Rewriting the Rules of the European Economy.* Brussels: Foundation for European Progressive Studies.

Stöhr, Walter. 1981. Development from Below: The Bottom-Up and Periphery-Inward Development Paradigm. In *Development from Above or Below? The Dialectics of Regional Planning in Developing Countries*, ed. Walter Stöhr and Fraser Taylor, 39–72. Chichester et al.: Wiley.

Stöhr, Walter, and Franz Tödtling. 1979. Spatial Equity: Some Anti-thesis to Current Regional Development Doctrine. In *Spatial Inequalities and Regional Development*, ed. Hendrik Folmer and Jan Oosterhaven, 133–160. Boston, The Hague, and London: Nijhoff.

Streeck, Wolfgang. 2016. *How Will Capitalism End? Essays on a Failing System*. London and New York: Verso.

Strickner, Alexandra, et al. 2017. Konzernmacht brechen. Zivilgesellschaftliche Ansätze und Strategien. In *Konzernmacht brechen! Von der Herrschaft des Kapitals zum Guten Leben für Alle*, ed. Attac, 248–276. Wien: Mandelbaum.

Vaitsos, Constantine. 1982. Conclusions: Economic Effects of the Second Enlargement. In *The Second Enlargement of the EEC: The Integration of Unequal Partners*, ed. Dudley Seers and Constantine Vaitsos with the assistance of Kiljunen, Marja-Liisa, 243–268. London and Basingstoke (= Studies in the Integration of Western Europe 2).

Wainwright, Hilary. 2016. Radicalizing the Movement-Party Relation: From Ralph Miliband to Jeremy Corbyn and Beyond. In *Socialist Register 2017: Rethinking Revolution*, ed. Leo Panitch and Greg Albo, 80–101. London: Merlin.

Weissenbacher, Rudy. 2005. *Jugoslawien. Politische Ökonomie einer Desintegration*. Wien: Promedia.

Weissenbacher, Rudy. 2008. Keeping Up Appearances: Uneven Global Development in a System of Structural Imbalances. *Journal Für Entwicklungspolitik* XXIV (4): 78–121.

Weissenbacher, Rudy. 2012a. "Wir wissen, dass wir das Spiel jetzt nach Euren Regeln spielen müssen…" Betrachtungen zu Hegemonie und ungleicher Entwicklung. *Z. Zeitschrift für marxistische Erneuerung* 23 (89): 60–79.

Weissenbacher, Rudy. 2012b. Berlusconismo mit guten Manieren. Anmerkungen Zur Regierungsumbildung in Italien. *Kurswechsel* 17 (2): 68–75.

Weissenbacher, Rudy. 2014. Reclaiming Public Ownership: Making Space for Economic Democracy. *Journal of Contemporary European Studies* 22 (2): 213–217.

Weissenbacher, Rudy. 2015. Keine andere Welt, nur ein anderes Europa. Die Lega Nord am rechten Weg. *Kurswechsel* 20 (3): 81–87.

Weissenbacher, Rudy. 2018. Die Krise als Normalität: Kapitalismus, Regionen und ungleiche Entwicklung. *Kurswechsel* 23 (2): 53–62.

Weissenbacher, Rudy. 2019. „In wenigen Monaten wird nichts mehr wie früher sein": Die gelb-grüne Regierung und der Abstieg Italiens im europäischen Kapitalismus. *Kurswechsel* 24 (1): 62–71.

Wistrich, Robert. 1983. *Wer war wer im Dritten Reich*. München: Harnack.

Wolff, Richard. 2017. Die Wut der Arbeiter und die Suche nach einer neuen Wirtschaftsordnung, Interview in Kontext. TV, 7.3. http://www.kontext-tv.de/de/sendungen/richard-wolff-die-wut-derarbeiter-und-die-suche-nach-einer-neuen-wirtschaftsordnung (February 2,2018).

Correction to: The Core-Periphery Divide in the European Union

Correction to:
R. Weissenbacher, *The Core-Periphery Divide in the European Union*,
https://doi.org/10.1007/978-3-030-28211-0

The original version of this book was inadvertently published with some references not cited and listed properly as per the supplied manuscript. These have now been corrected.

The updated version of the book can be found at
https://doi.org/10.1007/978-3-030-28211-0_1
https://doi.org/10.1007/978-3-030-28211-0_4
https://doi.org/10.1007/978-3-030-28211-0

R. Weissenbacher, *The Core-Periphery Divide in the European Union*,
https://doi.org/10.1007/978-3-030-28211-0_10

Bibliography

Abu-Lughod, Janet L. 1989. *Before European Hegemony: The World System A.D. 1250–1350*. New York and Oxford: Oxford University Press.

Adenauer, Konrad. 1954. *Freiheit, Wohlfahrt, Sicherheit für Deutschland und Europa. Regierungserklärung von Bundeskanzler Dr. Adenauer zur deutschen Außenpolitik vor dem Deutschen Bundestag am 15. Dez. 1954*. Bonn: Presse-uInformationsamt d Bundesregierung.

Adorno, Theodor. 1972 [1968]. Spätkapitalismus oder Industriegesellschaft. In *Gesammelte Schriften. Band 8. Soziologische Schriften I*, ed. Theodor Adorno, 354–370. Frankfurt/Main: Suhrkamp.

Agnoli, Johannes. 1977. Wahlkampf und Sozialer Konflikt. In *Auf dem Weg zum Einparteienstaat*, ed. Wolf-Dieter Narr, 213–241. Opladen: Westdeutscher.

Agnoli, Johannes. 1995 [1978]. Der Staat des Kapitals. „Zivilgesellschaft" oder bürgerliche Gesellschaft? In *Der Staat des Kapitals und weitere Schriften zur Kritik der Politik*, ed. Johannes Agnoli. Freiburg i.Br.: Ça ira, 21–89 (=Gesammelte Schriften 2).

Aiginger, Karl. 2019. Industriepolitik mit gesellschaftlichen Zielen verbinden – systemischer Ansatz statt Uraltkontroverse. *Wirtschaftsdienst* 99 (2): 101–105.

Albert, Michael. 2014. Partizipative Ökonomie – Eine Alternative zur Dauerkrise. Interview in Kontext. TV, 07.02. http://www.kontext-tv.de/de/sendungen/partizipative-oekonomie-eine-alternative-zur-dauerkrise (February 2,2018).

Altvater, Elmar. 1983. Bruch und Formwandel eines Entwicklungsmodells. Die gegenwärtige Krise ist ein Prozess gesellschaftlicher Transformation. In *Überproduktion, Unterkonsumtion, Depression. Analysen und Kontroversen zur Krisentheorie*, ed. Jürgen Hoffmann, 217–252. Hamburg: VSA.

R. Weissenbacher, *The Core-Periphery Divide in the European Union*, https://doi.org/10.1007/978-3-030-28211-0

Altvater, Elmar. 1988. Die Enttäuschung der Nachzügler oder: Der Bankrott "fordistischer" Industrialisierung. In *Der gewendete Kapitalismus: Kritische Beiträge zu einer Theorie der Regulation*, ed. Birgit Mahnkopf, 144–181. Münster: Westfälisches Dampfboot.

Amin, Samir. 1974. *Accumulation on a World Scale: Acritique of the Development of Underdevelopment*, vol. 1. New York and London: Monthly Review Press.

Amin, Samir. 1975 [1973]. *Die ungleiche Entwicklung. Essay über die Gesellschaftsformationen des peripheren Kapitalismus.* Aus dem Französischen von Hildegard und Hartmut Elsenhans. Hamburg.

Amin, Samir. 1981. Some Thoughts of Self-Reliant Development, Collective Self-Reliance and the New International Economic Order. In *The World Economic Order: Past and Prospects*, ed. Sven Grassman and Erik Lundberg, 534–552. London and Basingstoke: Macmillan.

Amin, Samir. 2017. Talk Given at the Plenary Session of the Conference 'Capitalist Development in Hostile Environments', June 6–8, June 6. Università della Calabria, Rende/Cosenza.

Anderson, Perry. 1978 [1974]. *Passages from Antiquity to Feudalism.* London: Verso.

Anderson, Perry. 1980 [1974]. *Lineages of the Absolutist State.* London: Verso.

Anderson, Perry. 2011 [2009]. *The New Old World.* London and Brooklyn: Verso.

Anderson, Perry. 2012. After the Event. *New Left Review* 73, 49–61.

Arrighi, Giovanni (ed.). 1985a. *Semiperipheral Development: The Politics of Southern Europe in the Twentieth Century: Beverly Hills, London, and New Delhi* (Explorations in the World-Economy 5).

Arrighi, Giovanni. 1985b. Introduction. In *Semiperipheral Development: The Politics of Southern Europe in the Twentieth Century*, ed. Giovanni Arrighi, 11–27. Beverly Hills, London, and New Delhi (=Explorations in the World-Economy 5).

Arrighi, Giovanni. 1985c. Fascism to Democratic Socialism: Logic and Limits of a Transition. In *Semiperipheral Development: The Politics of Southern Europe in the Twentieth Century*, ed. Giovanni Arrighi, 243–279. Beverly Hills, London, and New Delhi: Sage (=Explorations in the World-Economy 5).

Arrighi, Giovanni. 1990. The Developmentalist Illusion: A Reconceptualization of the Semiperiphery. In *Semiperipheral States in the World-Economy*, ed. William Martin, 11–42. Westport, CT: Greenwood Press.

Arrighi, Giovanni. 2008 [2007]. *Adam Smith in Beijing: Lineages of the Twenty-First Century.* London and New York: Verso.

Arrighi, Giovanni. 2010a. Postscript to the Second Edition of the Long Twentieth Century. In *The Long Twentieth Century: Money, Power, and the Origins of Our Times*, 371–386. London and New York: Verso.

Arrighi, Giovanni. 2010b [1994]. *The Long Twentieth Century: Money, Power, and the Origins of Our Times*, 2nd ed. London and New York: Verso.

Arrighi, Giovanni, and Fortunata Piselli. 1987. Capitalist Development in Hostile Environments: Feuds, Class Struggles, and Migrations in a Peripheral Region of Southern Italy. *Review* 10 (4): 649–751 (Fernand Braudel Center).

Arrighi, Giovanni, and Jessica Drangel. 1986. The Stratification of the World-Economy: An Exploration of the Semiperipheral Zone. *Review* 10 (1): 9–74 (=Anniversary Issue: The Work of the Fernand Braudel Center).

Arrighi, Giovanni, Beverly Silver, and Benjamin Brewer. 2003. Industrial Convergence, Globalization, and the Persistence of the North-South Divide. *Studies in Comparative International Development* 38 (1): 3–31.

Arrighi, Giovanni, Çağlar Keyder, and Immanuel Wallerstein. 1981. The Political Economy of Southern European Countries. *European Studies Newsletter* 9 (1): 6–11.

Arrighi, Giovanni, Terence Hopkins, and Immanuel Wallerstein. 1989. *Antisystemic Movements.* London and New York: Verso.

Arrighi Giovanni, Roberto Korzeniewicz, David Consiglio, and Timothy Moran. 1996. Modeling Zones of the World Economy: A Polynomial Regression Analysis (1964–1994). Paper Presented at the 1996 Annual Meeting of the American Sociological Association. New York, NY.

Attac, (ed.). 2017. *Entzauberte Union.* Wien: Mandelbaum.

AutorInnenkollektiv. 2016. Konzernmacht brechen – Zivilgesellschaftliche Ansätze und Strategien. In *Konzernmacht brechen!: von der Herrschaft des Kapitals zum guten Leben für alle*, Hg. Attac, 248–276. Wien: Mandelbaum.

Axt, Heinz-Jürgen. 1985. Self-Reliance and Reality in Greece. In *Endogenous Development: A Myth or a Path? Problems of Economic Self-Reliance in the European Periphery*, ed. Stefan Musto, 41–71. Tilburg: EADI.

Baade, Robert, and Jonathan Galloway. 1983. Monetary Integration in a 12-Member European Community: The Implications for Greece, Portugal, and Spain. In *The Contemporary Mediterranean World*, ed. Carl Pinkele and Adamantia Pollis, 221–236. New York: Praeger.

Bagnasco, Arnaldo. 1977. *Tre Italie. La Problematica territoriale dello svilluppo italiano.* Bologna: Il Mulino.

Bair, Jennifer. 2005. Global Capitalism and Commodity Chains: Looking Back. *Going Forward. in: Competition & Change* 9 (2): 153–180.

Bair, Jennifer. 2009. Global Commodity Chains: Genealogy and Review. In *Frontiers of Commodity Chain Research*, ed. Jennifer Bair, 1–34. Stanford: Stanford University Press.

Bair, Jennifer. 2014. Editor's Introduction: Commodity Chains in and of the World System. *Journal of World-Systems Research* 20 (1): 1–10.

Bassand, Michel, Ernst Brugger, John Bryden, John Friedmann, and Barbara Stuckey (eds.). 1986. *Self-Reliant Development in Europe.* Theory, Problems, Actions: Aldershot and Vermont.

Becker, Joachim. 2018. *Neo-Nationalismus in der EU: sozio-ökonomische Programmatik und Praxis*. Wien: AK (=Materialien zu Wirtschaft und Gesellschaft 179). https://emedien.arbeiterkammer.at/viewer/ppnresolver?id=AC15181468 (November 12, 2018).

Becker, Joachim, and Rudy Weissenbacher (eds.). 2009. *Sozialismen. Entwicklungsmodelle von Lenin bis Nyerere*. Wien: Promedia and Südwind (=Historische Sozialkunde/Internationale Entwicklung).

Becker, Joachim, and Rudy Weissenbacher. 2014. Berlin Consensus and Disintegration: Monetary Regime and Uneven Development in the EU. In *The Deepening Crisis of the European Union: The Case for Radical Change: Analysis and Proposals from EuroMemo Group*, ed. Włodzimierz Dymarski, Marica Frangakis, and Jeremy Leaman, 5–32. Poznań: Poznań University of Economics Press.

Becker, Joachim, and Rudy Weissenbacher. 2015. Changing Development Models: Dependency School Meets Regulation Theory. Contribution to Coloque International: Recherche & Regulation. Paris, June 10–12. https://www.eiseverywhere.com/retrieveupload.php?c3VibWlzc2lvbl84NTg3OF83NTYyMzIucGRmKmVzZWxlY3Q= (March 14, 2018).

Becker, Joachim, and Rudy Weissenbacher. 2016. Heterodoxy from the Right: Economic Policy Concepts of the Nationalist Right in Europe. Euro Memo Group: 22nd Conference on Alternative Economic Policy in Europe, Coimbra, Portugal, 15.9.–17.9. http://www2.euromemorandum.eu/uploads/becker_heterodoxy_from_the_right.pdf (February 2, 2018).

Becker, Joachim, Christina Plank, and Rudy Weissenbacher. 2018. Editorial. *Kurswechsel* 23 (2): 3–13.

Becker, Joachim, Franziska Disslbacher, and Rudy Weissenbacher. 2015. Zwischen Deutschland und Osteuropa: Österreichs neue Mittellage. In *Politische Ökonomie Österreichs. Kontinuitäten und Veränderungen seit dem EU-Beitritt*, ed. Beigewum, 132–155. Wien: Mandelbaum.

Becker, Joachim, Johannes Jäger, Bernhard Leubolt, and Rudy Weissenbacher. 2010. Peripheral Financialization and Vulnerability to Crisis: A Regulationist Perspective. *Competition and Change* 14 (3–4): 223–245.

Becker, Joachim, Johannes Jäger, and Rudy Weissenbacher. 2013. Abhängige Finanzialisierung und ungleiche Entwicklung. Zentrum und Peripherie im europäischen Integrationsprozess. *Journal für Entwicklungspolitik* XXIX (3): 34–54.

Becker, Joachim, Johannes Jäger, and Rudy Weissenbacher. 2015. Uneven and Dependent Development in Europe: The Crisis and Its Implications. In *Asymmetric Crisis in Europe and Possible Futures: Critical Political Economy and Post-Keynesian Perspectives*, ed. Johannes Jäger and Elisabeth Springler, 81–97. London and New York: Routledge (=RIPE Series in Global Political Economy).

Becker, Joachim, Predrag Ćetković, and Rudy Weissenbacher. 2016. Financialisation, Dependent Export Industrialization, and Deindustrialisation in Eastern Europe. In *Finance and Industrial Policy: Beyond Financial Regulation in Europe*, ed. Giovanni Cozzi, Susan Newman, and Jan Toporowski, 41–64. Oxford: Oxford University Press.

Becker, Joachim, and Rudy Weissenbacher. Forthcoming. Fordism in the Americas. In *Rethinking the Americas Vol. III: Key Topics in Political Economy and Governance*, ed. Anne Tittor, Bernhard Leubolt, and Daniel Hawkins.

Becker, Joachim, Rudy Weissenbacher, and Johannes Jäger. Forthcoming. Uneven Development in the EU: Processes of Core-Periphery Relations. In *The Routledge Handbook of Critical European Studies*, ed. Yannis Stivachtis et al. London: Routledge.

Benítez Zenteno, Raúl (ed.). 1998 [1973]. *Las clases sociales en américa latina. Congress at the Universidad Nacional Autónoma in Mérida, Yucatán*. Mexico: Siglo XXI.

Berend, Iván, and György Ránki. 1982. *The European Periphery and Industrialization 1780–1914*. Cambridge: Cambridge University Press.

Bernier, Aurélien. 2011. Der Süden zuerst. Die vergessene Weltkonferenz von 1974. *Le Monde diplomatique*, Dezember 2011, 1 und 8.

Bieling, Hans-Jürgen, and Jochen Steinhilber. 2000. Einleitung. In *Die Konfiguration Europas. Dimensionen einer kritischen Integrationstheorie*, ed. Hans-Jürgen Bieling and Jochen Steinhilber, 7–22. Münster.

Bienefeld, Manfred. 1980. Externalising Problems in a Future EEC. In *Integration and the Unequal Development: The Experience of the EEC*, ed. Dudley Seers and Constantine Vaitsos with the assistance of Marja-Liisa Kiljunen, 291–306. London and Basingstoke: Macmillan (=Studies in the Integration of Western Europe 1).

Bienefeld, Manfred. 1981. Dependency and the Newly Industrialising Countries (NICs): Towards a Reappraisal. In *Dependency Theory: A Critical Reassessment*, ed. Dudley Seers, 79–96. London: Pinter.

Bienefeld, Manfred. 1982a. Impact on Industry. In *The Second Enlargement of the EEC: The Integration of Unequal Partners*, ed. Dudley Seers and Constantine Vaitsos with the assistance of Marja-Liisa Kiljunen, 109–135. London and Basingstoke: Macmillan (=Studies in the Integration of Western Europe 2).

Bienefeld, Manfred. 1982b. The International Context of National Development Strategies: Constraints and Opportunities in a Changing World. In *The Struggle for Development: National Strategies in an International Context*, ed. Manfred Bienefeld and Martin Godfrey, 25–64. Chichester and New York: Wiley.

Bienefeld, Manfred. 1994. Capitalism and the Nation State in the Dog Days of the Twentieth Century. *Socialist Register 1994: Between Globalism and Nationalism*, ed. Ralph Miliband and Leo Panitch, 94–129. London: Merlin.

Bienefeld, Manfred, and Martin Godfrey. 1982. Introduction. In *The Struggle for Development: National Strategies in an International Context*, ed. Manfred Bienefeld and Martin Godfrey, 1–24. Chichester et al.: Wiley.

Blaut, James. 2000. *Eight Eurocentric Historians*. New York and London: Guilford Press (=The Colonizer's Model of the World, 2).

Bloch, Ernst. 2000 [1964, 1923]. *The Spirit of Utopia*. Stanford: University Press.

BMF—Bundesministerium für Finanzen. 2016. *Budgetbericht 2017*. Wien. https://www.bmf.gv.at/budget/das-budget/Budgetbericht_2017.pdf?67runp (November 12, 2018).

Bohlen, Celestine. 1997. Italian Government Falls in Fight Over Euro Austerity. *New York Times*, October 10. http://www.nytimes.com/1997/10/10/world/italian-government-falls-in-fight-over-euro-austerity.html (November 20, 2017).

Boianovsky, Mauro. 2015. Between Lévi-Strauss and Braudel: Furtado and the Historical-Structural Method in Latin American Political Economy. *Journal of Economic Methodology* 22 (4): 413–438.

Bordignon, Fabio. 2014. Matteo Renzi: A 'Leftist Berlusconi' for the Italian Democratic Party? *South European Society and Politics* 19 (1): 1–23.

Bourdieu, Pierre. 2005 [1997]. Neo-Liberalismus als konservative Restauration. In *Das PRAXIS-Konzept im Zentrum gesellschaftskritischer Wissenschaft*, ed. Horst Müller, 175–180. Norderstedt: Books on Demand.

Braudel, Fernand. 1992 [1985]. Chinesen, Araber … hatte nur Europa eine Chance? In *1492: die Welt zur Zeit des Kolumbus. Ein Lesebuch*, ed. Rainer Beck, 187–197. München (=Beck'sche Reihe 460).

Brenner, Robert. 1977. The Origins of Capitalist Development: A Critique of Neo-Smithian Marxism. *New Left Review* I/104 (July–August): 25–92.

Bristow, Gillian. 2005. Everyone's a 'Winner': Problematising the Discourse of Regional Competitiveness. *Journal of Economic Geography* 5 (3): 285–304.

Bristow, Gillian. 2010. *Critical Reflections on Regional Competitiveness: Theory, Policy and Practice*. London et al.: Routledge (=Routledge Studies in Human Geography 31).

Brown, Ken. 1994. Word for Word/Fernando Henrique Cardoso; Having Left Campus for the Arena, Winner in Brazil Shifts to Right. *New York Times*, November 20. http://www.nytimes.com/1994/11/20/weekinreview/word-for-word-fernando-henrique-cardoso-having-left-campus-for-arena-winner.html, http://www.nytimes.com/1994/11/20/weekinreview/word-for-word-fernando-henrique-cardoso-having-left-campus-for-arena-winner.html (November 26, 2014).

Brugger, Ernst, and Barbara Stuckey. 1986. Introduction: Self-Reliant Development in Europe. In *Self-Reliant Development in Europe: Theory, Problems, Actions*, ed. Michel Bassand, Ernst Brugger, John Bryden, John Friedmann, and Barbara Stuckey, 1–5. Aldershot and Vermont: Gower.

Bryden, John. 1979. Core-Periphery Problems: The Scottish Case. In *Underdeveloped Europe: Studies in Core-Periphery Relations*, ed. Dudley Seers, Bernard Schaffer, and Marja-Liisa Kiljunen, 257–277. Sussex: Harvester Press (=Harvester Studies in Development 1).

Caciagli, Mario. 1985. Dezentralisierung und Regionalpolitik in Italien. In *Ungleiche Entwicklung und Regionalpolitik in Südeuropa: Italien, Spanien, Portugal*, ed. Dieter Nohlen und Rainer-Olaf Schultze unter Mitwirkung von Wolfgang Merkel, 75–81. Bochum: Brockmeyer (=Politikwissenschaftliche Paperbacks 6).

Caporale, Antonello. 2015. Sfatiamo I falsi miti: si spende als Sud per arricchire il Nord. Interview with Gianfranco Viesti. In Il fatto quotidiano, August 1, 19.

Cardoso, Fernando Henrique. 1972. Dependency and Development in Latin America. *New Left Review* 74: 83–95.

Cardoso, Fernando Henrique. 1977a. The Consumption of Dependency Theory in the United States. *Latin American Research Review* 12 (3): 7–24.

Cardoso, Fernando Henrique. 1977b. Current Theses on Latin American Development and Dependency: A Critique. *Boletín de Estudios Latinoamericanos y del Caribe* 13 (22): 53–64.

Cardoso, Fernando Henrique, and Enzo Faletto. 1976. *Abhängigkeit und Entwicklung in Lateinamerika*. Frankfurt/Main: Suhrkamp.

Cardoso, Fernando Henrique, and Enzo Faletto. 1979. *Dependency and Development in Latin America*. Berkeley, Los Angeles, and London: University of California Press.

Carney, John. 1980. Regions in Crisis: Accumulation, Regional Problems and Crisis Formation. In *Regions in Crisis: New Perspectives in European Regional Theory*, ed. John Carney, Ray Hudson and Jim Lewis, 28–59. London: Croom Helm.

Casparis, John. 1985. Core Demand for Labor from Southern Europe: The Case of Switzerland. In *Semiperipheral Development: The Politics of Southern Europe in the Twentieth Century*, ed. Giovanni Arrighi, 107–131. Beverly Hills, London, and New Delhi: Sage (Explorations in the World-Economy 5).

Catanzaro, Raimondo. 1985. Unequal Development in Southern Italy: Features, Causes, and some Suggestions for Research: A Preliminary Report. In *Ungleiche Entwicklung und Regionalpolitik in Südeuropa: Italien, Spanien, Portugal*, ed. Dieter Nohlen und Rainer-Olaf Schultze unter Mitwirkung von Wolfgang Merkel, 83–94. Bochum: Brockmeyer (=Politikwissenschaftliche Paperbacks 6).

CDU—Christlich-Demokratische Union. 1995. Verantwortung für Deutschland und Europa. 50 Jahre CDU. UiD Extra 20/1995. Konrad Adenauer Stiftung. http://www.kas.de/wf/doc/kas_27628-544-1-30.pdf?110826092800 (July 3, 2018).

CEPAL (ed.). n.y. *Raúl Prebisch and the Challenges of Development of the XXI Century. Textos Esenciales: Introduction to Keynes.* http://prebisch.cepal.org/en/works/introduction-keynes (August 11, 2015).

Cesaratto, Sergio, and Antonella Stirati. 2010. Germany and the European and Global Crises. *International Journal of Political Economy* 39 (4): 56–86.

Chang, Ha-Joon. 2002. *Kicking Away the Ladder: Development Strategy in Historical Perspective.* London: Anthem Press.

Chase-Dunn, Christopher. 1980. Socialist States in the Capitalist World-Economy. *Social Problems* 27 (5): 505–525.

Chase-Dunn, Christopher (ed.). 1982. *Socialist States in the World System.* Beverly Hills: Sage.

Chenery, Hollis. 1960. Patterns of Industrial Growth. *American Economic Review* 50 (4): 624–654.

Chilcote, Ronald. 1978. A Question of Dependency. *Latin American Research Review* 13 (2): 55–68.

Chomsky, Noam. 1999. *The New Military Humanism: Lessons from Kosovo.* Monroe, ME: Common Courage Press.

Claus, Burghard, et al. 1977. Zur Erweiterung der Europäischen Gemeinschaft in Südeuropa. Berlin (=Schriften des Deutschen Instituts für Entwicklungspolitik (DIE) 52).

Cocoyoc Declaration, The. 1974. Adopted by the Participants in the United Nations Environmental Program (UNEP) and United Nations Conference on Trade and Development (UNCTAD) Symposium on 'Patterns of Resource Use, Environment and Development Strategies', October 8–12, Cocoyoc, Mexico.

CORPNET (ed.). 2017. Offshore Financial Centers and the Five Largest Value Conduits in the World. http://corpnet.uva.nl/ofcs/ (November 7, 2017).

Crafts, Nicholas, and Marco Magnani. 2013. The Golden Age and the Second Globalization in Italy. In *The Oxford Handbook of the Italian Economy Since Unification*, 69–106. Oxford et al.: Oxford University Press.

Crotty, Raymond. 1979. Capitalist Colonialism and Peripheralisation. In *Underdeveloped Europe: Studies in Core-Periphery Relations*, ed. Dudley Seers, Bernard Schaffer, and Marja-Liisa Kiljunen, 225–235. Sussex: Harvester Press (=Harvester Studies in Development 1).

Czichon, Eberhard. 1995. *Die Bank und die Macht. Hermann Josef Abs, die deutsche Bank und die Politik.* Köln.

Danescu, Elena Rodica. 2013. *A Rereading of the Werner Report of 8 October 1970 in the Light of the Pierre Werner Family Archives—A Detailed Study.* Sanem: Centre Virtuel de la Connaissance sur l'Europe.

De Bandt, Jacques, Péter Mándi, and Dudley Seers (eds.). 1980. European Studies in Development: New Trends in European Development Studies. London and Basingstoke: Palgrave Macmillan.

Demirović, Alex, et al. (ed.). 2011. *VielfachKrise. Im finanzmarktdominierten Kapitalismus*. Hamburg: VSA.

Der Standard. 2018. Kommission will höheres EU-Budget: Kurz lehnt Vorschlag als inakzeptabel ab, May 2. http://www.derstandard.at/2000079034573/Bruessel-will-hoeheres-EU-Budget-1-11-Prozent-der-Wirtschaftsleistung (November 12, 2018).

Deubner, Christian. 1982. West German Attitudes. In *The Second Enlargement of the EEC: The Integration of Unequal Partners*, ed. Dudley Seers and Constantine Vaitsos with the assistance of Marja-Liisa Kiljunen, 43–56. London and Basingstoke: Macmillan (=Studies in the Integration of Western Europe 2).

Dicken, Peter. 2007. Global Shift: Mapping the Changing Contours of the World Economy. 5th ed. London, Thousand Oaks, and New Delhi: Sage.

Dos Santos, Theotonio. 1970. The Structure of Dependence. *American Economic Review* 60 (2): 231–236.

Dosi, Giovanni. 2016. Beyond the 'Magic of the Market': The Slow Return of Industrial Policy (But Not yet in Italy). *Economia e Politica Industriale* 43 (3): 261–264.

Drucker, Jesse, and Simon Bowers. 2017. After a Tax Crackdown, Apple Found a New Shelter for Its Profits. *The New York Times*, November 6. https://www.nytimes.com/2017/11/06/world/apple-taxes-jersey.html?emc=edit_ta_20171106&nl=top-stories&nlid=58681655&ref=cta (November 7, 2017).

Duchêne, Francois. 1982. Community Attitudes. In *The Second Enlargement of the EEC: The Integration of Unequal Partners*, ed. Dudley Seers and Constantine Vaitsos with the assistance of Marja-Liisa Kiljunen, 25–42. London and Basingstoke: Macmillan (=Studies in the Integration of Western Europe 2).

Dunford, Michael, and Lidia Greco. 2006. *After the Three Italies: Wealth, Inequality and Industrial Change*. Malden, Oxford, and Carlton: Blackwell.

Eßer, Klaus. 1977. Integration zwischen Industrie- und teilindustrialisierten Ländern – Portugal in der EG. In *Zur Erweiterung der Europäischen Gemeinschaft in Südeuropa*, ed. Claus Burghard et al. Berlin (=Schriften des Deutschen Instituts für Entwicklungspolitik (DIE) 52).

Eßer, Klaus. 1978a. Industrie- und teilindustrialisierte Länder in der Europäischen Gemeinschaft. In *Europäische Gemeinschaft und südeuropäische Beitrittsländer*, ed. Klaus Eßer et al., 47–72. Berlin (=Schriften des Deutschen Instituts für Entwicklungspolitik (DIE) 54).

Eßer, Klaus. 1978b. Tendenzen regionaler Entwicklung in den Beitrittsländern. In *Europäische Gemeinschaft und südeuropäische Beitrittsländer*, ed. Klaus Eßer et al., 147–166. Berlin (=Schriften des Deutschen Instituts für Entwicklungspolitik (DIE) 54).

Eßer, Klaus. 1996. Nationaler Handlungsspielraum durch systematische Wettbewerbsfähigkeit. Einleitung. In *Globaler Wettbewerb und nationaler Handlungsspielraum: Neue Anforderungen an Wirtschaft, Staat und Gesellschaft*, ed. Klaus Eßer et al., 1–28. Köln: Weltforum.

Eßer, Klaus, et al. (eds.). 1978. *Europäische Gemeinschaft und südeuropäische Beitrittsländer*. Berlin (=Schriften des Deutschen Instituts für Entwicklungspolitik (DIE) 54).

Eßer, Klaus, et al. 1980. *Überlegungen zur portugiesischen Industriepolitik angesichts des Beitritts zur EG*. Berlin (=Schriften des Deutschen Instituts für Entwicklungspolitik (DIE) 60).

Eßer, Klaus, et al. (eds.). 1996. *Globaler Wettbewerb und nationaler Handlungsspielraum: neue Anforderungen an Wirtschaft, Staat und Gesellschaft*. Köln: Weltforum.

ECB—European Central Bank. 2015. Real Convergence in the Euro Area: Evidence, Theory and Policy Implications. *ECB Economic Bulletin* 5: 30–45.

Emmanuel, Arghiri. 1972. *Unequal Exchange: A Study of the Imperialism of Trade*. New York: Monthly Review Press.

Etxezarreta, Miren, et al. 2014. Boom and (Deep) Crisis in the Spanish Economy: The Role of the EU in Its Evolution. In *The Deepening Crisis of the European Union: The Case for Radical Change*, ed. Wlodzimierz Dymarski, Marica Frangakis, and Jeremy Leaman, 58–89. Poznan: Poznan University of Economics Press.

Eußner, Ansgar. 1983. *Industriepolitik und Süderweiterung der EG am Beispiel der Werftindustrie*. Berlin (=Schriften des Deutschen Instituts für Entwicklungspolitik (DIE) 72).

EU Commission (ed.). n.y. AMECO Database. http://ec.europa.eu/economy_finance/ameco/user/serie/SelectSerie.cfm (September 8, 2017).

EU Council. n.y. https://www.consilium.europa.eu/en/policies/eu-annual-budget/2017/ (November 12, 2018).

European Climate Foundation (ECF 2019): Planning for Net Zero: Assessing the Draft National Energy and Climate Plans. May. The Hague et al. https://europeanclimate.org/wp-content/uploads/2019/05/Planning-for-Net-Zero.-Assessing-the-draft-NECPs.pdf (May 16, 2019).

European Commission (EC), Access to European Union Law (EUR-Lex). n.y.1. Treaty Establishing the European Economic Community. http://eur-lex.europa.eu/legal-content/EN/TXT/?uri=celex:11957E/TXT (February 22, 2018).

European Commission (EC), Access to European Union Law (EUR-Lex). n.y.2. Consolidated version of the Treaty on the Functioning of the European Union—Part Three: Union Policies and Internal Actions—Title VII: Common Rules on Competition, Taxation and Approximation of Laws—Chapter 1: Rules on Competition—Section 2: Aids Granted by States—Article 107 (ex Article 87 TEC). http://eur-lex.europa.eu/legal-content/EN/ALL/?uri=CELEX:12008E107 (February 22, 2018).

European Council (ed.). 1972. Meetings of the Heads of State or Government. The First Summit Conference of the Enlarged Community, Paris, 19–21 October 1972. Bulletin of the European Communities, No. 10. Reproduced by Archive of European Integration (AEI), University of Pittsburgh.

Eurostat. 2018a. Regional GDP per Capita Ranged from 29% to 611% of the EU Average in 2016. Eurostat Newsrelease 33/2018. Brussels, February 28, https://ec.europa.eu/eurostat/documents/2995521/8700651/1-28022018-BP-EN/15f5fd90-ce8b-4927-9a3b-07dc255dc42a (November 7, 2018).

Eurostat. 2018b. Croatia and Latvia Are Most Dependent from International Remittances in the EU. https://ec.europa.eu/eurostat/statistics-explained/index.php/Personal_remittances_statistics#Croatia_and_Latvia_are_most_dependent_from_international_remittances_in_the_EU (April 12, 2019).

Eurostat (ed.). n.y.1. Glossary: Purchasing Power Standard (PPS). Brussels. http://ec.europa.eu/eurostat/statistics-explained/index.php/Glossary:Purchasing_power_standard_(PPS) (September 8, 2017).

Eurostat (ed.). n.y.2. Glossary: Purchasing Power Parities (PPPs). Brussels. http://ec.europa.eu/eurostat/statistics-explained/index.php/Glossary:Purchasing_power_parities_(PPPs) (September 8, 2017).

Eurostat (ed.). n.y.3. GDP at Regional Level. Brussels. https://ec.europa.eu/eurostat/statistics-explained/index.php/GDP_at_regional_level (November 7, 2018).

Evangelinides, Mary. 1979. Core-Periphery Relations in the Greek Case. In *Underdeveloped Europe: Studies in Core-Periphery Relations*, ed. Dudley Seers, Bernard Schaffer, and Marja-Liisa Kiljunen, 177–195. Sussex: Humanities Press (=Harvester Studies in Development 1).

Familienunternehmer, Die. 2018. *Satzung. Stand 13*, April 2018. https://www.familienunternehmer.eu/fileadmin/intranet/infothek/intern/satzung/satzung.pdf (July 3, 2018).

Farrant, Andrew, and Edward McPhail. 2014. Can a Dictator Turn a Constitution into a Can-Opener? F.A. Hayek and the Alchemy of Transitional Dictatorship in Chile. *Review of Political Economy* 26 (3): 331–348.

Fatto Quotidiano, Il. 2017. Nuova condanna per Umberto Bossi: due anni e mezzo per truffa allo Stato. Confiscati 48 milioni di euro al Carroccio. July 24. http://www.ilfattoquotidiano.it/2017/07/24/lega-nord-nuova-condanna-per-bossi-due-anni-e-mezzo-per-truffa-allo-stato-confiscati-48-milioni-di-euro-al-carroccio/3750650/ (October 18, 2017).

Ferdowsi, Mir. 1983. Editorisches Vorwort. In Galtung, Johan, *Self-Reliance. Beiträge zu einer alternativen Entwicklungsstrategie*, ed. Mir Ferdowsi, 5–11. München: Minerva.

Fiejka, Zdisław. 1981. Implementing the New International Economic Order (NIEO): Attempts at Regulating the Structure of World Industry. In *Dependency Theory: A Critical Reassessment*, ed. Dudley Seers, 150–159. London: F. Pinter.

Fischer, Karin, and Rudy Weissenbacher. 2016. Ungleicher Tausch – Grundannahmen, Widersprüche und aktuelle Bedeutung eines umstrittenen Theorems. *Z. Zeitschrift Marxistische Erneuerung* 27 (105): 140–157.

Fischer, Karin, Andreas Novy, and Christof Parnreiter. 1999. Globalisierung und Peripherie. In *Globalisierung und Peripherie*, ed. Karin Fischer, Andreas Novy, and Christof Parnreiter, 9–33. Frankfurt/Main: Brandes & Apsel and Südwind, (=Historische Sozialkunde 14).

Flassbeck, Heiner, and Friederike Spiecker. 2011. The Euro—Story of Misunderstanding. *Intereconomics* 46 (4): 180–187.

Foster-Carter, Aidan. 1979. Marxism Versus Dependency Theory? A Polemic. In *Millennium: Journal of International Studies* 8 (3): 214–234.

Frank, André Gunder. 1972. *Lumpenbourgeoisie: Lumpendevelopment. Dependence, Class, and Politics in Latin America*. New York and London: Monthly Review Press.

Frank, André Gunder. 1974. Dependence Is Dead, Long Live Dependence and the Class Struggle: An Answer to Critics. *Latin American Perspectives* 1 (1): 87–106.

Frank, Andre Gunder. n.y. Personal Research Interests for Public Policy Practice. In *Andre Gunder Frank Official Website*, ed. Róbinson Rojas. http://rrojasdatabank.info/agfrank/research.html#DEPENDENCE (April 26, 2016).

Friedmann, John. 1966. *Regional Development Policy: A Case Study of Venezuela*. Cambridge, MA: MIT Press.

Friedmann, John. 1967. *A General Theory of Polarized Development*. Santiago: The Ford Foundation: Urban and Regional Advisory Program in Chile.

Friedmann, John. 1983a. Life Space and Economic Space: Contradictions in Regional Development. *Seers/Öström* 1983: 148–162.

Friedmann, John. 1983b. Life Space and Economic Space: Contradictions in Regional Development. In *The Crises of the European Regions*, ed. Dudley Seers and Kjell Öström, 148–162. London: Palgrave Macmillan.

Friedmann, John. 1986. Regional Development in Industrialised Countries: Endogenous or Self-Reliant? In *Self-Reliant Development in Europe: Theory, Problems, Actions*, ed. Michel Bassand, Ernst Brugger, John Bryden, John Friedmann, and Barbara Stuckey, 203–216. Aldershot: Gower.

Friedmann, John, and Clyde Weaver. 1979. *Territory and Function: The Evolution of Regional Planning*. London: Edward Arnold.

Fröbel, Folker, Jürgen Heinrichs, and Otto Kreye. 1977. *Die neue internationale Arbeitsteilung: strukturelle Arbeitslosigkeit in den Industrieländern und die Industrialisierung der Entwicklungsländer.* Reinbek bei Hamburg: Rowohlt.

Fujita, Masahisa, Paul Krugman, and Anthony J. Venables. 2001 [1999]. *The Spatial Economy: Cities, Regions, and International Trade.* Cambridge, MA; London: MIT Press.

Furtado, Celso. 1967. La concentración del poder económico en los Estados Unidos y sus proyecciones en América Latina. *Estudios Internacionales* 1 (3–4): 323–336.

Galtung, Johan. 1971. A Structural Theory of Imperialism. *Journal of Peace Research* 8 (2): 81–117.

Galtung, Johan. 1972. Eine strukturelle Theorie des Imperialismus. In *Imperialismus und strukturelle Gewalt. Analysen über abhängige Reproduktion*, ed. Dieter Senghaas, 29–104. Frankfurt/Main: Suhrkamp.

Galtung, Johan. 1976a. Self-Reliance: Concept, Practice and Rationale. In *Transcend International.* https://www.transcend.org/galtung/papers/Self-Reliance%20-%20Concept,%20Practice%20and%20Rationale.pdf (May 23, 2017).

Galtung, Johan. 1976b. The Politics of Self-Reliance. In *Transcend International.* https://www.transcend.org/galtung/papers/The%20Politics%20of%20Self-Reliance.pdf (May 23, 2017).

Galtung, Johan. 1977. *Methodology and Ideology: Essays in Methodology*, vol. 1. Copenhagen: Christian Ejlers.

Galtung, Johan. 1983 [1978]. *Self-Reliance. Beiträge zu einer alternativen Entwicklungsstrategie*, ed. Mir Ferdowsi. München: Minerva.

Galtung, Johan. 1985. Towards a New Economics: On the Theory and Practice of Self-Reliance. In *Transcend International.* https://www.transcend.org/galtung/papers/Towards%20a%20New%20Economics-On%20the%20Theory%20and%20Practice%20of%20Self-Reliance.pdf (May 23, 2017).

Galtung, Johan (o.J.): The Cocoyoc Declaration, ed. Transcend. http://www.transcend.org/tms/2010/03/the-cocoyoc-declaration/ (November 12, 2014).

Garcia-Bernardo, Javier, Jan Fichtner, Frank W. Takes, and Eelke M. Heemskerk. 2017. Uncovering Offshore Financial Centers: Conduits and Sinks in the Global Corporate Ownership Network. *Scientific Reports* 7 (1): 6246. https://doi.org/10.1038/s41598-017-06322-9.

GFM EA&E. 2019. German Federal Ministry for Economic Affairs and Energy. 2019. National Industrial Strategy 2030. Strategic Guidelines for a German and European Industrial Policy. Berlin. https://www.bmwi.de/Redaktion/EN/Publikationen/Industry/national-industry-strategy-2030.html (June 13, 2019).

GFP—German Foreign Policy. 2018. *Europas Achsen*, July 3. https://www.german-foreign-policy.com/news/detail/7658/ (July 3, 2018).

GFP—German Foreign Policy. 2019. Reparationsabwehr aus der Trickkiste. https://www.german-foreign-policy.com/news/detail/7959/ (June 6, 2019).

Gindin, Sam. 2016. Chasing Utopia. *Jacobin*, October 3. https://www.jacobinmag.com/2016/03/workers-control-coops-wright-wolff-alperovitz (November 13, 2019).

Giner, Salvador. 1985. Political Economy, Legitimation and the State in Southern Europe. In *Uneven Development in Southern Europe: Studies of Accumulation, Class, Migration and the State*, ed. Ray Hudson and Jim Lewis, 309–350. London and New York: Methuen.

Giunta, Anna, and Flavia Martinelli. 1995. The Impact of Post-Fordist Corporate Restructuring in a Peripheral Region. In *Behind the Myth of European Union: Prospects for Cohesion*, ed. Ash Amin and John Tomaney, 190–225. London and New York: Routledge.

Goldberg, Jörg. 1983. Uberakkumulation von Kapital als Regulierungsproblem. In *Überproduktion, Unterkonsumtion, Depression. Analysen und Kontroversen zur Krisentheorie*, ed. Jürgen Hoffmann, 167–183. Hamburg: VSA.

Government of France. 2019. A Franco-German Manifesto for a European Industrial Policy Fit for the 21st Century. N°1043, February 19. Paris. https://www.gouvernement.fr/en/a-franco-german-manifesto-for-a-european-industrial-policy-fit-for-the-21st-century (May 10, 2019).

Grix, Jonathan. 2002. Introducing Students to the Generic Terminology of Social Research. *Politics* 22 (3): 175–186.

Guarascio, Dario, and Annamaria Simonazzi. 2016. A Polarized Country in a Polarized Europe: An Industrial Policy for Italy's Renaissance. *Economia a Politica Industriale* 43 (3): 315–322.

Hadjimichalis, Costis. 1983. Regional Crisis: The State and Regional Social Movements in Southern Europe. In *The Crisis of the European Regions*, ed. Dudley Seers and Kjell Öström, 127–147. London and Basingstoke: Palgrave Macmillan.

Hadjimichalis, Costis. 1984. The Geographical Transfer of Value: Notes on the Spatiality of Capitalism. *Environment and Planning D: Society and Space* 2 (3): 329–345.

Hadjimichalis, Costis. 1994. The Fringes of Europe and EU Integration: A View from the South. *European Urban and Regional Studies* 1 (1): 19–29.

Hadjimichalis, Costis. 2006. The End of Third Italy as We Knew It? *Antipode* 38 (1): 82–106.

Hadjimichalis, Costis, and Dina Varou-Hadjimichalis. 1980. Penetration of Multinational Capital into Backward Regions: A Policy Analysis in Greece. *Antipode* 12 (2): 17–24.

Hadjimichalis, Costis, and Nicos Papamichos. 1990. 'Local' Development in Southern Europe: Towards a New Mythology. *Antipode* 22 (3): 181–210.

Hadjimichalis, Costis, and Ray Hudson. 2014. Contemporary Crisis Across Europe and the Crisis of Regional Development Theories. *Regional Studies* 48 (1): 208–218.

Hager, Wolfgang. 1985. Fortress Europe: A Model? In *Europe at the Crossroads: Agendas of the Crisis*, ed. Stefan Musto and Carl Pinkele, 65–84. New York et al.: Praeger.

Haller, Max. 2009. *Die Europäische Union als Elitenprozess. Das Ende eines Traums?* Wiesbaden.

Hansen, Niles. 1981. Development from Above: The Centre-Down Development Paradigm. In *Development from Above or Below? The Dialectics of Regional Planning in Developing Countries*, ed. Walter Stöhr and Fraser Taylor, 15–38. Chichester et al.: Wiley.

Harris, Abram. 1942. Sombart and German (National) Socialism. *Journal of Political Economy* 50 (6): 805–835.

Harrod, Roy. 1958. The Possibility of Economic Satiety—Use of Economic Growth for Improving the Quality of Education and Leisure. In *Problems of United States Economic Development*, ed. Committee for Economic Development, vol. 1, 207–213. New York: Committee for Economic Development.

Harvey, David. 2003. *The New Imperialism*. New York: Oxford University Press.

Harvey, David. 2004. Die Geographie des 'neuen' Imperialismus: Akkumulation durch Enteignung. In *Die globale Enteignungsökonomie*, ed. Christian Zeller, 183–215. Münster: Westphälisches Dampfboot.

Hasenpflug, Hajo, and Beate Kohler (eds.). 1977. *Die Süd-Erweiterung der Europäischen Gemeinschaft. Wende oder Ende der Integration.* Hamburg: Weltarchiv (=Veröffentlichungen des HWWA-Instituts für Wirtschaftsforschung-Hamburg).

Haug, Frigga. 2014. Die Transformation muss am Herrschaftsknoten ansetzen. In *Futuring. Perspektiven der Transformation im Kapitalismus über ihn hinaus*, Hg. Michael Brie, 178–193. Münster: Westfälisches Dampfboot.

Hayek, Friedrich. 1958 [1948]. *Individualism and Economic Order*. London and Chicago: The University of Chicago Press.

Hayek, Friedrich. 1978. *Denationalisation of Money—The Argument Refined: An Analysis of the Theory and Practice of Concurrent Currencies*, 2nd ed., rev. and enlarged, n.p. London: The Institute of Economic Affairs.

Hayek, Friedrich. 1981 [1979]. *Law, Legislation and Liberty: Vol. 3: The Political Order of a Free People*. London and Chicago: The University of Chicago Press.

Hayek, Friedrich. 2011 [1960]. *The Constitution of Liberty: The Definitive Edition*, ed. Ronald Hamowy. Chicago and London: Chicago University Press.

Heimpold, Gerhard. 2010. Zwischen Deindustrialisierung und Reindustrialisierung. *Informationen zur Raumentwicklung* 37 (10/11): 727–743.

Hein, Wolfgang. 1980. Zusammenarbeit zwischen Entwicklungsländern – Ansatz für "Kollektive Self-Reliance" oder Voraussetzung für die weitere Entfaltung abhängiger Akkumulation? In *Self-Reliance als nationale und kollektive Entwicklungsstrategie*, ed. Khushi Khan, 67–127. München und London: Weltforum (=Weltwirtschaft und internationale Beziehungen 20).

Heller, Hermann. 1933. Autoritärer Liberalismus? In Hermann Heller. 1992. *Gesammelte Schriften*, ed. Christoph Müller. Zweiter Band. Recht, Staat, Macht, 2nd and rev. ed., Extented with an Epilog, 643–653. Tübingen: Mohr.

Herzog, Hubert, and Franz Tödtling. 1983. Versuch einer Einschätzung der österreichischen Regionalpolitik für periphere entwicklungsschwache Regionen. *Österreichische Zeitschrift Für Soziologie* 8 (3): 100–113.

Hettne, Björn. 1985. Development Theory and the European Crisis. In *Endogenous Development: A Myth or a Path? Problems of Economic Self-Reliance in the European Periphery*, ed. Stefan Musto, 41–71. Tilburg: EADI.

Hettne, Björn. 1997. Development, Security and World Order: A Regionalist Approach. In *European Journal of Development Studies* 9 (1): 83–106.

Hickel, Rudolf. 1983. Ökonomische Ursachen- und Politikprobleme der Massenarbeitslosigkeit. In *Überproduktion, Unterkonsumtion, Depression. Analysen und Kontroversen zur Krisentheorie*, ed. Jürgen Hoffmann, 55–88. Hamburg: VSA.

Hilberg, Raul. 1990 [1961]. *Die Vernichtung der europäischen Juden*. Band 3. Frankfurt/Main.

Hillebrand, Wolfgang. 1978. Hypothesen zur zukünftigen Entwicklung der Industriepolitik der Gemeinschaft. In *Europäische Gemeinschaft und südeuropäische Beitrittsländer*, ed. Klaus Eßer et al., 25–46. Berlin (=Schriften des Deutschen Instituts für Entwicklungspolitik (DIE) 54).

Hirsch, Joachim. 2001. Die Internationalisierung des Staates. Anmerkungen zu einigen aktuellen Fragen der Staatstheorie. In Joachim Hirsch, Bob Jessop, und Nicos Poulantzas: *Die Zukunft des Staates*, 101–138. Hamburg: VSA.

Hobsbawm, Eric. 1990. *Nations and Nationalism Since 1780: Programme, Myth, Reality*. Cambridge, New York, and Oakleigh: Cambridge University Press.

Hobsbawm, Eric. 1996. *The Age of the Extremes: A History of the World 1914–1991*. New York: Vintage.

Holland, Stuart. 1979. Dependent Development: Portugal as Periphery. In *Underdeveloped Europe: Studies in Core-Periphery Relations*, ed. Dudley Seers, Bernard Schaffer, and Marja-Liisa Kiljunen, 139–160. Sussex: Humanities Press (=Harvester Studies in Development 1).

Holland, Stuart. 1980. *The UnCommon Market*. London and Basingstoke: Macmillan.

Holman, Otto. 2002. Die Neue Europäische Peripherie. Ost- und Süderweiterung der Europäischen Union im Vergleich. *Prokla* 32 (2): 399–420.

Hübner, Kurt. 1983. Warum dauert die Krise so lange? Anmerkungen zum Verhältnis von Zyklus und Trend. In *Überproduktion, Unterkonsumtion, Depression, Analysen und Kontroversen zur Krisentheorie*, ed. Jürgen Hoffmann, 185–216. Hamburg: VSA.

Hudson, Ray, and Jim Lewis. 1984. Capital Accumulation: The Industrialisation of Southern Europe? In *Southern Europe Transformed: Political and Economic Change in Greece, Italy, Portugal and Spain*, ed. Allan Williams, 179–207. London: Harper & Row.

Hudson, Ray, and Jim Lewis (eds.). 1985a. *Uneven Development in Southern Europe: Studies of Accumulation, Class, Migration and the State*. London and New York: Methuen.

Hudson, Ray, and Jim Lewis. 1985b. Introduction: Recent Economic, Social and Political Changes in Southern Europe. In *Uneven Development in Southern Europe: Studies of Accumulation, Class, Migration and the State*, ed. Ray Hudson and Jim Lewis, 1–53. London and New York: Methuen.

Hummen, Wilhelm. 1977. *Greek Industry in the European Community—Prospects and Problems*. Berlin (=Schriften des Deutschen Instituts für Entwicklungspolitik (DIE) 45).

Hurtienne, Thomas. 1974. *Zur Ideologiekritik der lateinamerikanischen Theorien der Unterentwicklung und Abhängigkeit*. *Prokla* 4 (3): 213–283.

Hurtienne, Thomas. 1981. Peripherer Kapitalismus und autozentrierte Entwicklung – Zur Kritik des Erklärungsansatzes von Dieter Senghaas. *Prokla* 11 (3): 105–136.

Hurtienne, Thomas. 1984. Theoriegeschichtliche Grundlagen des sozialökonomischen Entwicklungsdenkens. Vol. 1. Rationalität und Sozialökonomische Entwicklung in der frühbürgerlichen Epoche. Saarbrücken et al. Breitenbach.

Hurtienne, Thomas, and Dirk Messner. 1996. Neue Konzepte internationaler Wettbewerbsfähigkeit in Industrie- und Entwicklungsländern. In *Globaler Wettbewerb und nationaler Handlungsspielraum: neue Anforderungen an Wirtschaft, Staat und Gesellschaft*, ed. Klaus Eßer et al., 39–72. Köln: Weltforum.

Hytten, Eyvind, and Marco Marchioni. 1970. *Industrializzazione senza sviluppo. Gela: una storia meridionale*. Milano: Franco Angeli.

Intergovernmental Committee of the Messina Conference. 1956. Report by the Heads of Delegations to the Foreign Ministers. Brussels, April 21. In University of Luxembourg (ed.), http://www.cvce.eu/obj/report_of_the_heads_of_delegation_to_the_foreign_ministers_brussels_21_april_1956-en-4dd69921-433b-4bc0-acec-808f72fec9ae.html (February 25, 2018).

International Monetary Fund (IMF). n.y. Portugal: Fast Facts, http://www.imf.org/external/np/exr/countryfacts/prt/ (May 27, 2015).

Jackson, Tim. 2009. *Prosperity without Growth: Economics for a Finite Planet*. London et al.: Earthscan.

James, Harold. 2001. *The Deutsche Bank and the Nazi Economic War Against the Jews*. Cambridge: Cambridge University Press.

James, Harold. 2004. *The Nazi Dictatorship and the Deutsche Bank*. Cambridge, MA: Cambridge University Press.

Jánossy, Ferenc. 1971 [1966]. *The End of the Economic Miracle: Appearance and Reality in Economic Development*. White Plains, NY: International Arts and Sciences Press.

Jessop, Bob. 1985. *Nicos Poulantzas: Marxist Theory and Political Strategy*. Basingstoke: Macmillan.

Johannison, Bengt. 1990. The Nordic Perspective: Self-Reliant Local Development in Four Scandinavian Countries. In *Global Challenge and Local Response: Initiatives for Economic Regeneration in Contemporary Europe*, ed. Walter Stöhr, 57–89. London, New York, and Tokyo: Mansell Publishing and United Nations University.

Kay, Cristóbal. 1989. *Latin American Theories of Development and Underdevelopment*. London and New York: Routledge.

Kay, Cristóbal. 1997. Introduction: Globalisation, Competitiveness and Human Security. *European Journal of Development Studies* 9 (1): 1–6.

Keen, Steve. 2011. *Debunking Economics: The Naked Emperor Dethroned?* Rev. and expanded ed. London: Zed Books.

Keyder, Çağlar. 1985. The American Recovery of Southern Europe. Aid and Hegemony. In *Semiperipheral Development: The Politics of Southern Europe in the Twentieth Century*, ed. Giovanni Arrighi, 135–148. Beverly Hills: Sage (=Explorations in the World-Economy 5).

Kiljunen, Kimmo. 1979. Finland in the International Division of Labour. In *Underdeveloped Europe: Studies in Core-Periphery Relations*, ed. Dudley Seers, Bernard Schaffer, and Marja-Liisa Kiljunen, 279–302. Sussex: Harvester Press (=Harvester Studies in Development 1).

Kiljunen, Marja-Liisa. 1979. Statistical Appendix. In *Underdeveloped Europe: Studies in Core-Periphery Relations*, ed. Dudley Seers, Bernard Schaffer, and Marja-Liisa Kiljunen, 303–320. Sussex: Harvester Press (=Harvester Studies in Development 1).

Kiljunen, Marja-Liisa. 1980. Regional Disparities and Policy in the EEC. In *Integration and the Unequal Development: The Experience of the EEC*, ed. Dudley Seers and Constantine Vaitsos with the assistance of Marja-Liisa Kiljunen, 199–222. London and Basingstoke: Macmillan (=Studies in the Integration of Western Europe 1).

Kirby, Peader. 2010. *Celtic Tiger in Collapse. Explaining the Weaknesses of the Irish Model*, Second Edition. Basingstoke and New York: Palgrave Macmillan.

Kojima, Kiyoshi. 1970. Towards a Theory of Agreed Specialization: The Economics of Integration. In *Induction, Growth and Trade: Essays in Honour of Roy Harrod*, ed. Walter Eltis et al., 305–324. Oxford: Clarendon Press.

Komlosy, Andrea. 2006. Österreichs Brückenfunktion und die Durchlässigkeit des „Eisernen Vorhangs". In *„Zarte Bande": Österreich und die europäischen planwirtschaftlichen Länder*, ed. Gertrude Enderle-Burcel, Dieter Stiefel, und Alice Teichova, 73–105. Wien: Studienverlag (=Mitteilungen des Österreichischen Staatsarchivs/Sonderband 9).

Kosta, Jiří. 1974. *Sozialistische Planwirtschaft. Theorie und Praxis.* Opladen: Westdeutscher Verlag.

Kramer, Ingo, Dieter Kempf, Eric Schweitzer, and Hans Peter Wollseifer. 2018. Aus Verantwortung für Deutschland und Europa. Gemeinsamer Appell der deutschen Wirtschaft, 29. Juni 2018. Bundesverband der deutschen Industrie (BDI). https://bdi.eu/#/publikation/news/gemeinsamer-appell-der-deutschen-wirtschaft/ (July 3, 2018).

Krugman, Paul. 1991. *Geography and Trade.* Leuven, Cambridge, and London: Leuven University Press and MIT Press.

Kynge, James, and Michael Peel. 2017. Eastern Europe's China Pivot. *Financial Times*, November 28, p. 7.

Lall, Sanjaya. 1975. Is 'Dependence' a Useful Concept in Analysing Underdevelopment? *World Development* 3 (11 and 12): 799–810.

Lange, Peter. 1980. Crisis and Consent, Change and Compromise: Dilemmas of Italian Communism in the 1970s. In *Italy in Transition. Conflict and Consensus*, ed. Peter Lange, and Sidney Tarrow, 110–132. London: Frank Cass.

Lange, Peter. 1985. Semiperiphery and Core in the European Context: Reflections on the Postwar Italian Experience. In *Semiperipheral Development: The Politics of Southern Europe in the Twentieth Century*, ed. Giovanni Arrighi, 179–214. Beverly Hills, London, and New Delhi: Sage (=Explorations in the World-Economy 5).

Lange, Peter, and Sidney Tarrow (eds.). 1980. *Italy in Transition: Conflict and Consensus.* London: Frank Cass.

Lapavitsas, Costas. 2013. *Profiting Without Producing: How Finance Exploits Us All.* London and New York: Verso.

Leggewie, Claus. 1975. Theoretische und empirische Aspekte des Abhängigkeitsverhältnisses der mediterranen Peripherie vom westeuropäischen Zentrum. In *Europäische Peripherie. Meisenheim am Glan*, ed. Claus Leggewie and Marios Nikolinakos, 13–94 (=Die Dritte Welt, Sonderheft 1975).

Leonard, Dick. 1992. *Guide to the European Community.* London: Economist.

Lipietz, Alain. 1987. *Mirages and Miracles. The Crisis of Global Fordism.* London: Verso.

Lissoni, Francesco. 1996. *Deindustrialization in Lombardy: An Empirical Assessment*. European Regional Science Association. 36th European Congress, August 26–30. ETH Zurich: Switzerland.

Logan, John. 1985. Democracy from Above: Limits to Change in Southern Europe. In *Semiperipheral Development: The Politics of Southern Europe in the Twentieth Century*, ed. Giovanni Arrighi, 149–177. Beverly Hills, London, and New Delhi: Sage (=Explorations in the World-Economy 5).

López, Isidro, and Emmanuel Rodríguez. 2010. *Fin de ciclo. Financiarización, territorio y sociedad de propietarios en la onda larga del capitalismo hispano (1959–2010)*. Madrid: Traficantes de Sueños.

Louri, Helen, and Ionna Pepelasis Minoglou. 2001. On the Determinants of (De-)Industrialization: A Quantitative Exploration. *International Review of Applied Economics*, 15 (4): 397–410.

Love, Joseph. 1996. *Crafting the Third World: Theorizing Underdevelopment in Rumania and Brazil*. Stanford: Stanford University Press.

Love, Joseph. 2011. The Latin American Contribution to Center-Periphery Perspectives: History and Prospect. In *Cores, Peripheries, and Globalization: Essays in Honor of Ivan Berend*, ed. Peter Hanns Reill and Balázs Szelényi, 15–42. Budapest and New York: Central European University Press.

Lucchese, Matteo, Leopoldo Nascia, and Mario Pianta. 2016. Industrial Policy and Technology in Italy. *Economic e Politica Industriale* 43 (3): 233–260.

Luif, Paul. 1988. Die Europäische Gemeinschaft. In *Der un-heimliche Anschluss. Österreich und die EG*, ed. Inge Morawetz and Margit Scherb, 1–18. Wien: Verlag für Gesellschaftskritik.

Lundvall, Bengt-Åke. 2016. From Manufacturing Nostalgia to a Strategy for Economic Transformation. *Economia e Politica Industriale* 43 (3): 265–271.

Maier, Gunther, Franz Tödtling, and Michaela Trippl. 2006. *Regional- und Stadtökonomik, Vol. 2. Regionalentwicklung und Regionalpolitik*. Wien/New York: Springer.

Mandel, Ernest. 1967. International Capitalism and "Supra-Nationality". In *Socialist Register 1967: A Survey of Movements and Ideas*, ed. Ralph Miliband and John Saville, 27–41. London: Merlin Press.

Mandel, Ernest. 1974 [1972]. *Der Spätkapitalismus. Versuch einer marxistischen Erklärung*. Frankfurt/Main: Suhrkamp.

Mania, Roberto. 2015. Mezzogiorno, la Grecia d'Italia. *La Repubblica, Affari & Finanza* 30 (27): 1–2 (July 20).

Manoilescu, Mihail. 1937. *Die nationalen Produktivkräfte und der Außenhandel*. Berlin: Junker und Dünnhaupt.

Marsh, David. 2011. *The Euro: The Battle for the New Global Currency*, New Edition. New Haven and London: Yale University Press.

Martinelli, Alberto. 1980. Organised Business and Italian Politics: Confindustria and the Christian Democrats in the Postwar Period. In *Italy in Transition: Conflict and Consensus*, ed. Peter Lange and Sidney Tarrow, 67–87. London: Frank Cass.

Marx, Karl. 1999 [1887]. *Capital: A Critique of Political Economy*, vol. I. Marx/Engels Internet Archive. https://www.marxists.org/archive/marx/works/download/pdf/Capital-Volume-I.pdf.

Massey, Doreen. 1979. In What Sense a Regional Problem? *Regional Studies* 13 (2): 233–243.

Meadows, Donella. 1972. *The Limits to Growth: A Report for the Club of Rome's Project on the Predicament of Mankind*. New York: Universe.

Mélenchon, Jean-Luc, Stefano Fassina, Zoe Konstantopoulou, Oskar Lafontaine, and Yanis Varoufakis. 2015. *A Plan B in Europe*. w/o place and publisher.

Monfort, Philippe. 2008. *Convergence of EU Regions: Measures and Evolution*. Brussels: European Union (=Directorate-General for Regional Policy 1/2008).

Mont Pèlerin-Society (MPS n.y.) F. A. Hayek. https://www.montpelerin.org/f-a-hayek/ (November 13, 2019).

Moravcsik, Andrew. 1998. *The Choice for Europe: Social Purpose and State Power from Messina to Maastricht*. Ithaca: Cornell University Press.

Morrice, David. 1994. C. B. Macpherson's Critique of Liberal Democracy and Capitalism. *Political Studies* 42 (4): 646–661.

Müller, Jan-Werner. 2012. Beyond Militant Democracy? *New Left Review* 73: 39–47.

Muñoz, Juan, Santiago Roldán, and Angel Serrano. 1979. The Growing Dependence of Spanish Industrialization on Foreign Investment. In *Underdeveloped Europe: Studies in Core-Periphery Relations*, ed. Dudley Seers, Bernard Schaffer, and Marja-Liisa Kiljunen, 161–175. Sussex: Humanities Press (=Harvester Studies in Development 1).

Musto, Stefan. 1977. Spanien und die Europäische Gemeinschaft. Der schwierige Weg zur Mitgliedschaft. Bonn (=Europäische Schriften des Instituts für Europäische Politik 48).

Musto, Stefan. 1981. Die Süderweiterung der Europäischen Gemeinschaft. *Kyklos* 34 (2): 242–273.

Musto, Stefan. 1982. Structural Implications. In *The Second Enlargement of the EEC: The Integration of Unequal Partners*, ed. Dudley Seers and Constantine Vaitsos (with the assistance of Marja-Liisa Kiljunen), 67–91. London and Basingstoke: Macmillan (=Studies in the Integration of Western Europe 2).

Musto, Stefan. 1985a. The Loss of Hegemony: Sensitive Industries and Industrial Policies in the European Community. In *Europe at the Crossroads: Agendas of the Crisis*, ed. Stefan Musto and Carl Pinkele, 85–102. New York et al.: Praeger.

Musto, Stefan (ed.). 1985b. *Endogenous Development: A Myth or a Path? Problems of Economic Self-Reliance in the European Periphery*. Tilburg (=European Association of Development Research and Training Institutes: EADI Book Series 5).

Musto, Stefan. 1985c. In Search of a New Paradigm. In *Endogenous Development: A Myth or a Path? Problems of Economic Self-Reliance in the European Periphery*, ed. Stefan Musto, 1–13. Tilburg: EADI (=European Association of Development Research and Training Institutes: EADI Book Series 5).

Musto, Stefan, and Carl Pinkele (eds.). 1985. *Europe at the Crossroads*. Agendas of the Crisis. New York et al.: Praeger.

Narr, Wolf-Dieter (ed.). 1977. *Auf dem Weg zum Einparteienstaat*. Opladen: Westdeutscher.

Nevradakis, Michael. 2014. Germany's Unpaid Debt to Greece: Economist Albrecht Ritschl on WWII Reparations That Never Were. *truthout*, November 7. http://www.truth-out.org/news/item/27261-germany-s-unpaid-debt-to-greece-albrecht-ritschl-on-germany-s-war-debts-and-reparations (August 8, 2016).

Nikolinakos, Marios. 1985a. The Impossibility of Self-Reliance. In *Europe at the Crossroads: Agendas of the Crisis*, ed. Stefan Musto, and Carl Pinkele, 327–342. New York et al.: Praeger.

Nikolinakos, Marios. 1985b. Transnationalization of Production, Location of Industry and the Deformation of Regional Development in Peripheral Countries: The Case of Greece. In *Uneven development in Southern Europe: Studies of Accumulation, Class, Migration and the State*, ed. Ray Hudson and Jim Lewis, 192–210. London and New York: Methuen.

Nohlen, Dieter. 1985. Ungleiche Entwicklung und Regionalpolitik in Südeuropa (Italien, Spanien, Portugal). Eine Einführung. In *Ungleiche Entwicklung und Regionalpolitik in Südeuropa: Italien, Spanien, Portugal*, ed. Dieter Nohlen und Rainer-Olaf Schultze unter Mitwirkung von Wolfgang Merkel, 9–15. Bochum (=Politikwissenschaftliche Paperbacks 6).

Nohlen, Dieter. n.y. Dieter Nohlen—Curriculum Vitae. http://www.nohlen.uni-hd.de/de/cv.html (December 2, 2014).

Nohlen, Dieter, and Rainer-Olaf Schultze. 1985a. Vorwort. In *Ungleiche Entwicklung und Regionalpolitik in Südeuropa: Italien, Spanien, Portugal*, ed. Dieter Nohlen and Rainer-Olaf Schultze unter Mitwirkung von Wolfgang Merkel, 7–8. Bochum (=Politikwissenschaftliche Paperbacks 6).

Nohlen, Dieter, und Rainer-Olaf Schultze. 1985b. Ungleiche Entwicklung und Regionalpolitik in Südeuropa. Externe Verursachungsdfaktoren und endogene Entwicklungschancen. In *Ungleiche Entwicklung und Regionalpolitik in Südeuropa: Italien, Spanien, Portugal*, Hg. Dieter Nohlen und Rainer-Olaf Schultze unter Mitwirkung von Wolfgang Merkel, 17–73. Bochum (=Politikwissenschaftliche Paperbacks 6).

Oberndorfer, Lukas. 2012a. Hegemoniekrise in Europa – Auf dem Weg zu einem autoritären Wettbewerbsetatismus? In *Die EU in der Krise. Zwischen autoritärem Etatismus und europäischen Frühling*, ed. Forschungsgruppe 'Staatsprojekt Europa', 49–71. Münster: Westfälisches Dampfboot.

Oberndorfer, Lukas. 2012b. Die Renaissance des autoritären Liberalismus? Carl Schmitt und der deutsche Neoliberalismus vor dem Hintergrund des Eintritts der "Massen" in die europäische Politik. *Prokla* 42 (3): 413–431.

Öström, Kjell. 1983. Introduction. In *The Crisis of the European Regions*, ed. Dudley Seers and Kjell Öström, 1–5. London and Basingstoke: Palgrave Macmillan.

Palloix, Christian. 1972 [1970]. The Question of Unequal Exchange: A Critique of Political Economy. *Bulletin of the Conference of Socialist Economists* 2 (1): 67–94.

Palma, Gabriel. 1978. Dependency: A Formal Theory of Underdevelopment or a Methodology for the Analysis of Concrete Situations of Underdevelopment. *World Development* 6 (7–8): 881–924.

Palma, Gabriel. 1981. Dependency and Development: A Critical Overview. In *Dependency Theory: A Critical Reassessment*, ed. Dudley Seers, 20–78. London: F. Pinter.

Palma, Gabriel. 2008. De-industrialization, 'Premature' De-industrialization and the Dutch Disease. In *The New Palgrave Dictionary of Economics*, 2nd ed., ed. Steven Durlauf and Lawrence Blume. Basingstoke. http://www.dictionaryo-feconomics.com/dictionary.

Panitch, Leo. 1994. Globalisation and the State. In *Socialist Register 1994. Between Globalism and Nationalism*, ed. Ralph Miliband, and Leo Panitch, 60–93. London: Merlin.

Panitch, Leo, et al. (eds.). 2004. *The Globalization Decade: A Critical Reader*. London: Merlin.

Panitch, Leo, and Sam Gindin. 2012. *The Making of Global Capitalism: The Political Economy of American Empire*. London and New York: Verso.

Panitch, Leo, and Sam Gindin. 2016. Class, Party and the Challenge of State Transformation. In *Socialist Register 2017: Rethinking Revolution*, ed. Leo Panitch and Greg Albo, 35–58. London: Merlin.

Papadantonakis, Kostis. 1985. Incorporation Is Peripheralization: Contradiction of Southern Europe's Economic Development. In *Semiperipheral Development: The Politics of Southern Europe in the Twentieth Century*, ed. Giovanni Arrighi, 86–106. Beverly Hills, London, and New Delhi: Sage (=Explorations in the World-Economy 5).

Papademetriou, Demetrios. 1983. A Retrospective Look at Mediterranean Labor Migrations to Europe. In *The Contemporary Mediterranean World*, ed. Carl Pinkele and Adamantia Pollis, 237–256. New York: Praeger.

Payno, Juan Antonio, and José Luis Sampedro (eds.). 1983. *The Enlargement of the European Community: Case-Studies of Greece, Portugal, and Spain*. London and Basingstoke: Macmillan (=Studies in the Integration of Western Europe 3).

Pimmer, Stefan. 2016. Ich war damals einfach interessiert an diesen neuen Paradigmen. In *Dieter Senghaas über die deutschsprachige Rezeption der Dependenztheorien*, ed. Mattersburger Kreis für Entwicklungspolitik. http://www.mattersburgerkreis.at/site/de/aktuelles/interviews/article/269.html (March 31, 2017).

Piselli, Fortunata. 2011. Reflections on Calabria: A Critique of the Concept of 'Primitive Accumulation'. *Austrian Journal of Development Policy* XXVII (1): 25–43.

Plehwe, Dieter. 1998. Ludwig Erhards D-Mark. Kontinuitätslinien des Rechtsliberalismus. In *Fünfzig Jahre Deutsche Mark*, ed. LAKS Hessen, 16–27. Berlin: Elefanten Press.

Pollin, Robert. 2018. De-Growth vs A Green New Deal. *New Left Review* 112, 5–25.

Pollis, Adamantia. 1983. The Southern European Semiperiphery and the European Community. In *The Contemporary Mediterranean World*, ed. Carl Pinkele and Adamantia Pollis, 202–220. New York: Praeger.

Pollis, Adamantia. 1985. International and Domestic Constraints on Socialist Transformation in Greece. In *Europe at the Crossroads: Agendas of the Crisis*, ed. Stefan Musto and Carl Pinkele, 197–217. New York et al.: Praeger.

Poma, Muruchi. 2018. Buen (Con)Vivir, das gute Leben für alle. Über die Prinzipien des guten Zusammenlebens und das Paradox von Entwicklung. In *Anders wachsen! Von der Krise der kapitalistischen Wachstumsgesellschaft und Ansätzen einer Transformation*, ed. Maximilian Becker and Mathilda Reinicke, 241–264. München: oekom.

Pomeranz, Kenneth. 2000. *The Great Divergence: China, Europe, and the Making of the Modern World Economy*. Princeton and Oxford: Princeton University Press.

Porter, Michael. 1990. *The Competitive Advantage of Nations*. London et al.: Macmillan.

Poulantzas, Nicos. 1974 [1973]. Die Internationalisierung der kapitalistischen Produktionsverhältnisse und der Nationalstaat. In Multinationale Konzerne. Entwicklungstendenzen im kapitalistischen System, ed. Otto Kreye, 81–129. München: Hanser.

Poulantzas, Nicos. 1976 [1975]. *The Crisis of the Dictatorships. Portugal, Greece, Spain*. London: NLB.

Poulantzas, Nicos. 2001 [1974]. Die Internationalisierung der kapitalistischen Verhältnisse und der Nationalstaat. In *Die Zukunft des Staates*, ed. Joachim Hirsch, Bob Jessop, and Nicos Poulantzas, 19–69. Hamburg: VSA.

Poulantzas, Nicos. 2008a [1976]. The Political Crisis and the Crisis of the State. In *The Poulantzas Reader: Marxism, Law and the State*, ed. James Martin, 294–322. London and New York: Verso.

Poulantzas, Nicos. 2008b [1976]. The Capitalist State: A Reply to Miliband and Laclau. In *The Poulantzas Reader: Marxism, Law and the State*, ed. James Martin, 270–293. London and New York: Verso.

Poulantzas, Nicos. 2008c [1965]. Preliminaries to the Study of Hegemony in the State. In *The Poulantzas Reader: Marxism, Law and the State*, ed. James Martin, 74–119. London and New York: Verso.

Poulantzas, Nicos. 2008d [1969]. The Problem of the Capitalist State. In The Poulantzas Reader: Marxism, Law and the State, ed. James Martin, 172–185. London and New York: Verso.

Poulantzas, Nicos. 2008e [1964]. Marxist Examination of the Contemporary State and Law and the Question of the 'Alternative'. In *The Poulantzas Reader: Marxism, Law and the State*, ed. James Martin, 25–46. London and New York: Verso.

Poulantzas, Nicos. 2008f [1972]. On Social Classes. In *The Poulantzas Reader: Marxism, Law and the State*, ed. James Martin, 186–219. London and New York: Verso.

Poulantzas, Nicos. 2008g [1979]. Interview with Nicos Poulantzas. In *The Poulantzas Reader: Marxism, Law and the State*, ed. James Martin, 387–402. London and New York: Verso.

Poulantzas, Nicos. 2014 [1978]. *State, Power, Socialism*. London and New York: Verso.

Ptak, Ralf. 2004. Vom Ordoliberalismus zur sozialen Marktwirtschaft: Stationen des Neoliberalismus in Deutschland. Opladen: Leske + Budrich.

Putnam, Robert, Robert Leonardi, and Raffaella Nonetti. 1993. *Making Democracy Work: Civic Traditions in Modern Italy*. Princeton: Princeton University Press.

Ránki, György. 1985. Problems of Southern European Economic Development (1918–38). In *Semiperipheral Development: The Politics of Southern Europe in the Twentieth Century*, ed. Giovanni Arrighi, 55–85. Beverly Hills, London, and New Delhi: Sage (Explorations in the World-Economy 5).

Reill, Peter Hanns. 2011. Introduction. In *Cores, Peripheries, and Globalization: Essays in Honor of Ivan Berend*, ed. Peter Hanns Reill and Balázs Szelényi, 1–11. Budapest and New York: Central European University Press.

Reuten, Geert. 2011. Economic Stagnation Postponed. Background of the 2008 Financial-Economic Crisis in the European Union and the United States. *International Journal of Political Economy* 40 (3): 50–58.

Rhenisch, Thomas. 1999. *Europäische Integration und industrielles Interesse. Die deutsche Industrie und die Gründung der Europäischen Wirtschaftsgemeinschaft*. Stuttgart: Franz Steiner (=VSWG Beihefte 152).

Ritschl, Albrecht. 2012. Germany, Greece and the Marshall Plan. *The Economist.* http://www.economist.com/blogs/freeexchange/2012/06/economic-history (March 18, 2015).

Roth, Karl Heinz. 1998. Das Ende eines Mythos. Ludwig Erhard und der Übergang der deutschen Wirtschaft von der Annexions- zur Nachkriegsplanung (1939 bis 1945). Teil II: 1943 bis 1945. *1999, Zeitschrift für Sozialgeschichte des 20. und 21. Jahrhunderts* 13 (1): 92–123.

Roth, Karl Heinz. 1999a. Das Ende eines Mythos. Ludwig Erhard und der Übergang der deutschen Wirtschaft von der Annexions- zur Nachkriegsplanung (1939 bis 1945). Teil II: 1943 bis 1945. Fortsetzung und Schluß. *1999, Zeitschrift für Sozialgeschichte des 20. und 21. Jahrhunderts* 14 (1): 73–91.

Roth, Karl Heinz. 1999b. Replik. *1999, Zeitschrift für Sozialgeschichte des 20. und 21. Jahrhunderts* 14 (1): 207f.

Roth, Karl Heinz. 2001. Klienten des Leviathan: Die Mont Pèlerin Society und das Bundeswirtschaftsministerium in den fünfziger Jahren. *1999, Zeitschrift für Sozialgeschichte des 20. und 21. Jahrhunderts* 16 (2): 13–41.

Roth, Karl Heinz, and Hartmut Rübner. 2017. *Reparationsschuld. Hypotheken der deutschen Besatzungsherrschaft in Griechenland und Europa.* Berlin: Metropol.

Rowthorn, Robert, and John Wells. 1987. *De-Industrialisation and Foreign Trade.* Cambridge: Cambridge University Press.

Santos, Vitor, and Ana Jacinto. 2006. A industria portuguesa: Desindustrialização – progresso ou declinio? In *A economia portuguesa 20 anos após a adesão*, ed. António Romão, 184–213. Coimbra.

Schaffer, Bernard. 1979. Regional Development and Institutions of Favor. In *Underdeveloped Europe: Studies in Core-Periphery Relations*, ed. Dudley Seers, Bernard Schaffer, and Marja-Liisa Kiljunen, 237–256. Sussex: Harvester Press (=Harvester Studies in Development 1).

Scherb, Margit. 1988. Die Europäische Gemeinschaft – Objekt österreichischer Begierden. In *Der un-heimliche Anschluss. Österreich und die EG.* ed. Inge Morawetz and Margit Scherb, 47–72. Wien: Verlag für Gesellschaftskritik.

Scheuerman, William. 1997. The Unholy Alliance of Carl Schmitt and Friedrich A. Hayek. *Constellations* 4 (2): 172–188.

Schlupp, Frieder. 1980. Federal Republic of Germany. In *Integration and the Unequal Development: The Experience of the EEC*, ed. Dudley Seers and Constantine Vaitsos (with the assistance of Marja-Liisa Kiljunen), 176–198. London and Basingstoke: Macmillan (=Studies in the Integration of Western Europe 1).

Schubert, Alexander. 1985. *Die internationale Verschuldung. Die Dritte Welt und das Transnationale Bankensystem.* Frankfurt/Main: Suhrkamp.

Schumann, Harald, and Árpád Bondy. 2015. *The Trail of the Troika*. RBB/ ARTE. https://www.youtube.com/watch?v=BLB3uu1IXM0 (June 13, 2018).

Schuurman, Frans. 1997. The Decentralisation Discourse: Post-Fordist Paradigm or Neo-liberal Cul-de-Sac? *European Journal of Development Research* 9 (1): 150–166.

Schwartz, Thomas Alan. 1990. Die Begnadigung deutscher Kriegsverbrecher. John J. McCloy und die Häftlinge von Landsberg. *Vierteljahrshefte für Zeitgeschichte* 38 (3): 375–414.

Secchi, Carlo. 1982. Impact on the Less Developed Regions of the EEC. In *The Second Enlargement of the EEC: The Integration of Unequal Partners*, ed. Dudley Seers and Constantine Vaitsos with the assistance of Marja-Liisa Kiljunen, 176–189. London and Basingstoke: Macmillan (=Studies in the Integration of Western Europe 2).

Seers, Dudley. 1977. Back to the Ivory Tower? The Professionalisation of Development Studies and Their Extension to Europe. *IDS Bulletin* 9 (2): 6–11.

Seers, Dudley. 1978. *Development Planning in Portugal: Report of a Mission Under the OECD Technical Co-operation Service*. Brighton: Institute of Development Studies (IDS), University of Sussex.

Seers, Dudley. 1979 [1977]. The Meaning of Development. With a Post Script. In *Development Theory: Four Critical Studies*, ed. David Lehmann, 9–30. London: Frank Cass.

Seers, Dudley. 1979a. Introduction. In *Underdeveloped Europe: Studies in Core-Periphery Relations*, ed. Dudley Seers, Bernard Schaffer, and Marja-Liisa Kiljunen, xiii–xxi. Sussex: Harvester Press (=Harvester Studies in Development 1).

Seers, Dudley. 1979b. The Periphery of Europe. In *Underdeveloped Europe: Studies in Core-Periphery Relations*, ed. Dudley Seers, Bernard Schaffer, and Marja-Liisa Kiljunen, 3–34. Sussex: Harvester Press (=Harvester Studies in Development 1).

Seers, Dudley. 1979c. Post Script: The New Meaning of Development. In *Development Theory: Four Critical Studies*, ed. David Lehmann, 25–30. London, UK: Frank Cass.

Seers, Dudley. 1979d. Post Script: The New Meaning of Development. In *Development Theory: Four Critical Studies*, ed. David Lehmann, 9–24. London: Routledge.

Seers, Dudley. 1980a. The Cultural Lag in Economics. In *The Relevance of Economic Theories*, ed. Josef Pajestka and Charles Feinstein, 3–16. London and Basingstoke: Macmillan.

Seers, Dudley. 1980b. Theoretical Aspects of Unequal Development at Different Spatial Levels. In *Integration and the Unequal Development: The Experience of the EEC*, ed. Dudley Seers and Constantine Vaitsos with the assistance of Marja-Liisa Kiljunen, 9–23. London and Basingstoke: Macmillan (=Studies in the Integration of Western Europe 1).

Seers, Dudley (ed.). 1981a. *Dependency Theory: A Critical Reassessment*. London: F. Pinter.

Seers, Dudley. 1981b. Development Options: The Strengths and Weaknesses of Dependency Theories in Explaining a Government's Room to Manoeuvre. In *Dependency Theory: A Critical Reassessment*, ed. Dudley Seers, 135–149. London: Pinter.

Seers, Dudley. 1982. Introduction: The Second Enlargement in Historical Perspective. In *The Second Enlargement of the EEC: The Integration of Unequal Partners*, ed. Dudley Seers and Constantine Vaitsos with the assistance of Marja-Liisa Kiljunen, 1–21. London and Basingstoke: Macmillan (=Studies in the Integration of Western Europe 2).

Seers, Dudley. 1983a. Preface: Regional Problems and Development Theory. In *The Crisis of the European Regions*, ed. Dudley Seers and Kjell Öström, ix–xiii. London and Basingstoke: Macmillan.

Seers, Dudley. 1983b. The Applications of Development Theories within Europe. In *Emerging Development Patterns: European Contributions*, ed. István Dobozi and Péter Mándi, 517–521. Selected Papers of the 3rd General Conference of EADI, November 11–14, 1981, Budapest, Hungary. Budapest, European Association of Development Research and Training Institutes (EADI) and Institute for World Economy of the Hungarian Academy of Sciences.

Seers, Dudley. 1983c. *The Political Economy of Nationalism*. London et al.: Oxford University Press.

Seers, Dudley, and Constantine Vaitsos. 1980. Introduction. In *Integration and the Unequal Development: The Experience of the EEC*, ed. Dudley Seers and Constantine Vaitsos (with the assistance of Marja-Liisa Kiljunen), 1–5. Macmillan: London and Basingstoke (=Studies in the Integration of Western Europe 1).

Seers, Dudley, and Constantine Vaitsos (with the assistance of Marja-Liisa Kiljunen) (eds.). 1982. *The Second Enlargement of the EEC: The Integration of Unequal Partners*. Macmillan: London and Basingstoke (=Studies in the Integration of Western Europe 2).

Seers, Dudley, and Kjell Öström (eds.). 1983. *The Crisis of the European Regions*. London and Basingstoke: Routledge.

Seers, Dudley, Bernard Schaffer, and Marja-Liisa Kiljunen (eds.). 1979. *Underdeveloped Europe: Studies in Core-Periphery Relations*. Sussex: Harvester Press (=Harvester Studies in Development 1).

Selwyn, Percy. 1979. Some Thoughts on Cores and Peripheries. In *Underdeveloped Europe: Studies in Core-periphery Relations*, ed. Dudley Seers, Bernard Schaffer, and Marja-Liisa Kiljunen, 35–43. Sussex: Harvester Press (=Harvester Studies in Development 1).

Senghaas, Dieter (ed.). 1972. *Imperialismus und strukturelle Gewalt. Analysen über abhängige Reproduktion*. Frankfurt/Main: Suhrkamp.

Senghaas, Dieter (ed.). 1974. *Peripherer Kapitalismus: Analysen über Abhängigkeit und Unterentwicklung*. Frankfurt/Main: Suhrkamp.

Senghaas, Dieter (ed.). 1979a. *Kapitalistische Weltökonomie. Kontroversen über ihren Ursprung und ihre Entwicklungsdynamik*. Frankfurt/Main: Suhrkamp.

Senghaas, Dieter. 1979b. Dissoziation und autozentrierte Entwicklung. Eine entwicklungspolitische Alternative für die Dritte Welt. In *Kapitalistische Weltökonomie. Kontroversen über ihren Ursprung und ihre Entwicklungsdynamik*, ed. Dieter Senghaas, 376–412. Frankfurt/Main: Suhrkamp.

Senghaas, Dieter, and Ulrich Menzel. 1979. Autozentrierte Entwicklung trotz internationalem Kompetenzgefälle. Warum wurden die heutigen Metropolen Metropolen und nicht Peripherien? In *Kapitalistische Weltökonomie. Kontroversen über ihre Entwicklungsdynamik*, ed. Dieter Senghaas, 280–313. Frankfurt/Main: Suhrkamp.

Serfati, Claude. 2004. Militarismus: der bewaffnete Arm der Globalisierung. In *Die globale Enteignungsökonomie*, ed. Christian Zeller, 21–59. Münster: Westphälisches Dapfboot.

Silver, Beverly, and Giovanni Arrighi. 2011. The End of the Long Twentieth Century. In *The Roots of Global Financial Meltdown*, ed. Craig Calhoun and Georgi Derluguian, 53–68. London and New York: New York University Press.

Simonazzi, Annamaria, Andrea Ginzburg, and Gianluigi Nocella. 2013. Economic Relations Between Germany and Southern Europe. *Cambridge Journal of Economics* 37 (3): 653–675.

Slater, Martin. 1984. Italy: Surviving into the 1980s. In *Southern Europe Transformed. Political and Economic Change in Greece, Italy, Portugal and Spain*, ed. Allan Williams, 61–83. London et al.: Harper & Row.

Smith, John. 2012. Outsourcing, Financialisation and the Crisis. *International Journal of Management Concepts and Philosophy* 6 (1–2): 19–44.

Sohn-Rethel, Alfred. 1973. *Ökonomie und Klassenstruktur des deutschen Faschismus. Aufzeichnungen und Analysen*. Frankfurt/Main: Suhrkamp.

Soja, Edward. 1980. The Socio-Spatial Dialectic. *Annals of the Association of American Geographers* 70 (2): 207–225.

Soja, Edward. 1985. Regions in Context: Spatiality, Periodicity, and the Historical Geography of the Regional Question. *Environment and Planning D: Society and Space* 3 (2): 175–190.

Soja, Edward, and Costis Hadjimichalis. 1979. Between Geographical Materialism and Spatial Fetishism: Some Observations on the Development of Marxist Spatial Analysis. *Antipode* 11 (3): 3–11.

Sombart, Werner. 1915. *Händler und Helden. Patriotische Besinnungen.* München und Leipzig: Duncker & Humblot.

Sombart, Werner. 1921. *Der moderne Kapitalismus. Historisch-systematische Darstellung des gesamteuropäischen Wirtschaftslebens von seinen Anfängen bis zur Gegenwart. Zweiter Band. Zweiter Halbband. Das europäische Wirtschaftsleben im Zeitalter des Frühkapitalismus, vornehmlich im 16., 17., und 18. Jahrhundert. Vierte, unveränderte Auflage.* München und Leipzig: Duncker & Humblot.

Sombart, Werner. 1927a. *Das Wirtschaftsleben im Zeitalter des Hochkapitalismus. Erster Halbband. Die Grundlagen – der Aufbau.* München und Leipzig: Duncker & Humblot (=Der moderne Kapitalismus. Dritter Band, erster Halbband).

Sombart, Werner. 1927b. *Das Wirtschaftsleben im Zeitalter des Hochkapitalismus. Zweiter Halbband. Der Hergang der hochkapitalistischen Wirtschaft. Die Gesamtwirtschaft.* München and Leipzig: Duncker & Humblot (=Der moderne Kapitalismus. Dritter Band, zweiter Halbband).

Sombart, Werner. 1934. *Deutscher Sozialismus.* Berlin: Buchholz & Weisswange.

Soms García, Esteban. 2010. ODEPLAN/MIDEPLAN: Una escuela para el cambio social. Ministerio de Planificación, Gobierno de Chile, Santiago.

Stahel, Walter. 2019. *The Circular Economy. A User's Guide.* London and New York: Routledge.

Stathakis, George. 2010. The Fiscal Crisis of the Greek Economy. In Kurswechsel, No. 3, 109–114. http://www.iippe.org/wiki/images/d/db/CONF_GREEKCRISIS_Stathakis.pdf.

Statistisches Bundesamt (ed.). 2015. *Foreign Trade: Overall Development in Foreign Trade Since 1950.* Wiesbaden.

Stiglitz, Joseph, Amartya Sen, and Jean-Paul Fitoussi. 2010. *Mis-measuring Our Lives: Why GDP Doesn't Add Up.* New York and London: New Press.

Stiglitz, Joseph, et al. 2019. *Rewriting the Rules of the European Economy.* Brussels: Foundation for European Progressive Studies.

Stöhr, Walter. 1975. *Regional Development: Experiences and Prospects in Latin America.* The Hague: Mouton.

Stöhr, Walter. 1981. Development from Below: The Bottom-Up and Periphery-Inward Development Paradigm. In *Development from Above or Below? The Dialectics of Regional Planning in Developing Countries*, ed. Walter Stöhr and Fraser Taylor, 39–72. Chichester et al.: Wiley.

Stöhr, Walter. 1983a. Alternative Strategies for Integrated Regional Development. In *The Crisis of the European Regions*, ed. Dudley Seers and Kjell Öström, 6–14. London and Basingstoke: Palgrave Macmillan.

Stöhr, Walter. 1983b. Alternative räumliche Entwicklungsstrategien endogener 'selektiver Eigenständigkeit'. *Österreichische Zeitschrift für Soziologie* 8 (3): 117–134.

Stöhr, Walter. 1983c. Changing External Conditions and a Paradigm Shift in Regional Development Strategies. In *Europe at the Crossroads: Agendas of the Crisis*, ed. Carl Pinkele and Stefan Musto, 283–307. New York: Praeger.

Stöhr, Walter. 1985a. Selective Self-Reliance and Endogenous Regional Development—Pre-conditions and Constraints. In *Ungleiche Entwicklung und Regionalpolitik in Südeuropa: Italien, Spanien, Portugal*, ed. Dieter Nohlen and Rainer-Olaf Schultze unter Mitwirkung von Wolfgang Merkel, 229–249. Bochum (=Politikwissenschaftliche Paperbacks 6).

Stöhr, Walter. 1985b. Industrial Structural Change and Regional Development Strategies: Towards a Conceptual Framework. Paper presented at the joint UNIDO/IGU Symposium on Regional Development Processes/Policies and the Changing International Division of Labour, Vienna, August 20–24, 1984. Wien (=IIR Discussion 21).

Stöhr, Walter. 1987. Regional Development Strategies and the Spatial Division of Labour. In *International Economic Restructuring and the Regional Community*, ed. Herman Muegge and Walter Stöhr with Paul Hesp and Barbara Stuckey, 167–179. Aldershot et al.: Avebury.

Stöhr, Walter. 1990a. Synthesis. In *Global Challenge and Local Response: Initiatives for Economic Regeneration in Contemporary Europe*, ed. Walter Stöhr, 1–19. London, New York, and Tokyo: Mansell Publishing and United Nations University.

Stöhr, Walter. 1990b. Introduction. In *Global Challenge and Local Response: Initiatives for Economic Regeneration in Contemporary Europe*, ed. Walter Stöhr, 20–34. London, New York, and Tokyo: Mansell Publishing and United Nations University.

Stöhr, Walter. 1990c. On the Theory and Practice of Local Development in Europe. In *Global Challenge and Local Response: Initiatives for Economic Regeneration in Contemporary Europe*, ed. Walter Stöhr, 35–45. London, New York, and Tokyo: Mansell Publishing and United Nations University.

Stöhr, Walter. 2001. Subsidiarity: A Key Concept for Regional Development Policy. In *New Regional Development Paradigms. Vol. 3. Decentralization, Governance, and the New Planning for Local-Level Development*, ed. Walter Stöhr, Josefa Edralin, and Devyani Mani, 35–51. Westport: Greenwood Press in cooperation with the United Nations Centre for Regional Development (=Contributions in Economics and Economic History 225).

Stöhr, Walter, and Franz Tödtling. 1977. Evaluation of Regional Policies: Experiences: Experiences in Market and Mixed Economies. Wien (=IIR-Discussion 1).

Stöhr, Walter, and Franz Tödtling. 1978. Evaluation of Regional Policies: Experiences in Market and Mixed Economies. In *Human Settlement System: International Perspectives on Structure, Change and Policy*, ed. Niles Hansen, 85–119. Cambridge, MA: Ballinger Publishing.

Stöhr, Walter, and Franz Tödtling. 1979. Spatial Equity: Some Anti-thesis to Current Regional Development Doctrine. In *Spatial Inequalities and Regional Development*, ed. Hendrik Folmer and Jan Oosterhaven, 133–160. Boston, The Hague, and London: Nijhoff.

Stöhr, Walter, and Fraser Taylor (eds.). 1981. *Development from Above or Below? The Dialectics of Regional Planning in Developing Countries*. Chichester et al.: Wiley.

Stöhr, Walter, Josefa Edralin, and Devyani Mani (eds.). 2001. *New Regional Development Paradigms. Vol. 3. Decentralization, Governance, and the New Planning for Local-level Development*. Westport: Greenwood Press in cooperation with the United Nations Centre for Regional Development (=Contributions in Economics and Economic History 225).

Stöllinger, Roman. 2016. Structural Change and Global Value Chains in the EU. *Empirica* 43 (4): 801–829.

Streeck, Wolfgang. 2016. *How Will Capitalism End? Essays on a Failing System*. London and New York: Verso.

Strickner, Alexandra, et al. 2017. Konzernmacht brechen. Zivilgesellschaftliche Ansätze und Strategien. In *Konzernmacht brechen! Von der Herrschaft des Kapitals zum Guten Leben für Alle*, ed. Attac, 248–276. Wien: Mandelbaum.

Sunkel, Osvaldo. 1972. Transnationale kapitalistische Integration und Nationale Desintegration: Der Fall Lateinamerika. In *Imperialismus und strukturelle Gewalt. Analysen über abhängige Reproduktion*, ed. Dieter Senghaas, 258–315. Frankfurt/Main: Suhrkamp.

Sunkel, Osvaldo. 1973. Transnational Capitalism and National Disintegration in Latin America. *Social and Economic Studies* 22 (1): 132–176 (Based on earlier works in 1968, see FN 2).

Sunkel, Osvaldo. 1977. The Development of Development Thinking. *The IDS Bulletin* 8 (3): 6–12.

Szentes, Tamás. 1983. The TNC Issue: Naive Illusions or Exorcism and Lip-Service. In *Emerging Development Patterns: European Contributions*, ed. István Dobozi and Péter Mándi, 97–118. Selected Papers of the 3rd General Conference of EADI. Budapest (=EADI Book Series 1).

Tarrow, Sidney. 1985. The Crisis of the Late 1960's in Italy and France: The Transition to Mature Capitalism. In *Semiperipheral Development. The Politics of Southern Europe in the Twentieth Century*, ed. Giovanni Arrighi, 215–241. Beverly Hills, London, and New Delhi (=Explorations in the World-Economy 5).

Tarrow, Sidney. 1990. Maintaining Hegemony in Italy: "The Softer They Rise, the Slower They Fall!" In *Uncommon Democracies: The One-Party Dominant Regimes*, ed. Thomas Jefferson Pempel, 306–332. Ithaca and London: Cornell University Press.

Teichova, Alice. 1988. *Kleinstaaten im Spannungsfeld der Großmächte. Wirtschaft und Politik in Mittel und Südosteuropa in der Zwischenkriegszeit.* Wien (=Sozial- und wirtschaftshistorische Studien 18).

The MacDougall Report. 1977. *Study Group on the Role of Public Finance in European Integration*, vol. I. Brussels: Commission of the European Communities. http://ec.europa.eu/economy_finance/emu_history/documentation/chapter8/19770401en73macdougallrepvol1.pdf (June 27, 2017).

Tödtling, Franz. 1983. Regionale Unterschiede der nichtlandwirtschaftlichen Betriebs- und Arbeitsplatzstruktur in Österreich. *Österreichische Zeitschrift für Soziologie* 8 (3): 36–44.

Tregenna, Fiona. 2011. *Manufacturing Productivity, Deindustrialization, and Reindustrialization.* Helsinki (=UNU-WIDER Working Paper 2011/57).

Triffin, Robert. 1980. The European Monetary System. In *Integration and Unequal Development: The Experience of the EEC*, ed. Dudley Seers and Constantine Vaitsos with the assistance of Marja-Liisa Kiljunen, 223–233. London and Basingstoke: Macmillan (=Studies in the Integration of Western Europe 1).

Tsoukalis, Loukas. 1981. *The European Community and Its Mediterranean Enlargement.* London, Boston, and Sydney: Allen and Unwin.

Tsoukalis, Loukas. 1982. Impact on the European Monetary System (EMS). In *The Second Enlargement of the EEC: The Integration of Unequal Partners*, ed. Dudley Seers and Constantine Vaitsos with the assistance of Marja-Liisa Kiljunen, 163–175. London and Basingstoke: Macmillan (=Studies in the Integration of Western Europe 2).

Tsoukalis, Loukas. 1997. *The New European Economy Revisited.* Oxford et al.: Oxford University Press.

UNCTAD (ed.). 2013. World Investment Report 2013. Global Value Chains: Investment and Trade for Development. New York and Geneva.

UNCTAD (ed.). 2016. World Investment Report 2016. Investor Nationality: Policy Challenges. New York and Geneva.

UNCTAD (ed.). 2017a. World Investment Report 2017. Investment and the Digital Economy. New York and Geneva.

UNCTAD (ed.). 2017b. World Investment Report 2017: Annex Tables. http://unctad.org/en/Pages/DIAE/World%20Investment%20Report/Annex-Tables.aspx (October 13, 2017).

UNIDO (ed.). 2013. *Industrial Development Report 2013. Sustaining Employment Growth: The Role of Manufacturing and Structural Change.* Vienna.

US Central Intelligence Agency. 1972. Europe 9–72. In Library of Congress, Washington, DC. https://urldefense.proofpoint.com/v2/url?u=https-3A__www.loc.gov_item_75693732_&d=DwIFAw&c=vh6FgFnduejNhPPD0fl_yRaSfZy8CWbWnIf4XJhSqx8&r=PQelu8ZjKbjEbRfu6o6YYu5Z6-FCD-MUN5ZxrvBFQbwSpLC9r6iMWlQG1R8s1JamK&m=C3u-s8CQ_iV-Qx-AEPP-jCYX52s_TZqLSUa1qrPQxRZY&s=nJu_jZWEGVsw5YDn8Qb-V1GHAOrF4fhIGQVkhNwKV8qQ&e= (August 30, 2019).

Vaitsos, Constantine. 1979. Transnational Corporations (TNCs) and Europe. In Underdeveloped Europe: Studies in Core-Periphery Relations, ed. Dudley Seers, Bernard Schaffer, and Marja-Liisa Kiljunen. Sussex, 97–102 (=Harvester Studies in Development 1).

Vaitsos, Constantine. 1980. Corporate Integration in World Production and Trade. In *Integration and Unequal Development: The Experience of the EEC*, ed. Dudley Seers and Constantine Vaitsos (with the assistance of Marja-Liisa Kiljunen), 24–45. London and Basingstoke: Macmillan (=Studies in the Integration of Western Europe 1).

Vaitsos, Constantine. 1982a. Transnational Corporate Behaviour and the Enlargement. In *The Second Enlargement of the EEC: The Integration of Unequal Partners*, ed. Dudley Seers and Constantine Vaitsos with the assistance of Marja-Liisa Kiljunen, 137–162. London and Basingstoke: Macmillan (=Studies in the Integration of Western Europe 2).

Vaitsos, Constantine. 1982b. Conclusions: Economic Effects of the Second Enlargement. In *The Second Enlargement of the EEC: The Integration of Unequal Partners*, ed. Dudley Seers and Constantine Vaitsos with the assistance of Marja-Liisa Kiljunen, 243–268. London and Basingstoke: Macmillan (=Studies in the Integration of Western Europe 2).

Van Bilsen, Anton. 1976. Report by the Chairman of the Provisional Committee. In *The New International Economic Order—Economic, Social and Political Imolications*, ed. European Association of Development Research and Training Institutes (EADI), 8–10. Report on the 1975 General Conference of EADI Linz/Austria, September 11–13, 1975. Vienna, EADI.

Viesti, Gianfranco. 2009. Mezzogiorno a tradimento. Il Nord, il Sud e la politica che non c'è. Roma and Bari: Laterza.

Villamil, José. 1977. Development Planning and Dependence. *IDS Bulletin* 9 (1): 57–61.

Villamil, José. 1979. Introduction. In *Transnational Capitalism and National Development*, ed. José Villamil, 1–15. Sussex: Harvester Press (=Harvester Studies in Development 2).

Wade, Robert. 1979. Fast Growth and Slow Development in South Italy. In: Dudley Seers, Bernard Schaffer, Bernard, and Marja-Liisa Kiljunen, (eds.) (1979): Underdeveloped Europe: Studies in Core-periphery Relations. Sussex: Harvester, 197–221 (=Harvester Studies in Development 1).

Wade, Robert. 1980. The Italian State and the Underdevelopment of South Italy. In *"Nation" and "State" in Europe*, ed. Ralph Grillo, 151–171. London et al.: Academic Press.

Wainwright, Hilary. 2016. Radicalizing the Movement-Party Relation: From Ralph Miliband to Jeremy Corbyn and Beyond. In *Socialist Register 2017: Rethinking Revolution*, ed. Leo Panitch and Greg Albo, 80–101. London: Merlin.

Wallerstein, Immanuel. 1978. World-System Analysis: Theoretical and Interpretative Issues. In *Social Change in the Capitalist World Economy*, ed. Barbara Hockey Kaplan, 219–235. Beverly Hills and London: Sage (=Political Economy of the World-System Annuals, 1).

Wallerstein, Immanuel. 1979a [1974]. The Rise and Future Demise of the World Capitalist System: Concepts for Comparative Analysis. In *The Capitalist World-Economy*, ed. Immanuel Wallerstein. Cambridge et al.: University Press and Editions de la Maison des Sciences de l'Homme, 1–36 (=Studies in modern capitalism).

Wallerstein, Immanuel. 1979b [1974]. Dependence in an Interdependent World: The Limited Possibilities of Transformation Within the Capitalist World Economy. In *The Capitalist World-Economy*, ed. Immanuel Wallerstein, 66–94. Cambridge et al.: University Press and Editions de la Maison des Sciences de l'Homme (=Studies in modern capitalism).

Wallerstein, Immanuel. 1979c [1976]. Semiperipheral Countries and the Contemporary World Crisis. In *The Capitalist World-Economy*, ed. Immanuel Wallerstein, 95–118. Cambridge et al.: University Press and Editions de la Maison des Sciences de l'Homme (=Studies in modern capitalism).

Wallerstein, Immanuel. 1985. The Relevance of the Concept of Semiperiphery to Southern Europe. In *Semiperipheral Development: The Politics of Southern Europe in the Twentieth Century*, ed. Giovanni Arrighi, 31–39. Beverly Hills, London, and New Delhi: Sage (=Explorations in the World-Economy 5).

Wallerstein, Immanuel. 2004. *World-Systems Analysis: An Introduction*. Durham: Duke University. Press.

Weissenbacher, Rudy. 2005. *Jugoslawien. Politische Ökonomie einer Desintegration*. Wien: Promedia.

Weissenbacher, Rudy. 2007. Historical Considerations of Uneven Development in East Central Europe. In *Dollarization, Euroization and Financial Instability: Central and Eastern European Countries Between Stagnation and Financial Crisis?* ed. Joachim Becker and Rudy Weissenbacher, 35–83. Marburg: Metropolis.

Weissenbacher, Rudy. 2008. Keeping Up Appearances: Uneven Global Development in a System of Structural Imbalances. *Journal Für Entwicklungspolitik XXIV* 4: 78–121.

Weissenbacher, Rudy. 2009. Sozialismus in Jugoslawien. Die Selbstauflösung des Entwicklungsstaats. In *Sozialismen. Entwicklungsmodelle von Lenin bis Nyerere*, ed. Joachim Becker and Rudy Weissenbacher, 74–97. Wien: Promedia and Südwind (=Historische Sozialkunde/Internationale Entwicklung 28).

Weissenbacher, Rudy. 2012a. "Wir wissen, dass wir das Spiel jetzt nach Euren Regeln spielen müssen…" Betrachtungen zu Hegemonie und ungleicher Entwicklung. *Z. Zeitschrift für marxistische Erneuerung* 23 (89): 60–79.

Weissenbacher, Rudy. 2012b. Berlusconismo mit guten Manieren. Anmerkungen Zur Regierungsumbildung in Italien. *Kurswechsel* 17 (2): 68–75.

Weissenbacher, Rudy. 2014a. From Dependent Industrialization to Peripheral De-industrialization in Europe: Considerations from Development Studies. Contribution to the 20th Conference on Alternative Economic Policy in Europe (EuroMemo), Rome, September 25–27. http://www2.euromemorandum.eu/uploads/weissenbacher_historical_fragments_of_an_alternative_development_paradigm.pdf (March 14, 2018).

Weissenbacher, Rudy. 2014b. Reclaiming Public Ownership: Making Space for Economic Democracy. *Journal of Contemporary European Studies* 22 (2): 213–217.

Weissenbacher, Rudy. 2015. Keine andere Welt, nur ein anderes Europa. Die Lega Nord am rechten Weg. *Kurswechsel* 20 (3): 81–87.

Weissenbacher, Rudy. 2018a. Die Krise als Normalität: Kapitalismus, Regionen und ungleiche Entwicklung. *Kurswechsel* 23 (2): 53–62.

Weissenbacher, Rudy. 2018b. Peripheral Integration and Disintegration in Europe: The 'European Dependency School' Revisited. *Journal of Contemporary European Studies* 26 (1): 81–98.

Weissenbacher, Rudy. 2019. „In wenigen Monaten wird nichts mehr wie früher sein": Die gelb-grüne Regierung und der Abstieg Italiens im europäischen Kapitalismus. *Kurswechsel* 24 (1): 62–71.

Wickham, James. 2012. After the Party's Over: The Irish Employment Model and the Paradoxes of Non-learning. In *A Triumph of Failed Ideas European Models of Capitalism in the Crisis*, ed. Steffen Lehndorff, 59–77. Brussels: ETUI.

Williams, Allan (ed.). 1984a. *Southern Europe Transformed: Political and Economic Change in Greece, Italy, Portugal and Spain*. London: Harper & Row.

Williams, Allan (ed.). 1984b. Introduction. In *Southern Europe Transformed: Political and Economic Change in Greece, Italy, Portugal and Spain*. London: Harper & Row, 1–29.

Wistrich, Robert. 1983. *Wer war wer im Dritten Reich*. München: Harnack.

Wohlmuth, Karl. 1980. Collective Self-Reliance und die Kontrolle Transnationaler Konzerne. In *Self-Reliance als nationale und kollektive Entwicklungsstrategie*, ed. Khushi Khan, 323–365. München and London: Weltforum (=Weltwirtschaft und internationale Beziehungen 20).

Wolff, Richard. 2017. Die Wut der Arbeiter und die Suche nach einer neuen Wirtschaftsordnung, Interview in Kontext. TV, 7.3. http://www.kontext-tv.de/de/sendungen/richard-wolff-die-wut-derarbeiter-und-die-suche-nach-einer-neuen-wirtschaftsordnung (February 2,2018).

Woodward, Susan. 1983. Political Changes in the European Mediterranean Arena: An Overview of Considerations for Policy Makers. In *The Contemporary Mediterranean World*, ed. Carl Pinkele and Adamantia Pollis, 175–201. New York: Praeger.

Woodward, Susan. 1985. The Economic Crisis in Southern Europe: Origins and Political Responses. In *Europe at the Crossroads: Agendas of the Crisis*, ed. Carl Pinkele and Stefan Musto, 103–132. New York: Praeger.

Wünsche, Horst Friedrich. 1999. Ludwig Erhard und die Grundlegung der Sozialen Marktwirtschaft 1943/44. *1999, Zeitschrift für Sozialgeschichte des 20. und 21. Jahrhunderts* 14 (1): 200–207.

Young, Andrew, Matthew Higgins, and Daniel Levy. 2008. Sigma Convergence Versus Beta Convergence: Evidence from U.S. County-Level Data. *Journal of Money, Credit and Banking* 40 (5): 1083–1093.

Ziltener, Patrick. 2000. Die Veränderung von Staatlichkeit in Europa – regulations- und staatstheoretische Überlegungen. In *Die Konfiguration Europas: Dimensionen einer kritischen Integrationstheorie*, ed. Hans-Jürgen Bieling and Jochen Steinhilber, 73–101. Münster.

Zingel, Wolfgang-Peter. 1976. Grundsätzliche Fragen einer europäischen Regionalpolitik. In *Möglichkeiten und Grenzen einer Europäischen Union. Band 2. Verteilung der wirtschaftlichen Kräfte im Raum*, ed. Hans von der Groeben and Hans Möller, 33–69. Baden-Baden.

Author Index

R. Weissenbacher, *The Core-Periphery Divide in the European Union*,
https://doi.org/10.1007/978-3-030-28211-0

Subject Index

R. Weissenbacher, *The Core-Periphery Divide in the European Union*,
https://doi.org/10.1007/978-3-030-28211-0

The manufacturer's authorised representative in the EU is Springer Nature Customer Service Centre GmbH, Europaplatz 3, 69115 Heidelberg, Germany. If you have any concerns regarding our products, please contact ProductSafety@springernature.com

Printed and bound by CPI Group (UK) Ltd, Croydon, CR0 4YY
30/09/2026
02225656-0019